Second Edition

Starting Out with

Programming Logic & Design

Second Edition

Starting Out with

Programming Logic & Design

Tony Gaddis

Haywood Community College

Addison-Wesley

Boston   Columbus   Indianapolis   New York   San Francisco   Upper Saddle River
Amsterdam   Cape Town   Dubai   London   Madrid   Milan   Munich   Paris   Montreal   Toronto
Delhi   Mexico City   Sao Paulo   Sydney   Hong Kong   Seoul   Singapore   Taipei   Tokyo

Editor in Chief: Michael Hirsch
Editorial Assistant: Stephanie Sellinger
Managing Editor: Jeff Holcomb
Media Producer: Katelyn Boller
Director of Marketing: Margaret Waples
Marketing Manager: Erin Davis
Marketing Coordinator: Kathryn Ferranti
Senior Manufacturing Buyer: Carol Melville
Senior Media Buyer: Ginny Michaud

Text Design: Joyce Cosentino Wells and Aptara®, Inc.
Project Management: Dennis Free, Aptara, Inc.
Composition and Illustrations: Aptara, Inc.
Cover Art Direction: Linda Knowles
Cover Design: Joyce Cosentino Wells
Cover Images: © Ingram Publishing / SuperStock
Printer/Binder: Edwards Brothers
Cover Printer: Lehigh Phoenix Hagerstown

Credits and acknowledgments borrowed from other sources and reproduced, with permission, in this textbook appear on the appropriate page within the text and as follows:

Figure 1-3, "The ENIAC computer," on page 4 is courtesy of U.S. Army Historic Computer Images.
Figure 1-4, "A lab technician holds a modern microprocessor," on page 4 is courtesy of Intel Corporation.
Figure 1-5, "Memory chips," on page 5 is courtesy of IBM Corporation.
Rendered art and photographic images in Figures 1-2, 1-14–1-16, 1-18, and 1-19 © 2007 JUPITERIMAGES and its licensors. All Rights Reserved.

Many of the designations by manufacturers and sellers to distinguish their products are claimed as trademarks. Where those designations appear in this book, and the publisher was aware of a trademark claim, the designations have been printed in initial caps or all caps.

Microsoft® and Windows® are registered trademarks of the Microsoft Corporation in the U.S.A. and other countries. Screen shots and icons reprinted with permission from the Microsoft Corporation. This book is not sponsored or endorsed by or affiliated with the Microsoft Corporation.

Library of Congress Cataloging-in-Publication Data

Gaddis, Tony.
    Starting out with programming logic & design / Tony Gaddis. — 2nd ed.
        p. cm.
    Includes index.
    ISBN-13: 978-0-13-607773-2
    ISBN-10: 0-13-607773-0
    1.   Computer programming.   I. Title.   II. Title: Starting out with programming logic and design.
    QA76.6.G315 2009
    005.1—dc22   2009031345

10 9 8 7 6 5 4 3 2 1—EB—13 12 11 10 09

Addison-Wesley
is an imprint of

www.pearsonhighered.com

ISBN 10: 0-13-607773-0
ISBN 13: 978-0-13-607773-2

Brief Contents

Contents

Chapter 4   Decision Structures and Boolean Logic   115

Chapter 5   Repetition Structures   163

Chapter 6   Functions   217

Chapter 7 Input Validation 257

Chapter 8 Arrays 269

Chapter 9 Sorting and Searching Arrays 323

Chapter 10 Files 361

Preface

Welcome to *Starting Out with Programming Logic and Design,* Second Edition. This book uses a language-independent approach to teach programming concepts and problem-solving skills, without assuming any previous programming experience. By using easy-to-understand pseudocode, flowcharts, and other tools, the student learns how to design the logic of programs without the complication of language syntax.

Fundamental topics such as data types, variables, input, output, control structures, modules, functions, arrays, and files are covered as well as object-oriented concepts, GUI development, and event-driven programming. As with all the books in the *Starting Out With . . .* series, this text is written with clear, easy-to-understand language that students find friendly and inviting.

Each chapter presents a multitude of program design examples. Short examples that highlight specific programming topics are provided, as well as more involved examples that focus on problem solving. Each chapter includes at least one case study that provides step-by-step analysis of a specific problem and demonstrates a solution to that problem.

This book is ideal for a programming logic course that is taught as a precursor to a language-specific introductory programming course, or for the first part of an introductory programming course in which a specific language is taught.

Changes in the Second Edition

This book's pedagogy, organization, and clear writing style remain the same as in the previous edition. Many improvements have been made, which are summarized here:

- **Online VideoNotes**

  An extensive series of online VideoNotes have been developed to accompany this text. Throughout the book, VideoNote icons alert the student to videos covering specific topics. Additionally, one programming exercise at the end of each chapter now has an accompanying VideoNote explaining how to develop the problem's solution. The videos are available at www.pearsonhighered.com/gaddis.

- **Programming Language Companions**

  Programming language companions specifically designed to accompany the Second Edition of this textbook are available for download. The companions introduce the Java™, Python®, and Visual Basic® programming languages, and correspond on a chapter-by-chapter basis with the textbook. Many of the pseudocode programs that appear in the textbook also appear in the companions, implemented in a specific programming language. The programming language companions are available at www.pearsonhighered.com/gaddis.

- **New Chapter on Text Processing**

  Chapter 12 in the Second Edition is a new chapter on Text Processing. This chapter discusses techniques for processing strings at the character level. Common library functions for processing characters and text are also discussed.

- **Additional Topics in Chapter 8: Arrays**

  Chapter 8: Arrays has a new section on partially filled arrays, and a new optional section on the For Each Loop.

- **Additional Programming Problems**

  Additional programming problems have been added to Chapters 4, 5, and 6. Several of these problems are simple games that will challenge and motivate students.

Brief Overview of Each Chapter

Chapter 1: Introduction to Computers and Programming

This chapter begins by giving a concise and easy-to-understand explanation of how computers work, how data is stored and manipulated, and why we write programs in high-level languages.

Chapter 2: Input, Processing, and Output

This chapter introduces the program development cycle, data types, variables, and sequence structures. The student learns to use pseudocode and flowcharts to design simple programs that read input, perform mathematical operations, and produce screen output.

Chapter 3: Modules

This chapter demonstrates the benefits of modularizing programs and using the top-down design approach. The student learns to define and call modules, pass arguments to modules, and use local variables. Hierarchy charts are introduced as a design tool.

Chapter 4: Decision Structures and Boolean Logic

In this chapter students explore relational operators and Boolean expressions and are shown how to control the flow of a program with decision structures. The If-Then, If-Then-Else, and If-Then-Else If statements are covered. Nested decision structures, logical operators, and the case structure are also discussed.

Chapter 5: Repetition Structures

This chapter shows the student how to use loops to create repetition structures. The While, Do-While, Do-Until, and For loops are presented. Counters, accumulators, running totals, and sentinels are also discussed.

Chapter 6: Functions

This chapter begins by discussing common library functions, such as those for generating random numbers. After learning how to call library functions and how to use values returned by functions, the student learns how to define and call his or her own functions.

Chapter 7: Input Validation

This chapter discusses the importance of validating user input. The student learns to write input validation loops that serve as error traps. Defensive programming and the importance of anticipating obvious as well as unobvious errors is discussed.

Chapter 8: Arrays

In this chapter the student learns to create and work with one- and two-dimensional arrays. Many examples of array processing are provided including examples illustrating how to find the sum, average, and highest and lowest values in an array, and how to sum the rows, columns, and all elements of a two-dimensional array. Programming techniques using parallel arrays are also demonstrated.

Chapter 9: Sorting and Searching Arrays

In this chapter the student learns the basics of sorting arrays and searching for data stored in them. The chapter covers the bubble sort, selection sort, insertion sort, and binary search algorithms.

Chapter 10: Files

This chapter introduces sequential file input and output. The student learns to read and write large sets of data, store data as fields and records, and design programs that work with both files and arrays. The chapter concludes by discussing control break processing.

Chapter 11: Menu-Driven Programs

In this chapter the student learns to design programs that display menus and execute tasks according to the user's menu selection. The importance of modularizing a menu-driven program is also discussed.

Chapter 12: Text Processing

This chapter discusses text processing at a detailed level. Algorithms that step through the individual characters in a string are discussed, and several common library functions for character and text processing are introduced.

Chapter 13: Recursion

This chapter discusses recursion and its use in problem solving. A visual trace of recursive calls is provided, and recursive applications are discussed. Recursive algorithms for many tasks are presented, such as finding factorials, finding a greatest common denominator (GCD), summing a range of values in an array, and performing a binary search. The classic Towers of Hanoi example is also presented.

Chapter 14: Object-Oriented Programming

This chapter compares procedural and object-oriented programming practices. It covers the fundamental concepts of classes and objects. Fields, methods, access specification, constructors, accessors, and mutators are discussed. The student learns how to model classes with UML and how to find the classes in a particular problem.

Chapter 15: GUI Applications and Event-Driven Programming

This chapter discusses the basic aspects of designing a GUI application. Building graphical user interfaces with visual design tools (such as Visual Studio® or NetBeans™) is discussed. The student learns how events work in a GUI application and how to write event handlers.

Appendix A: ASCII/Unicode Characters

This appendix lists the ASCII character set, which is the same as the first 127 Unicode character codes.

Appendix B: Flowchart Symbols

This appendix shows the flowchart symbols that are used in this book.

Appendix C: Answers to Checkpoint Questions

This appendix provides answers to the Checkpoint questions that appear throughout the text, and is located on the CD that accompanies this book.[1]

Organization of the Text

The text teaches programming logic and design in a step-by-step manner. Each chapter covers a major set of topics and builds knowledge as students progress through the book. Although the chapters can be easily taught in their existing sequence, there is some flexibility. Figure P-1 shows chapter dependencies. Each box represents a chapter or a group of chapters. A chapter to which an arrow points must be covered before the chapter from which the arrow originates. The dotted line indicates that only a portion of Chapter 10 depends on information presented in Chapter 8.

Features of the Text

Concept Statements. Each major section of the text starts with a concept statement. This statement concisely summarizes the main point of the section.

---

[1]If a CD did not come with your book or you can't locate your CD, you can also visit http://www.aw.com/cssupport/ to access this appendix.

Figure P-1 Chapter Dependencies

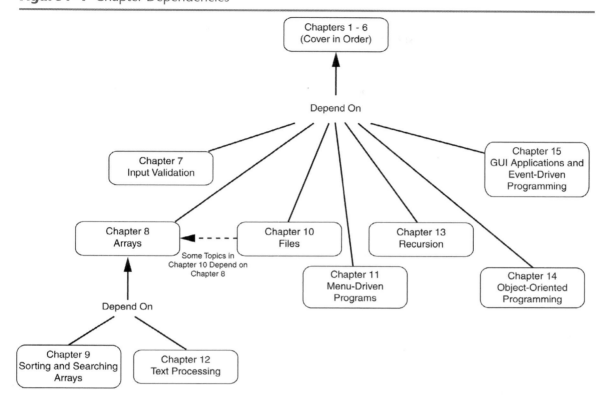

Example Programs. Each chapter has an abundant number of complete and partial example programs, each designed to highlight the current topic. Pseudocode, flow-charts, and other design tools are used in the example programs.

Case Studies. Each chapter has one or more *In the Spotlight* case studies that provide detailed, step-by-step analysis of problems, and show the student how to solve them.

VideoNote

VideoNotes. A series of online videos, developed specifically for this book, are available for viewing at `www.pearsonhighered.com/gaddis`. Icons appear throughout the text alerting the student to videos about specific topics.

NOTE: Notes appear at several places throughout the text. They are short explanations of interesting or often misunderstood points relevant to the topic at hand.

TIP: Tips advise the student on the best techniques for approaching different programming or animation problems.

WARNING! Warnings caution students about programming techniques or practices that can lead to malfunctioning programs or lost data.

Programming Language Companions. Many of the pseudocode programs shown in this book have also been written in Java, Python, and Visual Basic. These programs appear in the programming language companions that are available at www.pearsonhighered.com/gaddis. Icons appear next to each pseudocode program that also appears in the language companions.

Checkpoints. Checkpoints are questions placed at intervals throughout each chapter. They are designed to query the student's knowledge quickly after learning a new topic.

Review Questions. Each chapter presents a thorough and diverse set of Review Questions and exercises. They include Multiple Choice, True/False, Short Answer, and Algorithm Workbench.

Programming Exercises. Each chapter offers a pool of Programming Exercises designed to solidify the student's knowledge of the topics currently being studied.

Supplements

Student Resource CD

This CD includes:

- Answers to Checkpoint Questions (Appendix C)
- RAPTOR, a flowchart-based programming environment

If a CD did not come with your book or you can't locate your CD, you can visit http://www.aw.com/cssupport/ to access these supplements.

Programming Language Companions

Programming language companions specifically designed to accompany the Second Edition of this textbook are available for download. The companions introduce the Java, Python, and Visual Basic programming languages, and correspond on a chapter-by-chapter basis with the textbook. Many of the pseudocode programs that appear in the textbook also appear in the companions, implemented in a specific programming language. The programming language companions are available at www.pearsonhighered.com/gaddis.

Instructor Resources

The following supplements are available to qualified instructors only:

- Answers to all of the Review Questions
- Solutions for the Programming Exercises
- PowerPoint® presentation slides for each chapter
- Test bank

Visit the Addison-Wesley Instructor Resource Center (`http://www.pearsonhighered.com/irc`) or send an email to `computing@aw.com` for information on how to access them.

Acknowledgments

There have been many helping hands in the development and publication of this text. I would like to thank the following faculty reviewers:

Reni Abraham
Houston Community College

John P. Buerck
Saint Louis University

Jill Canine
Ivy Tech Community College of Indiana

Steven D. Carver
Ivy Tech Community College of Indiana

Katie Danko
Grand Rapids Community College

Coronicca Oliver
Coastal Georgia Community College

Dale T. Pickett
Baker College of Clinton Township

Tonya Pierce
Ivy Tech Community College

Larry Strain
Ivy Tech Community College–Bloomington

Donald Stroup
Ivy Tech Community College

Jim Turney
Austin Community College

I also want to thank everyone at Pearson Addison-Wesley for making the *Starting Out With . . .* series so successful. I have worked so closely with the team at Pearson Addison-Wesley that I consider them among my closest friends. I am extremely grateful that Michael Hirsch is my editor. He and Stephanie Sellinger, editorial assistant, have guided me through the process of revising this book. I am also thankful to have Erin Davis as marketing manager. Her energy and creativity are truly inspiring. The production team worked tirelessly to make this book a reality, and includes Jeff Holcomb, Katelyn Boller, Carol Melville, Linda Knowles, and Dennis Free. Thanks to you all!

Last, but not least, I want to thank my family for all the patience, love, and support they have shown me throughout this and my many other projects.

About the Author

Tony Gaddis is the principal author of the *Starting Out With . . .* series of textbooks. Tony has twenty years of experience teaching computer science courses, primarily at Haywood Community College. He is a highly acclaimed instructor who was previously selected as the North Carolina Community College "Teacher of the Year" and has received the Teaching Excellence award from the National Institute for Staff and Organizational Development. The *Starting Out With . . .* series includes introductory books covering Programming Logic and Design, C++, Java, Microsoft® Visual Basic, C#®, Python, and Alice, all published by Pearson Addison-Wesley.

1

Introduction to Computers and Programming

TOPICS

1.1 Introduction

Think about some of the different ways that people use computers. In school, students use computers for tasks such as writing papers, searching for articles, sending email, and participating in online classes. At work, people use computers to analyze data, make presentations, conduct business transactions, communicate with customers and coworkers, control machines in manufacturing facilities, and many other things. At home, people use computers for tasks such as paying bills, shopping online, communicating with friends and family, and playing computer games. And don't forget that cell phones, iPods®, BlackBerries®, car navigation systems, and many other devices are computers too. The uses of computers are almost limitless in our everyday lives.

Computers can do such a wide variety of things because they can be programmed. This means that computers are not designed to do just one job, but to do any job that their programs tell them to do. A *program* is a set of instructions that a computer follows to perform a task. For example, Figure 1-1 shows screens from two commonly used programs: Microsoft Word and Adobe® Photoshop®. Microsoft Word is a word processing program that allows you to create, edit, and print documents with your computer. Adobe Photoshop is an image editing program that allows you to work with graphic images, such as photos taken with your digital camera.

Figure 1-1 A word processing program and an image editing program

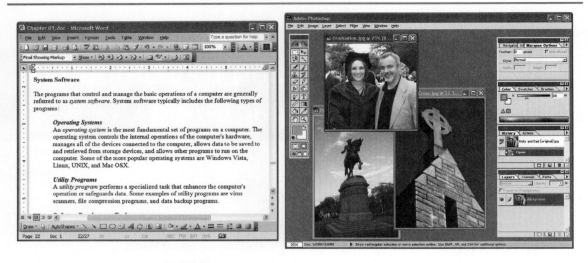

Programs are commonly referred to as *software*. Software is essential to a computer because without software, a computer can do nothing. All of the software that we use to make our computers useful is created by individuals known as programmers or software developers. A *programmer,* or *software developer,* is a person with the training and skills necessary to design, create, and test computer programs. Computer programming is an exciting and rewarding career. Today, you will find programmers working in business, medicine, government, law enforcement, agriculture, academics, entertainment, and almost every other field.

This book introduces you to the fundamental concepts of computer programming. Before we begin exploring those concepts, you need to understand a few basic things about computers and how they work. This chapter will build a solid foundation of knowledge that you will continually rely on as you study computer science. First, we will discuss the physical components that computers are commonly made of. Next, we will look at how computers store data and execute programs. Finally, we will discuss the major types of software that computers use.

1.2   Hardware

CONCEPT: The physical devices that a computer is made of are referred to as the computer's hardware. Most computer systems are made of similar hardware devices.

The term *hardware* refers to all of the physical devices, or *components,* that a computer is made of. A computer is not one single device, but a system of devices that all work together. Like the different instruments in a symphony orchestra, each device in a computer plays its own part.

If you have ever shopped for a computer, you've probably seen sales literature listing components such as microprocessors, memory, disk drives, video displays, graphics cards, and so on. Unless you already know a lot about computers, or at least have a friend who does, understanding what these different components do can be confusing. As shown in Figure 1-2, a typical computer system consists of the following major components:

- The central processing unit (CPU)
- Main memory
- Secondary storage devices
- Input devices
- Output devices

Figure 1-2 Typical components of a computer system

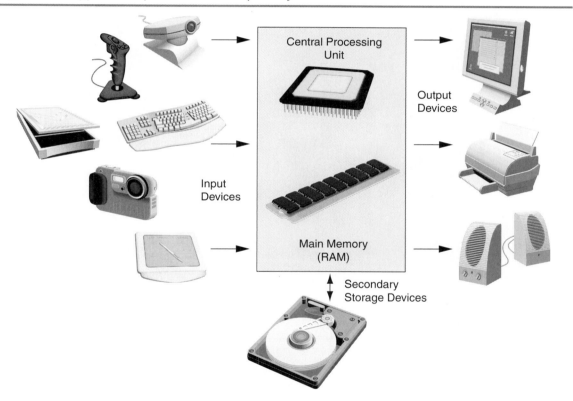

Let's take a closer look at each of these components.

The CPU

When a computer is performing the tasks that a program tells it to do, we say that the computer is *running* or *executing* the program. The *central processing unit*, or *CPU*, is the part of a computer that actually runs programs. The CPU is the most important component in a computer because without it, the computer could not run software.

In the earliest computers, CPUs were huge devices made of electrical and mechanical components such as vacuum tubes and switches. Figure 1-3 shows such a device. The two women in the photo are working with the historic ENIAC computer. The *ENIAC*, considered by many to be the world's first programmable electronic computer, was built in 1945 to calculate artillery ballistic tables for the U.S. Army. This machine, which was primarily one big CPU, was 8 feet tall, 100 feet long, and weighed 30 tons.

Today, CPUs are small chips known as *microprocessors*. Figure 1-4 shows a photo of a lab technician holding a modern-day microprocessor. In addition to being much smaller than the old electro-mechanical CPUs in early computers, microprocessors are also much more powerful.

Figure 1-3 The ENIAC computer (courtesy of U.S. Army Historic Computer Images)

Figure 1-4 A lab technician holds a modern microprocessor (photo courtesy of Intel Corporation)

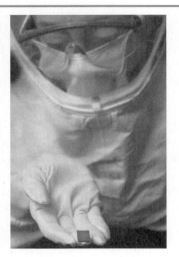

Main Memory

You can think of *main memory* as the computer's work area. This is where the computer stores a program while the program is running, as well as the data that the program is working with. For example, suppose you are using a word processing program to write an essay for one of your classes. While you do this, both the word processing program and the essay are stored in main memory.

Main memory is commonly known as *random-access memory,* or *RAM.* It is called this because the CPU is able to quickly access data stored at any random location in RAM. RAM is usually a *volatile* type of memory that is used only for temporary storage while a program is running. When the computer is turned off, the contents of RAM are erased. Inside your computer, RAM is stored in chips, similar to the ones shown in Figure 1-5.

Figure 1-5 Memory chips (photo courtesy of IBM Corporation)

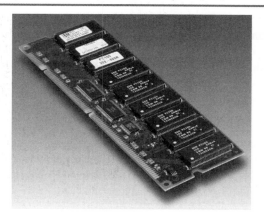

Secondary Storage Devices

Secondary storage is a type of memory that can hold data for long periods of time, even when there is no power to the computer. Programs are normally stored in secondary memory and loaded into main memory as needed. Important data, such as word processing documents, payroll data, and inventory records, is saved to secondary storage as well.

The most common type of secondary storage device is the disk drive. A *disk drive* stores data by magnetically encoding it onto a circular disk. Most computers have a disk drive mounted inside their case. External disk drives, which connect to one of the computer's communication ports, are also available. External disk drives can be used to create backup copies of important data or to move data to another computer.

In addition to external disk drives, many types of devices have been created for copying data, and for moving it to other computers. For many years floppy disk drives were popular. A *floppy disk drive* records data onto a small floppy disk, which can be removed from the drive. Floppy disks have many disadvantages, however. They hold only a small amount of data, are slow to access data, and are sometimes unreliable. The use of floppy disk drives has declined dramatically in recent years, in favor of superior devices such as USB drives. *USB drives* are small devices that plug into the computer's USB (universal serial bus) port, and appear to the system as a disk drive. These drives do not actually contain a disk, however. They store data in a special type of memory known as *flash memory*. USB drives, which are also known as *memory sticks* and *flash drives,* are inexpensive, reliable, and small enough to be carried in your pocket.

Optical devices such as the *CD* (compact disc) and the *DVD* (digital versatile disc) are also popular for data storage. Data is not recorded magnetically on an optical disc, but is encoded as a series of pits on the disc surface. CD and DVD drives use a laser to detect the pits and thus read the encoded data. Optical discs hold large amounts of data, and because recordable CD and DVD drives are now commonplace, they are good mediums for creating backup copies of data.

Input Devices

Input is any data the computer collects from people and from other devices. The component that collects the data and sends it to the computer is called an *input device*. Common input devices are the keyboard, mouse, scanner, microphone, and digital camera. Disk drives and optical drives can also be considered input devices because programs and data are retrieved from them and loaded into the computer's memory.

Output Devices

Output is any data the computer produces for people or for other devices. It might be a sales report, a list of names, or a graphic image. The data is sent to an *output device,* which formats and presents it. Common output devices are video displays and printers. Disk drives and CD recorders can also be considered output devices because the system sends data to them in order to be saved.

 **Checkpoint**

1.1 What is a program?

1.2 What is hardware?

1.3 List the five major components of a computer system.

1.4 What part of the computer actually runs programs?

1.5 What part of the computer serves as a work area to store a program and its data while the program is running?

1.6 What part of the computer holds data for long periods of time, even when there is no power to the computer?

1.7 What part of the computer collects data from people and from other devices?

1.8 What part of the computer formats and presents data for people or other devices?

1.3   How Computers Store Data

CONCEPT: All data that is stored in a computer is converted to sequences of 0s and 1s.

A computer's memory is divided into tiny storage locations known as *bytes*. One byte is only enough memory to store a letter of the alphabet or a small number. In order to do anything meaningful, a computer has to have lots of bytes. Most computers today have millions, or even billions, of bytes of memory.

Each byte is divided into eight smaller storage locations known as bits. The term *bit* stands for *binary digit*. Computer scientists usually think of bits as tiny switches that can be either on or off. Bits aren't actual "switches," however, at least not in the conventional sense. In most computer systems, bits are tiny electrical components that can hold either a positive or a negative charge. Computer scientists think of a positive charge as a switch in the *on* position, and a negative charge as a switch in the *off* position. Figure 1-6 shows the way that a computer scientist might think of a byte of memory: as a collection of switches that are each flipped to either the on or off position.

Figure 1-6 Think of a byte as eight switches

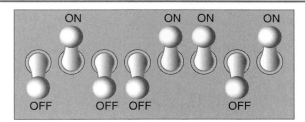

When a piece of data is stored in a byte, the computer sets the eight bits to an on/off pattern that represents the data. For example, the pattern shown on the left in Figure 1-7 shows how the number 77 would be stored in a byte, and the pattern on the right shows how the letter A would be stored in a byte. In a moment you will see how these patterns are determined.

Figure 1-7 Bit patterns for the number 77 and the letter A

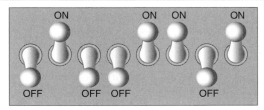
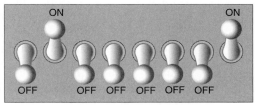

The number 77 stored in a byte.   The letter A stored in a byte.

Storing Numbers

A bit can be used in a very limited way to represent numbers. Depending on whether the bit is turned on or off, it can represent one of two different values. In computer systems, a bit that is turned off represents the number 0 and a bit that is turned on represents the number 1. This corresponds perfectly to the *binary numbering system*. In the binary numbering system (or *binary,* as it is usually called) all numeric values are written as sequences of 0s and 1s. Here is an example of a number that is written in binary:

10011101

The position of each digit in a binary number has a value assigned to it. Starting with the rightmost digit and moving left, the position values are 2^0, 2^1, 2^2, 2^3, and so forth, as shown in Figure 1-8. Figure 1-9 shows the same diagram with the position values calculated. Starting with the rightmost digit and moving left, the position values are 1, 2, 4, 8, and so forth.

Figure 1-8 The values of binary digits as powers of 2

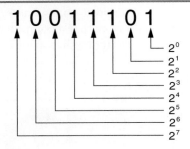

Figure 1-9 The values of binary digits

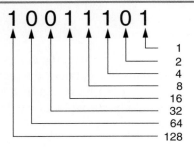

To determine the value of a binary number you simply add up the position values of all the 1s. For example, in the binary number 10011101, the position values of the 1s are 1, 4, 8, 16, and 128. This is shown in Figure 1-10. The sum of all of these position values is 157. So, the value of the binary number 10011101 is 157.

Figure 1-11 shows how you can picture the number 157 stored in a byte of memory. Each 1 is represented by a bit in the on position, and each 0 is represented by a bit in the off position.

Figure 1-10 Determining the value of 10011101

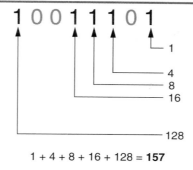

$1 + 4 + 8 + 16 + 128 = \textbf{157}$

Figure 1-11 The bit pattern for 157

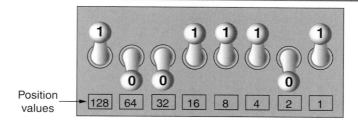

$128 + 16 + 8 + 4 + 1 = \textbf{157}$

When all of the bits in a byte are set to 0 (turned off), then the value of the byte is 0. When all of the bits in a byte are set to 1 (turned on), then the byte holds the largest value that can be stored in it. The largest value that can be stored in a byte is $1 + 2 + 4 + 8 + 16 + 32 + 64 + 128 = 255$. This limit exists because there are only eight bits in a byte.

What if you need to store a number larger than 255? The answer is simple: use more than one byte. For example, suppose we put two bytes together. That gives us 16 bits. The position values of those 16 bits would be 2^0, 2^1, 2^2, 2^3, and so forth, up through 2^{15}. As shown in Figure 1-12, the maximum value that can be stored in two bytes is 65,535. If you need to store a number larger than this, then more bytes are necessary.

Figure 1-12 Two bytes used for a large number

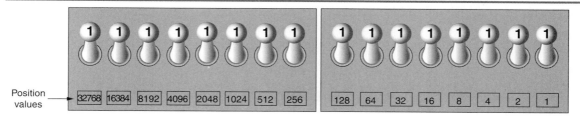

$32768 + 16384 + 8192 + 4096 + 2048 + 1024 + 512 + 256 + 128 + 64 + 32 + 16 + 8 + 4 + 2 + 1 = \textbf{65535}$

TIP: In case you're feeling overwhelmed by all this, relax! You will not have to actually convert numbers to binary while programming. Knowing that this process is taking place inside the computer will help you as you learn, and in the long term this knowledge will make you a better programmer.

Storing Characters

Any piece of data that is stored in a computer's memory must be stored as a binary number. That includes characters, such as letters and punctuation marks. When a character is stored in memory, it is first converted to a numeric code. The numeric code is then stored in memory as a binary number.

Over the years, different coding schemes have been developed to represent characters in computer memory. Historically, the most important of these coding schemes is *ASCII,* which stands for the *American Standard Code for Information Interchange.* ASCII is a set of 128 numeric codes that represent the English letters, various punctuation marks, and other characters. For example, the ASCII code for the uppercase letter A is 65. When you type an uppercase A on your computer keyboard, the number 65 is stored in memory (as a binary number, of course). This is shown in Figure 1-13.

Figure 1-13 The letter A is stored in memory as the number 65

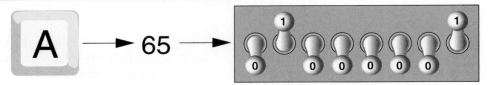

TIP: The acronym ASCII is pronounced "askee."

In case you are curious, the ASCII code for uppercase B is 66, for uppercase C is 67, and so forth. Appendix A shows all of the ASCII codes and the characters they represent.

The ASCII character set was developed in the early 1960s, and was eventually adopted by most all computer manufacturers. ASCII is limited, however, because it defines codes for only 128 characters. To remedy this, the Unicode character set was developed in the early 1990s. *Unicode* is an extensive encoding scheme that is compatible with ASCII, and can also represent the characters of many of the world's languages. Today, Unicode is quickly becoming the standard character set used in the computer industry.

Advanced Number Storage

Earlier you read about numbers and how they are stored in memory. While reading that section, perhaps it occurred to you that the binary numbering system can be used to represent only integer numbers, beginning with 0. Negative numbers and real numbers (such as 3.14159) cannot be represented using the simple binary numbering technique we discussed.

Computers are able to store negative numbers and real numbers in memory, but to do so they use encoding schemes along with the binary numbering system. Negative numbers are encoded using a technique known as *twos complement,* and real numbers are encoded in *floating-point notation.* You don't need to know how these encoding schemes work, only that they are used to convert negative numbers and real numbers to binary format.

Other Types of Data

Computers are often referred to as digital devices. The term *digital* can be used to describe anything that uses binary numbers. *Digital data* is data that is stored in binary, and a *digital device* is any device that works with binary data. In this section we have discussed how numbers and characters are stored in binary, but computers also work with many other types of digital data.

For example, consider the pictures that you take with your digital camera. These images are composed of tiny dots of color known as *pixels.* (The term pixel stands for *picture element.*) As shown in Figure 1-14, each pixel in an image is converted to a numeric code that represents the pixel's color. The numeric code is stored in memory as a binary number.

Figure 1-14 A digital image is stored in binary format

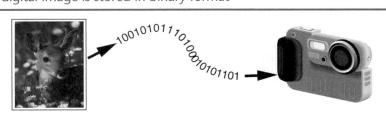

The music that you play on your CD player, iPod, or MP3 player is also digital. A digital song is broken into small pieces known as *samples.* Each sample is converted to a binary number, which can be stored in memory. The more samples that a song is divided into, the more it sounds like the original music when it is played back. A CD-quality song is divided into more than 44,000 samples per second!

Checkpoint

1.9 What amount of memory is enough to store a letter of the alphabet or a small number?

1.10 What do you call a tiny "switch" that can be set to either on or off?

1.11 In what numbering system are all numeric values written as sequences of 0s and 1s?

1.12 What is the purpose of ASCII?

1.13 What encoding scheme is extensive to represent all the characters of all the languages in the world?

1.14 What do the terms "digital data" and "digital device" mean?

1.4 How a Program Works

CONCEPT: A computer's CPU can only understand instructions that are written in machine language. Because people find it very difficult to write entire programs in machine language, other programming languages have been invented.

Earlier, we stated that the CPU is the most important component in a computer because it is the part of the computer that runs programs. Sometimes the CPU is called the "computer's brain," and is described as being "smart." Although these are common metaphors, you should understand that the CPU is not a brain, and it is not smart. The CPU is an electronic device that is designed to do specific things. In particular, the CPU is designed to perform operations such as the following:

- Reading a piece of data from main memory
- Adding two numbers
- Subtracting one number from another number
- Multiplying two numbers
- Dividing one number by another number
- Moving a piece of data from one memory location to another
- Determining whether one value is equal to another value
- And so forth . . .

As you can see from this list, the CPU performs simple operations on pieces of data. The CPU does nothing on its own, however. It has to be told what to do, and that's the purpose of a program. A program is nothing more than a list of instructions that cause the CPU to perform operations.

Each instruction in a program is a command that tells the CPU to perform a specific operation. Here's an example of an instruction that might appear in a program:

```
10110000
```

To you and me, this is only a series of 0s and 1s. To a CPU, however, this is an instruction to perform an operation[1]. It is written in 0s and 1s because CPUs only understand instructions that are written in *machine language,* and machine language instructions are always written in binary.

A machine language instruction exists for each operation that a CPU is capable of performing. For example, there is an instruction for adding numbers; there is an instruction for subtracting one number from another; and so forth. The entire set of instructions that a CPU can execute is known as the CPU's *instruction set.*

---

[1] The example shown is an actual instruction for an Intel microprocessor. It tells the microprocessor to move a value into the CPU.

NOTE: There are several microprocessor companies today that manufacture CPUs. Some of the more well-known microprocessor companies are Intel, AMD, and Motorola. If you look carefully at your computer, you might find a tag showing a logo for its microprocessor.

Each brand of microprocessor has its own unique instruction set, which is typically understood only by microprocessors of the same brand. For example, Intel microprocessors understand the same instructions, but they do not understand instructions for Motorola microprocessors.

The machine language instruction that was previously shown is an example of only one instruction. It takes a lot more than one instruction, however, for the computer to do anything meaningful. Because the operations that a CPU knows how to perform are so basic in nature, a meaningful task can be accomplished only if the CPU performs many operations. For example, if you want your computer to calculate the amount of interest that you will earn from your savings account this year, the CPU will have to perform a large number of instructions, carried out in the proper sequence. It is not unusual for a program to contain thousands, or even a million or more machine language instructions.

Programs are usually stored on a secondary storage device such as a disk drive. When you install a program on your computer, the program is typically copied to your computer's disk drive from a CD-ROM, or perhaps downloaded from a Web site.

Although a program can be stored on a secondary storage device such as a disk drive, it has to be copied into main memory, or RAM, each time the CPU executes it. For example, suppose you have a word processing program on your computer's disk. To execute the program you use the mouse to double-click the program's icon. This causes the program to be copied from the disk into main memory. Then, the computer's CPU executes the copy of the program that is in main memory. This process is illustrated in Figure 1-15.

Figure 1-15 A program is copied into main memory and then executed

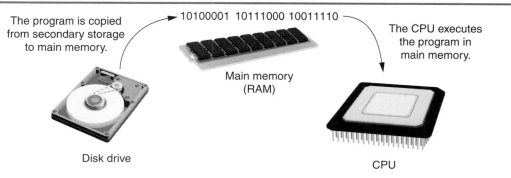

When a CPU executes the instructions in a program, it is engaged in a process that is known as the *fetch-decode-execute cycle*. This cycle, which consists of three steps, is repeated for each instruction in the program. The steps are:

1. **Fetch** A program is a long sequence of machine language instructions. The first step of the cycle is to fetch, or read, the next instruction from memory into the CPU.

2. **Decode** A machine language instruction is a binary number that represents a command that tells the CPU to perform an operation. In this step the CPU decodes the instruction that was just fetched from memory, to determine which operation it should perform.

3. **Execute** The last step in the cycle is to execute, or perform, the operation.

Figure 1-16 illustrates these steps.

Figure 1-16 The fetch-decode-execute cycle

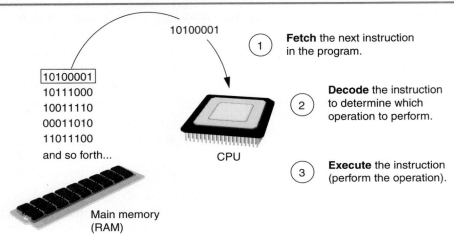

From Machine Language to Assembly Language

Computers can only execute programs that are written in machine language. As previously mentioned, a program can have thousands, or even a million or more binary instructions, and writing such a program would be very tedious and time consuming. Programming in machine language would also be very difficult because putting a 0 or a 1 in the wrong place will cause an error.

Although a computer's CPU only understands machine language, it is impractical for people to write programs in machine language. For this reason, *assembly language* was created in the early days of computing[2] as an alternative to machine language. Instead of using binary numbers for instructions, assembly language uses short words that are known as *mnemonics*. For example, in assembly language, the mnemonic add typically means to add numbers, mul typically means to multiply numbers, and mov typically means to move a value to a location in memory. When a programmer uses assembly language to write a program, he or she can write short mnemonics instead of binary numbers.

---

[2] The first assembly language was most likely developed in the 1940s at Cambridge University for use with a historical computer known as the EDSAC.

NOTE: There are many different versions of assembly language. It was mentioned earlier that each brand of CPU has its own machine language instruction set. Each brand of CPU typically has its own assembly language as well.

Assembly language programs cannot be executed by the CPU, however. The CPU only understands machine language, so a special program known as an *assembler* is used to translate an assembly language program to a machine language program. This process is shown in Figure 1-17. The machine language program that is created by the assembler can then be executed by the CPU.

Figure 1-17 An assembler translates an assembly language program to a machine language program

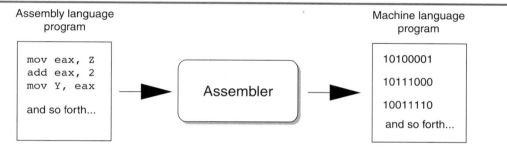

High-Level Languages

Although assembly language makes it unnecessary to write binary machine language instructions, it is not without difficulties. Assembly language is primarily a direct substitute for machine language, and like machine language, it requires that you know a lot about the CPU. Assembly language also requires that you write a large number of instructions for even the simplest program. Because assembly language is so close in nature to machine language, it is referred to as a *low-level language*.

In the 1950s, a new generation of programming languages known as *high-level languages* began to appear. A high-level language allows you to create powerful and complex programs without knowing how the CPU works, and without writing large numbers of low-level instructions. In addition, most high-level languages use words that are easy to understand. For example, if a programmer were using COBOL (which was one of the early high-level languages created in the 1950s), he or she would write the following instruction to display the message "Hello world" on the computer screen:

```
Display "Hello world"
```

Doing the same thing in assembly language would require several instructions, and an intimate knowledge of how the CPU interacts with the computer's video circuitry. As you can see from this example, high-level languages allow programmers to concentrate on the tasks they want to perform with their programs rather than the details of how the CPU will execute those programs.

Since the 1950s, thousands of high-level languages have been created. Table 1-1 lists several of the more well-known languages. If you are working toward a degree in computer science or a related field, you are likely to study one or more of these languages.

Table 1-1 Programming languages

Language	Description
Ada	Ada was created in the 1970s, primarily for applications used by the U.S. Department of Defense. The language is named in honor of Countess Ada Lovelace, an influential and historical figure in the field of computing.
BASIC	Beginners All-purpose Symbolic Instruction Code is a general-purpose language that was originally designed in the early 1960s to be simple enough for beginners to learn. Today, there are many different versions of BASIC.
FORTRAN	**FOR**mula **TRAN**slator was the first high-level programming language. It was designed in the 1950s for performing complex mathematical calculations.
COBOL	**C**ommon **B**usiness-**O**riented **L**anguage was created in the 1950s, and was designed for business applications.
Pascal	Pascal was created in 1970, and was originally designed for teaching programming. The language was named in honor of the mathematician, physicist, and philosopher Blaise Pascal.
C and C++	C and C++ (pronounced "c plus plus") are powerful, general-purpose languages developed at Bell Laboratories. The C language was created in 1972 and the C++ language was created in 1983.
C#	Pronounced "c sharp." This language was created by Microsoft around the year 2000 for developing applications based on the Microsoft .NET platform.
Java	Java was created by Sun Microsystems in the early 1990s. It can be used to develop programs that run on a single computer or over the Internet from a Web server.
JavaScript™	JavaScript, created in the 1990s, can be used in Web pages. Despite its name, JavaScript is not related to Java.
Python	Python is a general purpose language created in the early 1990s. It has become popular in business and academic applications.
Ruby	Ruby is a general purpose language that was created in the 1990s. It is increasingly becoming a popular language for programs that run on Web servers.
Visual Basic	Visual Basic (commonly known as VB) is a Microsoft programming language and software development environment that allows programmers to create Windows®-based applications quickly. VB was originally created in the early 1990s.

Each high-level language has its own set of words that the programmer must learn in order to use the language. The words that make up a high-level programming language are known as *key words* or *reserved words*. Each key word has a specific meaning, and cannot be used for any other purpose. You previously saw an example of a COBOL statement that uses the key word `display` to print a message on the screen. In the Python language the word `print` serves the same purpose.

In addition to key words, programming languages have *operators* that perform various operations on data. For example, all programming languages have math operators that perform arithmetic. In Java, as well as most other languages, the + sign is an operator that adds two numbers. The following adds 12 and 75:

```
12 + 75
```

In addition to key words and operators, each language also has it own *syntax*, which is a set of rules that must be strictly followed when writing a program. The syntax rules dictate how key words, operators, and various punctuation characters must be used in a program. When you are learning a programming language, you must learn the syntax rules for that particular language.

The individual instructions that you use to write a program in a high-level programming language are called *statements*. A programming statement can consist of key words, operators, punctuation, and other allowable programming elements, arranged in the proper sequence to perform an operation.

NOTE: Human languages also have syntax rules. Do you remember when you took your first English class, and you learned all those rules about infinitives, indirect objects, clauses, and so forth? You were learning the syntax of the English language.

Although people commonly violate the syntax rules of their native language when speaking and writing, other people usually understand what they mean. Unfortunately, computers do not have this ability. If even a single syntax error appears in a program, the program cannot be executed.

Compilers and Interpreters

VideoNote

Compiling and Executing a Program

Because the CPU understands only machine language instructions, programs that are written in a high-level language must be translated into machine language. Once a program has been written in a high-level language, the programmer will use a compiler or an interpreter to make the translation.

A *compiler* is a program that translates a high-level language program into a separate machine language program. The machine language program can then be executed any time it is needed. This is shown in Figure 1-18. As shown in the figure, compiling and executing are two different processes.

Figure 1-18 Compiling a high-level program and executing it

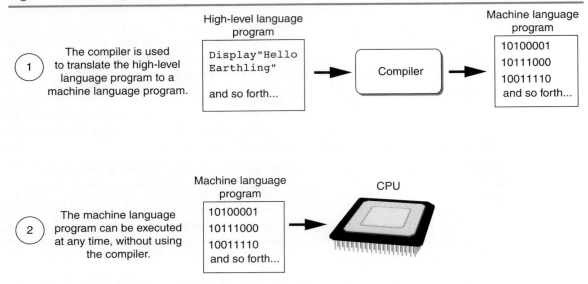

An *interpreter* is a program that both translates and executes the instructions in a high-level language program. As the interpreter reads each individual instruction in the program, it converts it to a machine language instruction and then immediately executes it. This process repeats for every instruction in the program. This process is illustrated in Figure 1-19. Because interpreters combine translation and execution, they typically do not create separate machine language programs.

Figure 1-19 Executing a high-level program with an interpreter

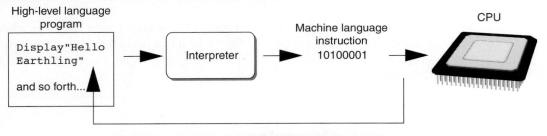

NOTE: Programs that are compiled generally execute faster than programs that are interpreted because a compiled program is already translated entirely to machine language when it is executed. A program that is interpreted must be translated at the time it is executed.

The statements that a programmer writes in a high-level language are called *source code*, or simply *code*. Typically, the programmer types a program's code into a text editor and then saves the code in a file on the computer's disk. Next, the programmer uses a compiler to translate the code into a machine language program, or an interpreter to translate and execute the code. If the code contains a syntax error, however, it cannot be translated. A *syntax error* is a mistake such as a misspelled key word, a missing punctuation character, or the incorrect use of an operator. When this happens the compiler or interpreter displays an error message indicating that the program contains a syntax error. The programmer corrects the error and then attempts once again to translate the program.

Integrated Development Environments

Although you can use a simple text editor such as Notepad (which is part of the Windows operating system) to write a program, most programmers use specialized software packages called *integrated development environments* or *IDEs*. Most IDEs combine the following programs into one software package:

- A text editor that has specialized features for writing statements in a high-level programming language
- A compiler or interpreter
- Useful tools for testing programs and locating errors

Figure 1-20 shows a screen from Microsoft Visual Studio, a popular IDE for developing programs in the C++, Visual Basic, and C# languages. Eclipse™, NetBeans, Dev-C++, and jGRASP™ are a few other popular IDEs.

Figure 1-20 An integrated development environment

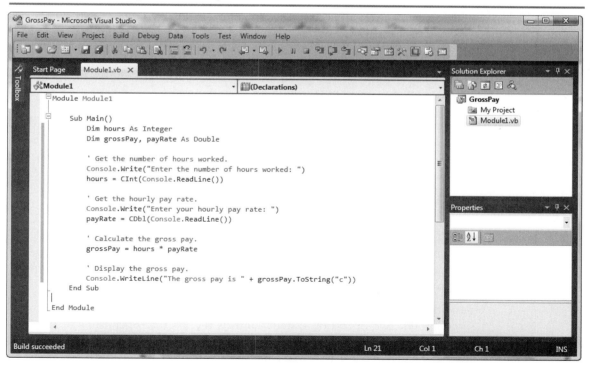

Checkpoint

1.15 A CPU understands instructions that are written only in what language?

1.16 A program has to be copied into what type of memory each time the CPU executes it?

1.17 When a CPU executes the instructions in a program, it is engaged in what process?

1.18 What is assembly language?

1.19 What type of programming language allows you to create powerful and complex programs without knowing how the CPU works?

1.20 Each language has a set of rules that must be strictly followed when writing a program. What is this set of rules called?

1.21 What do you call a program that translates a high-level language program into a separate machine language program?

1.22 What do you call a program that both translates and executes the instructions in a high-level language program?

1.23 What type of mistake is usually caused by a misspelled key word, a missing punctuation character, or the incorrect use of an operator?

 ## 1.5 Types of Software

CONCEPT: Programs generally fall into one of two categories: systems software or application software. System software is the set of programs that control or enhance the operation of a computer. Application software makes a computer useful for everyday tasks.

If a computer is to function, software is not optional. Everything that a computer does, from the time you turn the power switch on until you shut the system down, is under the control of software. There are two general categories of software: system software and application software. Most computer programs clearly fit into one of these two categories. Let's take a closer look at each.

System Software

The programs that control and manage the basic operations of a computer are generally referred to as *system software*. System software typically includes the following types of programs:

Operating Systems. An *operating system* is the most fundamental set of programs on a computer. The operating system controls the internal operations of the computer's hardware, manages all of the devices connected to the computer, allows data to be saved to and retrieved from storage devices, and allows other programs to run on the computer. Figure 1-21 shows screens from three popular operating systems: Windows, Mac OS X®, and Linux®.

Utility Programs. A *utility program* performs a specialized task that enhances the computer's operation or safeguards data. Examples of utility programs are virus scanners, file compression programs, and data backup programs.

Software Development Tools. *Software development tools* are the programs that programmers use to create, modify, and test software. Assemblers, compilers, and interpreters are examples of programs that fall into this category.

Figure 1-21 Screens from the Windows, Mac OS X, and Linux operating systems (continues on next page)

Windows

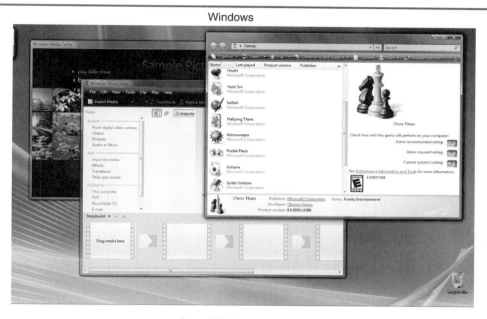

Mac OS X

Figure 1-21 Screens from the Windows, Mac OS X, and Linux operating systems (continued)

Application Software

Programs that make a computer useful for everyday tasks are known as *application software*. These are the programs that people normally spend most of their time running on their computers. Figure 1-1, at the beginning of this chapter, shows screens from two commonly used applications—Microsoft Word, a word processing program, and Adobe Photoshop, an image editing program. Some other examples of application software are spreadsheet programs, email programs, Web browsers, and game programs.

 Checkpoint

1.24 What fundamental set of programs control the internal operations of the computer's hardware?

1.25 What do you call a program that performs a specialized task, such as a virus scanner, a file compression program, or a data backup program?

1.26 Word processing programs, spreadsheet programs, email programs, Web browsers, and game programs belong to what category of software?

Review Questions

Multiple Choice

1. A(n) _____ is a set of instructions that a computer follows to perform a task.
   a. compiler
   b. program
   c. interpreter
   d. programming language

2. The physical devices that a computer is made of are referred to as _____.
   a. hardware
   b. software
   c. the operating system
   d. tools

3. The part of a computer that runs programs is called _____.
   a. RAM
   b. secondary storage
   c. main memory
   d. the CPU

4. Today, CPUs are small chips known as _____.
   a. ENIACs
   b. microprocessors
   c. memory chips
   d. operating systems

5. The computer stores a program while the program is running, as well as the data that the program is working with, in _____.
   a. secondary storage
   b. the CPU
   c. main memory
   d. the microprocessor

6. This is a volatile type of memory that is used only for temporary storage while a program is running.
   a. RAM
   b. secondary storage
   c. the disk drive
   d. the USB drive

7. A type of memory that can hold data for long periods of time—even when there is no power to the computer—is called _____.
   a. RAM
   b. main memory
   c. secondary storage
   d. CPU storage

8. A component that collects data from people or other devices and sends it to the computer is called _____.

   a. an output device
   b. an input device
   c. a secondary storage device
   d. main memory

9. A video display is a(n) _____.

   a. output device
   b. input device
   c. secondary storage device
   d. main memory

10. A _____ is enough memory to store a letter of the alphabet or a small number.

   a. byte
   b. bit
   c. switch
   d. transistor

11. A byte is made up of eight _____.

   a. CPUs
   b. instructions
   c. variables
   d. bits

12. In a(n) _____ numbering system, all numeric values are written as sequences of 0s and 1s.

   a. hexadecimal
   b. binary
   c. octal
   d. decimal

13. A bit that is turned off represents the following value: _____.

   a. 1
   b. −1
   c. 0
   d. "no"

14. A set of 128 numeric codes that represent the English letters, various punctuation marks, and other characters is _____.

   a. binary numbering
   b. ASCII
   c. Unicode
   d. ENIAC

15. An extensive encoding scheme that can represent the characters of many of the languages in the world is _____.

   a. binary numbering
   b. ASCII
   c. Unicode
   d. ENIAC

16. Negative numbers are encoded using the _____ technique.
    a. twos compliment
    b. floating point
    c. ASCII
    d. Unicode

17. Real numbers are encoded using the _____ technique.
    a. twos compliment
    b. floating point
    c. ASCII
    d. Unicode

18. The tiny dots of color that digital images are composed of are called _____.
    a. bits
    b. bytes
    c. color packets
    d. pixels

19. If you were to look at a machine language program, you would see _____.
    a. Java code
    b. a stream of binary numbers
    c. English words
    d. circuits

20. In the _____ part of the fetch-decode-execute cycle, the CPU determines which operation it should perform.
    a. fetch
    b. decode
    c. execute
    d. immediately after the instruction is executed

21. Computers can only execute programs that are written in _____.
    a. Java
    b. assembly language
    c. machine language
    d. C++

22. The _____ translates an assembly language program to a machine language program.
    a. assembler
    b. compiler
    c. translator
    d. interpreter

23. The words that make up a high-level programming language are called _____.
    a. binary instructions
    b. mnemonics
    c. commands
    d. key words

24. The rules that must be followed when writing a program are called _____.
    a. syntax
    b. punctuation
    c. key words
    d. operators

25. A(n) _____ program translates a high-level language program into a separate machine language program.
    a. assembler
    b. compiler
    c. translator
    d. utility

True or False

1. Today, CPUs are huge devices made of electrical and mechanical components such as vacuum tubes and switches.

2. Main memory is also known as RAM.

3. Any piece of data that is stored in a computer's memory must be stored as a binary number.

4. Images, like the ones you make with your digital camera, cannot be stored as binary numbers.

5. Machine language is the only language that a CPU understands.

6. Assembly language is considered a high-level language.

7. An interpreter is a program that both translates and executes the instructions in a high-level language program.

8. A syntax error does not prevent a program from being compiled and executed.

9. Windows Vista, Linux, UNIX®, and Mac OS X are all examples of application software.

10. Word processing programs, spreadsheet programs, email programs, Web browsers, and games are all examples of utility programs.

Short Answer

1. Why is the CPU the most important component in a computer?

2. What number does a bit that is turned on represent? What number does a bit that is turned off represent?

3. What would you call a device that works with binary data?

4. What are the words that make up a high-level programming language called?

5. What are the short words that are used in assembly language called?

6. What is the difference between a compiler and an interpreter?

7. What type of software controls the internal operations of the computer's hardware?

Exercises

1. Use what you've learned about the binary numbering system in this chapter to convert the following decimal numbers to binary:

   11
   65
   100
   255

VideoNote
Converting
Binary to
Decimal

2. Use what you've learned about the binary numbering system in this chapter to convert the following binary numbers to decimal:

   1101
   1000
   101011

3. Look at the ASCII chart in Appendix A on the CD that accompanies this book and determine the codes for each letter of your first name.

4. Use the Web to research the history of the BASIC, C++, Java, and Python programming languages, and answer the following questions:

   - Who was the creator of each of these languages?
   - When was each of these languages created?
   - Was there a specific motivation behind the creation of these languages? If so, what was it?

CHAPTER 2

Input, Processing, and Output

TOPICS

2.1 Designing a Program

CONCEPT: Programs must be carefully designed before they are written. During the design process, programmers use tools such as pseudocode and flowcharts to create models of programs.

In Chapter 1 you learned that programmers typically use high-level languages to write programs. However, all professional programmers will tell you that a program should be carefully designed before the code is actually written. When programmers begin a new project, they never jump right in and start writing code as the first step. They begin by creating a design of the program.

After designing the program, the programmer begins writing code in a high-level language. Recall from Chapter 1 that each language has its own rules, known as syntax, that must be followed when writing a program. A language's syntax rules dictate things such as how key words, operators, and punctuation characters can be used. A syntax error occurs if the programmer violates any of these rules.

If the program contains a syntax error, or even a simple mistake such as a misspelled key word, the compiler or interpreter will display an error message indicating what the error is. Virtually all code contains syntax errors when it is first written, so the programmer will typically spend some time correcting these. Once all of the syntax errors and simple typing mistakes have been corrected, the program can be compiled and translated into a machine language program (or executed by an interpreter, depending on the language being used).

Once the code is in an executable form, it is then tested to determine whether any logic errors exist. A *logic error* is a mistake that does not prevent the program from running, but causes it to produce incorrect results. (Mathematical mistakes are common causes of logic errors.)

If there are logic errors, the programmer *debugs* the code. This means that the programmer finds and corrects the code that is causing the error. Sometimes during this process, the programmer discovers that the original design must be changed. This entire process, which is known as the *program development cycle,* is repeated until no errors can be found in the program. Figure 2-1 shows the steps in the process.

Figure 2-1 The program development cycle

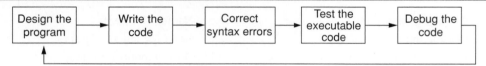

This book focuses entirely on the first step of the program development cycle: designing the program. The process of designing a program is arguably the most important part of the cycle. You can think of a program's design as its foundation. If you build a house on a poorly constructed foundation, eventually you will find yourself doing a lot of work to fix the house! A program's design should be viewed no differently. If your program is designed poorly, eventually you will find yourself doing a lot of work to fix the program.

Designing a Program

The process of designing a program can be summarized in the following two steps:

1. Understand the task that the program is to perform.
2. Determine the steps that must be taken to perform the task.

Let's take a closer look at each of these steps.

Understand the Task That the Program Is to Perform

It is essential that you understand what a program is supposed to do before you can determine the steps that the program will perform. Typically, a professional programmer gains this understanding by working directly with the customer. We use the term *customer* to describe the person, group, or organization that is asking you to write a program. This could be a customer in the traditional sense of the word, meaning someone who is paying you to write a program. It could also be your boss, or the manager of a department within your company. Regardless of whom it is, the customer will be relying on your program to perform an important task.

To get a sense of what a program is supposed to do, the programmer usually interviews the customer. During the interview, the customer will describe the task that the program should perform, and the programmer will ask questions to uncover as many details as possible about the task. A follow-up interview is usually needed because customers rarely mention everything they want during the initial meeting, and programmers often think of additional questions.

The programmer studies the information that was gathered from the customer during the interviews and creates a list of different software requirements. A *software requirement* is simply a single function that the program must perform in order to satisfy the customer. Once the customer agrees that the list of requirements is complete, the programmer can move to the next phase.

> **TIP:** If you choose to become a professional software developer, your customer will be anyone who asks you to write programs as part of your job. As long as you are a student, however, your customer is your instructor! In every programming class that you will take, it's practically guaranteed that your instructor will assign programming problems for you to complete. For your academic success, make sure that you understand your instructor's requirements for those assignments and write your programs accordingly.

Determine the Steps That Must Be Taken to Perform the Task

Once you understand the task that the program will perform, you begin by breaking down the task into a series of steps. This is similar to the way you would break down a task into a series of steps that another person can follow. For example, suppose your little sister asks you how to boil water. Assuming she is old enough to be trusted around the stove, you might break down that task into a series of steps as follows:

1. Pour the desired amount of water into a pot.
2. Put the pot on a stove burner.
3. Turn the burner to high.
4. Watch the water until you see large bubbles rapidly rising. When this happens, the water is boiling.

This is an example of an *algorithm,* which is a set of well-defined logical steps that must be taken to perform a task. Notice that the steps in this algorithm are sequentially ordered. Step 1 should be performed before Step 2, and so on. If your little sister follows these steps exactly as they appear, and in the correct order, she should be able to boil water successfully.

A programmer breaks down the task that a program must perform in a similar way. An algorithm is created, which lists all of the logical steps that must be taken. For example, suppose you have been asked to write a program to calculate and display the gross pay for an hourly paid employee. Here are the steps that you would take:

1. Get the number of hours worked.
2. Get the hourly pay rate.
3. Multiply the number of hours worked by the hourly pay rate.
4. Display the result of the calculation that was performed in Step 3.

Of course, this algorithm isn't ready to be executed on the computer. The steps in this list have to be translated into code. Programmers commonly use two tools to help them accomplish this: pseudocode and flowcharts. Let's look at each of these in more detail.

Pseudocode

Recall from Chapter 1 that each programming language has strict rules, known as syntax, that the programmer must follow when writing a program. If the programmer writes code that violates these rules, a syntax error will result and the program cannot be compiled or executed. When this happens, the programmer has to locate the error and correct it.

Because small mistakes like misspelled words and forgotten punctuation characters can cause syntax errors, programmers have to be mindful of such small details when writing code. For this reason, programmers find it helpful to write their programs in pseudocode (pronounced "sue doe code") before they write it in the actual code of a programming language.

The word "pseudo" means fake, so *pseudocode* is fake code. It is an informal language that has no syntax rules, and is not meant to be compiled or executed. Instead, programmers use pseudocode to create models, or "mock-ups" of programs. Because programmers don't have to worry about syntax errors while writing pseudocode, they can focus all of their attention on the program's design. Once a satisfactory design has been created with pseudocode, the pseudocode can be translated directly to actual code.

Here is an example of how you might write pseudocode for the pay calculating program that we discussed earlier:

```
Display "Enter the number of hours the employee worked."
Input hours
Display "Enter the employee's hourly pay rate."
Input payRate
Set grossPay = hours * payRate
Display "The employee's gross pay is $", grossPay
```

Each statement in the pseudocode represents an operation that can be performed in any high-level language. For example, all languages provide a way to display messages on the screen, read input that is typed on the keyboard, and perform mathematical calculations. For now, don't worry about the details of this particular pseudocode program. As you progress through this chapter you will learn more about each of the statements that you see here.

Flowcharts

Flowcharting is another tool that programmers use to design programs. A *flowchart* is a diagram that graphically depicts the steps that take place in a program. Figure 2-2 shows how you might create a flowchart for the pay calculating program.

Notice that there are three types of symbols in the flowchart: ovals, parallelograms, and rectangles. The ovals, which appear at the top and bottom of the flowchart, are called *terminal symbols*. The *Start* terminal symbol marks the program's starting point and the *End* terminal symbol marks the program's ending point.

Between the terminal symbols are parallelograms, which are used for both *input symbols* and *output symbols,* and rectangles, which are called *processing symbols*. Each of these symbols represents a step in the program. The symbols are connected by arrows that represent the "flow" of the program. To step through the symbols in the proper order, you begin at the *Start* terminal and follow the arrows until you reach the *End* terminal. Throughout this chapter we will look at each of these symbols in greater detail. For your reference, Appendix B summarizes all of the flowchart symbols that we use in this book.

There are a number of different ways that you can draw flowcharts, and your instructor will most likely tell you the way that he or she prefers you to draw them in class. Perhaps the simplest and least expensive way is to simply sketch the flowchart by hand with pencil and paper. If you need to make your hand-drawn flowcharts look more professional you can visit your local office supply store (or possibly your campus bookstore) and purchase a flowchart template, which is a small plastic sheet that has the flowchart symbols cut into it. You can use the template to trace the symbols onto a piece of paper.

The disadvantage to drawing flowcharts by hand is that mistakes have to be manually erased, and in many cases, require that the entire page be redrawn. A more efficient and professional way to create flowcharts is to use software. There are several specialized software packages available that allow you to create flowcharts.

Figure 2-2 Flowchart for the pay calculating program

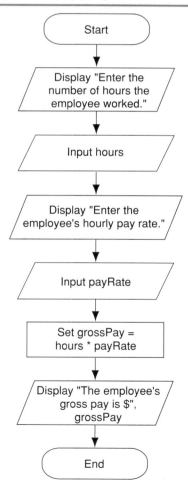

 **Checkpoint**

2.1 Who is a programmer's customer?

2.2 What is a software requirement?

2.3 What is an algorithm?

2.4 What is pseudocode?

2.5 What is a flowchart?

2.6 What are each of the following symbols in a flowchart?
- Oval
- Parallelogram
- Rectangle

 ## 2.2 Output, Input, and Variables

CONCEPT: Output is data that is generated and displayed by the program. Input is data that the program receives. When a program receives data, it stores it in variables, which are named storage locations in memory.

Computer programs typically perform the following three-step process:

1. Input is received.
2. Some process is performed on the input.
3. Output is produced.

Input is any data that the program receives while it is running. One common form of input is data that is typed on the keyboard. Once input is received, some process, such as a mathematical calculation, is usually performed on it. The results of the process are then sent out of the program as output.

Figure 2-3 illustrates these three steps in the pay calculating program that we discussed earlier. The number of hours worked and the hourly pay rate are provided as input. The program processes this data by multiplying the hours worked by the hourly pay rate. The results of the calculation are then displayed on the screen as output.

Figure 2-3 The input, processing, and output of the pay calculating program

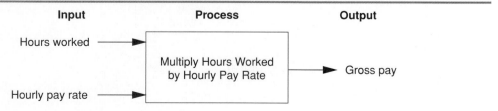

In this section, you will look at some simple programs that perform two of these steps: output and input. In the next section, we will discuss how to process data.

Displaying Screen Output

Perhaps the most fundamental thing that you can do in a program is to display a message on the computer screen. As previously mentioned, all high-level languages provide a way to display screen output. In this book, we use the word `Display` to write pseudocode statements for displaying output on the screen. Here is an example:

```
Display "Hello world"
```

The purpose of this statement is to display the message *Hello world* on the screen. Notice that after the word `Display`, we have written `Hello world` inside quotation marks. The quotation marks are not to be displayed. They simply mark the beginning and the end of the text that we wish to display.

Suppose your instructor tells you to write a pseudocode program that displays your name and address on the computer screen. The pseudocode shown in Program 2-1 is an example of such a program.

Program 2-1

```
Display "Kate Austen"
Display "123 Dharma Lane"
Display "Asheville, NC 28899"
```

It is important for you to understand that the statements in this program execute in the order that they appear, from the top of the program to the bottom. This is shown in Figure 2-4. If you translated this pseudocode into an actual program and ran it, the first statement would execute, followed by the second statement, and followed by the third statement. If you try to visualize the way this program's output would appear on the screen, you should imagine something like that shown in Figure 2-5. Each `Display` statement produces a line of output.

Figure 2-4 The statements execute in order

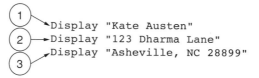

Figure 2-5 Output of Program 2-1

NOTE: Although this book uses the word Display for an instruction that displays screen output, some programmers use other words for this purpose. For example, some programmers use the word Print, and others use the word Write. Pseudocode has no rules that dictate the words that you may or may not use.

Figure 2-6 shows the way you would draw a flowchart for this program. Notice that between the *Start* and *End* terminal symbols there are three parallelograms. A parallelogram can be either an output symbol or an input symbol. In this program, all three parallelograms are output symbols. There is one for each of the Display statements.

Figure 2-6 Flowchart for Program 2-1

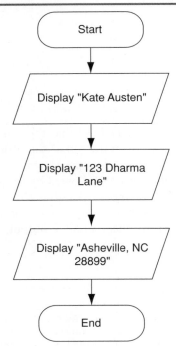

Sequence Structures

It was mentioned earlier that the statements in Program 2-1 execute in the order that they appear, from the top of the program to the bottom. A set of statements that execute in the order that they appear is called a *sequence structure*. In fact, all of the programs that you will see in this chapter are sequence structures.

A *structure*, also called a *control structure*, is a logical design that controls the order in which a set of statements execute. In the 1960s, a group of mathematicians proved that only three program structures are needed to write any type of program. The simplest of these structures is the sequence structure. Later in this book, you will learn about the other two structures—decision structures and repetition structures.

Strings and String Literals

Programs almost always work with data of some type. For example, Program 2-1 uses the following three pieces of data:

```
"Kate Austen"
"123 Dharma Lane"
"Asheville, NC 28899"
```

These pieces of data are sequences of characters. In programming terms, a sequence of characters that is used as data is called a *string*. When a string appears in the actual code of a program (or in pseudocode, as it does in Program 1-2) it is called a *string literal*. In program code, or pseudocode, a string literal is usually enclosed in quotation marks. As mentioned earlier, the quotation marks simply mark where the string begins and ends.

In this book, we will always enclose string literals in double quote marks ("). Most programming languages use this same convention, but a few use single quote marks (').

Variables and Input

VideoNote

Variables and Input

Quite often a program needs to store data in the computer's memory so it can perform operations on that data. For example, consider the typical online shopping experience: You browse a Web site and add the items that you want to purchase to the shopping cart. As you add items to the shopping cart, data about those items is stored in memory. Then, when you click the checkout button, a program running on the Web site's computer calculates the total of all the items you have in your shopping cart, applicable sales taxes, shipping costs, and the total of all these charges. When the program performs these calculations, it stores the results in the computer's memory.

Programs use variables to store data in memory. A *variable* is a storage location in memory that is represented by a name. For example, a program that calculates the sales tax on a purchase might use a variable named `tax` to hold that value in memory. And a program that calculates the distance from Earth to a distant star might use a variable named `distance` to hold that value in memory.

In this section, we will discuss a basic input operation: reading data that has been typed on the keyboard. When a program reads data from the keyboard, usually it stores that data in a variable so it can be used later by the program. In pseudocode we will read data from the keyboard with the `Input` statement. As an example, look at the following statement, which appeared earlier in the pay calculating program:

```
Input hours
```

The word `Input` is an instruction to read a piece of data from the keyboard. The word `hours` is the name of the variable in which that the data will be stored. When this statement executes, two things happen:

- The program pauses and waits for the user to type something on the keyboard, and then press the ⏎Enter⏎ key.
- When the ⏎Enter⏎ key is pressed, the data that was typed is stored in the `hours` variable.

Program 2-2 is a simple pseudocode program that demonstrates the Input statement. Before we examine the program, we should mention a couple of things. First, you will notice that each line in the program is numbered. The line numbers are not part of the pseudocode. We will refer to the line numbers later to point out specific parts of the program. Second, the program's output is shown immediately following the pseudocode. From now on, all pseudocode programs will be shown this way.

Program 2-2

```
1 Display "What is your age?"
2 Input age
3 Display "Here is the value that you entered:"
4 Display age
```

Program Output (with Input Shown in Bold)

```
What is your age?
24 [Enter]
Here is the value that you entered:
24
```

The statement in line 1 displays the string "What is your age?" Then, the statement in line 2 waits for the user to type a value on the keyboard and press Enter. The value that is typed will be stored in the age variable. In the example execution of the program, the user has entered 24. The statement in line 3 displays the string "Here is the value that you entered:" and the statement in line 4 displays the value that is stored in the age variable.

Notice that in line 4 there are no quotation marks around age. If quotation marks were placed around age, it would have indicated that we want to display the word "age" instead of the contents of the age variable. In other words, the following statement is an instruction to display the contents of the age variable:

```
Display age
```

This statement, however, is an instruction to display the word "age":

```
Display "age"
```

NOTE: In this section, we have mentioned the user. The *user* is simply any hypothetical person that is using a program and providing input for it. The user is sometimes called the *end user*.

Figure 2-7 shows a flowchart for Program 2-2. Notice that the Input operation is also represented by a parallelogram.

Figure 2-7 Flowchart for Program 2-2

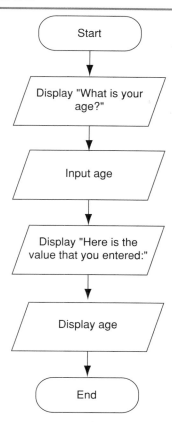

Variable Names

All high-level programming languages allow you to make up your own names for the variables that you use in a program. You don't have complete freedom in naming variables, however. Every language has its own set of rules that you must abide by when creating variable names.

Although the rules for naming variables differ slightly from one language to another, there are some common restrictions:

- Variable names must be one word. They cannot contain spaces.
- In most languages, punctuation characters cannot be used in variable names. It is usually a good idea to use only alphabetic letters and numbers in variable names.
- In most languages, the first character of a variable name cannot be a number.

In addition to following the programming language rules, you should always choose names for your variables that give an indication of what they are used for. For example, a variable that holds the temperature might be named `temperature`, and a variable that holds a car's speed might be named `speed`. You may be tempted to give variables names like `x` and `b2`, but names like these give no clue as to what the variable's purpose is.

Because a variable's name should reflect the variable's purpose, programmers often find themselves creating names that are made of multiple words. For example, consider the following variable names:

```
grosspay
payrate
hotdogssoldtoday
```

Unfortunately, these names are not easily read by the human eye because the words aren't separated. Because we can't have spaces in variable names, we need to find another way to separate the words in a multiword variable name, and make it more readable to the human eye.

One way to do this is to use the underscore character to represent a space. For example, the following variable names are easier to read than those previously shown:

```
gross_pay
pay_rate
hot_dogs_sold_today
```

Another way to address this problem is to use the *camelCase* naming convention. camelCase names are written in the following manner:

- You begin writing the variable name with lowercase letters.
- The first character of the second and subsequent words is written in uppercase.

For example, the following variable names are written in camelCase:

```
grossPay
payRate
hotDogsSoldToday
```

Because the camelCase convention is very popular with programmers, we will use it from this point forward. In fact, you have already seen several programs in this chapter that use camelCase variable names. The pay calculating program shown at the beginning of the chapter uses the variable name payRate. In addition, Program 2-7 uses the variable names originalPrice and salePrice, and Program 2-9 uses the variable names futureValue and presentValue.

> **NOTE:** This style of naming is called camelCase because the uppercase characters that appear in a name are sometimes reminiscent of a camel's humps.

Displaying Multiple Items with One Display Statement

If you refer to Program 2-2 you will see that we used the following two Display statements in lines 3 and 4:

```
Display "Here is the value that you entered:"
Display age
```

We used two Display statements because we needed to display two pieces of data. Line 3 displays the string literal "Here is the value that you entered:" and line 4 displays the contents of the age variable.

Most programming languages provide a way to display multiple pieces of data with one statement. Because this is a common feature of programming languages, frequently we will write `Display` statements in our pseudocode that display multiple items. We will simply separate the items with a comma, as shown in line 3 of Program 2-3.

Program 2-3

```
1 Display "What is your age?"
2 Input age
3 Display "Here is the value that you entered: ", age
```

Program Output (with Input Shown in Bold)

```
What is your age?
24 [Enter]
Here is the value that you entered: 24
```

String Input

The previous two programs read numbers from the keyboard, which were stored in variables by `Input` statements. Programs can also read string input. For example, the pseudocode in Program 2-4 uses two `Input` statements: one to read a string and one to read a number.

Program 2-4

```
1 Display "Enter your name."
2 Input name
3 Display "Enter your age."
4 Input age
5 Display "Hello ", name
6 Display "You are ", age, " years old."
```

Program Output (with Input Shown in Bold)

```
Enter your name.
Andrea [Enter]
Enter your age.
24 [Enter]
Hello Andrea
You are 24 years old.
```

The `Input` statement in line 2 reads input from the keyboard and stores it in the `name` variable. In the example execution of the program, the user entered Andrea. The `Input` statement in line 4 reads input from the keyboard and stores it in the `age` variable. In the example execution of the program, the user entered 24.

Prompting the User

Getting keyboard input from the user is normally a two-step process:

1. Display a prompt on the screen.
2. Read a value from the keyboard.

A *prompt* is a message that tells (or asks) the user to enter a specific value. For example, the pseudocode in Program 2-3 gets the user to enter his or her age with the following statements:

```
Display "What is your age?"
Input age
```

In most programming languages, the statement that reads keyboard input does not display instructions on the screen. It simply causes the program to pause and wait for the user to type something on the keyboard. For this reason, whenever you write a statement that reads keyboard input, you should also write a statement just before it that tells the user what to enter. Otherwise, the user will not know what they are expected to do. For example, suppose we remove line 1 from Program 2-3, as follows:

```
Input age
Display "Here is the value that you entered: ", age
```

If this were an actual program, can you see what would happen when it is executed? The screen would appear blank because the `Input` statement would cause the program to wait for something to be typed on the keyboard. The user would probably think the computer was malfunctioning.

The term *user-friendly* is commonly used in the software business to describe programs that are easy to use. Programs that do not display adequate or correct instructions are frustrating to use, and are not considered user-friendly. One of the simplest things that you can do to increase a program's user-friendliness is to make sure that it displays clear, understandable prompts prior to each statement that reads keyboard input.

TIP: Sometimes we computer science instructors jokingly tell our students to write programs as if "Uncle Joe" or "Aunt Sally" were the user. Of course, these are not real people, but imaginary users who are prone to making mistakes if not told exactly what to do. When you are designing a program, you should imagine that someone who knows nothing about the program's inner workings will be using it.

Checkpoint

2.7 What are the three operations that programs typically perform?

2.8 What is a sequence structure?

2.9 What is a string? What is a string literal?

2.10 A string literal is usually enclosed inside a set of what characters?

2.11 What is a variable?

2.12 Summarize three common rules for naming variables.

2.13 What variable naming convention do we follow in this book?

2.14 Look at the following pseudocode statement:

```
Input temperature
```

What happens when this statement executes?

2.15 Who is the user?

2.16 What is a prompt?

2.17 What two steps usually take place when a program prompts the user for input?

2.18 What does the term "user-friendly" mean?

2.3   Variable Assignment and Calculations

CONCEPT: You can store a value in a variable with an assignment statement. The value can be the result of a calculation, which is created with math operators.

Variable Assignment

In the previous section, you saw how the Input statement gets a value typed on the keyboard and stores it in a variable. You can also write statements that store specific values in variables. The following is an example, in pseudocode:

```
Set price = 20
```

This is called an assignment statement. An *assignment statement* sets a variable to a specified value. In this case, the variable price is set to the value 20. When we write an assignment statement in pseudocode, we will write the word Set, followed by the name of the variable, followed by an equal sign (=), followed by the value we want to store in the variable. The pseudocode in Program 2-5 shows another example.

Program 2-5

```
1 Set dollars = 2.75
2 Display "I have ", dollars, " in my account."
```

Program Output

```
I have 2.75 in my account.
```

In line 1, the value 2.75 is stored in the dollars variable. Line 2 displays the message "I have 2.75 in my account." Just to make sure you understand how the Display statement in line 2 is working, let's walk through it. The word Display is followed by three pieces of data, so that means it will display three things. The first thing it displays is the string literal "I have ". Next, it displays the contents of the dollars variable, which is 2.75. Last, it displays the string literal " in my account."

Variables are called "variable" because they can hold different values while a program is running. Once you set a variable to a value, that value will remain in the variable until you store a different value in the variable. For example, look at the pseudocode in Program 2-6.

Program 2-6

```
1 Set dollars = 2.75
2 Display "I have ", dollars, " in my account."
3 Set dollars = 99.95
4 Display "But now I have ", dollars, " in my account!"
```

Program Output

```
I have 2.75 in my account.
But now I have 99.95 in my account!
```

Line 1 sets the dollars variable to the 2.75, so when the statement in line 2 executes, it displays "I have 2.75 in my account." Then, the statement in line 3 sets the dollars variable to 99.95. As a result, the value 99.95 replaces the value 2.75 that was previously stored in the variable. When line 4 executes, it displays "But now I have 99.95 in my account!" This program illustrates two important characteristics of variables:

- A variable holds only one value at a time.
- When you store a value in a variable, that value replaces the previous value that was in the variable.

NOTE: When writing an assignment statement, all programming languages require that you write the name of the variable that is receiving the value on the left side of the = operator. For example, the following statement is incorrect:

Set 99.95 = dollars   ◄── This is an error!

A statement such as this would be considered a syntax error.

NOTE: In this book, we have chosen to start variable assignment statements with the word `Set` because it makes it clear that we are setting a variable to a value. In most programming languages, however, assignment statements do not start with the word `Set`. In most languages, an assignment statement looks similar to the following:

```
dollars = 99.95
```

If your instructor allows it, it is permissible to write assignment statements without the word `Set` in your pseudocode. Just be sure to write the name of the variable that is receiving the value on the left side of the equal sign.

In flowcharts, an assignment statement appears in a processing symbol, which is a rectangle. Figure 2-8 shows a flowchart for Program 2-6.

Figure 2-8 Flowchart for Program 2-6

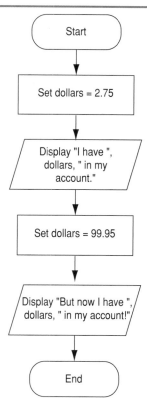

VideoNote

Performing
Calculations

Performing Calculations

Most real-world algorithms require calculations to be performed. A programmer's tools for performing calculations are *math operators*. Programming languages commonly provide the operators shown in Table 2-1.

Table 2-1 Common math operators

Symbol	Operator	Description
+	Addition	Adds two numbers
−	Subtraction	Subtracts one number from another
*	Multiplication	Multiplies one number by another
/	Division	Divides one number by another and gives the quotient
MOD	Modulus	Divides one number by another and gives the remainder
^	Exponent	Raised a number to a power

Programmers use the operators shown in Table 2-1 to create math expressions. A *math expression* performs a calculation and gives a value. The following is an example of a simple math expression:

    12 + 2

The values on the right and left of the + operator are called *operands*. These are values that the + operator adds together. The value that is given by this expression is 14.

Variables may also be used in a math expression. For example, suppose we have two variables named hours and payRate. The following math expression uses the * operator to multiply the value in the hours variable by the value in the payRate variable:

    hours * payRate

When we use a math expression to calculate a value, normally we want to save that value in memory so we can use it again in the program. We do this with an assignment statement. Program 2-7 shows an example.

Program 2-7

```
1 Set price = 100
2 Set discount = 20
3 Set sale = price - discount
4 Display "The total cost is $", sale
```

Program Output

```
The total cost is $80
```

Line 1 sets the price variable to 100, and line 2 sets the discount variable to 20. Line 3 sets the sale variable to the result of the expression price − discount. As you can see from the program output, the sale variable holds the value 80.

In the Spotlight:

Calculating a Percentage

Determining percentages is a common calculation in computer programming. In mathematics, the % symbol is used to indicate a percentage, but most programming languages don't use the % symbol for this purpose. In a program, you usually have to convert a percentage to a decimal number. For example, 50 percent would be written as 0.5 and 2 percent would be written as 0.02.

Let's step through the process of writing a program that calculates a percentage. Suppose a retail business is planning to have a storewide sale where the prices of all items will be 20 percent off. We have been asked to write a program to calculate the sale price of an item after the discount is subtracted. Here is the algorithm:

1. Get the original price of the item.
2. Calculate 20 percent of the original price. This is the amount of the discount.
3. Subtract the discount from the original price. This is the sale price.
4. Display the sale price.

In Step 1 we get the original price of the item. We will prompt the user to enter this data on the keyboard. Recall from the previous section that prompting the user is a two-step process: (1) display a message telling the user to enter the desired data, and (2) reading that data from the keyboard. We will use the following pseudocode statements to do this. Notice that the value entered by the user will be stored in a variable named originalPrice.

```
Display "Enter the item's original price: "
Input originalPrice
```

In Step 2, we calculate the amount of the discount. To do this we multiply the original price by 20 percent. The following statement performs this calculation and stores the result in the discount variable.

```
Set discount = originalPrice * 0.2
```

In Step 3, we subtract the discount from the original price. The following statement does this calculation and stores the result in the salePrice variable.

```
Set salePrice = originalPrice - discount
```

Last, in Step 4, we will use the following statement to display the sale price:

```
Display "The sale price is $", salePrice
```

Program 2-8 shows the entire pseudocode program, with example output. Figure 2-9 shows the flowchart for this program.

Program 2-8

```
1 Display "Enter the item's original price."
2 Input originalPrice
3 Set discount = originalPrice * 0.2
4 Set salePrice = originalPrice - discount
5 Display "The sale price is $", salePrice
```

Program Output (with Input Shown in Bold)

```
Enter the item's original price.
100 [Enter]
The sale price is $80
```

Figure 2-9 Flowchart for Program 2-8

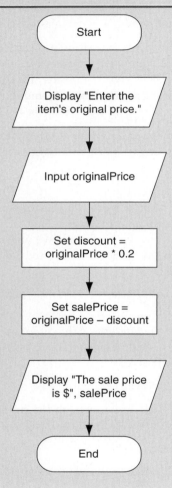

The Order of Operations

It is possible to build mathematical expressions with several operators. The following statement assigns the sum of 17, the variable x, 21, and the variable y to the variable answer.

```
Set answer = 17 + x + 21 + y
```

Some expressions are not that straightforward, however. Consider the following statement:

```
Set outcome = 12 + 6 / 3
```

What value will be stored in `outcome`? The number 6 is used as an operand for both the addition and division operators. The `outcome` variable could be assigned either 6 or 14, depending on when the division takes place. The answer is 14 because the *order of operations* dictates that the division operator works before the addition operator does.

In most programming languages, the order of operations can be summarized as follows:

1. Perform any operations that are enclosed in parentheses.
2. Perform any operations that use the exponent operator to raise a number to a power.
3. Perform any multiplications, divisions, or modulus operations as they appear from left to right.
4. Perform any additions or subtractions as they appear from left to right.

Mathematical expressions are evaluated from left to right. When two operators share an operand, the order of operations determines which operator works first. Multiplication and division are always performed before addition and subtraction, so the statement

```
Set outcome = 12 + 6 / 3
```

works like this:

1. 6 is divided by 3, yielding a result of 2
2. 12 is added to 2, yielding a result of 14

It could be diagrammed as shown in Figure 2-10.

Figure 2-10 The order of operations at work

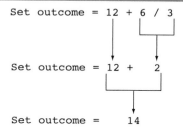

Table 2-2 shows some other sample expressions with their values.

Table 2-2 Some expressions

Expression	Value
5 + 2 * 4	13
10 / 2 − 3	2
8 + 12 * 2 − 4	28
6 − 3 * 2 + 7 − 1	6

Grouping with Parentheses

Parts of a mathematical expression may be grouped with parentheses to force some operations to be performed before others. In the following statement, the variables a and b are added together, and their sum is divided by 4:

```
Set result = (a + b) / 4
```

Without the parentheses, however, b would be divided by 4 and the result added to a. Table 2-3 shows more expressions and their values.

Table 2-3 More expressions and their values

Expression	Value
(5 + 2) * 4	28
10 / (5 − 3)	5
8 + 12 * (6 − 2)	56
(6 − 3) * (2 + 7) / 3	9

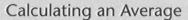

In the Spotlight:

Calculating an Average

Determining the average of a group of values is a simple calculation: You add all of the values and then divide the sum by the number of values. Although this is a straightforward calculation, it is easy to make a mistake when writing a program that calculates an average. For example, let's assume that the variables a, b, and c each hold a value and we want to calculate the average of those values. If we are careless, we might write a statement such as the following to perform the calculation:

```
Set average = a + b + c / 3
```

Can you see the error in this statement? When it executes, the division will take place first. The value in c will be divided by 3, and then the result will be added to a + b. That is not the correct way to calculate an average. To correct this error we need to put parentheses around a + b + c, as shown here:

```
Set average = (a + b + c) / 3
```

Let's step through the process of writing a program that calculates an average. Suppose you have taken three tests in your computer science class, and you want to write a program that will display the average of the test scores. Here is the algorithm:

1. Get the first test score.
2. Get the second test score.
3. Get the third test score.
4. Calculate the average by adding the three test scores and dividing the sum by 3.
5. Display the average.

In steps 1, 2, and 3 we will prompt the user to enter the three test scores. We will store those test scores in the variables test1, test2, and test3. In Step 4 we will calculate the average of the three test scores. We will use the following statement to perform the calculation and store the result in the average variable:

```
Set average = (test1 + test2 + test3) / 3
```

Last, in Step 5, we display the average. Program 2-9 shows the pseudocode for this program, and Figure 2-11 shows the flowchart.

Program 2-9

```
1 Display "Enter the first test score."
2 Input test1
3 Display "Enter the second test score."
4 Input test2
5 Display "Enter the third test score."
6 Input test3
7 Set average = (test1 + test2 + test3) / 3
8 Display "The average score is ", average
```

Program Output (with Input Shown in Bold)

```
Enter the first test score.
90 [Enter]
Enter the second test score.
80 [Enter]
Enter the third test score.
100 [Enter]
The average score is 90
```

Figure 2-11 Flowchart for Program 2-9

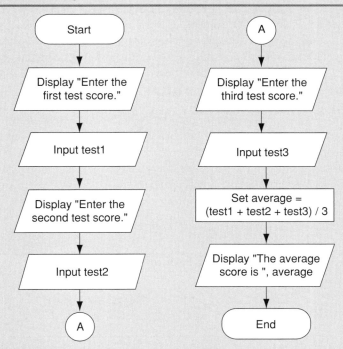

Notice that the flowchart uses a new symbol:

This is called a *connector symbol* and is used when a flowchart is broken into two or more smaller flowcharts. This is necessary when a flowchart does not fit on a single page, or must be divided into sections. A connector symbol, which is a small circle with a letter or number inside it, allows you to connect two flowcharts. In Figure 2-11 the A connector indicates that the second flowchart segment begins where the first flowchart segment ends.

Advanced Arithmetic Operators: Exponent and Modulus

In addition to the basic math operators for addition, subtraction, multiplication, and division, many languages provide an exponent operator and a modulus operator. The ^ symbol is commonly used as the exponent operator, and its purpose it to raise a number to a power. For example, the following pseudocode statement raises the length variable to the power of 2 and stores the result in the area variable:

```
Set area = length^2
```

The word MOD is used in many languages as the modulus operator. (Some languages use the % symbol for the same purpose.) The modulus operator performs division, but instead of returning the quotient, it returns the remainder. The following statement assigns 2 to leftover:

```
Set leftover = 17 MOD 3
```

This statement assigns 2 to leftover because 17 divided by 3 is 5 with a remainder of 2. You will not use the modulus operator frequently, but it is useful in some situations. It is commonly used in calculations that detect odd or even numbers, determine the day of the week, measure the passage of time, and other specialized operations.

Converting Math Formulas to Programming Statements

You probably remember from algebra class that the expression $2xy$ is understood to mean 2 times x times y. In math, you do not always use an operator for multiplication. Programming languages, however, require an operator for any mathematical operation. Table 2-4 shows some algebraic expressions that perform multiplication and the equivalent programming expressions.

Table 2-4 Algebraic expressions

Algebraic Expression	Operation Being Performed	Programming Expression
$6B$	6 times B	6 * B
(3)(12)	3 times 12	3 * 12
$4xy$	4 times x times y	4 * x * y

When converting some algebraic expressions to programming expressions, you may have to insert parentheses that do not appear in the algebraic expression. For example, look at the following formula:

$$x = \frac{a+b}{c}$$

To convert this to a programming statement, $a + b$ will have to be enclosed in parentheses:

```
Set x = (a + b) / c
```

Table 2-5 shows additional algebraic expressions and their pseudocode equivalents.

Table 2-5 Algebraic and programming expressions

Algebraic Expression	Pseudocode Statement
$y = 3\dfrac{x}{2}$	`Set y = x / 2 * 3`
$z = 3bc + 4$	`Set z = 3 * b * c + 4`
$a = \dfrac{x+2}{a-1}$	`Set a = (x + 2) / (a - 1)`

In the Spotlight:
Converting a Math Formula
to a Programming Statement

Suppose you want to deposit a certain amount of money into a savings account, and then leave it alone to draw interest for the next 10 years. At the end of 10 years you would like to have $10,000 in the account. How much do you need to deposit today to make that happen? You can use the following formula to find out

$$P = \frac{F}{(1+r)^n}$$

The terms in the formula are as follows:

- P is the present value, or the amount that you need to deposit today.
- F is the future value that you want in the account. (In this case, F is $10,000.)
- r is the annual interest rate.
- n is the number of years that you plan to let the money sit in the account.

It would be nice to write a computer program to perform the calculation, because then we can experiment with different values for the terms. Here is an algorithm that we can use:

1. Get the desired future value.
2. Get the annual interest rate.
3. Get the number of years that the money will sit in the account.
4. Calculate the amount that will have to be deposited.
5. Display the result of the calculation in Step 4.

In steps 1 through 3, we will prompt the user to enter the specified values. We will store the desired future value in a variable named `futureValue`, the annual interest rate in a variable named `rate`, and the number of years in a variable named `years`.

In Step 4, we calculate the present value, which is the amount of money that we will have to deposit. We will convert the formula previously shown to the following pseudocode statement. The statement stores the result of the calculation in the `presentValue` variable.

```
Set presentValue = futureValue / (1 + rate)^years
```

In Step 5, we display the value in the `presentValue` variable. Program 2-10 shows the pseudocode for this program, and Figure 2-12 shows the flowchart.

Program 2-10

```
1 Display "Enter the desired future value."
2 Input futureValue
3 Display "Enter the annual interest rate."
4 Input rate
5 Display "How many years will you let the money grow?"
6 Input years
7 Set presentValue = futureValue / (1 + rate)^years
8 Display "You will need to deposit $", presentValue
```

Program Output (with Input Shown in Bold)

```
Enter the desired future value.
10000 [Enter]
Enter the annual interest rate.
0.05 [Enter]
How many years will you let the money grow?
10 [Enter]
You need to deposit $6139
```

Figure 2-12 Flowchart for Program 2-10

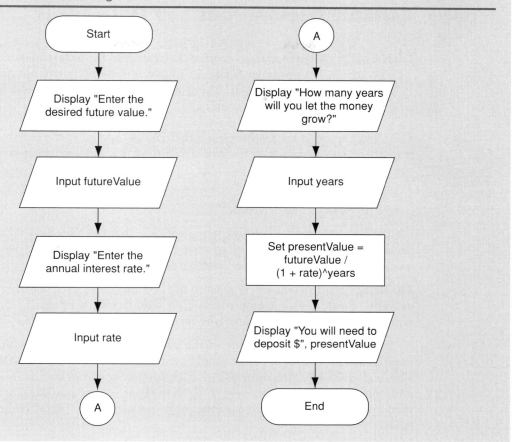

Checkpoint

2.19 What is an assignment statement?

2.20 When you assign a value to a variable, what happens to any value that is already stored in the variable?

2.21 Summarize the mathematical order of operations, as it works in most programming languages.

2.22 What is the purpose of the exponent operator?

2.23 What is the purpose of the modulus operator?

2.4 Variable Declarations and Data Types

CONCEPT: Most languages require that variables be declared before they are used in a program. When a variable is declared, it can optionally be initialized with a value. Using an uninitialized variable is the source of many errors in programming.

VideoNote

Variable
Declarations

Most programming languages require that you *declare* all of the variables that you intend to use in a program. A *variable declaration* is a statement that typically specifies two things about a variable:

- The variable's name
- The variable's data type

A variable's *data type* is simply the type of data that the variable will hold. Once you declare a variable, it can be used to store values of only the specified data type. In most languages, an error occurs if you try to store values of other types in the variable.

The data types that you are allowed to use depend on the programming language. For example, the Java language provides four data types for integer numbers, two data types for real numbers, one data type for strings, and others.

So far, we haven't declared any of the variables that we have used in our example pseudocode programs. We have simply used the variables without first declaring them. This is permissible with short pseudocode programs, but as programs grow in length and complexity, it makes sense to declare them. When you declare variables in a pseudocode program, it will make the job of translating the pseudocode to actual code easier.

In most of the programs in this book, we will use only three data types when we declare variables: `Integer`, `Real`, and `String`. Here is a summary of each:

- A variable of the `Integer` data type can hold whole numbers. For example, an `Integer` variable can hold values such as 42, 0, and –99. An `Integer` variable cannot hold numbers with a fractional part, such as 22.1 or –4.9.
- A variable of the `Real` data type can hold either whole numbers or numbers with a fractional part. For example, a `Real` variable can hold values such as 3.5, –87.95, and 3.0.
- A variable of the `String` data type can hold any string of characters, such as someone's name, address, password, and so on.

In this book, we will begin variable declarations with the word `Declare`, followed by a data type, followed by the variable's name. Here is an example:

```
Declare Integer length
```

This statement declares a variable named `length`, of the `Integer` data type. Here is another example:

```
Declare Real grossPay
```

This statement declares a variable named `grossPay`, of the `Real` data type. Here is one more example:

```
Declare String name
```

This statement declares a variable named `name`, of the `String` data type.

If we need to declare more than one variable of the same data type, we can use one declaration statement. For example, suppose we want to declare three variables, `length`, `width`, and `height`, all of the `Integer` data type. We can declare all three with one statement, as shown here:

```
Declare Integer length, width, height
```

> **NOTE:** In addition to a `String` data type, many programming languages also provide a `Character` data type. The difference between a `String` variable and a `Character` variable is that a `String` variable can hold a sequence of characters of virtually any length, and a `Character` variable can hold only one character. In this book, we will keep things simple. We will use `String` variables to hold all character data.

Declaring Variables Before Using Them

The purpose of a variable declaration statement is to tell the compiler or interpreter that you plan to use a particular variable in the program. A variable declaration statement typically causes the variable to be created in memory. For this reason, you have to write a variable's declaration statement *before* any other statements in the program that use the variable. This makes perfect sense because you cannot store a value in a variable if the variable has not been created in memory.

For example, look at the following pseudocode. If this code were converted to actual code in a language like Java or C++, it would cause an error because the `Input` statement uses the `age` variable before the variable has been declared.

```
Display "What is your age?"
Input age
Declare Integer age
```
This pseudocode has an error!

Program 2-11 shows the correct way to declare a variable. Notice that the declaration statement for the `age` variable appears before any other statements that use the variable.

Program 2-11

```
1 Declare Integer age
2 Display "What is your age?"
3 Input age
4 Display "Here is the value that you entered:"
5 Display age
```

Program Output (with Input Shown in Bold)

```
What is your age?
24 [Enter]
Here is the value that you entered:
24
```

Program 2-12 shows another example. This program declares a total of four variables: three to hold test scores and another to hold the average of those test scores.

Program 2-12

```
 1 Declare Real test1
 2 Declare Real test2
 3 Declare Real test3
 4 Declare Real average
 5
 6 Set test1 = 88.0
 7 Set test2 = 92.5
 8 Set test3 = 97.0
 9 Set average = (test1 + test2 + test3) / 3
10 Display "Your average test score is ", average
```

Program Output (with Input Shown in Bold)

```
Your average test score is 92.5
```

This program shows a common technique for declaring variables: they are all declared at the beginning of the program, before any other statements. This is one way of making sure that all variables are declared before they are used.

Notice that line 5 in this program is blank. This blank line does *not* affect the way the program works because most compilers and interpreters ignore blank lines. For the human reader, however, this blank line visually separates the variable declarations from the other statements. This makes the program appear more organized and easier for people to read.

Programmers commonly use blank lines and indentations in their code to create a sense of organization visually. This is similar to the way that authors visually arrange the text on the pages of a book. Instead of writing each chapter as one long series of sentences, they break it into paragraphs. This does not change the information in the book; it only makes it easier to read.

Although you are generally free to place blank lines and indentations anywhere in your code, you should not do this haphazardly. Programmers follow certain conventions when it comes to this. For example, you have just learned that one convention is to use a blank line to separate a group of variable declaration statements from the rest of the statements in a program. These conventions are known as *programming style*. As you progress through this book you will see many other programming style conventions.

Variable Initialization

When you declare a variable, you can optionally assign a value to it in the declaration statement. This is known as *initialization*. For example, the following statement declares a variable named `price` and assigns the value 49.95 to it:

```
Declare Real price = 49.95
```

We would say that this statement *initializes* the `price` variable with the value 49.95. The following statement shows another example:

```
Declare Integer length = 2, width = 4, height = 8
```

This statement declares and initializes three variables. The `length` variable is initialized with the value 2, `width` is initialized with the value 4, and `height` is initialized with the value 8.

Uninitialized Variables

An *uninitialized variable* is a variable that has been declared, but has not been initialized or assigned a value. Uninitialized variables are a common cause of logic errors in programs. For example, look at the following pseudocode:

```
Declare Real dollars
Display "I have ", dollars, " in my account."
```

In this pseudocode, we have declared the `dollars` variable, but we have not initialized it or assigned a value to it. Therefore, we do not know what value the variable holds. Nevertheless, we have used the variable in a `Display` statement.

You're probably wondering what a program like this would display. An honest answer would be "I don't know." This is because each language has its own way of handling uninitialized variables. Some languages assign a default value such as 0 to uninitialized variables. In many languages, however, uninitialized variables hold unpredictable values. This is because those languages set aside a place in memory for the variable, but do not alter the contents of that place in memory. As a result, an uninitialized variable holds the value that happens to be stored in its memory location. Programmers typically refer to unpredictable values such as this as "garbage."

Uninitialized variables can cause logic errors that are hard to find in a program. This is especially true when an uninitialized variable is used in a calculation. For example, look at the following pseudocode, which is a modified version of Program 2-12. Can you spot the error?

```
1   Declare Real test1
2   Declare Real test2
3   Declare Real test3
4   Declare Real average
5
6   Set test1 = 88.0
7   Set test2 = 92.5
8   Set average = (test1 + test2 + test3) / 3
9   Display "Your average test score is ", average
```

This pseudocode contains an error!

This program will not work properly because the `test3` variable is never assigned a value. The `test3` variable will contain garbage when it is used in the calculation in line 8. This means that the calculation will result in an unpredictable value, which will be assigned to the `average` variable. A beginning programmer might have trouble finding this error because he or she would initially assume that something is wrong with the math in line 8.

In the next section, we will discuss a debugging technique that will help uncover errors such as the one in Program 2-12. However, as a rule you should always make sure that your variables either (1) are initialized with the correct value when you declare them, or (2) receive the correct value from an assignment statement or an `Input` statement before they are used for any other purpose.

Numeric Literals and Data Type Compatibility

Many of the programs that you have seen so far have numbers written into their pseudocode. For example, the following statement, which appears in Program 2-6, has the number 2.75 written into it.

```
Set dollars = 2.75
```

And, the following statement, which appears in Program 2-7, has the number 100 written into it.

```
Set price = 100
```

A number that is written into a program's code is called a *numeric literal*. In most programming languages, if a numeric literal is written with a decimal point, such as 2.75, that numeric literal will be stored in the computer's memory as a `Real` and it will be treated as a `Real` when the program runs. If a numeric literal does not have a decimal point, such as 100, that numeric literal will be stored in the computer's memory as an `Integer` and it will be treated as an `Integer` when the program runs.

This is important to know when you are writing assignment statements or initializing variables. In many languages, an error will occur if you try to store a value of one data type in a variable of another data type. For example, look at the following pseudocode:

```
Declare Integer i
Set i = 3.7  ◄──────── This is an error!
```

The assignment statement will cause an error because it attempts to assign a real number, 3.7, in an `Integer` variable. The following pseudocode will also cause an error.

```
Declare Integer i
Set i = 3.0  ◄──────── This is an error!
```

Even though the numeric literal 3.0 does not have a fractional value (it is mathematically the same as the integer 3), it is still treated as a real number by the computer because it is written with a decimal point.

NOTE: Most languages do not allow you to assign real numbers to `Integer` variables because `Integer` variables cannot hold fractional amounts. In many languages, however, you are allowed to assign an integer value to a `Real` variable without causing an error. Here is an example:

```
Declare Real r
Set r = 77
```

Even though the numeric literal 77 is treated as an `Integer`, it can be assigned to a `Real` variable without the loss of data.

Integer Division

Be careful when dividing an integer by another integer. In many programming languages, when an integer is divided by an integer the result will also be an integer. This behavior is known as *integer division*. For example, look at the following pseudocode:

```
Set number = 3 / 2
```

This statement divides 3 by 2 and stores the result in the `number` variable. What will be stored in `number`? You would probably assume that 1.5 would be stored in `number` because that's the result your calculator shows when you divide 3 by 2. However, that's not what will happen in many programming languages. Because the numbers 3 and 2 are both treated as integers, the programming language that you are using might throw away the fractional part of the answer. (Throwing away the fractional part of a number is called *truncation*.) As a result, the statement will store 1 in the `number` variable, not 1.5.

If you are using a language that behaves this way and you want to make sure that a division operation yields a real number, at least one of the operands must be a real number or a `Real` variable.

NOTE: In Java, C++, C, and Python, the / operator throws away the fractional part of the result when both operands are integers. In these languages the result of the expression 3/2 would be 1. In Visual Basic, the / operator does not throw away the fractional part of the answer. In Visual Basic the result of the expression 3/2 would be 1.5.

 Checkpoint

2.24 What two items do you usually specify with a variable declaration?

2.25 Does it matter where you write the variable declarations in a program?

2.26 What is variable initialization?

2.27 Do uninitialized variables pose any danger in a program?

2.28 What is an uninitialized variable?

2.5   Named Constants

CONCEPT: A named constant is a name that represents a value that cannot be changed during the program's execution.

Assume that the following statement appears in a banking program that calculates data pertaining to loans:

```
Set amount = balance * 0.069
```

In such a program, two potential problems arise. First, it is not clear to anyone other than the original programmer what 0.069 is. It appears to be an interest rate, but in some situations there are fees associated with loan payments. How can the purpose of this statement be determined without painstakingly checking the rest of the program?

The second problem occurs if this number is used in other calculations throughout the program and must be changed periodically. Assuming the number is an interest rate, what if the rate changes from 6.9 percent to 7.2 percent? The programmer would have to search through the source code for every occurrence of the number.

Both of these problems can be addressed by using named constants. A *named constant* is a name that represents a value that cannot be changed during the program's execution. The following is an example of how we will declare named constants in our pseudocode:

```
Constant Real INTEREST_RATE = 0.069
```

This creates a constant named `INTEREST_RATE`. The constant's value is the `Real` number 0.069. Notice that the declaration looks a lot like a variable declaration, except that we use the word `Constant` instead of `Declare`. Also, notice that the name of the constant is written in all uppercase letters. This is a standard practice in most programming languages because it makes named constants easily distinguishable from regular variable names. An initialization value must be given when declaring a named constant.

An advantage of using named constants is that they make programs more self-explanatory. The following statement:

```
Set amount = balance * 0.069
```

can be changed to read

```
Set amount = balance * INTEREST_RATE
```

A new programmer can read the second statement and know what is happening. It is evident that `balance` is being multiplied by the interest rate. Another advantage to this approach is that widespread changes can easily be made to the program. Let's say the interest rate appears in a dozen different statements throughout the program. When the rate changes, the initialization value in the declaration of the named constant is the only value that needs to be modified. If the rate increases to 7.2 percent, the declaration can be changed to the following:

```
Constant Real INTEREST_RATE = 0.072
```

The new value of 0.072 will then be used in each statement that uses the `INTEREST_RATE` constant.

> **NOTE:** A named constant cannot be assigned a value with a `Set` statement. If a statement in a program attempts to change the value of a named constant, an error will occur.

2.6 Hand Tracing a Program

CONCEPT: Hand tracing is a simple debugging process for locating hard to find errors in a program.

Hand tracing is a debugging process where you imagine that you are the computer executing a program. (This process is also known as *desk checking*.) You step through each of the program's statements one by one. As you carefully look at a statement, you record the contents that each variable will have after the statement executes. This process is often helpful in finding mathematical mistakes and other logic errors.

To hand trace a program, you construct a chart that has a column for each variable, and a row for each line in the program. For example, Figure 2-13 shows how we would construct a hand trace chart for the program that you saw in the previous section. The chart has a column for each of the four variables: `test1`, `test2`, `test3`, and `average`. The chart also has nine rows, one for each line in the program.

Figure 2-13 A program with a hand trace chart

```
1   Declare Real test1
2   Declare Real test2
3   Declare Real test3
4   Declare Real average
5
6   Set test1 = 88.0
7   Set test2 = 92.5
8   Set average = (test1 + test2 + test3) / 3
9   Display "Your average test score is ", average
```

	test1	test2	test3	average
1				
2				
3				
4				
5				
6				
7				
8				
9				

To hand trace this program, you step through each statement, observing the operation that is taking place, and then record the value that each variable will hold *after* the statement executes. When the process is complete, the chart will appear as shown in Figure 2-14. We have written question marks in the chart to indicate that a variable is uninitialized.

Figure 2-14 Program with the hand trace chart completed

```
1   Declare Real test1
2   Declare Real test2
3   Declare Real test3
4   Declare Real average
5
6   Set test1 = 88.0
7   Set test2 = 92.5
8   Set average = (test1 + test2 + test3) / 3
9   Display "Your average test score is ", average
```

	test1	test2	test3	average
1	?	?	?	?
2	?	?	?	?
3	?	?	?	?
4	?	?	?	?
5	?	?	?	?
6	88	?	?	?
7	88	92.5	?	?
8	88	92.2	?	undefined
9	88	92.5	?	undefined

When we get to line 8 we will carefully do the math. This means we look at the values of each variable in the expression. At that point we discover that one of the variables, test3, is uninitialized. Because it is uninitialized, we have no way of knowing the value that it contains. Consequently, the result of the calculation will be undefined. After making this discovery, we can correct the problem by adding a line that assigns a value to test3.

Hand tracing is a simple process that focuses your attention on each statement in a program. Often this helps you locate errors that are not obvious.

2.7 Documenting a Program

CONCEPT: A program's external documentation describes aspects of the program for the user. The internal documentation is for the programmer, and explains how parts of the program work.

A program's documentation explains various things about the program. There are usually two types of program documentation: external and internal. *External documentation* is typically designed for the user. It consists of documents such as a reference guide that describes the program's features, and tutorials that teach the user how to operate the program.

Sometimes the programmer is responsible for writing all or part of a program's external documentation. This might be the case in a small organization, or in a company that has a relatively small programming staff. Some organizations, particularly large companies, will employ a staff of technical writers whose job is to produce external documentation. These documents might be in printed manuals, or in files that can be viewed on the computer. In recent years it has become common for software companies to provide all of a program's external documentation in PDF (Portable Document Format) files.

Internal documentation appears as *comments* in a program's code. Comments are short notes placed in different parts of a program, explaining how those parts of the program work. Although comments are a critical part of a program, they are ignored by the compiler or interpreter. Comments are intended for human readers of a program's code, not the computer.

Programming languages provide special symbols or words for writing comments. In several languages, including Java, C, and C++, you begin a comment with two forward slashes (//). Everything that you write on the same line, after the slashes, is ignored by the compiler. Here is an example of a comment in any of those languages:

```
// Get the number of hours worked.
```

Some languages use symbols other than the two forward slashes to indicate the beginning of a comment. For example, Visual Basic uses an apostrophe ('), and Python uses the # symbol. In this book, we will use two forward slashes (//) in pseudocode.

Block Comments and Line Comments

Programmers generally write two types of comments in a program: block comments and line comments. *Block comments* take up several lines and are used when lengthy explanations are required. For example, a block comment often appears at the beginning of a program, explaining what the program does, listing the name of the author, giving the date that the program was last modified, and any other necessary information. The following is an example of a block comment:

```
// This program calculates an employee's gross pay.
// Written by Matt Hoyle.
// Last modified on 12/14/2010
```

NOTE: Some programming languages provide special symbols to mark the beginning and ending of a block comment.

Line comments are comments that occupy a single line, and explain a short section of the program. The following statements show an example:

```
// Calculate the interest.
Set interest = balance * INTEREST_RATE
// Add the interest to the balance.
Set balance = balance + interest
```

A line comment does not have to occupy an entire line. Anything appearing after the // symbol, to the end of the line, is ignored, so a comment can appear after an executable statement. Here is an example:

```
Input age     // Get the user's age.
```

As a beginning programmer, you might be resistant to the idea of liberally writing comments in your programs. After all, it's a lot more fun to write code that actually does something! It is crucial that you take the extra time to write comments, however. They will almost certainly save you time in the future when you have to modify or debug the program. Even large and complex programs can be made easy to read and understand if they are properly commented.

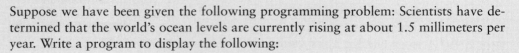

In the Spotlight:
Using Named Constants, Style Conventions, and Comments

Suppose we have been given the following programming problem: Scientists have de-termined that the world's ocean levels are currently rising at about 1.5 millimeters per year. Write a program to display the following:

- The number of millimeters that the oceans will rise in five years
- The number of millimeters that the oceans will rise in seven years
- The number of millimeters that the oceans will rise in ten years

Here is the algorithm:

1. Calculate the amount that the oceans will rise in five years.
2. Display the result of the calculation in Step 1.
3. Calculate the amount that the oceans will rise in seven years.
4. Display the result of the calculation in Step 3.
5. Calculate the amount that the oceans will rise in ten years.
6. Display the result of the calculation in Step 5.

This program is straightforward. It performs three calculations and displays the results of each. The calculations should give the amount the oceans will rise in five, seven, and ten years. Each of these values can be calculated with the following formula:

Amount of yearly rise × Number of years

The amount of yearly rise is the same for each calculation, so we will create a constant to represent that value. Program 2-13 shows the pseudocode for the program.

Program 2-13

```
 1 // Declare the variables
 2 Declare Real fiveYears
 3 Declare Real sevenYears
 4 Declare Real tenYears
 5
 6 // Create a constant for the yearly rise
 7 Constant Real YEARLY_RISE = 1.5
 8
 9 // Display the amount of rise in five years
10 Set fiveYears = YEARLY_RISE * 5
11 Display "The ocean levels will rise ", fiveYears,
12     " millimeters in five years."
13
14 // Display the amount of rise in seven years
15 Set sevenYears = YEARLY_RISE * 7
16 Display "The ocean levels will rise ", sevenYears,
17     " millimeters in seven years."
18
19 // Display the amount of rise in ten years
20 Set tenYears = YEARLY_RISE * 10
21 Display "The ocean levels will rise ", tenYears,
22     " millimeters in ten years."
```

Program Output (with Input Shown in Bold)

```
The ocean levels will rise 7.5 millimeters in five years.
The ocean levels will rise 10.5 millimeters in seven years.
The ocean levels will rise 15 millimeters in ten years.
```

Three variables fiveYears, sevenYears, and tenYears are declared in lines 2 through 4. These variables will hold the amount that the ocean levels will rise in five, seven, and ten years.

Line 7 creates a constant, YEARLY_RISE, which is set to the value 1.5. This is the amount that the oceans rise per year. This constant will be used in each of the program's calculations.

Lines 10 through 12 calculate and display the amount that the oceans will rise in five years. The same values for seven years and ten years is calculated and displayed in lines 15 through 17 and 20 through 22.

This program illustrates the following programming style conventions:

- Several blank lines appear throughout the program (see lines 5, 8, 13, and 18). These blank lines do not affect the way the program works, but make the pseudocode easier to read.
- Line comments are used in various places to explain what the program is doing.
- Notice that each of the Display statements are too long to fit on one line. (See lines 11 and 12, 16 and 17, 21 and 22.) Most programming languages allow you to write long statements across several lines. When we do this in pseudocode, we will indent the second and subsequent lines. This will give a visual indication that the statement spans more than one line.

Figure 2-15 shows a flowchart for the program.

Figure 2-15 Flowchart for Program 2-13

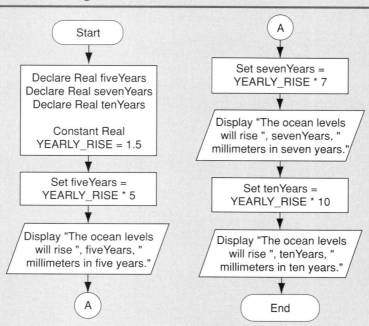

Checkpoint

2.29 What is external documentation?

2.30 What is internal documentation?

2.31 What are the two general types of comments that programmers write in a program's code? Describe each.

Review Questions

Multiple Choice

1. A _____ error does not prevent the program from running, but causes it to produce incorrect results.
   a. syntax
   b. hardware
   c. logic
   d. fatal

2. A _____ is a single function that the program must perform in order to satisfy the customer.
   a. task
   b. software requirement
   c. prerequisite
   d. predicate

3. A(n) _____ is a set of well-defined logical steps that must be taken to perform a task.
   a. logarithm
   b. plan of action
   c. logic schedule
   d. algorithm

4. An informal language that has no syntax rules, and is not meant to be compiled or executed is called _____.
   a. faux code
   b. pseudocode
   c. Java
   d. a flowchart

5. A _____ is a diagram that graphically depicts the steps that take place in a program.
   a. flowchart
   b. step chart
   c. code graph
   d. program graph

6. A(n) _____ is a set of statements that execute in the order that they appear.
   a. serial program
   b. sorted code
   c. sequence structure
   d. ordered structure

7. A _____ is a sequence of characters that is used as data.
   a. sequence structure
   b. character collection
   c. string
   d. text block

8. A _____ is a storage location in memory that is represented by a name.
   a. variable
   b. register
   c. RAM slot
   d. byte

9. A _____ is any hypothetical person that is using a program and providing input for it.
   a. designer
   b. user
   c. guinea pig
   d. test subject

10. A(n) _____ is a message that tells (or asks) the user to enter a specific value.
    a. inquiry
    b. input statement
    c. directive
    d. prompt

11. A(n) _____ sets a variable to a specified value.
    a. variable declaration
    b. assignment statement
    c. math expression
    d. string literal

12. In the expression 12 + 7, the values on the right and left of the + symbol are called _____.
    a. operands
    b. operators
    c. arguments
    d. math expressions

13. A(n) _____ operator raises a number to a power.
    a. modulus
    b. multiplication
    c. exponent
    d. operand

14. A(n) _____ operator performs division, but instead of returning the quotient it returns the remainder.

    a. modulus
    b. multiplication
    c. exponent
    d. operand

15. A(n) _____ specifies a variable's name and data type.

    a. assignment
    b. variable specification
    c. variable certification
    d. variable declaration

16. Assigning a value to a variable in a declaration statement is called _____.

    a. allocation
    b. initialization
    c. certification
    d. programming style

17. A(n) _____ variable is one that has been declared, but has not been initialized or assigned a value.

    a. undefined
    b. uninitialized
    c. empty
    d. default

18. A(n) _____ is a variable whose content has a value that is read only and cannot be changed during the program's execution.

    a. static variable
    b. uninitialized variable
    c. named constant
    d. locked variable

19. A debugging process in which you imagine that you are the computer executing a program is called _____.

    a. imaginative computing
    b. role playing
    c. mental simulation
    d. hand tracing

20. Short notes placed in different parts of a program, explaining how those parts of the program work are called _____.

    a. comments
    b. reference manuals
    c. tutorials
    d. external documentation

True or False

1. Programmers must be careful not to make syntax errors when writing pseudocode programs.

2. In a math expression, multiplication and division takes place before addition and subtraction.

3. Variable names can have spaces in them.

4. In most languages, the first character of a variable name cannot be a number.

5. The name `gross_pay` is written in the camelCase convention.

6. In languages that require variable declarations, a variable's declaration must appear before any other statements that use the variable.

7. Uninitialized variables are a common cause of errors.

8. The value of a named constant cannot be changed during the program's execution.

9. Hand tracing is the process of translating a pseudocode program into machine language by hand.

10. Internal documentation refers to books and manuals that document a program, and are intended for use within a company's programming department.

Short Answer

1. What does a professional programmer usually do first to gain an understanding of a problem?

2. What is pseudocode?

3. Computer programs typically perform what three steps?

4. What does the term "user-friendly" mean?

5. What two things must you normally specify in a variable declaration?

6. What value is stored in uninitialized variables?

Algorithm Workbench

1. Design an algorithm that prompts the user to enter his or her height and stores the user's input in a variable named `height`.

2. Design an algorithm that prompts the user to enter his or her favorite color and stores the user's input in a variable named `color`.

3. Write assignment statements that perform the following operations with the variables `a`, `b`, and `c`.

   a. Adds 2 to `a` and stores the result in `b`
   b. Multiplies `b` times 4 and stores the result in `a`
   c. Divides `a` by 3.14 and stores the result in `b`
   d. Subtracts 8 from `b` and stores the result in `a`

4. Assume the variables result, w, x, y, and z are all integers, and that w = 5, x = 4, y = 8, and z = 2. What value will be stored in result in each of the following statements?

   a. Set result = x + y
   b. Set result = z * 2
   c. Set result = y / x
   d. Set result = y - z

5. Write a pseudocode statement that declares the variable cost so it can hold real numbers.

6. Write a pseudocode statement that declares the variable total so it can hold integers. Initialize the variable with the value 0.

7. Write a pseudocode statement that assigns the value 27 to the variable count.

8. Write a pseudocode statement that assigns the sum of 10 and 14 to the variable total.

9. Write a pseudocode statement that subtracts the variable downPayment from the variable total and assigns the result to the variable due.

10. Write a pseudocode statement that multiplies the variable subtotal by 0.15 and assigns the result to the variable totalfee.

11. If the following pseudocode were an actual program, what would it display?

```
Declare Integer a = 5
Declare Integer b = 2
Declare Integer c = 3
Declare Integer result

Set result = a + b * c
Display result
```

12. If the following pseudocode were an actual program, what would it display?

```
Declare Integer num = 99
Set num = 5
Display num
```

Programming Exercises

1. **Personal Information**

   Design a program that displays the following information:

   - Your name
   - Your address, with city, state, and ZIP
   - Your telephone number
   - Your college major

2. **Sales Prediction**

   A company has determined that its annual profit is typically 23 percent of total sales. Design a program that asks the user to enter the projected amount of total sales, and then displays the profit that will be made from that amount.

   Hint: Use the value 0.23 to represent 23 percent.

3. **Land Calculation**

   One acre of land is equivalent to 43,560 square feet. Design a program that asks the user to enter the total square feet in a tract of land and calculates the number of acres in the tract.

   Hint: Divide the amount entered by 43,560 to get the number of acres.

4. **Total Purchase**

   A customer in a store is purchasing five items. Design a program that asks for the price of each item, and then displays the subtotal of the sale, the amount of sales tax, and the total. Assume the sales tax is 6 percent.

5. **Distance Traveled**

   Assuming there are no accidents or delays, the distance that a car travels down the interstate can be calculated with the following formula:

   $$Distance = Speed \times Time$$

   A car is traveling at 60 miles per hour. Design a program that displays the following:
   - The distance the car will travel in 5 hours
   - The distance the car will travel in 8 hours
   - The distance the car will travel in 12 hours

6. **Sales Tax**

   Design a program that will ask the user to enter the amount of a purchase. The program should then compute the state and county sales tax. Assume the state sales tax is 4 percent and the county sales tax is 2 percent. The program should display the amount of the purchase, the state sales tax, the county sales tax, the total sales tax, and the total of the sale (which is the sum of the amount of purchase plus the total sales tax).

   Hint: Use the value 0.02 to represent 2 percent, and 0.04 to represent 4 percent.

7. **Miles-per-Gallon**

   A car's miles-per-gallon (MPG) can be calculated with the following formula:

   $$MPG = Miles\ driven\ /\ Gallons\ of\ gas\ used$$

   Design a program that asks the user for the number of miles driven and the gallons of gas used. It should calculate the car's miles-per-gallon and display the result on the screen.

VideoNote
The Tip, Tax, and Total Problem

8. **Tip, Tax, and Total**

   Design a program that calculates the total amount of a meal purchased at a restaurant. The program should ask the user to enter the charge for the food, and then calculate the amount of a 15 percent tip and 7 percent sales tax. Display each of these amounts and the total.

9. **Celsius to Fahrenheit Temperature Converter**

   Design a program that converts Celsius temperatures to Fahrenheit temperatures. The formula is as follows:

   $$F = \frac{9}{5}C + 32$$

The program should ask the user to enter a temperature in Celsius, and then display the temperature converted to Fahrenheit.

10. **Stock Transaction Program**

    Last month Joe purchased some stock in Acme Software, Inc. Here are the details of the purchase:

    - The number of shares that Joe purchased was 1,000.
    - When Joe purchased the stock, he paid $32.87 per share.
    - Joe paid his stockbroker a commission that amounted to 2 percent of the amount he paid for the stock.

    Two weeks later Joe sold the stock. Here are the details of the sale:

    - The number of shares that Joe sold was 1,000.
    - He sold the stock for $33.92 per share.
    - He paid his stockbroker another commission that amounted to 2 percent of the amount he received for the stock.

    Design a program that displays the following information:

    - The amount of money Joe paid for the stock.
    - The amount of commission Joe paid his broker when he bought the stock.
    - The amount that Joe sold the stock for.
    - The amount of commission Joe paid his broker when he sold the stock.
    - Did Joe make money or lose money? Display the amount of profit or loss after Joe sold the stock and paid his broker (both times).

3.1   Introduction to Modules

CONCEPT: A module is a group of statements that exist within a program for the purpose of performing a specific task.

In Chapter 1 you learned that a program is a set of instructions that a computer follows to perform a task. Then, in Chapter 2 you saw a simple program that performs the task of calculating an employee's pay. Recall that the program multiplied the number of hours that the employee worked by the employee's hourly pay rate. A more realistic payroll program, however, would do much more than this. In a real-world application, the overall task of calculating an employee's pay would consist of several subtasks, such as the following:

- Getting the employee's hourly pay rate
- Getting the number of hours worked
- Calculating the employee's gross pay
- Calculating overtime pay
- Calculating withholdings for taxes and benefits
- Calculating the net pay
- Printing the paycheck

Most programs perform tasks that are large enough to be broken down into several subtasks. For this reason, programmers usually break down their programs into modules. A *module* is a group of statements that exist within a program for the purpose

75

of performing a specific task. Instead of writing a large program as one long sequence of statements, it can be written as several small modules, each one performing a specific part of the task. These small modules can then be executed in the desired order to perform the overall task.

This approach is sometimes called *divide and conquer* because a large task is divided into several smaller tasks that are easily performed. Figure 3-1 illustrates this idea by comparing two programs: one that uses a long, complex sequence of statements to perform a task, and another that divides a task into smaller tasks, each of which are performed by a separate module.

When using modules in a program, you generally isolate each task within the program in its own module. For example, a realistic pay calculating program might have the following modules:

- A module that gets the employee's hourly pay rate
- A module that gets the number of hours worked
- A module that calculates the employee's gross pay
- A module that calculates the overtime pay
- A module that calculates the withholdings for taxes and benefits
- A module that calculates the net pay
- A module that prints the paycheck

Although every modern programming language allows you to create modules, they are not always referred to as modules. Modules are commonly called *procedures, subroutines, subprograms, methods,* and *functions.* (A function is a special type of module that we will discuss in Chapter 6.)

Benefits of Using Modules

A program benefits in the following ways when it is modularized:

Simpler Code

A program's code tends to be simpler and easier to understand when it is modularized. Several small modules are much easier to read than one long sequence of statements.

Code Reuse

Modules also reduce the duplication of code within a program. If a specific operation is performed in several places in a program, a module can be written once to perform that operation, and then be executed any time it is needed. This benefit of using modules is known as *code reuse* because you are writing the code to perform a task once and then reusing it each time you need to perform the task.

Better Testing

When each task within a program is contained in its own module, testing and debugging becomes simpler. Programmers can test each module in a program individually, to determine whether it correctly performs its operation. This makes it easier to isolate and fix errors.

Figure 3-1 Using modules to divide and conquer a large task

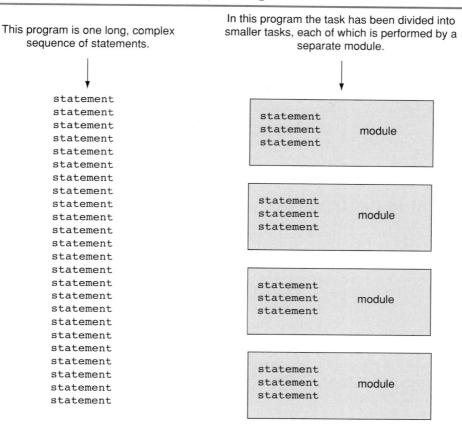

Faster Development

Suppose a programmer or a team of programmers is developing multiple programs. They discover that each of the programs perform several common tasks, such as asking for a username and a password, displaying the current time, and so on. It doesn't make sense to write the code for these tasks multiple times. Instead, modules can be written for the commonly needed tasks, and those modules can be incorporated into each program that needs them.

Easier Facilitation of Teamwork

Modules also make it easier for programmers to work in teams. When a program is developed as a set of modules that each performs an individual task, then different programmers can be assigned the job of writing different modules.

 **Checkpoint**

3.1 What is a module?

3.2 What is meant by the phrase "divide and conquer"?

3.3 How do modules help you reuse code in a program?

3.4 How can modules make the development of multiple programs faster?

3.5 How can modules make it easier for programs to be developed by teams of programmers?

3.2 Defining and Calling a Module

CONCEPT: The code for a module is known as a module definition. To execute the module, you write a statement that calls it.

Module Names

Before we discuss the process of creating and using modules, we should mention a few things about module names. Just as you name the variables that you use in a program, you also name the modules. A module's name should be descriptive enough so that anyone reading your code can reasonably guess what the module does.

Because modules perform actions, most programmers prefer to use verbs in module names. For example, a module that calculates gross pay might be named `calculateGrossPay`. This name would make it evident to anyone reading the code that the module calculates something. What does it calculate? The gross pay, of course. Other examples of good module names would be `getHours`, `getPayRate`, `calculateOvertime`, `printCheck`, and so on. Each module name describes what the module does.

When naming a module, most languages require that you follow the same rules that you follow when naming variables. This means that module names cannot contain spaces, cannot typically contain punctuation characters, and usually cannot begin with a number. These are only general rules, however. The specific rules for naming a module will vary slightly with each programming language. (Recall that we discussed the common variable naming rules in Chapter 2.)

VideoNote

Defining and Calling a Module

Defining and Calling a Module

To create a module you write its *definition*. In most languages, a module definition has two parts: a header and a body. The *header* indicates the starting point of the module, and the *body* is a list of statements that belong to the module. Here is the general format that we will follow when we write a module definition in pseudocode:

```
Module name()
    statement
    statement        } These statements are the body of the module.
    etc.
End Module
```

The first line is the module header. In our pseudocode the header begins with the word `Module`, followed by the name of the module, followed by a set of parentheses. It is a common practice in most programming languages to put a set of parentheses after a module name. Later in this chapter, you will see the actual purpose of the parentheses, but for now, just remember that they come after the module name.

Beginning at the line after the module header, one or more statements will appear. These statements are the module's body, and are performed any time the module is executed. The last line of the definition, after the body, reads `End Module`. This line marks the end of the module definition.

Let's look at an example. Keep in mind that this is not a complete program. We will show the entire pseudocode program in a moment.

```
Module showMessage()
   Display "Hello world."
End Module
```

This pseudocode defines a module named `showMessage`. As its name implies, the purpose of this module is to show a message on the screen. The body of the `showMessage` module contains one statement: a `Display` statement that displays the message "Hello world."

Notice in the previous example that the statement in the body of the module is indented. Indenting the statements in the body of a module is not usually required,[1] but it makes your code much easier to read. By indenting the statements inside a module, you visually set them apart. As a result, you can tell at a glance which statements are inside the module. This practice is a programming style convention that virtually all programmers follow

Calling a Module

A module definition specifies what a module does, but it does not cause the module to execute. To execute a module, we must *call* it. In pseudocode we will use the word `Call` to call a module. This is how we would call the `showMessage` module:

```
Call showMessage()
```

When a module is called, the computer jumps to that module and executes the statements in the module's body. Then, when the end of the module is reached, the computer jumps back to the part of the program that called the module, and the program resumes execution at that point.

To fully demonstrate how module calling works, we will look at Program 3-1.

Program 3-1

```
1 Module main()
2    Display "I have a message for you."
3    Call showMessage()
4    Display "That's all, folks!"
5 End Module
6
```

---

[1]The Python language requires you to indent the statements inside a module.

```
7 Module showMessage()
8    Display "Hello world"
9 End Module
```

Program Output

```
I have a message for you.
Hello world
That's all, folks!
```

First, notice that Program 3-1 has two modules: a module named `main` appears in lines 1 through 5, and the `showMessage` module appears in lines 7 through 9. Many programming languages require that programs have a *main module*. The main module is the program's starting point, and it generally calls other modules. When the end of the main module is reached, the program stops executing. In this book, any time you see a pseudocode program with a module named `main`, we are using that module as the program's starting point. Likewise, when the end of the `main` module is reached, the program will stop executing. This is shown in Figure 3-2.

Figure 3-2 The main module

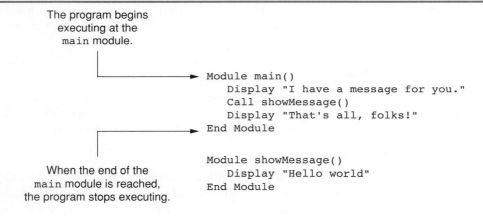

 NOTE: Many languages, including Java, C, and C++, require that the main module actually be named `main`, as we have shown in Program 3-1.

Let's step through the program. When the program runs, the `main` module starts and the statement in line 2 displays "I have a message for you." Then, line 3 calls the `showMessage` module. As shown in Figure 3-3, the computer jumps to the `showMessage` module and executes the statements in its body. There is only one statement in the body of the `showMessage` module: the `Display` statement in line 8. This statement displays "Hello world" and then the module ends. As shown in Figure 3-4, the computer jumps back to the part of the program that called `showMessage`, and resumes execution from that point. In this case, the program resumes execution at line 4, which displays "That's all folks!" The main module ends at line 5, so the program stops executing.

Figure 3-3 Calling the showMessage module

The computer jumps to the showMessage module and executes the statements in its body.

```
Module main()
    Display "I have a message for you."
   ─Call showMessage()
    Display "That's all, folks!"
 End Module


►Module showMessage()
    Display "Hello world"
 End Module
```

Figure 3-4 The showMessage module returns

When the showMessage module ends, the computer jumps back to the part of the program that called it, and resumes execution from that point.

```
Module main()
    Display "I have a message for you."
    Call showMessage()
  ►Display "That's all, folks!"
 End Module

 Module showMessage()
    Display "Hello world"
  ─End Module
```

When the computer encounters a module call, such as the one in line 3 of Program 3-1, it has to perform some operations "behind the scenes" so it will know where to return after the module ends. First, the computer saves the memory address of the location that it should return to. This is typically the statement that appears immediately after the module call. This memory location is known as the *return point*. Then, the computer jumps to the module and executes the statements in its body. When the module ends, the computer jumps back to the return point and resumes execution.

NOTE: When a program calls a module, programmers commonly say that the *control* of the program transfers to that module. This simply means that the module takes control of the program's execution.

Flowcharting a Program with Modules

In a flowchart, a module call is shown with a rectangle that has vertical bars at each side, as shown in Figure 3-5. The name of the module that is being called is written on the symbol. The example shown in Figure 3-5 shows how we would represent a call to the showMessage module.

Figure 3-5 Module call symbol

Programmers typically draw a separate flowchart for each module in a program. For example, Figure 3-6 shows how Program 3-1 would be flowcharted. Notice that the figure shows two flowcharts: one for the main module and another for the showMessage module.

Figure 3-6 Flowchart for Program 3-1

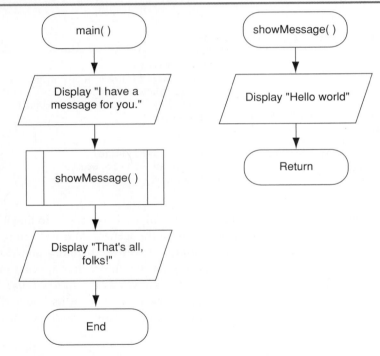

When drawing a flowchart for a module, the starting terminal symbol usually shows the name of the module. The ending terminal symbol in the main module reads End because it marks the end of the program's execution. The ending terminal symbol for all other modules reads Return because it marks the point where the computer returns to the part of the program that called the module.

Top-Down Design

In this section, we have discussed and demonstrated how modules work. You've seen how the computer jumps to a module when it is called, and returns to the part of the program that called the module when the module ends. It is important that you understand these mechanical aspects of modules.

Just as important as understanding how modules work is understanding how to design a modularized program. Programmers commonly use a technique known as *top-down design* to break down an algorithm into modules. The process of top-down design is performed in the following manner:

- The overall task that the program is to perform is broken down into a series of subtasks.
- Each of the subtasks is examined to determine whether it can be further broken down into more subtasks. This step is repeated until no more subtasks can be identified.
- Once all of the subtasks have been identified, they are written in code.

This process is called top-down design because the programmer begins by looking at the topmost level of tasks that must be performed, and then breaks down those tasks into lower levels of subtasks.

 NOTE: The top-down design process is sometimes called *stepwise refinement*.

Hierarchy Charts

Flowcharts are good tools for graphically depicting the flow of logic inside a module, but they do not give a visual representation of the relationships between modules. Programmers commonly use *hierarchy charts* for this purpose. A hierarchy chart, which is also known as a *structure chart*, shows boxes that represent each module in a program. The boxes are connected in a way that illustrates their relationship to one another. Figure 3-7 shows an example of a hierarchy chart for a pay calculating program.

Figure 3-7 A hierarchy chart

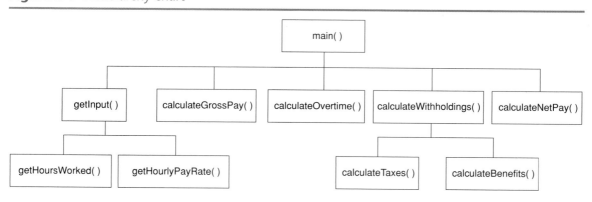

The chart shown in Figure 3-7 shows the main module as the topmost module in the hierarchy. The main module calls five other modules: getInput, calculateGrossPay, calculateOvertime, calculateWithholdings, and calculateNetPay. The getInput module calls two additional modules: getHoursWorked and getHourlyPayRate. The calculateWithholdings module also calls two modules: calculateTaxes and calculateBenefits.

Notice that the hierarchy chart does not show the steps that are taken inside a module. Because they do not reveal any details about how modules work, they do not replace flowcharts or pseudocode.

In the Spotlight:
Defining and Calling Modules

Professional Appliance Service, Inc. offers maintenance and repair services for household appliances. The owner wants to give each of the company's service technicians a small handheld computer that displays step-by-step instructions for many of the repairs that they perform. To see how this might work, the owner has asked you to develop a program that displays the following instructions for disassembling an ACME laundry dyer:

Step 1: Unplug the dryer and move it away from the wall.
Step 2: Remove the six screws from the back of the dryer.
Step 3: Remove the dryer's back panel.
Step 4: Pull the top of the dryer straight up.

During your interview with the owner, you determine that that the program should display the steps one at a time. You decide that after each step is displayed, the user will be asked to press a key to see the next step. Here is the algorithm for the program:

1. Display a starting message, explaining what the program does.
2. Ask the user to press a key to see Step 1.
3. Display the instructions for Step 1.
4. Ask the user to press a key to see the next step.
5. Display the instructions for Step 2.
6. Ask the user to press a key to see the next step.
7. Display the instructions for Step 3.
8. Ask the user to press a key to see the next step.
9. Display the instructions for Step 4.

This algorithm lists the top level of tasks that the program needs to perform, and becomes the basis of the program's main module. Figure 3-8 shows the program's structure in a hierarchy chart.

Figure 3-8 Hierarchy chart for the program

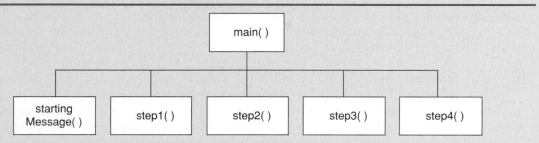

As you can see from the hierarchy chart, the main module will call several other modules. Here are summaries of those modules:

- startingMessage—This module will display the starting message that tells the technician what the program does.
- step1—This module will display the instructions for Step 1.
- step2—This module will display the instructions for Step 2.
- step3—This module will display the instructions for Step 3.
- step4—This module will display the instructions for Step 4.

Between calls to these modules, the main module will instruct the user to press a key to see the next step in the instructions. Program 3-2 shows the pseudocode for the program. Figure 3-9 shows the flowchart for the main module, and Figure 3-10 shows the flowcharts for the startingMessage, step1, step2, step3, and step4 modules.

Program 3-2

```
 1 Module main()
 2     // Display the starting message.
 3     Call startingMessage()
 4     Display "Press a key to see Step 1."
 5     Input
 6
 7     // Display Step 1.
 8     Call step1()
 9     Display "Press a key to see Step 2."
10     Input
11
12     // Display Step 2.
13     Call step2()
14     Display "Press a key to see Step 3."
15     Input
16
17     // Display Step 3.
18     Call step3()
19     Display "Press a key to see Step 4."
20     Input
21
22     // Display Step 4.
23     Call step4()
24 End Module
25
26 // The startingMessage module displays
27 // the program's starting message.
28 Module startingMessage()
29     Display "This program tells you how to"
30     Display "disassemble an ACME laundry dryer."
31     Display "There are 4 steps in the process."
32 End Module
33
34 // The step1 module displays the instructions
35 // for Step 1.
```

```
36 Module step1()
37    Display "Step 1: Unplug the dryer and"
38    Display "move it away from the wall."
39 End Module
40
41 // The step2 module displays the instructions
42 // for Step 2.
43 Module step2()
44    Display "Step 2: Remove the six screws"
45    Display "from the back of the dryer."
46 End Module
47
48 // The step3 module displays the instructions
49 // for Step 3.
50 Module step3()
51    Display "Step 3: Remove the dryer's"
52    Display "back panel."
53 End Module
54
55 // The step4 module displays the instructions
56 // for Step 4.
57 Module step4()
58    Display "Step 4: Pull the top of the"
59    Display "dryer straight up."
60 End Module
```

Program Output

```
This program tells you how to
disassemble an ACME laundry dryer.
There are 4 steps in the process.
Press a key to see Step 1.
[Enter]
Step 1: Unplug the dryer and
move it away from the wall.
Press a key to see Step 2.
[Enter]
Step 2: Remove the six screws
from the back of the dryer.
Press a key to see Step 3.
[Enter]
Step 3: Remove the dryer's
back panel.
Press a key to see Step 4.
[Enter]
Step 4: Pull the top of the
dryer straight up.
```

NOTE: Lines 5, 10, 15, and 20 show an `Input` statement with no variable specified. In our pseudocode, this is the way we will read a keystroke from the keyboard without saving the character that was pressed. Most programming languages provide a way to do this.

Figure 3-9 Flowchart for the `main` module in Program 3-2

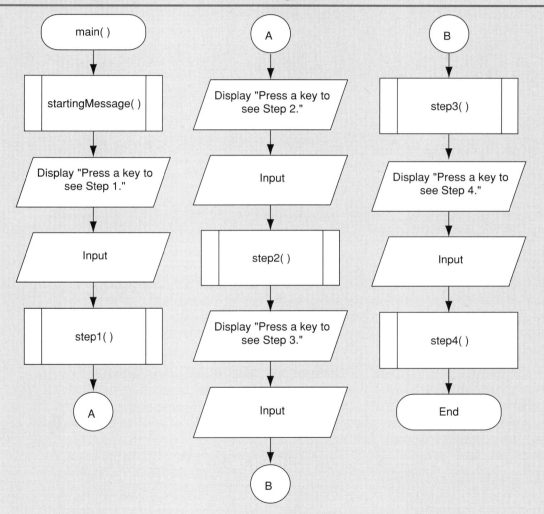

Figure 3-10 Flowcharts for the other modules in Program 3-2

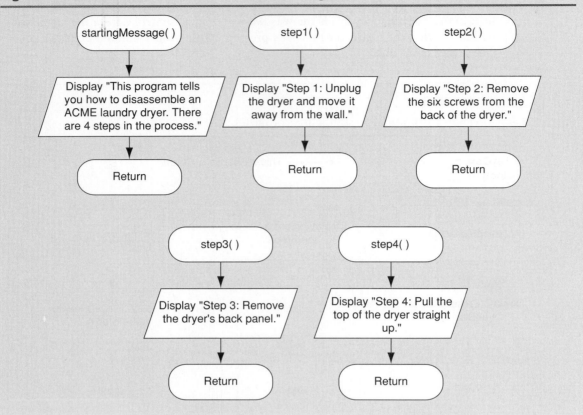

 Checkpoint

3.6 In most languages, a module definition has what two parts?

3.7 What does the phrase "calling a module" mean?

3.8 When a module is executing, what happens when the end of the module is reached?

3.9 Describe the steps involved in the top-down design process.

 3.3   Local Variables

CONCEPT: A local variable is declared inside a module and cannot be accessed by statements that are outside the module. Different modules can have local variables with the same names because the modules cannot see each other's local variables.

In most programming languages, a variable that is declared inside a module is called a *local variable*. A local variable belongs to the module in which it is declared, and only statements inside that module can access the variable. (The term *local* is meant to indicate that the variable can be used only locally, within the module in which it is declared.)

An error will occur if a statement in one module tries to access a local variable that belongs to another module. For example, look at the pseudocode in Program 3-3.

Program 3-3

```
 1 Module main()
 2    Call getName()
 3    Display "Hello ", name      ←———————— This will cause an error!
 4 End Module
 5
 6 Module getName()
 7    Declare String name    ←———————— This is local variable.
 8    Display "Enter your name."
 9    Input name
10 End Module
```

The `name` variable is declared in line 7, inside the `getName` module. Because it is declared inside the `getName` module, it is a local variable belonging to that module. Line 8 prompts the user to enter his or her name, and the `Input` statement in line 9 stores the user's input in the `name` variable.

The `main` module calls the `getName` module in line 2. Then, the `Display` statement in line 3 tries to access the `name` variable. This results in an error because the `name` variable is local to the `getName` module, and statements in the `main` module cannot access it.

Scope and Local Variables

Programmers commonly use the term *scope* to describe the part of a program in which a variable may be accessed. A variable is visible only to statements inside the variable's scope.

A local variable's scope usually begins at the variable's declaration and ends at the end of the module in which the variable is declared. The variable cannot be accessed by statements that are outside this region. This means that a local variable cannot be accessed by code that is outside the module, or inside the module but before the variable's declaration. For example, look at the following code. It has an error because the `Input` statement tries to store a value in the `name` variable, but the statement is outside the variable's scope. Moving the variable declaration to a line before the `Input` statement will fix this error.

```
Module getName()
   Display "Enter your name."
   Input name    ←———————————— This statement will cause an error because
   Declare String name         the name variable has not been declared yet.
End Module
```

Duplicate Variable Names

In most programming languages, you cannot have two variables with the same name in the same scope. For example, look at the following module:

```
Module getTwoAges()
    Declare Integer age
    Display "Enter your age."
    Input age

    Declare Integer age    ←——————————— This will cause an error!
    Display "Enter your pet's age."      A variable named age has
    Input age                            already been declared.
End Module
```

This module declares two local variables named age. The second variable declaration will cause an error because a variable named age has already been declared in the module. Renaming one of the variables will fix this error.

> **TIP:** You cannot have two variables with the same name in the same module because the compiler or interpreter would not know which variable to use when a statement tries to access one of them. All variables that exist within the same scope must have unique names.

Although you cannot have two local variables with the same name in the same module, it is usually okay for a local variable in one module to have the same name as a local variable in a different module. For example, suppose a program has two modules: getPersonAge and getPetAge. It would be legal for both modules to have a local variable named age.

Checkpoint

3.10 What is a local variable? How is access to a local variable restricted?

3.11 What is a variable's scope?

3.12 Is it usually permissible to have more than one variable with the same name in the same scope? Why or why not?

3.13 Is it usually permissible for a local variable in one module to have the same name as a local variable in a different module?

3.4 ## Passing Arguments to Modules

VideoNote

Passing
Arguments
to a Module

> **CONCEPT:** An argument is any piece of data that is passed into a module when the module is called. A parameter is a variable that receives an argument that is passed into a module.

Sometimes it is useful not only to call a module, but also to send one or more pieces of data into the module. Pieces of data that are sent into a module are known as *arguments*. The module can use its arguments in calculations or other operations.

If you want a module to receive arguments when it is called, you must equip the module with one or more parameter variables. A *parameter variable*, often simply called a *parameter*, is a special variable that receives an argument when a module is called. Here is an example of a pseudocode module that has a parameter variable:

```
Module doubleNumber(Integer value)
    Declare Integer result
    Set result = value * 2
    Display result
End Module
```

This module's name is doubleNumber. Its purpose is to accept an integer number as an argument and display the value of that number doubled. Look at the module header and notice the words Integer value that appear inside the parentheses. This is the declaration of a parameter variable. The parameter variable's name is value and its data type is Integer. The purpose of this variable is to receive an Integer argument when the module is called. Program 3-4 demonstrates the module in a complete program.

Program 3-4

```
1 Module main()
2     Call doubleNumber(4)
3 End Module
4
5 Module doubleNumber(Integer value)
6     Declare Integer result
7     Set result = value * 2
8     Display result
9 End Module
```

Program Output

```
8
```

When this program runs, the main module will begin executing. The statement in line 2 calls the doubleNumber module. Notice that the number 4 appears inside the parentheses. This is an argument that is being passed to the doubleNumber module. When this statement executes, the doubleNumber module will be called with the number 4 copied into the value parameter variable. This is shown in Figure 3-11.

Figure 3-11 The argument 4 is copied into the value parameter variable

```
Module main()
    Call doubleNumber(4)          The argument 4 is copied into
End Module                        the value parameter variable.


Module doubleNumber(Integer value)
    Declare Integer result
    Set result = value * 2
    Display result
End Module
```

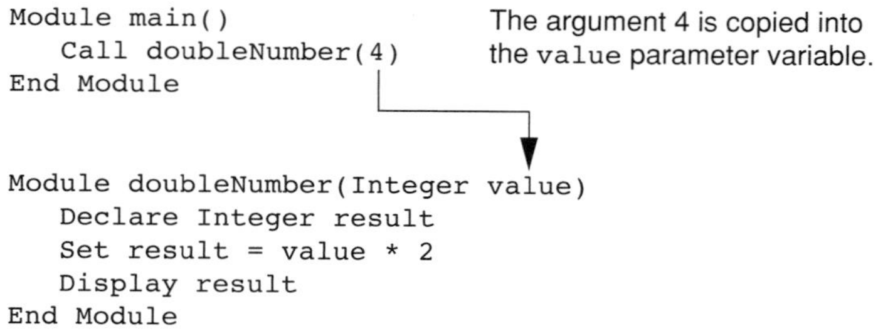

Let's step through the `doubleNumber` module. As we do, remember that the `value` parameter variable will contain the number that was passed into it as an argument. In this program, that number is 4.

Line 6 declares a local `Integer` variable named `result`. Then, line 7 assigns the value of the expression `value * 2` to result. Because the `value` variable contains 4, this line assigns 8 to result. Line 8 displays the contents of the `result` variable. The module ends at line 9.

For example, if we had called the module as follows:

```
Call doubleNumber(5)
```

the module would have displayed 10.

We can also pass the contents of a variable as an argument. For example, look at Program 3-5. The `main` module declares an `Integer` variable named `number` in line 2. Lines 3 and 4 prompt the user to enter a number, and line 5 reads the user's input into the `number` variable. Notice that in line 6 `number` is passed as an argument to the `doubleNumber` module, which causes the `number` variable's contents to be copied into the `value` parameter variable. This is shown in Figure 3-12.

Program 3-5

```
 1 Module main()
 2    Declare Integer number
 3    Display "Enter a number and I will display"
 4    Display "that number doubled."
 5    Input number
 6    Call doubleNumber(number)
 7 End Module
 8
 9 Module doubleNumber(Integer value)
10    Declare Integer result
11    Set result = value * 2
12    Display result
13 End Module
```

Program Output (with Input Shown in Bold)

```
Enter a number and I will display
that number doubled.
20 [Enter]
40
```

Argument and Parameter Compatibility

When you pass an argument to a module, most programming languages require that the argument and the receiving parameter variable be of the same data type. If you try to pass an argument of one type into a parameter variable of another type, an error usually occurs. For example, Figure 3-13 shows that you cannot pass a real number or a `Real` variable into an `Integer` parameter.

Figure 3-12 The contents of the number variable passed as an argument

```
Module main()
   Declare Integer number
   Display "Enter a number and I will display"
   Display "that number doubled."
   Input number
   Call doubleNumber(number)
End Module

Module doubleNumber(Integer value)
   Declare Integer result
   Set result = value * 2
   Display result
End Module
```

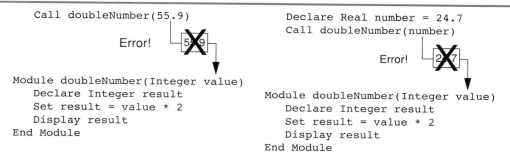

The contents of the number variable are copied into the value parameter variable.

Figure 3-13 Arguments and parameter variables must be of the same type

```
Call doubleNumber(55.9)


   Error!          5 9



Module doubleNumber(Integer value)
   Declare Integer result
   Set result = value * 2
   Display result
End Module
```

```
Declare Real number = 24.7
Call doubleNumber(number)


             Error!      2 7



Module doubleNumber(Integer value)
   Declare Integer result
   Set result = value * 2
   Display result
End Module
```

NOTE: Some languages allow you to pass an argument into a parameter variable of a different type as long as no data will be lost. For example, some languages allow you to pass integer arguments into real parameters because real variables can hold whole numbers. If you pass a real argument, such as 24.7, into an integer parameter, the fractional part of the number would be lost.

Parameter Variable Scope

Earlier in this chapter, you learned that a variable's scope is the part of the program in which the variable may be accessed. A variable is visible only to statements inside the variable's scope. A parameter variable's scope is usually the entire module in which the parameter is declared. No statement outside the module can access the parameter variable.

Passing Multiple Arguments

Most languages allow you to write modules that accept multiple arguments. Program 3-6 shows a pseudocode module named showSum, that accepts two Integer arguments. The module adds the two arguments and displays their sum.

Program 3-6

```
 1 Module main()
 2    Display "The sum of 12 and 45 is:"
 3    Call showSum(12, 45)
 4 End Module
 5
 6 Module showSum(Integer num1, Integer num2)
 7    Declare Integer result
 8    Set result = num1 + num2
 9    Display result
10 End Module
```

Program Output

```
The sum of 12 and 45 is:
57
```

Notice that two parameter variables, num1 and num2, are declared inside the parentheses in the module header. This is often referred to as a *parameter list*. Also notice that a comma separates the declarations.

The statement in line 3 calls the showSum module and passes two arguments: 12 and 45. The arguments are passed into the parameter variables in the order that they appear in the module call. In other words, the first argument is passed into the first parameter variable, and the second argument is passed into the second parameter variable. So, this statement causes 12 to be passed into the num1 parameter and 45 to be passed into the num2 parameter, as shown in Figure 3-14.

Figure 3-14 Two arguments passed into two parameters

```
Module main()
   Display "The sum of 12 and 45 is"
   Call showSum(12, 45)
End Module



Module showSum(Integer num1, Integer num2)
   Declare Integer result
   Set result = num1 + num2
   Display result
End Module
```

Suppose we were to reverse the order in which the arguments are listed in the module call, as shown here:

```
Call showSum(45, 12)
```

This would cause 45 to be passed into the num1 parameter and 12 to be passed into the num2 parameter. The following pseudocode code shows one more example. This time we are passing variables as arguments.

```
Declare Integer value1 = 2
Declare Integer value2 = 3
Call showSum(value1, value2)
```

When the showSum methods executes as a result of this code, the num1 parameter will contain 2 and the num2 parameter will contain 3.

In the Spotlight:
Passing an Argument to a Module

Your friend Michael runs a catering company. Some of the ingredients that his recipes require are measured in cups. When he goes to the grocery store to buy those ingredients, however, they are sold only by the fluid ounce. He has asked you to write a simple program that converts cups to fluid ounces.

You design the following algorithm:

1. Display an introductory screen that explains what the program does.
2. Get the number of cups.
3. Convert the number of cups to fluid ounces and display the result.

This algorithm lists the top level of tasks that the program needs to perform, and becomes the basis of the program's main module. Figure 3-15 shows the program's structure in a hierarchy chart.

Figure 3-15 Hierarchy chart for the program

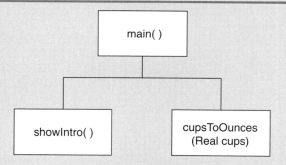

As shown in the hierarchy chart, the main module will call two other modules.

Here are summaries of those modules:

- showIntro—This module will display a message on the screen that explains what the program does.
- cupsToOunces—This module will accept the number of cups as an argument and calculate and display the equivalent number of fluid ounces.

In addition to calling these modules, the main module will ask the user to enter the number of cups. This value will be passed to the cupsToOunces module. Program 3-7 shows the pseudocode for the program, and Figure 3-16 shows a flowchart.

Program 3-7

```
 1 Module main()
 2    // Declare a variable for the
 3    // number of cups needed.
 4    Declare Real cupsNeeded
 5
 6    // Display an intro message.
 7    Call showIntro()
 8
 9    // Get the number of cups.
10    Display "Enter the number of cups."
11    Input cupsNeeded
12
13    // Convert cups to ounces.
14    Call cupsToOunces(cupsNeeded)
15 End Module
16
17 // The showIntro module displays an
18 // introductory screen.
19 Module showIntro()
20    Display "This program converts measurements"
21    Display "in cups to fluid ounces. For your"
22    Display "reference the formula is:"
23    Display "    1 cup = 8 fluid ounces."
24 End Module
25
26 // The cupsToOunces module accepts a number
27 // of cups and displays the equivalent number
28 // of ounces.
29 Module cupsToOunces(Real cups)
30    // Declare variables.
31    Declare Real ounces
32
33    // Convert cups to ounces.
34    Set ounces = cups * 8
35
36    // Display the result.
37    Display "That converts to ",
38            ounces, " ounces."
39 End Module
```

Program Output (with Input Shown in Bold)

```
This program converts measurements
in cups to fluid ounces. For your
reference the formula is:
    1 cup = 8 fluid ounces.
Enter the number of cups.
2 [Enter]
That converts to 16 ounces.
```

Figure 3-16 Flowchart for Program 3-7

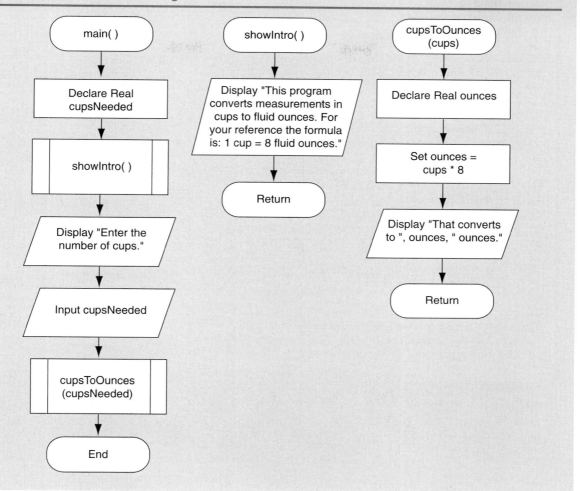

Passing Arguments by Value and by Reference

Many programming languages provide two different ways to pass arguments: by value and by reference. Before studying these techniques in detail, we should mention that different languages have their own way of doing each. In this book, we will teach you the fundamental concepts behind these techniques, and show you how to model them in pseudocode. When you begin to use these techniques in an actual language, you will need to learn the details of how they are carried out in that language.

Passing Arguments by Value

All of the example programs that we have looked at so far pass arguments by value. Arguments and parameter variables are separate items in memory. Passing an argument *by value* means that only a copy of the argument's value is passed into the parameter variable. If the contents of the parameter variable are changed inside the module, it has no effect on the argument in the calling part of the program. For example, look at Program 3-8.

Program 3-8

```
1 Module main()
2    Declare Integer number = 99
3
4    // Display the value stored in number.
5    Display "The number is ", number
6
7    // Call the changeMe module, passing
8    // the number variable as an argument.
9    Call changeMe(number)
10
11    // Display the value of number again.
12    Display "The number is", number
13 End Module
14
15 Module changeMe(Integer myValue)
16    Display "I am changing the value."
17
18    // Set the myValue parameter variable
19    // to 0.
20    Set myValue = 0
21
22    // Display the value in myValue.
23    Display "Now the number is ", myValue
24 End Module
```

Program Output

```
The number is 99
I am changing the number.
Now the value is 0
The number is 99
```

The main module declares a local variable named number in line 2, and initializes it to the value 99. As a result, the Display statement in line 5 displays "The number is 99." The number variable's value is then passed as an argument to the changeMe module in line 9. This means that in the changeMe module the value 99 will be copied into the myValue parameter variable.

Inside the changeMe module, in line 20, the myValue parameter variable is set to 0. As a result, the Display statement in line 23 displays "Now the number is 0." The module ends, and control of the program returns to the main module.

The next statement to execute is the Display statement in line 12. This statement displays "The number is 99." Even though the parameter variable myValue was changed in the changeMe method, the argument (the number variable in main) was not modified.

Passing an argument is a way that one module can communicate with another module. When the argument is passed by value, the communication channel works in only one direction: the calling module can communicate with the called module. The called module, however, cannot use the argument to communicate with the calling module.

Passing Arguments by Reference

Passing an argument *by reference* means that the argument is passed into a special type of parameter known as a *reference variable*. When a reference variable is used as a parameter in a module, it allows the module to modify the argument in the calling part of the program.

A reference variable acts as an alias for the variable that was passed into it as an argument. It is called a reference variable because it references the other variable. Anything that you do to the reference variable is actually done to the variable it references.

Reference variables are useful for establishing two-way communication between modules. When a module calls another module and passes a variable by reference, communication between the modules can take place in the following ways:

- The calling module can communicate with the called module by passing an argument.
- The called module can communicate with the calling module by modifying the value of the argument via the reference variable.

In pseudocode we will declare that a parameter is a reference variable by writing the word `Ref` before the parameter variable's name in the module header. For example, look at the following pseudocode module:

```
Module setToZero(Integer Ref value)
   Set value = 0
End Module
```

The word `Ref` indicates that `value` is a reference variable. The module stores 0 in the `value` parameter. Because `value` is a reference variable, this action is actually performed on the variable that was passed to the module as an argument. Program 3-9 demonstrates this module.

Program 3-9

```
 1 Module main()
 2    // Declare and initialize some variables.
 3    Declare Integer x = 99
 4    Declare Integer y = 100
 5    Declare Integer z = 101
 6
 7    // Display the values in those variables.
 8    Display "x is set to ", x
 9    Display "y is set to ", y
10    Display "z is set to ", z
11
12    // Pass each variable to setToZero.
13    Call setToZero(x)
14    Call setToZero(y)
15    Call setToZero(z)
16
17    // Display the values now.
18    Display "----------------"
19    Display "x is set to ", x
```

```
20    Display "y is set to ", y
21    Display "z is set to ", z
22 End Module
23
24 Module setToZero(Integer Ref value)
25    Set value = 0
26 End Module
```

Program Output

```
x is set to 99
y is set to 100
z is set to 101
---------------
x is set to 0
y is set to 0
z is set to 0
```

In the main module the variable x is initialized with 99, the variable y is initialized with 100, and the variable z is initialized with 101. Then, in lines 13 through 15 those variables are passed as arguments to the setToZero module. Each time setToZero is called, the variable that is passed as an argument is set to 0. This is shown when the values of the variables are displayed in lines 19 through 21.

NOTE: In an actual program you should never use variable names like x, y, and z. This particular program is meant for demonstration purposes, however, and these simple names are adequate.

NOTE: Normally, only variables may be passed by reference. If you attempt to pass a non-variable argument into a reference variable parameter, an error will result. Using the setToZero module as an example, the following statement will generate an error:

```
// This is an error!
setToZero(5);
```

In the Spotlight:
Passing an Argument by Reference

In the previous *In the Spotlight* case study, we developed a program that your friend Michael can use in his catering business. The program does exactly what Michael wants it to do: it converts cups to fluid ounces. After studying the program that we initially wrote, however, you believe that you can improve the design. As shown in the following pseudocode, the main module contains the code that reads the user's input. This code should really be treated as a separate subtask, and put in its own module. If this change is made, the program will be like the new hierarchy chart shown in Figure 3-17.

```
Module main()
    // Declare a variable for the
    // number of cups needed.
    Declare Real cupsNeeded

    // Display an intro message.
    showIntro()

    // Get the number of cups.
    Display "Enter the number of cups."
    Input cupsNeeded

    // Convert cups to ounces.
    cupsToOunces(cupsNeeded)
End Module
```

This code can be put in its own module.

Figure 3-17 Revised hierarchy chart

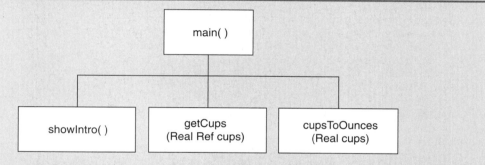

This version of the hierarchy chart shows a new module: getCups. Here is the pseudocode for the getCups module:

```
Module getCups(Real Ref cups)
    Display "Enter the number of cups."
    Input cups
End Module
```

The getCups module has a parameter, cups, which is a reference variable. The module prompts the user to enter the number of cups and then stores the user's input in the cups parameter. When the main module calls getCups, it will pass the local variable cupsNeeded as an argument. Because it will be passed by reference, it will contain the user's input when the module returns. Program 3-10 shows the revised pseudocode for the program, and Figure 3-18 shows a flowchart.

NOTE: In this case study, we improved the design of an existing program without changing the behavior of the program. In a nutshell, we "cleaned up" the design. Programmers call this *refactoring*.

Program 3-10

```
 1 Module main()
 2    // Declare a variable for the
 3    // number of cups needed.
 4    Declare Real cupsNeeded
 5
 6    // Display an intro message.
 7    Call showIntro()
 8
 9    // Get the number of cups.
10    Call getCups(cupsNeeded)
11
12    // Convert cups to ounces.
13    Call cupsToOunces(cupsNeeded)
14 End Module
15
16 // The showIntro module displays an
17 // introductory screen.
18 Module showIntro()
19    Display "This program converts measurements"
20    Display "in cups to fluid ounces. For your"
21    Display "reference the formula is:"
22    Display "    1 cup = 8 fluid ounces."
23 End Module
24
25 // The getCups module gets the number of cups
26 // and stores it in the reference variable cups.
27 Module getCups(Real Ref cups)
28    Display "Enter the number of cups."
29    Input cups
30 End Module
31
32 // The cupsToOunces module accepts a number
33 // of cups and displays the equivalent number
34 // of ounces.
35 Module cupsToOunces(Real cups)
36    // Declare variables.
37    Declare Real ounces
38
39    // Convert cups to ounces.
40    Set ounces = cups * 8
41
42    // Display the result.
43    Display "That converts to ",
44            ounces, " ounces."
45 End Module
```

Program Output (with Input Shown in Bold)

```
This program converts measurements
in cups to fluid ounces. For your
reference the formula is:
    1 cup = 8 fluid ounces.
Enter the number of cups.
2 [Enter]
That converts to 16 ounces.
```

Figure 3-18 Flowchart for Program 3-10

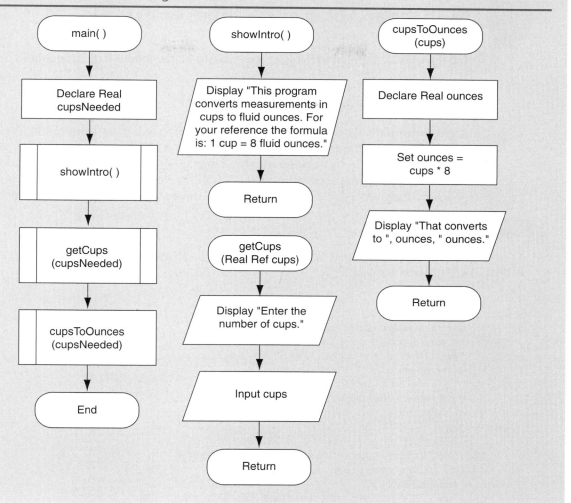

Checkpoint

3.14 What are the pieces of data that are passed into a module called?

3.15 What are the variables that receive pieces of data in a module called?

3.16 Does it usually matter if an argument's data type is different than the data type of the parameter that it is being passed to?

3.17 Typically, what is a parameter variable's scope?

3.18 Explain the difference between passing by value and passing by reference.

3.5 Global Variables and Global Constants

CONCEPT: A global variable is accessible to all the modules in a program.

Global Variables

A *global variable* is a variable that is visible to every module in the program. A global variable's scope is the entire program, so all of the modules in the program can access a global variable. In most programming languages, you create a global variable by writing its declaration statement outside of all the modules, usually at the top of the program. Program 3-11 shows how you can declare a global variable in pseudocode.

Program 3-11

```
 1 // The following declares a global Integer variable.
 2 Declare Integer number
 3
 4 // The main module
 5 Module main()
 6    // Get a number from the user and store it
 7    // in the global variable number.
 8    Display "Enter a number."
 9    Input number
10
11    // Call the showNumber module.
12    Call showNumber()
13 End Module
14
15 // The showNumber module displays the contents
16 // of the global variable number.
17 Module showNumber()
18    Display "The number you entered is ", number
19 End Module
```

Program Output (with Input Shown in Bold)

```
Enter a number.
22 [Enter]
The number you entered is 22
```

Line 2 declares an Integer variable named number. Because the declaration does not appear inside a module, the number variable is a global variable. All of the modules that are defined in the program have access to the variable. When the Input statement in line 9 (inside the main module) executes, the value entered by the user is stored in the global variable number. When the Display statement in line 18 (inside the showNumber module) executes, it is the value of the same global variable that is displayed.

Most programmers agree that you should restrict the use of global variables, or not use them at all. The reasons are as follows:

- Global variables make debugging difficult. Any statement in a program can change the value of a global variable. If you find that the wrong value is being stored in a global variable, you have to track down every statement that accesses it to determine where the bad value is coming from. In a program with thousands of lines of code, this can be difficult.
- Modules that use global variables are usually dependent on those variables. If you want to use such a module in a different program, most likely you will have to redesign it so it does not rely on the global variable.
- Global variables make a program hard to understand. A global variable can be modified by any statement in the program. If you are to understand any part of the program that uses a global variable, you have to be aware of all the other parts of the program that access the global variable.

In most cases, you should declare variables locally and pass them as arguments to the modules that need to access them.

Global Constants

Although you should try to avoid the use of global variables, it is permissible to use global constants in a program. A *global constant* is a named constant that is available to every module in the program. Because a global constant's value cannot be changed during the program's execution, you do not have to worry about many of the potential hazards that are associated with the use of global variables.

Global constants are typically used to represent unchanging values that are needed throughout a program. For example, suppose a banking program uses a named constant to represent an interest rate. If the interest rate is used in several modules, it is easier to create a global constant, rather than a local named constant in each module. This also simplifies maintenance. If the interest rate changes, only the declaration of the global constant has to be changed, instead of several local declarations.

In the Spotlight:
Using Global Constants

Marilyn works for Integrated Systems, Inc., a software company that has a reputation for providing excellent fringe benefits. One of their benefits is a quarterly bonus that is paid to all employees. Another benefit is a retirement plan for each employee. The company contributes 5 percent of each employee's gross pay and bonuses to their retirement plans. Marilyn wants to design a program that will calculate the company's contribution to an employee's retirement account for a year. She wants the program to show the amount of contribution for the employee's gross pay and for the bonuses separately.

Here is an algorithm for the program:

1. Get the employee's annual gross pay.
2. Get the amount of bonuses paid to the employee.
3. Calculate and display the contribution for the gross pay.
4. Calculate and display the contribution for the bonuses.

Figure 3-19 shows a hierarchy chart for the program. The pseudocode for the program is shown in Program 3-12, and a set of flowcharts is shown in Figure 3-20.

Figure 3-19 Hierarchy chart

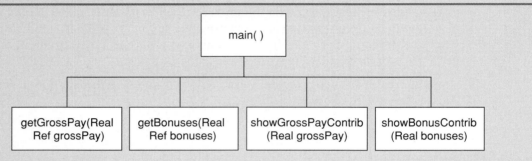

Program 3-12

```
 1 // Global constant for the rate of contribution.
 2 Constant Real CONTRIBUTION_RATE = 0.05
 3
 4 // main module
 5 Module main()
 6    // Local variables
 7    Declare Real annualGrossPay
 8    Declare Real totalBonuses
 9
10    // Get the annual gross pay.
11    Call getGrossPay(annualGrossPay)
12
13    // Get the total of the bonuses.
14    Call getBonuses(totalBonuses)
15
16    // Display the contribution for
17    // the gross pay.
18    Call showGrossPayContrib(annualGrossPay)
19
20    // Display the contribution for
21    // the bonuses.
22    Call showBonusContrib(totalBonuses)
23 End Module
24
25 // The getGrossPay module gets the
26 // gross pay and stores it in the
27 // grossPay reference variable.
28 Module getGrossPay(Real Ref grossPay)
29    Display "Enter the total gross pay."
```

```
30      Input grossPay
31 End Module
32
33 // The getBonuses module gets the
34 // amount of bonuses and stores it
35 // in the bonuses reference variable.
36 Module getBonuses(Real Ref bonuses)
37      Display "Enter the amount of bonuses."
38      Input bonuses
39 End Module
40
41 // The showGrossPayContrib module
42 // accepts the gross pay as an argument
43 // and displays the retirement contribution
44 // for gross pay.
45 Module showGrossPayContrib(Real grossPay)
46      Declare Real contrib
47      Set contrib = grossPay * CONTRIBUTION_RATE
48      Display "The contribution for the gross pay"
49      Display "is $", contrib
50 End Module
51
52 // The showBonusContrib module accepts
53 // the bonus amount as an argument and
54 // displays the retirement contribution
55 // for bonuses.
56 Module showBonusContrib(Real bonuses)
57      Declare Real contrib
58      Set contrib = bonuses * CONTRIBUTION_RATE
59      Display "The contribution for the bonuses"
60      Display "is $", contrib
61 End Module
```

Program Output (with Input Shown in Bold)

```
Enter the total gross pay.
80000.00 [Enter]
Enter the amount of bonuses.
20000.00 [Enter]
The contribution for the gross pay
is $4000
The contribution for the bonuses
is $1000
```

A global constant named CONTRIBUTION_RATE is declared in line 2, and initialized with the value 0.05. The constant is used in the calculation in line 47 (in the showGrossPayContrib module) and again in line 58 (in the showBonusContrib module). Marilyn decided to use this global constant to represent the 5 percent contribution rate for two reasons:

- It makes the program easier to read. When you look at the calculations in lines 47 and 58 it is apparent what is happening.
- Occasionally the contribution rate changes. When this happens, it will be easy to update the program by changing the declaration statement in line 2.

Figure 3-20 Flowchart for Program 3-12

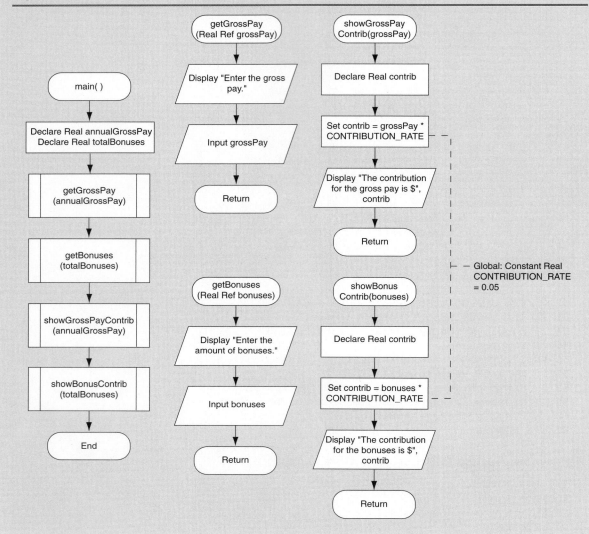

 **Checkpoint**

3.19 What is the scope of a global variable?

3.20 Give one good reason that you should not use global variables in a program.

3.21 What is a global constant? Is it permissible to use global constants in a program?

Review Questions

Multiple Choice

1. A group of statements that exist within a program for the purpose of performing a specific task is a(n) _____.
   a. block
   b. parameter
   c. module
   d. expression

2. A benefit of using modules that helps to reduce the duplication of code within a program is _____.
   a. code reuse
   b. divide and conquer
   c. debugging
   d. facilitation of teamwork

3. The first line of a module definition is known as the _____.
   a. body
   b. introduction
   c. initialization
   d. header

4. You _____ the module to execute it.
   a. define
   b. call
   c. import
   d. export

5. A _____ point is the memory address of the location in the program that the computer will return to when a module ends.
   a. termination
   b. module definition
   c. return
   d. reference

6. A design technique that programmers use to break down an algorithm into modules is known as _____.
   a. top-down design
   b. code simplification
   c. code refactoring
   d. hierarchical subtasking

7. A _____ is a diagram that gives a visual representation of the relationships between modules in a program.
   a. flowchart
   b. module relationship chart
   c. symbol chart
   d. hierarchy chart

8. A _____ is a variable that is declared inside a module.

   a. global variable
   b. local variable
   c. hidden variable
   d. none of the above; you cannot declare a variable inside a module

9. A(n) _____ is the part of a program in which a variable may be accessed.

   a. declaration space
   b. area of visibility
   c. scope
   d. mode

10. A(n) _____ is a piece of data that is sent into a module.

    a. argument
    b. parameter
    c. header
    d. packet

11. A(n) _____ is a special variable that receives a piece of data when a module is called.

    a. argument
    b. parameter
    c. header
    d. packet

12. When _____, only a copy of the argument's value is passed into the parameter variable.

    a. passing an argument by reference
    b. passing an argument by name
    c. passing an argument by value
    d. passing an argument by data type

13. When _____, the module can modify the argument in the calling part of the program.

    a. passing an argument by reference
    b. passing an argument by name
    c. passing an argument by value
    d. passing an argument by data type

14. A variable that is visible to every module in the program is a _____.

    a. local variable
    b. universal variable
    c. program-wide variable
    d. global variable

15. When possible, you should avoid using _____ variables in a program.

    a. local
    b. global
    c. reference
    d. parameter

True or False

1. The phrase "divide and conquer" means that all of the programmers on a team should be divided and work in isolation.

2. Modules make it easier for programmers to work in teams.

3. Module names should be as short as possible.

4. Calling a module and defining a module mean the same thing.

5. A flowchart shows the hierarchical relationships between modules in a program.

6. A hierarchy chart does not show the steps that are taken inside a module.

7. A statement in one module can access a local variable in another module.

8. In most programming languages, you cannot have two variables with the same name in the same scope.

9. Programming languages typically require that arguments be of the same data type as the parameters that they are passed to.

10. Most languages do not allow you to write modules that accept multiple arguments.

11. When an argument is passed by reference, the module can modify the argument in the calling part of the program.

12. Passing an argument by value is a means of establishing two-way communication between modules.

Short Answer

1. How do modules help you to reuse code in a program?

2. Name and describe the two parts that a module definition has in most languages.

3. When a module is executing, what happens when the end of the module is reached?

4. What is a local variable? What statements are able to access a local variable?

5. In most languages, where does a local variable's scope begin and end?

6. What is the difference between passing an argument by value and passing it by reference?

7. Why do global variables make a program difficult to debug?

Algorithm Workbench

1. Design a module named `timesTen`. The module should accept an `Integer` argument. When the module is called, it should display the product of its argument multiplied times 10.

2. Examine the following pseudocode module header, and then write a statement that calls the module, passing 12 as an argument.

```
Module showValue(Integer quantity)
```

3. Look at the following pseudocode module header:

   ```
   Module myModule(Integer a, Integer b, Integer c)
   ```

   Now look at the following call to myModule:

   ```
   Call myModule(3, 2, 1)
   ```

   When this call executes, what value will be stored in a? What value will be stored in b? What value will be stored in c?

4. Assume that a pseudocode program contains the following module:

   ```
   Module display(Integer arg1, Real arg2, String arg3)
      Display "Here are the values:"
      Display arg1, " ", arg2, " ", arg3
   End Module
   ```

   Assume that the same program has a main module with the following variable declarations:

   ```
   Declare Integer age
   Declare Real income
   Declare String name
   ```

   Write a statement that calls the display module and passes these variables to it.

5. Design a module named getNumber, which uses a reference parameter variable to accept an Integer argument. The module should prompt the user to enter a number and then store the input in the reference parameter variable.

6. What will the following pseudocode program display?

   ```
   Module main()
      Declare Integer x = 1
      Declare Real y = 3.4
      Display x, " ", y
      Call changeUs(x, y)
      Display x, " ", y
   End Module

   Module changeUs(Integer a, Real b)
      Set a = 0
      Set b = 0
      Display a, " ", b
   End Module
   ```

7. What will the following pseudocode program display?

   ```
   Module main()
      Declare Integer x = 1
      Declare Real y = 3.4
      Display x, " ", y
      Call changeUs(x, y)
      Display x, " ", y
   End Module

   Module changeUs(Integer Ref a, Real Ref b)
      Set a = 0
      Set b = 0.0
      Display a, " ", b
   End Module
   ```

Programming Exercises

1. **Kilometer Converter**

   Design a modular program that asks the user to enter a distance in kilometers, and then converts that distance to miles. The conversion formula is as follows:

   $$Miles = Kilometers \times 0.6214$$

2. **Sales Tax Program Refactoring**

   Programming Exercise 6 in Chapter 2 was the Sales Tax program. For that exercise you were asked to design a program that calculates and displays the county and state sales tax on a purchase. If you have already designed that program, refactor it so the subtasks are in modules. If you have not already designed that program, create a modular design for it.

3. **How Much Insurance?**

   Many financial experts advise that property owners should insure their homes or buildings for at least 80 percent of the amount it would cost to replace the structure. Design a modular program that asks the user to enter the replacement cost of a building and then displays the minimum amount of insurance he or she should buy for the property.

4. **Automobile Costs**

   Design a modular program that asks the user to enter the monthly costs for the following expenses incurred from operating his or her automobile: loan payment, insurance, gas, oil, tires, and maintenance. The program should then display the total monthly cost of these expenses, and the total annual cost of these expenses.

5. **Property Tax**

   A county collects property taxes on the assessment value of property, which is 60 percent of the property's actual value. For example, if an acre of land is valued at $10,000, its assessment value is $6,000. The property tax is then 64¢ for each $100 of the assessment value. The tax for the acre assessed at $6,000 will be $38.40. Design a modular program that asks for the actual value of a piece of property and displays the assessment value and property tax.

6. **Body Mass Index**

   Design a modular program that calculates and displays a person's body mass index (BMI). The BMI is often used to determine whether a person with a sedentary lifestyle is overweight or underweight for their height. A person's BMI is calculated with the following formula:

   $$BMI = Weight \times 703/Height^2$$

7. **Calories from Fat and Carbohydrates**

   A nutritionist who works for a fitness club helps members by evaluating their diets. As part of her evaluation, she asks members for the number of fat grams and carbohydrate grams that they consumed in a day. Then, she calculates the number of calories that result from the fat, using the following formula:

   $$Calories\ from\ Fat = Fat\ Grams \times 9$$

Next, she calculates the number of calories that result from the carbohydrates, using the following formula:

$$Calories\ from\ Carbs = Carb\ Grams \times 4$$

The nutritionist asks you to design a modular program that will make these calculations.

8. **Stadium Seating**

There are three seating categories at a stadium. For a softball game, Class A seats cost $15, Class B seats cost $12, and Class C seats cost $9. Design a modular program that asks how many tickets for each class of seats were sold, and then displays the amount of income generated from ticket sales.

9. **Paint Job Estimator**

A painting company has determined that for every 115 square feet of wall space, one gallon of paint and eight hours of labor will be required. The company charges $20.00 per hour for labor. Design a modular program that asks the user to enter the square feet of wall space to be painted and the price of the paint per gallon. The program should display the following data:

- The number of gallons of paint required
- The hours of labor required
- The cost of the paint
- The labor charges
- The total cost of the paint job

10. **Monthly Sales Tax**

A retail company must file a monthly sales tax report listing the total sales for the month, and the amount of state and county sales tax collected. The state sales tax rate is 4 percent and the county sales tax rate is 2 percent. Design a modular program that asks the user to enter the total sales for the month. From this figure, the application should calculate and display the following:

- The amount of county sales tax
- The amount of state sales tax
- The total sales tax (county plus state)

In the pseudocode, represent the county tax rate (0.02) and the state tax rate (0.04) as named constants.

4 Decision Structures and Boolean Logic

TOPICS

4.1 Introduction to Decision Structures

CONCEPT: A decision structure allows a program to perform actions only under certain conditions.

VideoNote

The Single Alternative Decision Structure

A control structure is a logical design that controls the order in which a set of statements execute. So far in this book we have used only the simplest type of control structure: the sequence structure. Recall from Chapter 2 that a sequence structure is a set of statements that execute in the order that they appear. For example, the following pseudocode is a sequence structure because the statements execute from top to bottom.

```
Declare Integer age
Display "What is your age?"
Input age
Display "Here is the value that you entered:"
Display age
```

Even in Chapter 3, where you learned about modules, each module was written as a sequence structure. For example, the following module is a sequence structure because the statements in it execute in the order that they appear, from the beginning of the module to the end.

```
Module doubleNumber(Integer value)
    Declare Integer result
    Set result = value * 2
    Display result
End Module
```

Although the sequence structure is heavily used in programming, it cannot handle every type of task. Some problems simply cannot be solved by performing a set of ordered steps, one after the other. For example, consider a pay calculating program that determines whether an employee has worked overtime. If the employee has worked more than 40 hours, he or she gets paid extra for all the hours over 40. Otherwise, the overtime calculation should be skipped. Programs like this require a different type of control structure: one that can execute a set of statements only under certain circumstances. This can be accomplished with a *decision structure*. (Decision structures are also known as *selection structures*.)

In a decision structure's simplest form, a specific action is performed only if a certain condition exists. If the condition does not exist, the action is not performed. The flowchart shown in Figure 4-1 shows how the logic of an everyday decision can be diagrammed as a decision structure. The diamond symbol represents a true/false condition. If the condition is true, we follow one path, which leads to an action being performed. If the condition is false, we follow another path, which skips the action.

Figure 4-1 A simple decision structure

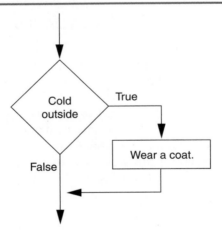

In the flowchart, the diamond symbol indicates some condition that must be tested. In this case, we are determining whether the condition *Cold outside* is true or false. If this condition is true, the action *Wear a coat* is performed. If the condition is false, the action is skipped. The action is *conditionally executed* because it is performed only when a certain condition is true.

Programmers call the type of decision structure shown in Figure 4-1 a *single alternative decision structure*. This is because it provides only one alternative path of execution. If the condition in the diamond symbol is true, we take the alternative path. Otherwise, we exit the structure.

Combining Structures

You cannot use decision structures alone to create a complete program. You use a decision structure to handle any part of a program that needs to test a condition and conditionally execute an action depending on the outcome of the condition. For other parts of a program you need to use other structures. For example, Figure 4-2 shows a complete flowchart that combines a decision structure with two sequence structures.

The flowchart in the figure starts with a sequence structure. Assuming you have an outdoor thermometer in your window, the first step is *Go to the window,* and the next step is *Read thermometer*. A decision structure appears next, testing the condition *Cold outside*. If this is true, the action *Wear a coat* is performed. Another sequence structure appears next. The step *Open the door* is performed, followed by *Go outside*.

Quite often, structures must be nested inside of other structures. For example, look at the partial flowchart in Figure 4-3. It shows a decision structure with a sequence structure nested inside it. The decision structure tests the condition *Cold outside*. If that condition is true, the steps in the sequence structure are executed.

Figure 4-2 Combining sequence structures with a decision structure

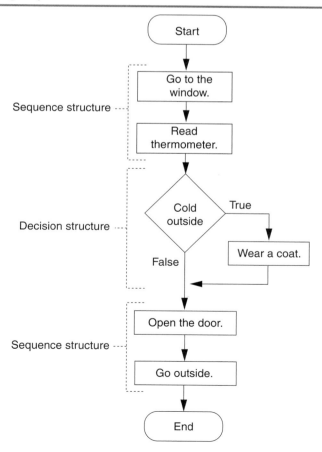

Figure 4-3 A sequence structure nested inside a decision structure

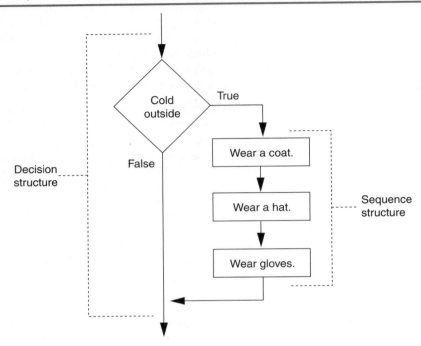

Writing a Decision Structure in Pseudocode

In pseudocode we use the If-Then statement to write a single alternative decision structure. Here is the general format of the If-Then statement:

```
If condition Then
      statement
      statement
      etc.
End If
```

These statements are conditionally executed

For simplicity, we will refer to the line that begins with the word If as the *If clause,* and we will refer to the line that reads End If as the *End If clause.* In the general format, the *condition* is any expression that can be evaluated as either true or false. When the If-Then statement executes, the *condition* is tested. If it is true, the statements that appear between the If clause and the End If clause are executed. The End If clause marks the end of the If-Then statement.

Boolean Expressions and Relational Operators

All programming languages allow you to create expressions that can be evaluated as either true or false. These are called *Boolean expressions,* named in honor of the English mathematician George Boole. In the 1800s Boole invented a system of mathematics in which the abstract concepts of true and false can be used in computations. The condition that is tested by an If-Then statement must be a Boolean expression.

Typically, the Boolean expression that is tested by an If-Then statement is formed with a relational operator. A *relational operator* determines whether a specific relationship exists between two values. For example, the greater than operator (>) determines whether one value is greater than another. The equal to operator (==) determines whether two values are equal. Table 4-1 lists the relational operators that are commonly available in most programming languages.

Table 4-1 Relational operators

Operator	Meaning
>	Greater than
<	Less than
>=	Greater than or equal to
<=	Less than or equal to
==	Equal to
!=	Not equal to

The following is an example of an expression that uses the greater than (>) operator to compare two variables, length and width:

```
length > width
```

This expression determines whether the value of length is greater than the value of width. If length is greater than width, the value of the expression is true. Otherwise, the value of the expression is false. Because the expression can be only true or false, it is a Boolean expression. The following expression uses the less than operator to determine whether length is less than width:

```
length < width
```

Table 4-2 shows examples of several Boolean expressions that compare the variables x and y.

Table 4-2 Boolean expressions using relational operators

Expression	Meaning
x > y	Is x greater than y?
x < y	Is x less than y?
x >= y	Is x greater than or equal to y?
x <= y	Is x less than or equal to y?
x == y	Is x equal to y?
x != y	Is x not equal to y?

The >= and <= Operators

Two of the operators, >= and <=, test for more than one relationship. The >= operator determines whether the operand on its left is greater than *or* equal to the operand on its right. For example, assuming that a is 4, b is 6, and c is 4, both of the expressions b >= a and a >= c are true and a >= 5 is false.

The <= operator determines whether the operand on its left is less than *or* equal to the operand on its right. Once again, assuming that a is 4, b is 6, and c is 4, both a <= c and b <= 10 are true, but b <= a is false.

The == Operator

The == operator determines whether the operand on its left is equal to the operand on its right. If both operands have the same value, the expression is true. Assuming that a is 4, the expression a == 4 is true and the expression a == 2 is false.

In this book, we use two = characters as the equal to operator to avoid confusion with the assignment operator, which is one = character. Several programming languages, most notably Java, C, and C++, also follow this practice.

> **WARNING!** When programming in a language that uses == as the equal to operator, take care not to confuse this operator with the assignment operator, which is one = sign. In languages such as Java, C, and C++ the == operator determines whether a variable is equal to another value, but the = operator assigns the value to a variable.

The != Operator

The != operator is the not equal to operator. It determines whether the operand on its left is not equal to the operand on its right, which is the opposite of the == operator. As before, assuming a is 4, b is 6, and c is 4, both a != b and b != c are true because a is not equal to b and b is not equal to c. However, a != c is false because a is equal to c.

Note that != is the same character sequence used by several languages for the not equal to operator, including Java, C, and C++. Some languages, such as Visual Basic, use <> as the not equal to operator.

Putting It All Together

Let's look at the following example of the If-Then statement in pseudocode:

```
If sales > 50000 Then
    Set bonus = 500.0
End If
```

This statement uses the > operator to determine whether sales is greater than 50,000. If the expression sales > 50000 is true, the variable bonus is assigned 500.0. If the expression is false, however, the assignment statement is skipped. Figure 4-4 shows a flowchart for this section of code.

The following example conditionally executes a set of statements. Figure 4-5 shows a flowchart for this section of code.

```
If sales > 50000 Then
    Set bonus = 500.0
    Set commissionRate = 0.12
    Display "You've met your sales quota!"
End If
```

Figure 4-4 Example decision structure

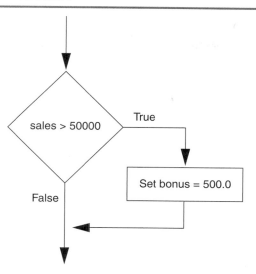

Figure 4-5 Example decision structure

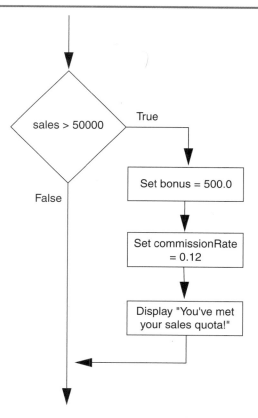

The following pseudocode uses the == operator to determine whether two values are equal. The expression `balance == 0` will be true if the `balance` variable is set to 0. Otherwise the expression will be false.

```
If balance == 0 Then
    // Statements appearing here will
    // be executed only if balance is
    // equal to 0.
End If
```

The following pseudocode uses the != operator to determine whether two values are *not* equal. The expression choice != 5 will be true if the choice variable is not set to 5. Otherwise the expression will be false.

```
If choice != 5 Then
    // Statements appearing here will
    // be executed only if choice is
    // not equal to 5.
End If
```

Programming Style and the If-Then Statement

As shown in Figure 4-6, you should use the following conventions when you write an If-Then statement:

- Make sure the If clause and the End If clause are aligned.
- Indent the conditionally executed statements that appear between the If clause and the End If clause.

By indenting the conditionally executed statements you visually set them apart from the surrounding code. This makes your program easier to read and debug. Most programmers use this style of writing If-Then statements in both pseudocode and actual code.

Figure 4-6 Programming Style with an If-Then statement

```
                          If sales > 50000 Then
Align the If                  Set bonus = 500.0                      Indent the
and End If                    Set commissionRate = 0.12             conditionally
clauses.                      Display "You've met your sales quota!" executed
                          End If                                     statements.
```

In the Spotlight:
Using the If-Then Statement

Kathryn teaches a science class and her students are required to take three tests. She wants to write a program that her students can use to calculate their average test score. She also wants the program to congratulate the student enthusiastically if the average is greater than 95. Here is the algorithm:

1. Get the first test score.
2. Get the second test score.
3. Get the third test score.
4. Calculate the average.
5. Display the average.
6. If the average is greater than 95, congratulate the user.

Program 4-1 shows the pseudocode, and Figure 4-7 shows a flowchart for the program.

Program 4-1

```
 1 // Declare variables
 2 Declare Real test1, test2, test3, average
 3
 4 // Get test 1
 5 Display "Enter the score for test #1."
 6 Input test1
 7
 8 // Get test 2
 9 Display "Enter the score for test #2."
10 Input test2
11
12 // Get test 3
13 Display "Enter the score for test #3."
14 Input test3
15
16 // Calculate the average score.
17 Set average = (test1 + test2 + test3) / 3
18
19 // Display the average.
20 Display "The average is ", average
21
22 // If the average is greater than 95
23 // congratulate the user.
24 If average > 95 Then
25     Display "Congratulations! Great average!"
26 End If
```

Program Output (with Input Shown in Bold)

```
Enter the score for test #1.
82 [Enter]
Enter the score for test #2.
76 [Enter]
Enter the score for test #3.
91 [Enter]
The average is 83
```

Program Output (with Input Shown in Bold)

```
Enter the score for test #1.
93 [Enter]
Enter the score for test #2.
99 [Enter]
Enter the score for test #3.
96 [Enter]
The average is 96
Congratulations! Great average!
```

Figure 4-7 Flowchart for Program 4-1

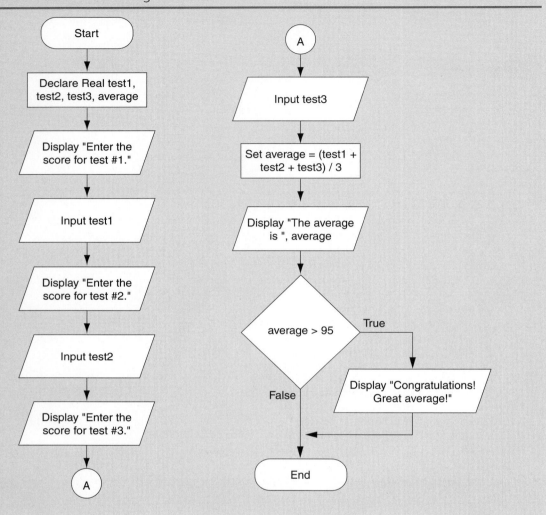

 **Checkpoint**

4.1 What is a control structure?

4.2 What is a decision structure?

4.3 What is a single alternative decision structure?

4.4 What is a Boolean expression?

4.5 What types of relationships between values can you test with relational operators?

4.6 Write a pseudocode If-Then statement that assigns 0 to x if y is equal to 20.

4.7 Write a pseudocode If-Then statement that assigns 0.2 to commission if sales is greater than or equal to 10000.

4.2 Dual Alternative Decision Structures

CONCEPT: A dual alternative decision structure will execute one group of state-ments if its Boolean expression is true, or another group if its Boolean expression is false.

VideoNote

The Dual Alternative Decision Structure

A *dual alternative decision structure* has two possible paths of execution—one path is taken if a condition is true, and the other path is taken if the condition is false. Figure 4-8 shows a flowchart for a dual alternative decision structure.

Figure 4-8 A dual alternative decision structure

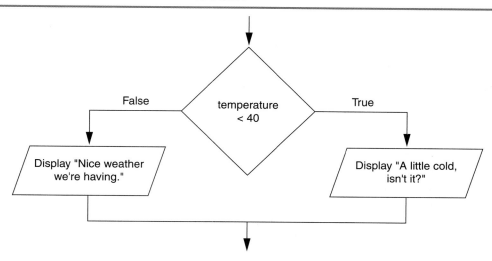

The decision structure in the flowchart tests the condition `temperature < 40`. If this condition is true, the statement `Display "A little cold, isn't it?"` is performed. If the condition is false, the statement `Display "Nice weather we're having."` is performed.

In pseudocode we write a dual alternative decision structure as an `If-Then-Else` statement. Here is the general format of the `If-Then-Else` statement:

```
If condition Then
    statement
    statement        } These statements are executed if the condition is true.
    etc.
Else
    statement
    statement        } These statements are executed if the condition is false.
    etc.
End If
```

In the general format, the *condition* is any Boolean expression. If the expression is true, the statements that appear next are executed, up to the line that reads `Else`. If the ex-pression is false, the statements that appear between `Else` and `End If` are executed. The line that reads `End If` marks the end of the `If-Then-Else` statement.

The following pseudocode shows an example of an `If-Then-Else` statement. This pseudocode matches the flowchart that was shown in Figure 4-8.

```
If temperature < 40 Then
    Display "A little cold, isn't it?"
Else
    Display "Nice weather we're having."
End If
```

We will refer to the line that reads `Else` as the *Else clause*. When you write an `If-Then-Else` statement, use the following style conventions:

- Make sure the `If` clause, the `Else` clause, and the `End If` clause are aligned.
- Indent the conditionally executed statements that appear between the `If` clause and the `Else` clause, and between the `Else` clause and the `End If` clause.

This is shown in Figure 4-9.

Figure 4-9 Programming style with an `If-Then-Else` statement

Align the If, Else, and End If clauses.
```
If temperature < 40 Then
    Display "A little cold, isn't it?"
Else
    Display "Nice weather we're having."
End If
```
Indent the conditionally executed statements.

In the Spotlight:
Using the `If-Then-Else` Statement

Chris owns an auto repair business and has several employees. If an employee works over 40 hours in a week, Chris pays that employee 1.5 times his or her regular hourly pay rate for all hours over 40. Chris has asked you to design a simple payroll program that calculates an employee's gross pay, including any overtime wages. You design the following algorithm:

1. Get the number of hours worked.
2. Get the hourly pay rate.
3. If the employee worked more than 40 hours, calculate the gross pay with overtime. Otherwise, calculate the gross pay as usual.
4. Display the gross pay.

You go through the top-down design process and create the hierarchy chart shown in Figure 4-10. As shown in the hierarchy chart, the main module will call four other modules. The following are summaries of those modules:

- `getHoursWorked`—This module will ask the user to enter the number of hours worked.
- `getPayRate`—This module will ask the user to enter the hourly pay rate.
- `calcPayWithOT`—This module will calculate an employee's pay with overtime.
- `calcRegularPay`—This module will calculate the gross pay for an employee with no overtime.

The `main` module, which executes when the program is run, will call these modules and then display the gross pay. The pseudocode for the program is shown in Program 4-2. Figures 4-11 and show flowcharts for each of the modules.

Figure 4-10 Hierarchy chart

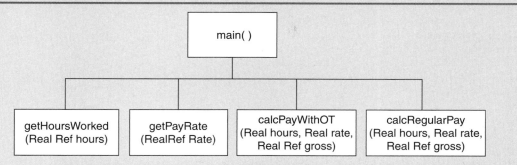

Program 4-2

```
 1 // Global constants
 2 Constant Integer BASE_HOURS = 40
 3 Constant Real OT_MULTIPLIER = 1.5
 4
 5 Module main()
 6    // Local variables
 7    Declare Real hoursWorked, payRate, grossPay
 8
 9    // Get the number of hours worked.
10    Call getHoursWorked(hoursWorked)
11
12    // Get the hourly pay rate.
13    Call getPayRate(payRate)
14
15    // Calculate the gross pay.
16    If hoursWorked > BASE_HOURS Then
17       Call calcPayWithOT(hoursWorked, payRate,
18                     grossPay)
19    Else
20       Call calcRegularPay(hoursWorked, payRate,
21                     grossPay)
22    End If
23
24    // Display the gross pay.
25    Display "The gross pay is $", grossPay
26 End Module
27
28 // The getHoursWorked module gets the number
29 // of hours worked and stores it in the
```

```
30 // hours parameter.
31 Module getHoursWorked(Real Ref hours)
32     Display "Enter the number of hours worked."
33     Input hours
34 End Module
35
36 // The getPayRate module gets the hourly
37 // pay rate and stores it in the rate
38 // parameter.
39 Module getPayRate(Real Ref rate)
40     Display "Enter the hourly pay rate."
41     Input rate
42 End Module
43
44 // The calcPayWithOT module calculates pay
45 // with overtime. The gross pay is stored
46 // in the gross parameter.
47 Module calcPayWithOT(Real hours, Real rate,
48                      Real Ref gross)
49     // Local variables
50     Declare Real overtimeHours, overtimePay
51
52     // Calculate the number of overtime hours.
53     Set overtimeHours = hours - BASE_HOURS
54
55     // Calculate the overtime pay
56     Set overtimePay = overtimeHours * rate *
57                       OT_MULTIPLIER
58
59     // Calculate the gross pay.
60     Set gross = BASE_HOURS * rate + overtimePay
61 End Module
62
63 // The calcRegularPay module calculates
64 // pay with no overtime and stores it in
65 // the gross parameter.
66 Module calcRegularPay(Real hours, Real rate,
67                       Real Ref gross)
68     Set gross = hours * rate
69 End Module
```

Program Output (with Input Shown in Bold)

Enter the number of hours worked.
40 [Enter]
Enter the hourly pay rate.
20 [Enter]
The gross pay is $800

Program Output (with Input Shown in Bold)

Enter the number of hours worked.
50 [Enter]
Enter the hourly pay rate.
20 [Enter]
The gross pay is $1100

Notice that two global constants are declared in lines 2 and 3. The BASE_HOURS constant is set to 40, which is the number of hours an employee can work in a week without getting paid overtime. The OT_MULTIPLIER constant is set to 1.5, which is the pay rate multiplier for overtime hours. This means that the employee's hourly pay rate is multiplied by 1.5 for all overtime hours.

Figure 4-11 Flowchart for the main module

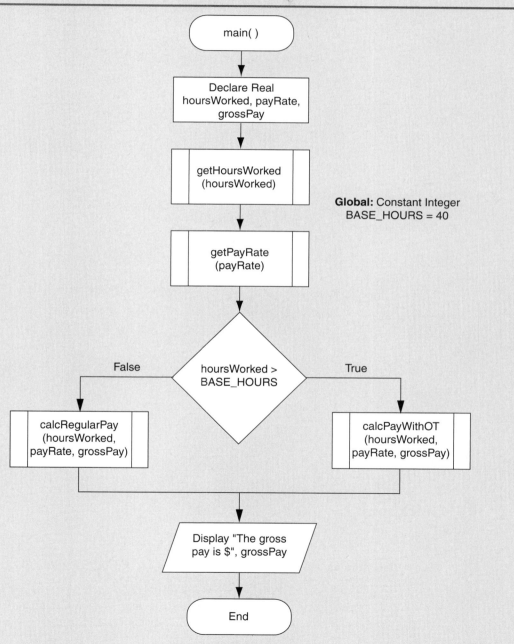

Figure 4-12 Flowcharts for the other modules

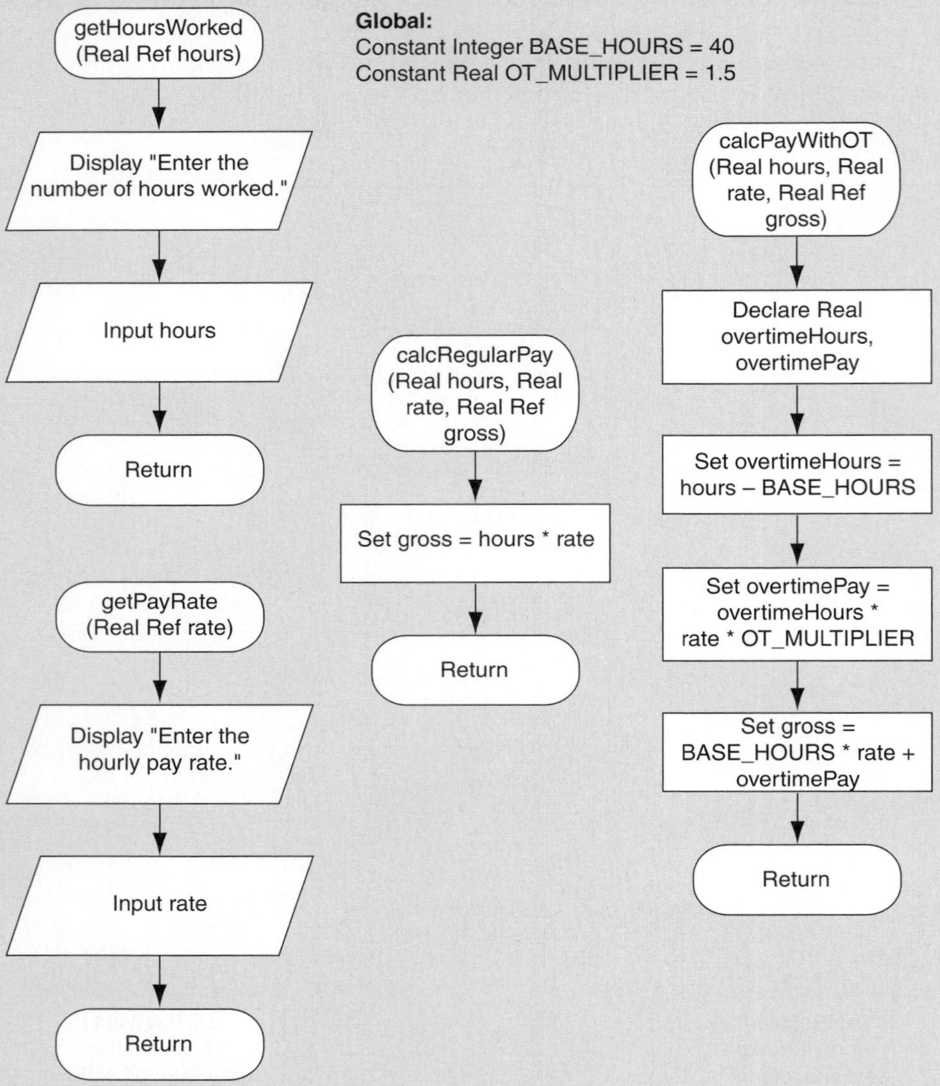
getHoursWorked (Real Ref hours)
Display "Enter the number of hours worked."
Input hours
Return
getPayRate (Real Ref rate)
Display "Enter the hourly pay rate."
Input rate
Return
Global:
Constant Integer BASE_HOURS = 40
Constant Real OT_MULTIPLIER = 1.5
calcRegularPay (Real hours, Real rate, Real Ref gross)
Set gross = hours * rate
Return
calcPayWithOT (Real hours, Real rate, Real Ref gross)
Declare Real overtimeHours, overtimePay
Set overtimeHours = hours – BASE_HOURS
Set overtimePay = overtimeHours * rate * OT_MULTIPLIER
Set gross = BASE_HOURS * rate + overtimePay
Return

Checkpoint

4.8 How does a dual alternative decision structure work?

4.9 What statement do you use in pseudocode to write a dual alternative decision structure?

4.10 When you write an `If-Then-Else` statement, under what circumstances do the statements that appear between `Else` and `End If` execute?

4.3 Comparing Strings

> **CONCEPT:** Most programming languages allow you to compare strings. This allows you to create decision structures that test the value of a string.

You saw in the preceding examples how numbers can be compared. Most programming languages also allow you to compare strings. For example, look at the following pseudocode:

```
Declare String name1 = "Mary"
Declare String name2 = "Mark"
If name1 == name2 Then
    Display "The names are the same"
Else
    Display "The names are NOT the same"
End If
```

The == operator tests name1 and name2 to determine whether they are equal. Since the strings "Mary" and "Mark" are not equal, the Else clause will display the message "The names are NOT the same."

You can compare String variables with string literals as well. Assume month is a String variable. The following pseudocode sample uses the != operator to determine whether month is not equal to "October."

```
If month != "October" Then
    statement
End If
```

The pseudocode in Program 4-3 demonstrates how two strings can be compared. The program prompts the user to enter a password and then determines whether the string entered is equal to "prospero."

Program 4-3

```
 1 // A variable to hold a password.
 2 Declare String password
 3
 4 // Prompt the user to enter the password.
 5 Display "Enter the password."
 6 Input password
 7
 8 // Determine whether the correct password
 9 // was entered.
10 If password == "prospero" Then
11    Display "Password accepted."
12 Else
13    Display "Sorry, that is not the correct password."
14 End If
```

Program Output (with Input Shown in Bold)

```
Enter the password.
ferdinand [Enter]
Sorry, that is not the correct password.
```

Program Output (with Input Shown in Bold)

```
Enter the password.
prospero [Enter]
Password accepted.
```

NOTE: In most languages, string comparisons are case sensitive. For example, the strings `"saturday"` and `"Saturday"` are not equal because the "s" is lowercase in the first string, but uppercase in the second string.

Other String Comparisons

In addition to determining whether strings are equal or not equal, many languages allow you to determine whether one string is greater than or less than another string. This is a useful capability because programmers commonly need to design programs that sort strings in some order.

Recall from Chapter 1 that computers do not actually store characters, such as A, B, C, and so on, in memory. Instead, they store numeric codes that represent the characters. We mentioned in Chapter 1 that ASCII (the American Standard Code for Information Interchange) is the most commonly used character coding system. You can see the set of ASCII codes in Appendix A on the student CD, but here are some facts about it:

- The uppercase characters "A" through "Z" are represented by the numbers 65 through 90.
- The lowercase characters "a" through "z" are represented by the numbers 97 through 122.
- When the digits "0" through "9" are stored in memory as characters, they are represented by the numbers 48 through 57. (For example, the string `"abc123"` would be stored in memory as the codes 97, 98, 99, 49, 50, and 51.)
- A blank space is represented by the number 32.

In addition to establishing a set of numeric codes to represent characters in memory, ASCII also establishes an order for characters. The character "A" comes before the character "B," which comes before the character "C," and so on.

When a program compares characters, it actually compares the codes for the characters. For example, look at the following pseudocode:

```
If "a" < "b" Then
    Display "The letter a is less than the letter b."
End If
```

This `If` statement determines whether the ASCII code for the character "a" is less than the ASCII code for the character "b." The expression `"a" < "b"` is true because the code for "a" is less than the code for "b." So, if this were part of an actual program it would display the message "The letter a is less than the letter b."

Let's look at how strings containing more than one character are typically compared. Suppose we have the strings `"Mary"` and `"Mark"` stored in memory, as follows:

```
Declare String name1 = "Mary"
Declare String name2 = "Mark"
```

Figure 4-13 shows how the strings `"Mary"` and `"Mark"` would actually be stored in memory, using ASCII codes.

Figure 4-13 Character codes for the strings "Mary" and "Mark"

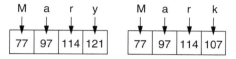

When you use relational operators to compare these strings, they are compared character-by-character. For example, look at the following pseudocode:

```
Declare String name1 = "Mary"
Declare String name2 = "Mark"
If name1 > name2 Then
    Display "Mary is greater than Mark"
Else
    Display "Mary is not greater than Mark"
End If
```

The > operator compares each character in the strings `"Mary"` and `"Mark,"` beginning with the first, or leftmost, characters. This is shown in Figure 4-14.

Figure 4-14 Comparing each character in a string

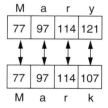

Here is how the comparison typically takes place:

1. The "M" in "Mary" is compared with the "M" in "Mark." Since these are the same, the next characters are compared.
2. The "a" in "Mary" is compared with the "a" in "Mark." Since these are the same, the next characters are compared.

3. The "r" in "Mary" is compared with the "r" in "Mark." Since these are the same, the next characters are compared.

4. The "y" in "Mary" is compared with the "k" in "Mark." Since these are not the same, the two strings are not equal. The character "y" has a higher ASCII code (121) than "k" (107), so it is determined that the string "Mary" is greater than the string "Mark."

If one of the strings in a comparison is shorter than the other, many languages compare only the corresponding characters. If the corresponding characters are identical, then the shorter string is considered less than the longer string. For example, suppose the strings "High" and "Hi" were being compared. The string "Hi" would be considered less than "High" because it is shorter.

The pseudocode in Program 4-4 shows a simple demonstration of how two strings can be compared with the < operator. The user is prompted to enter two names and the program displays those two names in alphabetical order.

Program 4-4

```
 1 // Declare variables to hold two names.
 2 Declare String name1
 3 Declare String name2
 4
 5 // Prompt the user for two names.
 6 Display "Enter a name (last name first)."
 7 Input name1
 8 Display "Enter another name (last name first)."
 9 Input name2
10
11 // Display the names in alphabetical order.
12 Display "Here are the names, listed alphabetically:"
13 If name1 < name2 Then
14     Display name1
15     Display name2
16 Else
17     Display name2
18     Display name1
19 End If
```

Program Output

```
Enter a name (last name first).
Jones, Richard [Enter]
Enter another name (last name first).
Costa, Joan [Enter]
Here are the names, listed alphabetically:
Costa, Joan
Jones, Richard
```

Checkpoint

4.11 If the following pseudocode were an actual program, what would it display?

```
If "z" < "a" Then
    Display "z is less than a."
Else
    Display "z is not less than a."
End If
```

4.12 If the following pseudocode were an actual program, what would it display?

```
Declare String s1 = "New York"
Declare String s2 = "Boston"
If s1 > s2 Then
    Display s2
    Display s1
Else
    Display s1
    Display s2
End If
```

4.4 Nested Decision Structures

> **CONCEPT:** To test more than one condition, a decision structure can be nested inside another decision structure.

In Section 4.1, we mentioned that programs are usually designed as combinations of different control structures. In that section you saw an example of a sequence structure nested inside a decision structure (see Figure 4-3). You can also nest decision structures inside of other decision structures. In fact, this is a common requirement in programs that need to test more than one condition.

For example, consider a program that determines whether a bank customer qualifies for a loan. To qualify, two conditions must exist: (1) the customer must earn at least $30,000 per year, and (2) the customer must have been employed at his or her current job for at least two years. Figure 4-15 shows a flowchart for an algorithm that could be used in such a program. Assume that the salary variable contains the customer's annual salary, and the yearsOnJob variable contains the number of years that the customer has worked on his or her current job.

If we follow the flow of execution, we see that the condition salary >= 30000 is tested. If this condition is false, there is no need to perform further tests; we know that the customer does not qualify for the loan. If the condition is true, however, we need to test the second condition. This is done with a nested decision structure that tests the condition yearsOnJob >= 2. If this condition is true, then the customer qualifies for the loan. If this condition is false, then the customer does not qualify. Program 4-5 shows the pseudocode for the complete program.

Figure 4-15 A nested decision structure

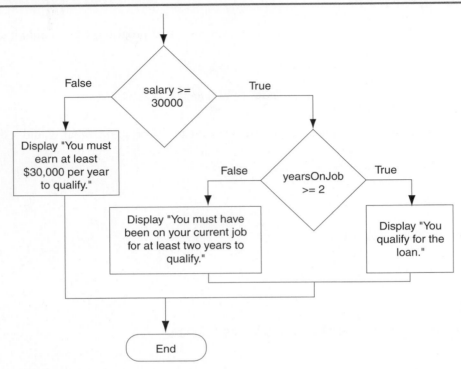

Program 4-5

```
 1 // Declare variables
 2 Declare Real salary, yearsOnJob
 3
 4 // Get the annual salary.
 5 Display "Enter your annual salary."
 6 Input salary
 7
 8 // Get the number of years on the current job.
 9 Display "Enter the number of years on your"
10 Display "current job."
11 Input yearsOnJob
12
13 // Determine whether the user qualifies.
14 If salary >= 30000 Then
15    If yearsOnJob >= 2 Then
16       Display "You qualify for the loan."
17    Else
18       Display "You must have been on your current"
19       Display "job for at least two years to qualify."
20    End If
21 Else
22    Display "You must earn at least $30,000"
23    Display "per year to qualify."
24 End If
```

Program Output (with Input Shown in Bold)

```
Enter your annual salary.
35000 [Enter]
Enter the number of years on your
current job.
1 [Enter]
You must have been on your current
job for at least two years to qualify.
```

Program Output (with Input Shown in Bold)

```
Enter your annual salary.
25000 [Enter]
Enter the number of years on your
current job.
5 [Enter]
You must earn at least $30,000
per year to qualify.
```

Program Output (with Input Shown in Bold)

```
Enter your annual salary.
35000 [Enter]
Enter the number of years on your
current job.
5 [Enter]
You qualify for the loan.
```

Look at the If-Then-Else statement that begins in line 14. It tests the condition salary >= 30000. If this condition is true, the If-Then-Else statement that begins in line 15 is executed. Otherwise the program jumps to the Else clause in line 21 and executes the two Display statements in lines 22 and 23. The program then leaves the decision structure and the program ends.

Programming Style and Nested Decision Structures

For debugging purposes, it's important to use proper alignment and indentation in a nested decision structure. This makes it easier to see which actions are performed by each part of the structure. For example, in most languages the following pseudocode is functionally equivalent to lines 14 through 24 in Program 4-5. Although this pseudocode is logically correct, it would be very difficult to debug because it is not properly indented.

```
If salary >= 30000 Then
If yearsOnJob >= 2 Then                          Don't write
Display "You qualify for the loan."             pseudocode
Else                                             like this!
Display "You must have been on your current"
Display "job for at least two years to qualify."
End If
```

```
Else
Display "You must earn at least $30,000"
Display "per year to qualify.
End If
```

Proper indentation and alignment also makes it easier to see which If, Else, and End If clauses belong together, as shown in Figure 4-16.

Figure 4-16 Alignment of If, Else, and End If clauses

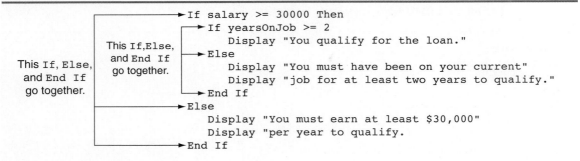

Testing a Series of Conditions

In the previous example you saw how a program can use nested decision structures to test more than one condition. It is not uncommon for a program to have a series of conditions to test, and then perform an action depending on which condition is true. One way to accomplish this is to have a decision structure with numerous other decision structures nested inside it. For example, consider the program presented in the following *In the Spotlight* section.

In the Spotlight:
Multiple Nested Decision Structures

Dr. Suarez teaches a literature class and uses the following 10 point grading scale for all of his exams:

Test Score	Grade
90 and above	A
80–89	B
70–79	C
60–69	D
Below 60	F

He has asked you to write a program that will allow a student to enter a test score and then display the grade for that score. Here is the algorithm that you will use:

1. Ask the user to enter a test score.
2. Determine the grade in the following manner:

If the score is less than 60, then the grade is "F."
Otherwise, if the score is less than 70, then the grade is "D."
Otherwise, if the score is less than 80, then the grade is "C."
Otherwise, if the score is less than 90, then the grade is "B."
Otherwise, the grade is "A."

You decide that the process of determining the grade will require several nested decisions structures, as shown in Figure 4-17. Program 4-6 shows the pseudocode for the complete program. The code for the nested decision structures is in lines 9 through 25.

Figure 4-17 Nested decision structure to determine a grade

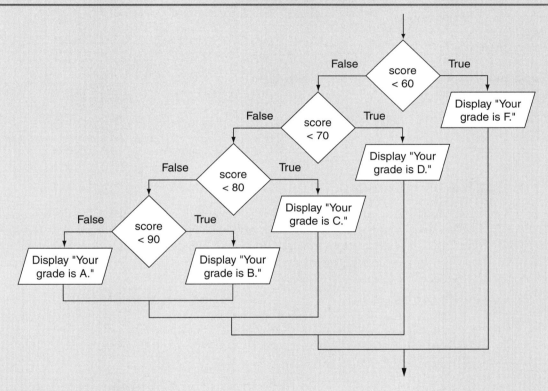

Program 4-6

```
 1 // Variable to hold the test score
 2 Declare Real score
 3
 4 // Get the test score.
 5 Display "Enter your test score."
 6 Input score
 7
 8 // Determine the grade.
 9 If score < 60 Then
10     Display "Your grade is F."
11 Else
12     If score < 70 Then
13         Display "Your grade is D."
14     Else
15         If score < 80 Then
```

```
16          Display "Your grade is C."
17      Else
18          If score < 90 Then
19              Display "Your grade is B."
20          Else
21              Display "Your grade is A."
22          End If
23      End If
24    End If
25 End If
```

Program Output (with Input Shown in Bold)

Enter your test score.
78 [Enter]
Your grade is C.

Program Output (with Input Shown in Bold)

Enter your test score.
84 [Enter]
Your grade is B.

The If-Then-Else If Statement

Even though Program 4-6 is a simple example, the logic of the nested decision structure is fairly complex. Most languages provide a special version of the decision structure known as the If-Then-Else If statement, which makes this type of logic simpler to write. In pseudocode we will write the If-Then-Else If statement using the following general format:

```
If condition_1 Then
    statement
    statement
    etc.
```
If *condition_1* is true these statements are executed, and the rest of the structure is ignored.
```
Else If condition_2 Then
    statement
    statement
    etc.
```
If *condition_2* is true these statements are executed, and the rest of the structure is ignored.

Insert as many Else If *clauses as necessary*

```
Else
    statement
    statement
    etc.
End If
```
These statements are executed if none of the conditions above are true.

When the statement executes, *condition_1* is tested. If *condition_1* is true, the statements that immediately follow are executed, up to the Else If clause. The rest of the structure is ignored. If *condition_1* is false, however, the program jumps to the very next Else If clause and tests *condition_2*. If it is true, the statements that immediately follow are executed, up to the next Else If clause. The rest of the structure is then ignored. This process continues until a condition is found to be true, or no more Else

If clauses are left. If none of the conditions are true, the statements following the Else clause are executed.

The pseudocode in Program 4-7 shows an example of the If-Then-Else If statement. This program works the same as Program 4-6. Instead of using a nested decision structure, this program uses the If-Then-Else If statement in lines 9 through 19.

Program 4-7

```
 1 // Variable to hold the test score
 2 Declare Real score
 3
 4 // Get the test score.
 5 Display "Enter your test score."
 6 Input score
 7
 8 // Determine the grade.
 9 If score < 60 Then
10     Display "Your grade is F."
11 Else If score < 70 Then
12     Display "Your grade is D."
13 Else If score < 80 Then
14     Display "Your grade is C."
15 Else If score < 90 Then
16     Display "Your grade is B."
17 Else
18     Display "Your grade is A."
19 End If
```

Program Output (with Input Shown in Bold)

```
Enter your test score.
78 [Enter]
Your grade is C.
```

Program Output (with Input Shown in Bold)

```
Enter your test score.
84 [Enter]
Your grade is B.
```

Notice the alignment and indentation that is used with the If-Then-Else If statement: The If, Else If, Else, and End If clauses are all aligned, and the conditionally executed statements are indented.

You never have to use the If-Then-Else If statement because its logic can be coded with nested If-Then-Else statements. However, a long series of nested If-Then-Else statements has two particular disadvantages when you are debugging code:

- The code can grow complex and become difficult to understand.
- Because indenting is important in nested statements, a long series of nested If-Then-Else statements can become too long to be displayed on the computer screen without horizontal scrolling. Also, long statements tend to "wrap around" when printed on paper, making the code even more difficult to read.

The logic of an `If-Then-Else If` statement is usually easier to follow than a long series of nested `If-Then-Else` statements. And, because all of the clauses are aligned in an `If-Then-Else If` statement, the lengths of the lines in the statement tend to be shorter.

 Checkpoint

4.13   How does a dual alternative decision structure work?

4.14   What statement do you use in pseudocode to write a dual alternative decision structure?

4.15   When you write an `If-Then-Else` statement, under what circumstances do the statements that appear between the `Else` clause and the `End If` clause execute?

4.16   Convert the following pseudocode to an `If-Then-Else If` statement:

```
If number == 1 Then
    Display "One"
Else
    If number == 2 Then
        Display "Two"
    Else
        If number == 3 Then
            Display "Three"
        Else
            Display "Unknown"
        End If
    End If
End If
```

4.5 The Case Structure

CONCEPT: The case structure lets the value of a variable or an expression determine which path of execution the program will take.

VideoNote
The Case Structure

The *case structure* is a *multiple alternative decision structure*. It allows you to test the value of a variable or an expression and then use that value to determine which statement or set of statements to execute. Figure 4-18 shows an example of how a case structure looks in a flowchart.

In the flowchart, the diamond symbol contains the name of a variable. If the variable contains the value 1, the statement `Display "January"` is executed. If the variable contains the value 2 the statement `Display "February"` is executed. If the variable contains the value 3 the statement `Display "March"` is executed. If the variable contains none of these values, the statement labeled `Default` is executed. In this case, the statement `Display "Error: Invalid month"` is executed.

To write a case structure in pseudocode we will use a `Select Case` statement. The general format follows Figure 4-18.

Figure 4-18 A case structure

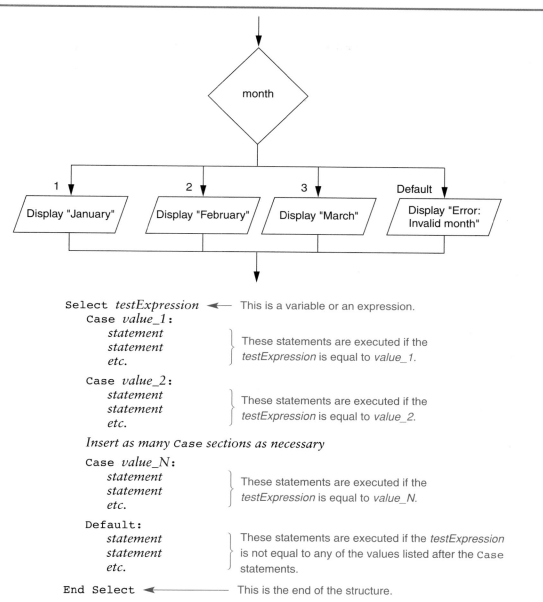

The first line of the structure starts with the word Select, followed by a *testExpression*. The *testExpression* is usually a variable, but in many languages it can also be anything that gives a value (such as a math expression). Inside the structure there is one or more blocks of statements that begin with a Case statement. Notice that the word Case is followed by a value.

When the Select Case statement executes, it compares the value of the *testExpression* with the values that follow each of the Case statements (from top to bottom). When it finds a Case value that matches the *testExpression*'s value, the program branches to the Case statement. The statements that immediately follow the Case statement are executed, and then the program jumps out of the structure. If the *testExpression* does not match any of the Case values, the program branches to the Default statement and executes the statements that immediately follow it.

For example, the following pseudocode performs the same operation as the flowchart shown in Figure 4-18:

```
Select month
   Case 1:
       Display "January"
   Case 2:
       Display "February"
   Case 3:
       Display "March"
   Default:
       Display "Error: Invalid month"
End Select
```

In this example, the *testExpression* is the month variable. If the value in the month variable is 1, the program will branch to the Case 1: section and execute the Display "January" statement that immediately follows it. If the value in the month variable is 2, the program will branch to the Case 2: section and execute the Display "February" statement that immediately follows it. If the value in the month variable is 3, the program will branch to the Case 3: section and execute the Display "March" statement that immediately follows it. If the value in the month variable is not 1, 2, or 3, the program will branch to the Default: section and if the value in the month variable is 1, the program will branch to the Case 1: section and execute the Display "Error: Invalid month" statement that immediately follows it.

 NOTE: In many languages the case structure is called a switch statement.

Case structures are never required because the same logic can be achieved with nested decision structures. For example, Figure 4-19 shows nested decision structures that are equivalent to the case structure in Figure 4-18. In situations where they can be used, however, case structures are more straightforward.

Figure 4-19 Nested decision structures

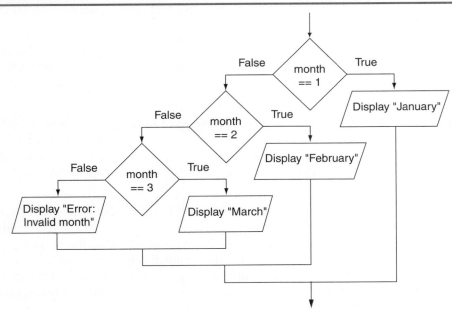

In the Spotlight:
Using a Case Structure

Lenny, who owns Lenny's Stereo and Television, has asked you to write a program that will let a customer pick one of three TV models and then displays the price and size of the selected model. Here is the algorithm:

1. Get the TV model number.
2. If the model is 100, then display the information for that model.
   Otherwise, if the model is 200, then display the information for that model.
   Otherwise, if the model is 300, then display the information for that model.

At first, you consider designing a nested decision structure to determine the model number and display the correct information. But you realize that a case structure will work just as well because a single value, the model number, will be used to determine the action that the program will perform. The model number can be stored in a variable, and that variable can be tested by the case structure. Assuming that the model number is stored in a variable named modelNumber, Figure 4-20 shows a flowchart for the case structure. Program 4-8 shows the pseudocode for the program.

Figure 4-20 Flowchart for the case structure

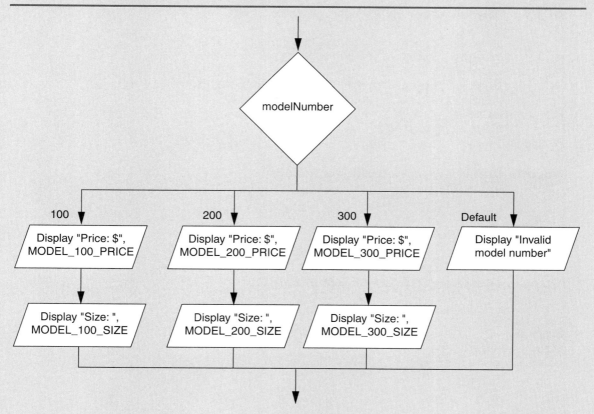

Program 4-8

```
 1 // Constants for the TV prices
 2 Constant Real MODEL_100_PRICE = 199.99
 3 Constant Real MODEL_200_PRICE = 269.99
 4 Constant Real MODEL_300_PRICE = 349.99
 5
 6 // Constants for the TV sizes
 7 Constant Integer MODEL_100_SIZE = 24
 8 Constant Integer MODEL_200_SIZE = 27
 9 Constant Integer MODEL_300_SIZE = 32
10
11 // Variable for the model number
12 Declare Integer modelNumber
13
14 // Get the model number.
15 Display "Which TV are you interested in?"
16 Display "The 100, 200, or 300?"
17 Input modelNumber
18
19 // Display the price and size.
20 Select modelNumber
21    Case 100:
22        Display "Price: $", MODEL_100_PRICE
23        Display "Size: ", MODEL_100_SIZE
24    Case 200:
25        Display "Price: $", MODEL_200_PRICE
26        Display "Size: ", MODEL_200_SIZE
27    Case 300:
28        Display "Price $", MODEL_300_PRICE
29        Display "Size: ", MODEL_300_SIZE
30    Default:
31        Display "Invalid model number"
32 End Select
```

Program Output (with Input Shown in Bold)

```
Which TV are you interested in?
The 100, 200, or 300?
100 [Enter]
Price: $199.99
Size: 24
```

Program Output (with Input Shown in Bold)

```
Which TV are you interested in?
The 100, 200, or 300?
200 [Enter]
Price: $269.99
Size: 27
```

Program Output (with Input Shown in Bold)

```
Which TV are you interested in?
The 100, 200, or 300?
300 [Enter]
Price: $349.99
Size: 32
```

Program Output (with Input Shown in Bold)

```
Which TV are you interested in?
The 100, 200, or 300?
500 [Enter]
Invalid model number
```

NOTE: The details of writing a case structure differ from one language to another. Because of the specific rules that each language uses for writing case structures, you might not be able to use the case structure for every multiple alternative decision. In such an event, you can use the If-Then-Else If statement or a nested decision structure.

 **Checkpoint**

4.17 What is a multiple alternative decision structure?

4.18 How do you write a multiple alternative decision structure in pseudocode?

4.19 What does the case structure test, in order to determine which set of statements to execute?

4.20 You need to write a multiple alternative decision structure, but the language you are using will not allow you to perform the test you need in a Select Case statement. What can you do to achieve the same results?

4.6 Logical Operators

CONCEPT: The logical **AND** operator and the logical **OR** operator allow you to connect multiple Boolean expressions to create a compound expression. The logical **NOT** operator reverses the truth of a Boolean expression.

Programming languages provide a set of operators known as *logical operators*, which you can use to create complex Boolean expressions. Table 4-3 describes these operators.

Table 4-4 shows examples of several compound Boolean expressions that use logical operators.

Table 4-3 Logical operators

Operator	Meaning
AND	The AND operator connects two Boolean expressions into one compound expression. Both subexpressions must be true for the compound expression to be true.
OR	The OR operator connects two Boolean expressions into one compound expression. One or both subexpressions must be true for the compound expression to be true. It is only necessary for one of the subexpressions to be true, and it does not matter which.
NOT	The NOT operator is a unary operator, meaning it works with only one operand. The operand must be a Boolean expression. The NOT operator reverses the truth of its operand. If it is applied to an expression that is true, the operator returns false. If it is applied to an expression that is false, the operator returns true.

Table 4-4 Compound Boolean expressions using logical operators

Expression	Meaning
x > y AND a < b	Is x greater than y AND is a less than b?
x == y OR x == z	Is x equal to y OR is x equal to z?
NOT (x > y)	Is the expression x > y NOT true?

NOTE: In many languages, most notably C, C++, and Java, the AND operator is written as &&, the OR operator is written as ||, and the NOT operator is written as !.

The AND Operator

The AND operator takes two Boolean expressions as operands and creates a compound Boolean expression that is true only when both subexpressions are true. The following is an example of an If-Then statement that uses the AND operator:

```
If temperature < 20 AND minutes > 12 Then
    Display "The temperature is in the danger zone."
End If
```

In this statement, the two Boolean expressions temperature < 20 and minutes > 12 are combined into a compound expression. The Display statement will be executed only if temperature is less than 20 AND minutes is greater than 12. If either of the Boolean subexpressions is false, the compound expression is false and the message is not displayed.

Table 4-5 shows a truth table for the AND operator. The truth table lists expressions showing all the possible combinations of true and false connected with the AND operator. The resulting values of the expressions are also shown.

Table 4-5 Truth table for the AND operator

Expression	Value of the Expression
true AND false	false
false AND true	false
false AND false	false
true AND true	true

As the table shows, both sides of the AND operator must be true for the operator to return a true value.

The OR Operator

The OR operator takes two Boolean expressions as operands and creates a compound Boolean expression that is true when either of the subexpressions is true. The following is an example of an If-Then statement that uses the OR operator:

```
If temperature < 20 OR temperature > 100 Then
    Display "The temperature is in the danger zone."
End If
```

The Display statement will execute only if temperature is less than 20 OR temperature is greater than 100. If either subexpression is true, the compound expression is true. Table 4-6 shows a truth table for the OR operator.

Table 4-6 Truth table for the OR operator

Expression	Value of the Expression
true OR false	true
false OR true	true
false OR false	false
true OR true	true

All it takes for an OR expression to be true is for one side of the OR operator to be true. It doesn't matter if the other side is false or true.

Short-Circuit Evaluation

In many languages both the AND and OR operators perform *short-circuit evaluation*. Here's how it works with the AND operator: If the expression on the left side of the AND operator is false, the expression on the right side will not be checked. Because the compound expression will be false if only one of the subexpressions is false, it would waste CPU time to check the remaining expression. So, when the AND operator finds that the expression on its left is false, it short-circuits and does not evaluate the expression on its right.

Here's how short-circuit evaluation works with the OR operator: If the expression on the left side of the OR operator is true, the expression on the right side will not be checked. Because it is only necessary for one of the expressions to be true, it would waste CPU time to check the remaining expression.

The NOT Operator

The NOT operator is a unary operator that takes a Boolean expression as its operand and reverses its logical value. In other words, if the expression is true, the NOT operator returns false, and if the expression is false, the NOT operator returns true. The following is an If-Then statement using the NOT operator:

```
If NOT(temperature > 100) Then
    Display "This is below the maximum temperature."
End If
```

First, the expression (temperature > 100) is tested and a value of either true or false is the result. Then the NOT operator is applied to that value. If the expression (temperature > 100) is true, the NOT operator returns false. If the expression (temperature > 100) is false, the NOT operator returns true. The previous code is equivalent to asking: "Is the temperature not greater than 100?"

> **NOTE:** In this example, we have put parentheses around the expression temperature > 100. The reason for this is that, in many languages, the NOT operator has higher precedence than the relational operators. Suppose we wrote the expression as follows:
>
> ```
> NOT temperature > 100
> ```
>
> In many languages this expression would not work correctly because the NOT operator would be applied to the temperature variable, not the expression temperature > 100. To make sure that the operator is applied to the expression, we enclose it in parentheses.

Table 4-7 shows a truth table for the NOT operator.

Table 4-7 Truth table for the NOT operator

Expression	Value of the Expression
NOT true	false
NOT false	true

The Loan Qualifier Program Revisited

In some situations the AND operator can be used to simplify nested decision structures. For example, recall that the loan qualifier program in Program 4-5 uses the following nested If-Then-Else statements:

```
If salary >= 30000 Then
    If yearsOnJob >= 2 Then
        Display "You qualify for the loan."
    Else
        Display "You must have been on your current"
        Display "job for at least two years to qualify."
    End If
Else
    Display "You must earn at least $30,000"
    Display "per year to qualify."
End If
```

The purpose of this decision structure is to determine that a person's salary is at least $30,000 and that he or she has been at their current job for at least two years. Program 4-9 shows a way to perform a similar task with simpler code.

Program 4-9

```
 1 // Declare variables
 2 Declare Real salary, yearsOnJob
 3
 4 // Get the annual salary.
 5 Display "Enter your annual salary."
 6 Input salary
 7
 8 // Get the number of years on the current job.
 9 Display "Enter the number of years on your ",
10         "current job."
11 Input yearsOnJob
12
13 // Determine whether the user qualifies.
14 If salary >= 30000 AND yearsOnJob >= 2 Then
15     Display "You qualify for the loan."
16 Else
17     Display "You do not qualify for this loan."
18 End If
```

Program Output (with Input Shown in Bold)

Enter your annual salary.
35000 [Enter]
Enter the number of years on your current job.
1 [Enter]
You do not qualify for this loan.

Program Output (with Input Shown in Bold)

Enter your annual salary.
25000 [Enter]
Enter the number of years on your current job.
5 [Enter]
You do not qualify for this loan.

Program Output (with Input Shown in Bold)

Enter your annual salary.
35000 [Enter]
Enter the number of years on your current job.
5 [Enter]
You qualify for the loan.

The If-Then-Else statement in lines 14 through 18 tests the compound expression salary >= 30000 AND yearsOnJob >= 2. If both subexpressions are true, the compound expression is true and the message "You qualify for the loan" is displayed. If either of the subexpressions is false, the compound expression is false and the message "You do not qualify for this loan" is displayed.

> **NOTE:** A careful observer will realize that Program 4-9 is similar to Program 4-5, but it is not equivalent. If the user does not qualify for the loan, Program 4-9 displays only the message "You do not qualify for this loan" whereas Program 4-5 displays one of two possible messages explaining why the user did not qualify.

Yet Another Loan Qualifier Program

Suppose the bank is losing customers to a competing bank that isn't as strict about whom it loans money to. In response, the bank decides to change its loan requirements. Now, customers have to meet only one of the previous conditions, not both. Program 4-10 shows the pseudocode for the new loan qualifier program. The compound expression that is tested by the If-Then-Else statement in line 14 now uses the OR operator.

Program 4-10

```
 1 // Declare variables
 2 Declare Real salary, yearsOnJob
 3
 4 // Get the annual salary.
 5 Display "Enter your annual salary."
 6 Input salary
 7
 8 // Get the number of years on the current job.
 9 Display "Enter the number of years on your"
10 Display "current job."
11 Input yearsOnJob
12
13 // Determine whether the user qualifies.
14 If salary >= 30000 OR yearsOnJob >= 2 Then
15     Display "You qualify for the loan."
16 Else
17     Display "You do not qualify for this loan."
18 End If
```

Program Output (with Input Shown in Bold)

```
Enter your annual salary.
35000 [Enter]
Enter the number of years on your current job.
1 [Enter]
You qualify for the loan.
```

Program Output (with Input Shown in Bold)

```
Enter your annual salary.
25000 [Enter]
Enter the number of years on your current job.
5 [Enter]
You qualify for the loan.
```

Program Output (with Input Shown in Bold)

```
Enter your annual salary.
12000 [Enter]
Enter the number of years on your current job.
1 [Enter]
You do not qualify for this loan.
```

Checking Numeric Ranges with Logical Operators

Sometimes you will need to design an algorithm that determines whether a numeric value is within a specific range of values or outside a specific range of values. When determining whether a number is inside a range, it is best to use the AND operator. For example, the following If-Then statement checks the value in x to determine whether it is in the range of 20 through 40:

```
If x >= 20 AND x <= 40 Then
    Display "The value is in the acceptable range."
End If
```

The compound Boolean expression being tested by this statement will be true only when x is greater than or equal to 20 AND less than or equal to 40. The value in x must be within the range of 20 through 40 for this compound expression to be true.

When determining whether a number is outside a range, it is best to use the OR operator. The following statement determines whether x is outside the range of 20 through 40:

```
If x < 20 OR x > 40 Then
    Display "The value is outside the acceptable range."
End If
```

It is important not to get the logic of the logical operators confused when testing for a range of numbers. For example, the compound Boolean expression in the following pseudocode would never test true:

```
// This is an error!
If x < 20 AND x > 40 Then
    Display "The value is outside the acceptable range."
End If
```

Obviously, x cannot be less than 20 and at the same time be greater than 40.

 **Checkpoint**

4.21 What is a compound Boolean expression?

4.22 The following truth table shows various combinations of the values true and false connected by a logical operator. Complete the table by circling T or F to indicate whether the result of such a combination is true or false.

Logical Expression	Result (circle T or F)	
True AND False	T	F
True AND True	T	F

(continues next page)

Logical Expression	Result (circle T or F)	
False AND True	T	F
False AND False	T	F
True OR False	T	F
True OR True	T	F
False OR True	T	F
False OR False	T	F
NOT True	T	F
NOT False	T	F

4.23 Assume the variables a = 2, b = 4, and c = 6. Circle the T or F for each of the following conditions to indicate whether its value is true or false.

a == 4 OR b > 2	T	F
6 <= c AND a > 3	T	F
1 != b AND c != 3	T	F
a >= -1 OR a <= b	T	F
NOT (a > 2)	T	F

4.24 Explain how short-circuit evaluation works with the AND and OR operators.

4.25 Write an If-Then statement that displays the message "The number is valid" if the variable speed is within the range 0 through 200.

4.26 Write an If-Then statement that displays the message "The number is not valid" if the variable speed is outside the range 0 through 200.

4.7 Boolean Variables

CONCEPT: A Boolean variable can hold one of two values: true or false. Boolean variables are commonly used as flags, which indicate whether specific conditions exist.

So far in this book we have worked with Integer, Real, and String variables. In addition to numeric and string data types, most programming languages provide a Boolean data type. The Boolean data type allows you to create variables that may hold one of two possible values: True or False. Here is an example of the way we declare Boolean variables in this book:

```
Declare Boolean isHungry
```

Most programming languages have key words such as True and False that can be assigned to Boolean variables. Here are examples of how we assign values to a Boolean variable:

```
Set isHungry = True
Set isHungry = False
```

Boolean variables are most commonly used as flags. A *flag* is a variable that signals when some condition exists in the program. When the flag variable is set to False, it indicates the condition does not exist. When the flag variable is set to `True`, it means the condition does exist.

For example, suppose a salesperson has a quota of $50,000. Assuming the `sales` variable holds the amount that the salesperson has sold, the following pseudocode determines whether the quota has been met:

```
If sales >= 50000 Then
    Set salesQuotaMet = True
Else
    Set salesQuotaMet = False
End If
```

As a result of this code, the `salesQuotaMet` variable can be used as a flag to indicate whether the sales quota has been met. Later in the program we might test the flag in the following way:

```
If salesQuotaMet Then
    Display "You have met your sales quota!"
End If
```

This code displays the message "You have met your sales quota!" if the `Boolean` variable `salesQuotaMet` equals `True`. Notice that we did not have to use the `==` operator to explicitly compare the `salesQuotaMet` variable with the value `True`. This code is equivalent to the following:

```
If salesQuotaMet == True Then
    Display "You have met your sales quota!"
End If
```

 ## Checkpoint

4.27 What values can you store in a Boolean variable?

4.28 What is a flag variable?

Review Questions

Multiple Choice

1. A _____ structure can execute a set of statements only under certain circumstances.
   a. sequence
   b. circumstantial
   c. decision
   d. Boolean

2. A _____ structure provides one alternative path of execution.
   a. sequence
   b. single alternative decision
   c. one path alternative
   d. single execution decision

3. In pseudocode, the `If-Then` statement is an example of a _____.

   a. sequence structure
   b. decision structure
   c. pathway structure
   d. class structure

4. A(n) _____ expression has a value of either true or false.

   a. binary
   b. decision
   c. unconditional
   d. Boolean

5. The symbols >, <, and == are all _____ operators.

   a. relational
   b. logical
   c. conditional
   d. ternary

6. A(n) _____ structure tests a condition and then takes one path if the condition is true, or another path if the condition is false.

   a. `If-Then` statement
   b. single alternative decision
   c. dual alternative decision
   d. sequence

7. You use a(n) _____ statement in pseudocode to write a single alternative decision structure.

   a. `Test-Jump`
   b. `If-Then`
   c. `If-Then-Else`
   d. `If-Call`

8. You use a(n) _____ statement in pseudocode to write a dual alternative decision structure.

   a. `Test-Jump`
   b. `If-Then`
   c. `If-Then-Else`
   d. `If-Call`

9. A _____ structure allows you to test the value of a variable or an expression and then use that value to determine which statement or set of statements to execute.

   a. variable test decision
   b. single alternative decision
   c. dual alternative decision
   d. multiple alternative decision

10. A(n) _____ section of a `Select Case` statement is branched to if none of the case values match the expression listed after the `Select` statement.

   a. `Else`
   b. `Default`
   c. `Case`
   d. `Otherwise`

11. `AND`, `OR`, and `NOT` are _____ operators.

   a. relational
   b. logical
   c. conditional
   d. ternary

12. A compound Boolean expression created with the _____ operator is true only if both of its subexpressions are true.

   a. `AND`
   b. `OR`
   c. `NOT`
   d. `BOTH`

13. A compound Boolean expression created with the _____ operator is true if either of its subexpressions is true.

   a. `AND`
   b. `OR`
   c. `NOT`
   d. `EITHER`

14. The _____ operator takes a Boolean expression as its operand and reverses its logical value.

   a. `AND`
   b. `OR`
   c. `NOT`
   d. `EITHER`

15. A _____ is a Boolean variable that signals when some condition exists in the program.

   a. flag
   b. signal
   c. sentinel
   d. siren

True or False

1. You can write any program using only sequence structures.

2. A program can be made of only one type of control structure. You cannot combine structures.

3. A single alternative decision structure tests a condition and then takes one path if the condition is true, or another path if the condition is false.

4. A decision structure can be nested inside another decision structure.

5. A compound Boolean expression created with the AND operator is true only when both subexpressions are true.

Short Answer

1. Explain what is meant by the term "conditionally executed."

2. You need to test a condition and then execute one set of statements if the condition is true. If the condition is false, you need to execute a different set of statements. What structure will you use?

3. If you need to test the value of a variable and use that value to determine which statement or set of statements to execute, which structure would be the most straightforward to use?

4. Briefly describe how the AND operator works.

5. Briefly describe how the OR operator works.

6. When determining whether a number is inside a range, which logical operator is it best to use?

7. What is a flag and how does it work?

Algorithm Workbench

1. Design an If-Then statement (or a flowchart with a single alternative decision structure) that assigns 20 to the variable y and assigns 40 to the variable z if the variable x is greater than 100.

2. Design an If-Then statement (or a flowchart with a single alternative decision structure) that assigns 0 to the variable b and assigns 1 to the variable c if the variable a is less than 10.

3. Design an If-Then-Else statement (or a flowchart with a dual alternative decision structure) that assigns 0 to the variable b if the variable a is less than 10. Otherwise, it should assign 99 to the variable b.

4. The following pseudocode contains several nested If-Then-Else statements. Unfortunately, it was written without proper alignment and indentation. Rewrite the code and use the proper conventions of alignment and indentation.

```
If score < 60 Then
Display "Your grade is F."
Else
If score < 70 Then
Display "Your grade is D."
Else
If score < 80 Then
Display "Your grade is C."
Else
```

```
If score < 90 Then
Display "Your grade is B."
Else
Display "Your grade is A."
End If
End If
End If
End If
```

5. Design nested decision structures that perform the following: If `amount1` is greater than 10 and `amount2` is less than 100, display the greater of `amount1` and `amount2`.

6. Rewrite the following `If-Then-Else If` statement as a `Select Case` statement.

```
If selection == 1 Then
    Display "You selected A."
Else If selection == 2 Then
    Display "You selected 2."
Else If selection == 3 Then
    Display "You selected 3."
Else If selection == 4 Then
    Display "You selected 4."
Else
    Display "Not good with numbers, eh?"
End If
```

7. Design an `If-Then-Else` statement (or a flowchart with a dual alternative decision structure) that displays "Speed is normal" if the `speed` variable is within the range of 24 to 56. If speed holds a value outside this range, display "Speed is abnormal."

8. Design an `If-Then-Else` statement (or a flowchart with a dual alternative decision structure) that determines whether the `points` variable is outside the range of 9 to 51. If the variable holds a value outside this range it should display "Invalid points." Otherwise, it should display "Valid points."

9. Design a case structure that tests the `month` variable and does the following:
   - If the `month` variable is set to 1, it displays "January has 31 days."
   - If the `month` variable is set to 2, it displays "February has 28 days."
   - If the `month` variable is set to 3, it displays "March has 31 days."
   - If the `month` variable is set to anything else, it displays "Invalid selection."

10. Write an `If-Then` statement that sets the variable `hours` to 10 when the flag variable `minimum` is set.

Programming Exercises

1. Roman Numerals

Design a program that prompts the user to enter a number within the range of 1 through 10. The program should display the Roman numeral version of that number. If the number is outside the range of 1 through 10, the program should display an error message.

VideoNote

The Areas of
Rectangles
Problem

2. **Areas of Rectangles**

The area of a rectangle is the rectangle's length times its width. Design a program that asks for the length and width of two rectangles. The program should tell the user which rectangle has the greater area, or if the areas are the same.

3. **Mass and Weight**

Scientists measure an object's mass in kilograms and its weight in Newtons. If you know the amount of mass of an object, you can calculate its weight, in Newtons, with the following formula:

$$Weight = Mass \times 9.8$$

Design a program that asks the user to enter an object's mass, and then calculates its weight. If the object weighs more than 1000 Newtons, display a message indicating that it is too heavy. If the object weighs less than 10 Newtons, display a message indicating that it is too light.

4. **Magic Dates**

The date June 10, 1960, is special because when it is written in the following format, the month times the day equals the year:

$$6/10/60$$

Design a program that asks the user to enter a month (in numeric form), a day, and a two-digit year. The program should then determine whether the month times the day equals the year. If so, it should display a message saying the date is magic. Otherwise, it should display a message saying the date is not magic.

5. **Color Mixer**

The colors red, blue, and yellow are known as the primary colors because they cannot be made by mixing other colors. When you mix two primary colors, you get a secondary color, as shown here:

- When you mix red and blue, you get purple.
- When you mix red and yellow, you get orange.
- When you mix blue and yellow, you get green.

Design a program that prompts the user to enter the names of two primary colors to mix. If the user enters anything other than "red," "blue," or "yellow," the program should display an error message. Otherwise, the program should display the name of the secondary color that results.

6. **Book Club Points**

Serendipity Booksellers has a book club that awards points to its customers based on the number of books purchased each month. The points are awarded as follows:

- If a customer purchases 0 books, he or she earns 0 points.
- If a customer purchases 1 book, he or she earns 5 points.
- If a customer purchases 2 books, he or she earns 15 points.
- If a customer purchases 3 books, he or she earns 30 points.
- If a customer purchases 4 or more books, he or she earns 60 points.

Design a program that asks the user to enter the number of books that he or she has purchased this month and displays the number of points awarded.

7. **Software Sales**

    A software company sells a package that retails for $99. Quantity discounts are given according to the following table:

Quantity	Discount
10–19	20%
20–49	30%
50–99	40%
100 or more	50%

    Design a program that asks the user to enter the number of packages purchased. The program should then display the amount of the discount (if any) and the total amount of the purchase after the discount.

8. **Change for a Dollar Game**

    Design a change-counting game that gets the user to enter the number of coins required to make exactly one dollar. The program should ask the user to enter the number of pennies, nickels, dimes, and quarters. If the total value of the coins entered is equal to one dollar, the program should congratulate the user for winning the game. Otherwise, the program should display a message indicating whether the amount entered was more than or less than one dollar.

9. **Shipping Charges**

    The Fast Freight Shipping Company charges the following rates:

Weight of Package	Rate per Pound
2 pounds or less	$1.10
Over 2 pounds but not more than 6 pounds	$2.20
Over 6 pounds but not more than 10 pounds	$3.70
Over 10 pounds	$3.80

    Design a program that asks the user to enter the weight of a package and then displays the shipping charges.

10. **Body Mass Index Program Enhancement**

    In Programming Exercise 6 in Chapter 3 you were asked to design a program that calculates a person's body mass index (BMI). Recall from that exercise that the BMI is often used to determine whether a person with a sedentary lifestyle is overweight or underweight for their height. A person's BMI is calculated with the following formula:

    $$BMI = Weight \times 703 / Height^2$$

    In the formula, weight is measured in pounds and height is measured in inches. Enhance the program so it displays a message indicating whether the person has optimal weight, is underweight, or is overweight. A sedentary person's weight is considered to be optimal if his or her BMI is between 18.5 and 25. If the BMI is less than 18.5, the person is considered to be underweight. If the BMI value is greater than 25, the person is considered to be overweight.

11. **Time Calculator**

    Design a program that asks the user to enter a number of seconds, and works as follows:

    - There are 60 seconds in a minute. If the number of seconds entered by the user is greater than or equal to 60, the program should display the number of minutes in that many seconds.
    - There are 3,600 seconds in an hour. If the number of seconds entered by the user is greater than or equal to 3,600, the program should display the number of hours in that many seconds.
    - There are 86,400 seconds in a day. If the number of seconds entered by the user is greater than or equal to 86,400, the program should display the number of days in that many seconds.

CHAPTER

5 Repetition Structures

TOPICS

5.1 Introduction to Repetition Structures

5.2 Condition-Controlled Loops: `While`, `Do-While`, and `Do-Until`

5.3 Count-Controlled Loops and the `For` Statement

5.4 Calculating a Running Total

5.5 Sentinels

5.6 Nested Loops

5.1 Introduction to Repetition Structures

CONCEPT: A repetition structure causes a statement or set of statements to execute repeatedly.

Programmers commonly have to write code that performs the same task over and over. For example, suppose you have been asked to write a program that calculates a 10 percent sales commission for several salespeople. Although it would not be a good design, one approach would be to write the code to calculate one salesperson's commission, and then repeat that code for each salesperson. For example, look at the following pseudocode:

```
// Variables for sales and commission.
Declare Real sales, commission

// Constant for the commission rate.
Constant Real COMMISSION_RATE = 0.10

// Get the amount of sales.
Display "Enter the amount of sales."
Input sales

// Calculate the commission.
Set commission = sales * COMMISSION_RATE

// Display the commission
Display "The commission is $", commission
```

This calculates the first salesperson's commission.

163

```
// Get the amount of sales.
Display "Enter the amount of sales."
Input sales

// Calculate the commission.
Set commission = sales * COMMISSION_RATE

// Display the commission
Display "The commission is $", commission
```

This calculates the second salesperson's commission.

And this code goes on and on . . .

As you can see, this is one long sequence structure containing a lot of duplicated code. There are several disadvantages to this approach, including the following:

- The duplicated code makes the program large.
- Writing a long sequence of statements can be time consuming.
- If part of the duplicated code has to be corrected or changed then the correction or change has to be done many times.

Instead of writing the same sequence of statements over and over, a better way to repeatedly perform an operation is to write the code for the operation once, and then place that code in a structure that makes the computer repeat it as many times as necessary. This can be done with a *repetition structure*, which is more commonly known as a *loop*.

Condition-Controlled and Count-Controlled Loops

In this chapter, we will look at two broad categories of loops: condition-controlled and count-controlled. A *condition-controlled loop* uses a true/false condition to control the number of times that it repeats. A *count-controlled loop* repeats a specific number of times. We will also discuss the specific ways that most programming languages allow you to construct these types of loops.

 Checkpoint

5.1 What is a repetition structure?

5.2 What is a condition-controlled loop?

5.3 What is a count-controlled loop?

5.2

Condition-Controlled Loops:
`While`, `Do-While`, and `Do-Until`

CONCEPT: Both the `While` and `Do-While` loops cause a statement or set of statements to repeat as long as a condition is true. The `Do-Until` loop causes a statement or set of statements to repeat until a condition is true.

The While Loop

The While loop gets its name from the way it works: *While a condition is true, do some task*. The loop has two parts: (1) a condition that is tested for a true or false value, and (2) a statement or set of statements that is repeated as long as the condition is true. Figure 5-1 shows the logic of a While loop.

Figure 5-1 The logic of a While loop

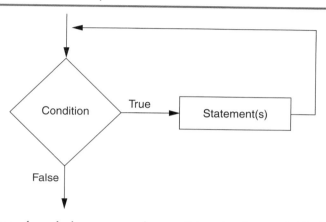

VideoNote

The While Loop

The diamond symbol represents the condition that is tested. Notice what happens if the condition is true: one or more statements are executed and the program's execution flows back to the point just above the diamond symbol. The condition is tested again, and if it is true, the process repeats. If the condition is false, the program exits the loop. In a flowchart, you will always recognize a loop when you see a flow line going back to a previous part of the flowchart.

Writing a While Loop in Pseudocode

In pseudocode, we will use the While statement to write a While loop. Here is the general format of the While statement:

```
While condition
    statement
    statement      These statements are the body of the loop. They are
    etc.           repeated while the condition is true.
End While
```

In the general format, the *condition* is a Boolean expression, and the statements that appear on the lines between the While and the End While clauses are called the *body of the loop*. When the loop executes, the *condition* is tested. If it is true, the statements that appear in the body of the loop are executed, and then the loop starts over. If the *condition* is false, the program exits the loop.

As shown in the general format, you should use the following conventions when you write a While statement:

• Make sure the While clause and the End While clause are aligned.
• Indent the statements in the body of the loop.

By indenting the statements in the body of the loop you visually set them apart from the surrounding code. This makes your program easier to read and debug. Also, this is similar to the style that most programmers follow when writing loops in actual code.

Program 5-1 shows how we might use a While loop to write the commission calculating program that was described at the beginning of this chapter.

Program 5-1

```
 1 // Variable declarations
 2 Declare Real sales, commission
 3 Declare String keepGoing = "y"
 4
 5 // Constant for the commission rate
 6 Constant Real COMMISSION_RATE = 0.10
 7
 8 While keepGoing == "y"
 9     // Get the amount of sales.
10     Display "Enter the amount of sales."
11     Input sales
12
13     // Calculate the commission.
14     Set commission = sales * COMMISSION_RATE
15
16     // Display the commission
17     Display "The commission is $", commission
18
19     Display "Do you want to calculate another"
20     Display "commission? (Enter y for yes.)"
21     Input keepGoing
22 End While
```

Program Output (with Input Shown in Bold)

```
Enter the amount of sales.
10000.00 [Enter]
The commission is $1000
Do you want to calculate another
commission? (Enter y for yes.)
y [Enter]
Enter the amount of sales.
5000.00 [Enter]
The commission is $500
Do you want to calculate another
commission? (Enter y for yes.)
y [Enter]
Enter the amount of sales.
12000.00 [Enter]
The commission is $1200
Do you want to calculate another
commission? (Enter y for yes.)
n [Enter]
```

In line 2, we declare the `sales` variable, which will hold the amount of sales, and the `commission` variable, which will hold the amount of commission. Then, in line 3 we declare a `String` variable named `keepGoing`. Notice that the variable is initialized with the value "y." This initialization value is important, and in a moment you will see why. In line 6 we declare a constant, `COMMISSION_RATE`, which is initialized with the value 0.10. This is the commission rate that we will use in our calculation.

Line 8 is the beginning of a `While` loop, which starts like this:

```
While keepGoing == "y"
```

Notice the condition that is being tested: `keepGoing == "y"`. The loop tests this condition, and if it is true, the statements in the body of the loop (lines 9 through 21) are executed. Then, the loop starts over at line 8. It tests the expression `keepGoing == "y"` and if it is true, the statements in the body of the loop are executed again. This cycle repeats until the expression `keepGoing == "y"` is tested in line 8 and found to be false. When that happens, the program exits the loop. This is illustrated in Figure 5-2.

In order for this loop to stop executing, something has to happen inside the loop to make the expression `keepGoing == "y"` false. The statements in lines 19 through 21 take care of this. Lines 19 and 20 display a message asking "Do you want to calculate another commission? (Enter y for yes)." Then, the `Input` statement in line 21 reads the user's input and stores it in the `keepGoing` variable. If the user enters y (and it must be a lowercase y), then the expression `keepGoing == "y"` will be true when the loop starts over. This will cause the statements in the body of the loop to execute again. But, if the user enters anything other than lowercase y, the expression will be false when the loop starts over, and the program will exit the loop.

Figure 5-2 The `While` loop

```
                        This condition is tested.
                               |
                    While keepGoing == "y"

                        // Get the amount of sales.
                        Display "Enter the amount of sales."
 If the condition is true,    Input sales
 these statements are
 executed, and then the   // Calculate the commission.
 loop starts over.        Set commission = sales * COMMISSION_RATE

                        // Display the commission
 If the condition is false,  Display "The commission is $", commission
 these statements are
 skipped and the          Display "Do you want to calculate another"
 program exits the loop.    Display "commission? (Enter y for yes.)"
                          Input keepGoing

                    End While
```

Now that you have examined the pseudocode, look at the program output in the sample run. First, the program prompted the user to enter the amount of sales. The user entered 10000.00, and then the program displayed the commission for that amount, which is $1000.00. Then, the user is prompted "Do you want to calculate another commission? (Enter y for yes.)" The user entered y, and the loop started the steps over. In the sample run, the user went through this process three times. Each execution of the body of a loop is known as an *iteration*. In the sample run, the loop iterated three times.

Figure 5-3 shows a flowchart for Program 5-1. By looking at this flowchart you can see that we have a repetition structure (the While loop) with a sequence structure (the body of the loop) nested inside it. The fundamental structure of the While loop is still present, however. A condition is tested, and if it is true one or more statements are executed and the flow of execution returns to the point just above the conditional test.

Figure 5-3 Flowchart for Program 5-1

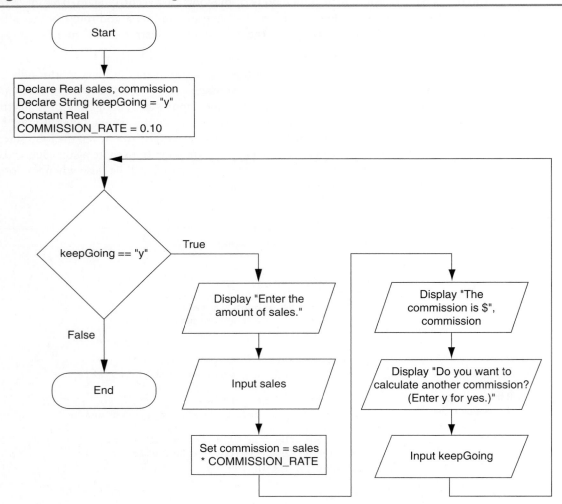

The While Loop Is a Pretest Loop

The While loop is known as a *pretest* loop, which means it tests its condition *before* performing an iteration. Because the test is done at the beginning of the loop, you usually have to perform some steps prior to the loop to make sure that the loop executes at least once. For example, the loop in Program 5-1 starts like this:

```
While keepGoing == "y"
```

The loop will perform an iteration only if the expression keepGoing == "y" is true. To make sure the expression is true the first time that the loop executes, we declared and initialized the keepGoing variable in line 3 as follows:

```
Declare String keepGoing = "y"
```

If keepGoing had been initialized with any other value (or not initialized at all), the loop would never execute. This is an important characteristic of the While loop: it will never execute if its condition is false to start with. In some programs, this is exactly what you want. The following *In the Spotlight* section gives an example.

In the Spotlight:

Designing a While Loop

A project currently underway at Chemical Labs, Inc. requires that a substance be continually heated in a vat. A technician must check the substance's temperature every 15 minutes. If the substance's temperature does not exceed 102.5, then the technician does nothing. However, if the temperature is greater than 102.5, the technician must turn down the vat's thermostat, wait five minutes, and check the temperature again. The technician repeats these steps until the temperature does not exceed 102.5. The director of engineering has asked you to design a program that guides the technician through this process.

Here is the algorithm:

1. Get the substance's temperature.
2. Repeat the following steps as long as the temperature is greater than 102.5:
   a. Tell the technician to turn down the thermostat, wait five minutes, and check the temperature again.
   b. Get the substance's temperature.
3. After the loop finishes, tell the technician that the temperature is acceptable and to check it again in 15 minutes.

After reviewing this algorithm, you realize that steps 2(a) and 2(b) should not be performed if the test condition (temperature is greater than 102.5) is false to begin with. The While loop will work well in this situation, because it will not execute even once if its condition is false. Program 5-2 shows the pseudocode for the program, and Figure 5-4 shows a flowchart.

Program 5-2

```
1  // Variable to hold the temperature
2  Declare Real temperature
3
4  // Constant for the maximum temperature
5  Constant Real MAX_TEMP = 102.5
6
7  // Get the substance's temperature.
8  Display "Enter the substance's temperature."
9  Input temperature
10
11 // If necessary, adjust the thermostat.
12 While temperature > MAX_TEMP
13     Display "The temperature is too high."
14     Display "Turn the thermostat down and wait"
15     Display "five minutes. Take the temperature"
16     Display "again and enter it here."
17     Input temperature
18 End While
19
20 // Remind the user to check the temperature
21 // again in 15 minutes.
22 Display "The temperature is acceptable."
23 Display "Check it again in 15 minutes."
```

Program Output (with Input Shown in Bold)

```
Enter the substance's temperature.
104.7 [Enter]
The temperature is too high.
Turn the thermostat down and wait
five minutes. Take the temperature
again and enter it here.
103.2 [Enter]
The temperature is too high.
Turn the thermostat down and wait
five minutes. Take the temperature
again and enter it here.
102.1 [Enter]
The temperature is acceptable.
Check it again in 15 minutes.
```

Program Output (with Input Shown in Bold)

```
Enter the substance's temperature.
102.1 [Enter]
The temperature is acceptable.
Check it again in 15 minutes.
```

Figure 5-4 Flowchart for Program 5-2

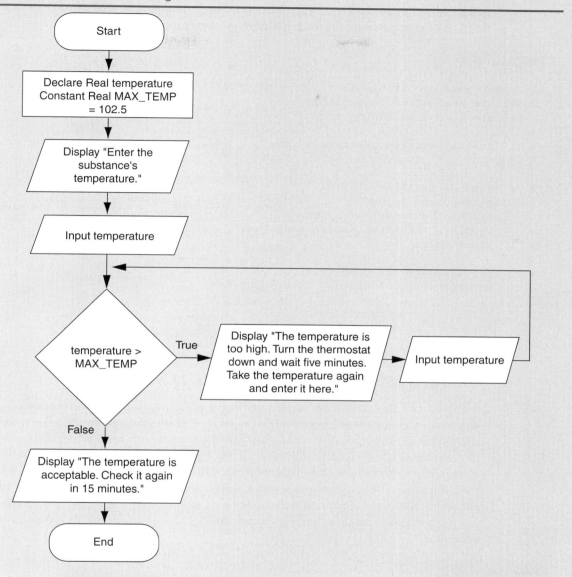

Infinite Loops

In all but rare cases, loops must contain within themselves a way to terminate. This means that something inside the loop must eventually make the test condition false. The loop in Program 5-1 stops when the expression keepGoing == "y" is false. If a loop does not have a way of stopping, it is called an infinite loop. An *infinite loop* continues to repeat until the program is interrupted. Infinite loops usually occur when the programmer forgets to write code inside the loop that makes the test condition false. In most circumstances you should avoid writing infinite loops.

The pseudocode in Program 5-3 demonstrates an infinite loop. This is a modified version of the commission calculating program. In this version, we have removed the code that modifies the keepGoing variable in the body of the loop. Each time the expression keepGoing == "y" is tested in line 9, keepGoing will contain the string "y". As a consequence, the loop has no way of stopping.

Program 5-3

```
 1 // Variable declarations
 2 Declare Real sales, commission
 3 Declare String keepGoing = "y"
 4
 5 // Constant for the commission rate
 6 Constant Real COMMISSION_RATE = 0.10
 7
 8 // Warning! Infinite loop!
 9 While keepGoing == "y"
10      // Get the amount of sales.
11      Display "Enter the amount of sales."
12      Input sales
13
14      // Calculate the commission.
15      Set commission = sales * COMMISSION_RATE
16
17      // Display the commission
18      Display "The commission is $", commission
19 End While
```

Modularizing the Code in the Body of a Loop

Modules can be called from statements in the body of a loop. In fact, modularizing the code in a loop often improves the design. For example, in Program 5-1, the statements that get the amount of sales, calculate the commission, and display the commission can easily be placed in a module. That module can then be called in the loop. Program 5-4 shows how this might be done. This program has a main module, which executes when the program runs, and a showCommission module that handles all of the steps related to calculating and displaying a commission. Figure 5-5 shows a flowchart for the main module, and Figure 5-6 shows a flowchart for the showCommission module.

Program 5-4

```
 1 Module main()
 2      // Local variable
 3      Declare String keepGoing = "y"
 4
 5      // Calculate as many commissions
 6      // as needed.
 7      While keepGoing == "y"
 8          // Display a salesperson's commission.
 9          Call showCommission()
10
```

```
11          // Do it again?
12          Display "Do you want to calculate another?"
13          Display "commission? (Enter y for yes.)"
14          Input keepGoing
15      End While
16 End Module
17
18 // The showCommission module gets the
19 // amount of sales and displays the
20 // commission.
21 Module show Commission()
22      // Local variables
23      Declare Real sales, commission
24
25      // Constant for the commission rate
26      Constant Real COMMISSION_RATE = 0.10
27
28      // Get the amount of sales.
29      Display "Enter the amount of sales."
30      Input sales
31
32      // Calculate the commission.
33      Set commission = sales * COMMISSION_RATE
34
35      // Display the commission
36      Display "The commission is $", commission
37 End Module
```

The output of this program is the same as that of Program 5-1

Figure 5-5 The main module of Program 5-3

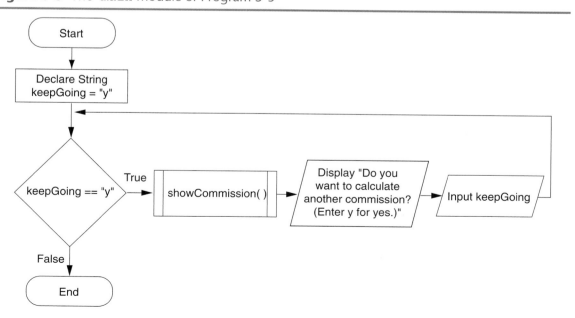

Figure 5-6 The showCommission module

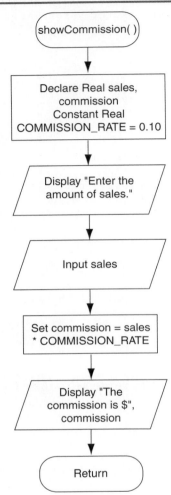

The Do-While Loop

You have learned that the While loop is a pretest loop, which means it tests its condition before performing an iteration. The Do-While loop is a *posttest* loop. This means it performs an iteration before testing its condition. As a result, the Do-While loop always performs at least one iteration, even if its condition is false to begin with. The logic of a Do-While loop is shown in Figure 5-7.

In the flowchart, one or more statements are executed, and then a condition is tested. If the condition is true, the program's execution flows back to the point just above the first statement in the body of the loop, and this process repeats. If the condition is false, the program exits the loop.

Figure 5-7 The logic of a Do-While loop

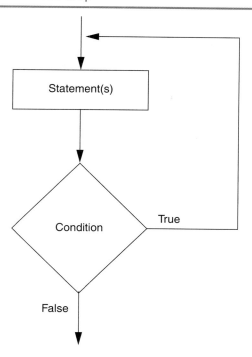

Writing a Do-While Loop in Pseudocode

In pseudocode, we will use the Do-While statement to write a Do-While loop. Here is the general format of the Do-While statement:

```
Do
    statement
    statement
    etc.
While condition
```

These statements are the body of the loop. They are always performed once, and then repeated while the condition is true.

In the general format, the statements that appear in the lines between the Do and the While clauses are the body of the loop. The *condition* that appears after the While clause is a Boolean expression. When the loop executes, the statements in the body of the loop are executed, and then the *condition* is tested. If the *condition* is true, the loop starts over and the statements in the body are executed again. If the condition is false, however, the program exits the loop.

As shown in the general format, you should use the following conventions when you write a Do-While statement:

- Make sure the Do clause and the While clause are aligned.
- Indent the statements in the body of the loop.

As shown in Program 5-5, the commission calculating program can be easily modified to use a Do-While loop instead of a While loop. Notice that in this version of the program, in line 3, we do not initialize the keepGoing variable with the string "y". It isn't necessary because the Do-While loop, in lines 7 through 15, will always execute at least once. This means that the Input statement in line 14 will read a value into the keepGoing variable before the condition is ever tested in line 15.

Figure 5-8 shows a flowchart for the main module.

Program 5-5

```
 1 Module main()
 2     // Local variable
 3     Declare String keepGoing
 4
 5     // Calculate commissions as many
 6     // times as needed.
 7     Do
 8         // Display a salesperson's commission.
 9         Call showCommission()
10
11         // Do it again?
12         Display "Do you want to calculate another"
13         Display "commission? (Enter y for yes.)"
14         Input keepGoing
15     While keepGoing == "y"
16 End Module
17
18 // The showCommission module gets the
19 // amount of sales and displays the
20 // commission.
21 Module showCommission()
22     // Local variables
23     Declare Real sales, commission
24
25     // Constant for the commission rate
26     Constant Real COMMISSION_RATE = 0.10
27
28     // Get the amount of sales.
29     Display "Enter the amount of sales."
30     Input sales
31
32     // Calculate the commission.
33     Set commission = sales * COMMISSION_RATE
34
35     // Display the commission
36     Display "The commission is $", commission
37 End Module
```

The output of this program is the same as that of Program 5-1

Figure 5-8 Flowchart for the main module in Program 5-4

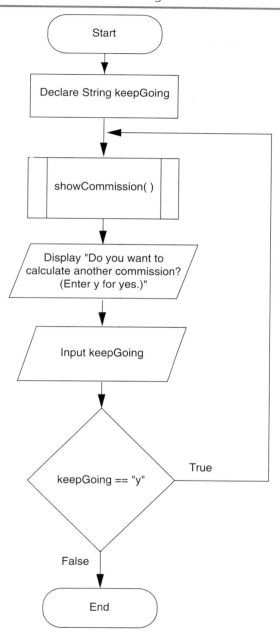

Although the Do-While loop is convenient to use in some circumstances, it is never required. Any loop that can be written as a Do-While loop can also be written as a While loop. As previously mentioned, some circumstances require that you initialize data prior to executing a While loop, to ensure that it executes at least once.

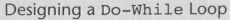

In the Spotlight:
Designing a Do-While Loop

Samantha owns an import business and she calculates the retail prices of her products with the following formula:

Retail Price = Wholesale Cost × 2.5

She has asked you to design a program to do this calculation for each item that she receives in a shipment. You learn that each shipment contains various numbers of items, so you decide to use a loop that calculates the price for one item, and then asks her if she has another item. The loop will iterate as long as she indicates that she has another item. Program 5-6 shows the pseudocode for the program, and Figure 5-9 shows the flowchart.

Program 5-6

```
1 Module main()
2    // Local variable
3    Declare String doAnother
4
5    Do
6        // Calculate and display a retail price.
7        Call showRetail()
8
9        // Do this again?
10       Display "Do you have another item? (Enter y for yes.)"
11       Input doAnother
12    While doAnother == "y" OR doAnother == "Y"
13 End Module
14
15 // The showRetail module gets an item's wholesale cost
16 // from the user and displays its retail price.
17 Module showRetail()
18    // Local variables
19    Declare Real wholesale, retail
20
21    // Constant for the markup percentage
22    Constant Real MARKUP = 2.50
23
24    // Get the wholesale cost.
25    Display "Enter an item's wholesale cost."
26    Input wholesale
27
28    // Calculate the retail price.
29    Set retail = wholesale * MARKUP
30
31    // Display the retail price.
32    Display "The retail price is $", retail
33 End Module
```

Program Output (with Input Shown in Bold)

```
Enter an item's wholesale cost.
10.00 [Enter]
The retail price is $25
Do you have another item? (Enter y for yes.)
y [Enter]
Enter an item's wholesale cost.
15.00 [Enter]
The retail price is $37.50
Do you have another item? (Enter y for yes.)
y [Enter]
Enter an item's wholesale cost.
12.50 [Enter]
The retail price is $31.25
Do you have another item? (Enter y for yes.)
n [Enter]
```

Figure 5-9 Flowchart for Program 5-6

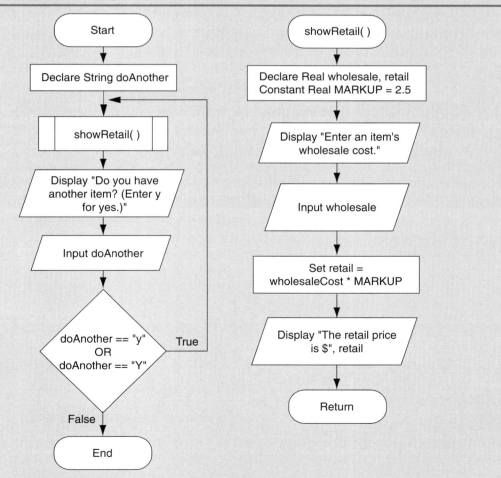

This program has two modules: main, which executes when the program runs, and showRetail, which calculates and displays an item's retail price. In the main module, a Do-While loop appears in lines 5 through 12. In line 7, the loop calls the showRetail module. Then, in line 10 the user is prompted "Do you have another item? (Enter y for yes.)" In line 11, the user's input is stored in the doAnother variable. In line 12, the following statement is the end of the Do-While loop:

```
While doAnother == "y" OR doAnother == "Y"
```

Notice that we are using the logical OR operator to test a compound Boolean expression. The expression on the left side of the OR operator will be true if doAnother is equal to lowercase "y". The expression on the right side of the OR operator will be true if doAnother is equal to uppercase "Y". If either of these subexpressions is true, the loop will iterate. This is a simple way to make a case insensitive comparison, which means that it does not matter whether the user enters uppercase or lowercase letters.

The Do-Until Loop

Both the While and the Do-While loops iterate as long as a condition is true. Sometimes, however, it is more convenient to write a loop that iterates *until* a condition is true—that is, a loop that iterates as long as a condition is false, and then stops when the condition becomes true.

For example, consider a machine in an automobile factory that paints cars as they move down the assembly line. When there are no more cars to paint, the machine stops. If you were programming such a machine, you would want to design a loop that causes the machine to paint cars until there are no more cars on the assembly line.

A loop that iterates until a condition is true is known as a Do-Until loop. Figure 5-10 shows the general logic of a Do-Until loop.

Figure 5-10 The logic of a Do-Until loop

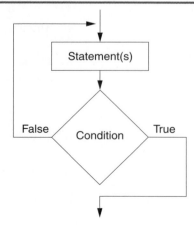

Notice that the Do-Until loop is a posttesp loop. First, one or more statements are executed, and then a condition is tested. If the condition is false, the program's execution flows back to the point just above the first statement in the body of the loop, and this process repeats. If the condition is true, the program exits the loop.

Writing a Do-Until Loop in Pseudocode

In pseudocode, we will use the Do-Until statement to write a Do-Until loop. Here is the general format of the Do-Until statement:

```
Do
     statement
     statement          These statements are the body of the loop. They are always
     etc.               performed once, and then repeated until the condition is true.
Until condition
```

In the general format, the statements that appear in the lines between the Do and the Until clauses are the body of the loop. The *condition* that appears after the While clause is a Boolean expression. When the loop executes, the statements in the body of the loop are executed, and then the *condition* is tested. If the *condition* is true, the program exits the loop. If the *condition* is false, the loop starts over and the statements in the body are executed again.

As shown in the general format, you should use the following conventions when you write a Do-Until statement:

- Make sure the Do clause and the Until clause are aligned.
- Indent the statements in the body of the loop.

The pseudocode in Program 5-7 shows an example of the Do-Until loop. The loop in lines 6 through 16 repeatedly asks the user to enter a password until the string "prospero" is entered. Figure 5-11 shows a flowchart for the program.

Program 5-7

```
 1 // Declare a variable to hold the password.
 2 Declare String password
 3
 4 // Repeatedly ask the user to enter a password
 5 // until the correct one is entered.
 6 Do
 7     // Prompt the user to enter the password.
 8     Display "Enter the password."
 9     Input password
10
11     // Display an error message if the wrong
12     // password was entered.
13     If password != "prospero" Then
14         Display "Sorry, try again."
15     End If
16 Until password == "prospero"
17
18 // Indicate that the password is confirmed.
19 Display "Password confirmed."
```

Program Output (with Input Shown in Bold)

```
Enter the password.
ariel [Enter]
Sorry, try again.
Enter the password.
caliban [Enter]
Sorry, try again.
Enter the password.
prospero [Enter]
Password confirmed.
```

Figure 5-11 Flowchart for Program 5-7

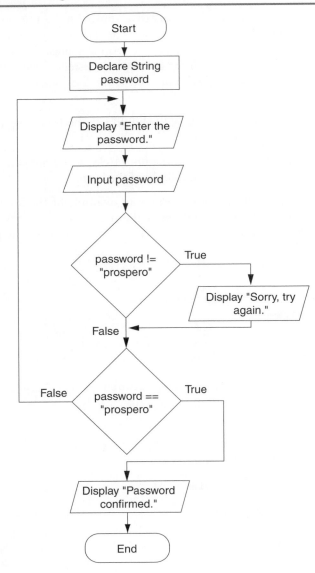

> **NOTE:** Not all programming languages provide a Do-Until loop because you can write a Do-While loop that is logically equivalent to any Do-Until loop.

Deciding Which Loop to Use

In this section, we have introduced three different types of condition-controlled loop: the While loop, the Do-While loop, and the Do-Until loop. When you write a program that requires a condition-controlled loop, you will have to decide which loop to use.

You want to use the While loop to repeat a task as long as a condition is true. The While loop is ideal in situations where the condition might be false to start with, and in such cases you do not want the loop to iterate at all. The pseudocode that you saw in Program 5-2 is a good example.

The Do-While loop is also a candidate in situations where a task must be repeated as long as a condition is true. It is the best choice, however, when you always want the task to be performed at least once, regardless of whether the condition is true or false to start with.

The Do-Until loop also performs a task at least once. It is the best choice, however, when you want to perform a task *until* a condition is true. The Do-Until loop will repeat as long as its condition is false. When the condition is true, the Do-Until loop stops.

 Checkpoint

5.4 What is a loop iteration?

5.5 What is the difference between a pretest loop and a posttest loop?

5.6 Does the While loop test its condition before or after it performs an iteration?

5.7 Does the Do-While loop test its condition before or after it performs an iteration?

5.8 What is an infinite loop?

5.9 What is the difference between a Do-While loop and a Do-Until loop?

5.3 Count-Controlled Loops and the For Statement

CONCEPT: A count-controlled loop iterates a specific number of times. Although you can write the logic of a condition-controlled loop so it iterates a specific number of times, most languages provide a loop known as the **For** loop, which is specifically designed as a count-controlled loop.

As mentioned at the beginning of this chapter, a count-controlled loop iterates a specific number of times. Count-controlled loops are commonly used in programs. For example, suppose a business is open six days per week, and you are going to write a program that calculates the total sales for a week. You will need a loop that iterates exactly six times. Each time the loop iterates, it will prompt the user to enter the sales for one day.

The way that a count-controlled loop works is simple: the loop keeps a count of the number of times that it iterates, and when the count reaches a specified amount, the loop stops. A count-controlled loop uses a variable known as a *counter variable,* or simply *counter,* to store the number of iterations that it has performed. Using the counter variable, the loop typically performs the following three actions: *initialization, test,* and *increment:*

1. **Initialization:** Before the loop begins, the counter variable is initialized to a starting value. The starting value that is used will depend on the situation.
2. **Test:** The loop tests the counter variable by comparing it to a maximum value. If the counter variable is less than or equal to the maximum value, the loop iterates. If the counter is greater than the maximum value, the program exits the loop.
3. **Increment:** To *increment* a variable means to increase its value. During each iteration, the loop increments the counter variable by adding 1 to it.

Figure 5-12 shows the general logic of a count-controlled loop. The initialization, test, and increment operations are indicated with the ①, ②, and ③ callouts.

Figure 5-12 Logic of a count-controlled loop

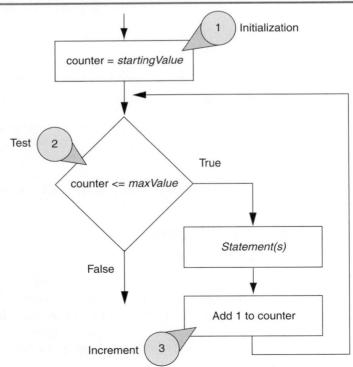

In the flowchart, assume that counter is an Integer variable. The first step is to set counter to the appropriate starting value. Then, determine whether counter is less than or equal to the maximum value. If this is true, the body of the loop executes. Otherwise, the program exits the loop. Notice that in the body of the loop one or more statements are executed, and then 1 is added to counter.

For example, look at the flowchart in Figure 5-13. First, an Integer variable named counter is declared and initialized with the starting value 1. Then, the expression counter <= 5 is tested. If this expression is true the message "Hello world" is displayed and 1 is added to counter. Otherwise, the program exits the loop. If you follow the logic of this program you will see that the loop will iterate five times.

Figure 5-13 A count-controlled loop

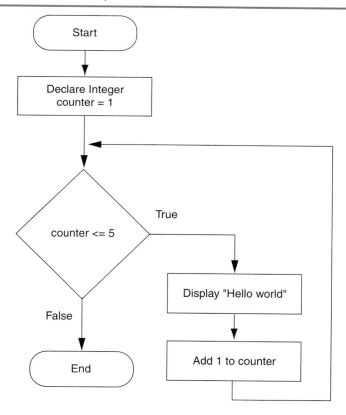

The For Statement

Count-controlled loops are so common in programming that most languages provide a statement just for them. This is usually called the For statement. The For statement is specifically designed to initialize, test, and increment a counter variable. Here is the general format that we will use to write the For statement in pseudocode:

For *counterVariable* = *startingValue* To *maxValue*
>   *statement*
>   *statement*   } These statements are the body of the loop.
>   *statement*
>   *etc.*
End For

In the general format, *counterVariable* is the name of a variable that is used as a counter, *startingValue* is the value that the counter will be initially set to, and *maxValue* is the maximum value that the counter can contain. When the loop executes, the following actions are performed:

1. The *counterVariable* is set to the *startingValue*.
2. The *counterVariable* is compared to the *maxValue*. If the *counterVariable* is greater than *maxValue*, the loop stops. Otherwise:
   a. The statements that appear in the body of the loop are executed.
   b. The *counterVariable* is incremented.
   c. The loop starts over again at Step 2.

An actual For loop is easy to understand, so let's look at one. The pseudocode in Program 5-8 uses a For loop to display "Hello world" five times. The flowchart in Figure 5-14 shows the logic of the program.

Program 5-8

```
1 Declare Integer counter
2 Constant Integer MAX_VALUE = 5
3
4 For counter = 1 To MAX_VALUE
5    Display "Hello world"
6 End For
```

Program Output

```
Hello world
Hello world
Hello world
Hello world
Hello world
```

Line 1 declares an Integer variable that will be used as the counter variable. You do not have to name the variable counter (you are free to name it anything you wish), but in many cases that is an appropriate name. Line 2 declares a constant named MAX_VALUE that will be used as the counter's maximum value. The For loop begins in line 4 with the statement For counter = 1 To MAX_VALUE. This specifies that the counter variable will start with the value 1 and will end with the value 5. At the end of each loop iteration, the counter variable will be incremented by 1, so this loop will iterate five times. Each time it iterates, it displays "Hello world."

Notice that the loop does not contain a statement to increment the counter variable. This happens automatically in a For loop, at the end of each iteration. For that reason, you should be careful not to place a statement that modifies the counter variable inside the body of a For loop. Doing so will usually disrupt the way the For loop works.

Figure 5-14 Flowchart for Program 5-8

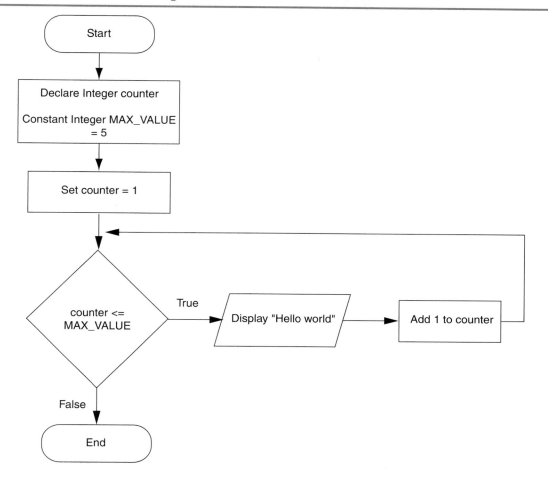

 TIP: Program 5-8 has a constant, MAX_VALUE, that represents the counter variable's maximum value. The first line of the loop could have been written as follows, to achieve the same result:

```
For counter = 1 To 5
```

Although creating the named constant is not necessary for this simple program, creating named constants to represent important values is a good habit. Recall from Chapter 2 that named constants make a program easier to read and easier to maintain.

Using the Counter Variable in the Body of the Loop

In a count-controlled loop, the primary purpose of the counter variable is to store the number of times that the loop has iterated. In some situations, it is also helpful to use the counter variable in a calculation or other task within the body of the loop. For example, suppose you need to write a program that displays the numbers 1 through 10 and their squares, in a table similar to the following:

Number	Square
1	1
2	4
3	9
4	16
5	25
6	36
7	49
8	64
9	81
10	100

This can be accomplished by writing a count-controlled loop that iterates 10 times. During the first iteration, the counter variable will be set to 1, during the second iteration it will be set to 2, and so forth. Because the counter variable will take on the values 1 through 10 during the loop's execution, you can use it in the calculation inside the loop.

The flowchart in Figure 5-15 shows the logic of such a program. Notice that in the body of the loop, the `counter` variable is used in the following calculation:

```
Set square = counter^2
```

This assigns the result of `counter^2` to the `square` variable. After performing this calculation, the contents of the `counter` variable and the `square` variable are displayed. Then, 1 is added to `counter` and the loop starts over again.

Program 5-9 shows the pseudocode for the program. Notice that the word `Tab` is used in the `Display` statements in lines 8 and 18. This is simply a way of indicating in pseudocode that we are indenting the screen output. For example, look at the following statement, which appears in line 18:

```
Display counter, Tab, square
```

This statement displays the contents of the `counter` variable, indents (or "tabs over"), and then displays the contents of the `square` variable. As a result, the numbers that are displayed will be aligned in two columns. Most programming languages provide a way to indent, or tab, screen output.

Figure 5-15 Displaying the numbers 1 through 10 and their squares

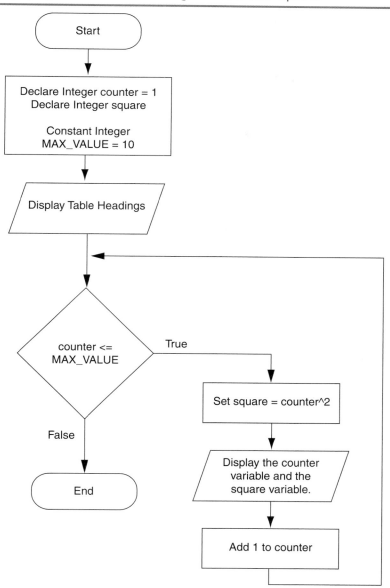

Program 5-9

```
 1 // Variables
 2 Declare Integer counter, square
 3
 4 // Constant for the maximum value
 5 Constant Integer MAX_VALUE = 10
 6
 7 // Display table headings.
 8 Display "Number", Tab, "Square"
 9 Display "----------------------"
10
11 // Display the numbers 1 through 10 and
12 // their squares.
13 For counter = 1 To MAX_VALUE
14     // Calculate number squared.
15     Set square = counter^2
16
17     // Display number and number squared.
18     Display counter, Tab, square
19 End For
```

Program Output

```
Number              Square
----------------------
   1                   1
   2                   4
   3                   9
   4                  16
   5                  25
   6                  36
   7                  49
   8                  64
   9                  81
  10                 100
```

Incrementing by Values Other Than 1

The amount by which the counter variable is incremented in a For loop is known as the *step amount*. By default, the step amount is 1. Most languages provide a way to change the step amount. This gives you the ability to increment the counter variable by any value you wish.

In pseudocode, we will use the Step clause to specify a step value in a For loop. For example, look at the following pseudocode:

```
For counter = 0 To 100 Step 10
    Display counter
End For
```

In this loop, the starting value of the `counter` variable is 0, and its ending value is 100. The `step` clause specifies a step value of 10, which means that 10 is added to the `counter` variable at the end of each iteration. During the first iteration, `counter` is 0, during the second iteration, `counter` is 10, during the third iteration, `counter` is 20, and so forth.

The pseudocode in Program 5-10 gives another demonstration. The program displays all of the odd numbers from 1 through 11.

Program 5-10

```
 1 // Declare a counter variable
 2 Declare Integer counter
 3
 4 // Constant for the maximum value
 5 Constant Integer MAX_VALUE = 11
 6
 7 // Display the odd numbers from 1 through 11.
 8 For counter = 1 To MAX_VALUE Step 2
 9    Display counter
10 End For
```

Program Output

```
1
3
5
7
9
11
```

In the Spotlight:
Designing a Count-Controlled Loop with the For Statement

Your friend Amanda just inherited a European sports car from her uncle. Amanda lives in the United States, and she is afraid she will get a speeding ticket because the car's speedometer works in kilometers per hour. She has asked you to write a program that displays a table of speeds in kilometers per hour with their values converted to miles per hour. The formula for converting kilometers per hour to miles per hour is:

$$MPH = KPH \times 0.6214$$

In the formula, *MPH* is the speed in miles per hour and *KPH* is the speed in kilometers per hour.

The table that your program displays should show speeds from 60 kilometers per hour through 130 kilometers per hour, in increments of 10, along with their values converted to miles per hour. The table should look something like this:

KPH	MPH
60	37.284
70	43.498
80	49.712
etc....	
130	80.782

After thinking about this table of values, you decide that you will write a For loop that uses a counter variable to hold the kilometer-per-hour speeds. The counter's starting value will be 60, its ending value will be 130, and a step value of 10 will be used. Inside the loop you will use the counter variable to calculate a speed in miles-per-hour. Program 5-11 shows the pseudocode for the program, and Figure 5-16 shows a flowchart.

Program 5-11

```
 1 // Declare variables to hold speeds in MPH and KPH.
 2 Declare Real mph
 3 Declare Integer kph
 4
 5 // Display the table headings.
 6 Display "KPH", Tab, "MPH"
 7 Display "----------------------"
 8
 9 // Display the speeds.
10 For kph = 60 To 130 Step 10
11     // Calculate the miles-per-hour.
12     Set mph = kph * 0.6214
13
14     // Display KPH and MPH.
15     Display kph, Tab, mph
16 End For
```

Program Output

```
KPH                  MPH
----------------------
60                   37.284
70                   43.498
80                   49.712
90                   55.926
100                  62.14
110                  68.354
120                  74.568
130                  80.782
```

Notice that a variable named kph is used as the counter. Until now we have used the name counter for our counter variables. In this program, however, kph is a better name for the counter because it will hold speeds in kilometers-per-hour.

Figure 5-16 Flowchart for Program 5-11

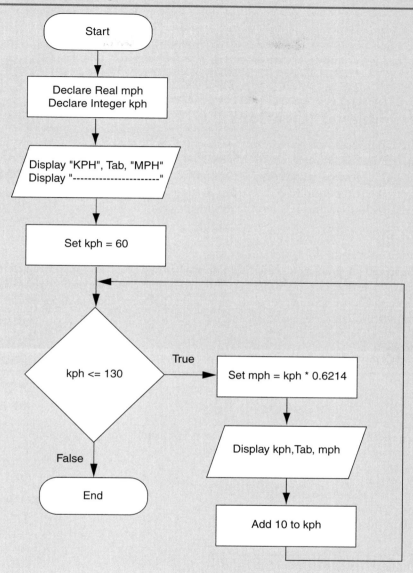

Counting Backward by Decrementing the Counter Variable

Although the counter variable is usually incremented in a count-controlled loop, you can alternatively decrement the counter variable. To *decrement* a variable means to decrease its value. In a For statement, you specify a negative step value to decrement the counter variable. For example, look at the following loop:

```
For counter = 10 To 1 Step -1
    Display counter
End For
```

In this loop, the starting value of the counter variable is 10, and its ending value is 1. The step value is –1, which means that 1 is subtracted from counter at the end of each iteration. During the first iteration, counter is 10; during the second iteration, counter is 9; and so forth. If this were an actual program, it would display the numbers 10, 9, 8, and so forth, down to 1.

Letting the User Control the Number of Iterations

In many cases, the programmer knows the exact number of iterations that a loop must perform. For example, recall Program 5-9, which displays a table showing the numbers 1 through 10 and their squares. When the pseudocode was written, the programmer knew that the loop had to iterate 10 times. A constant named MAX_VALUE was initialized with the value 10, and the loop was written as follows:

```
For counter = 1 To MAX_VALUE
```

As a result, the loop iterates exactly 10 times. Sometimes, however, the programmer needs to let the user decide the number of times that a loop should iterate. For example, what if you want Program 5-9 to be a bit more versatile by allowing the user to specify the maximum value displayed by the loop? The pseudocode in Program 5-12 shows how you can accomplish this.

Program 5-12

```
 1 // Variables
 2 Declare Integer counter, square, upperLimit
 3
 4 // Get the upper limit.
 5 Display "This program displays numbers, starting at 1,"
 6 Display "and their squares. How high should I go?"
 7 Input upperLimit
 8
 9 // Display table headings.
10 Display "Number", Tab, "Square"
11 Display "----------------------"
12
13 // Display the numbers and their squares.
14 For counter = 1 To upperLimit
15    // Calculate number squared.
16    Set square = counter^2
17
18    // Display number and number squared.
19    Display counter, Tab, square
20 End For
```

Program Output

```
This program displays numbers, starting at 1,
and their squares. How high should I go?
5 [Enter]
```

```
Number          Square
--------------------
   1                1
   2                4
   3                9
   4               16
   5               25
```

Lines 5 and 6 ask the user how high the numbers in the table should go, and the statement in line 7 stores the user's input in the upperLimit variable. Then, the For loop uses the upperLimit variable as the counter's ending value:

```
For counter = 1 To upperLimit
```

As a result, the counter variable starts with 1, and ends with the value in upperLimit. In addition to specifying the counter's ending value, you can also specify its starting value. The pseudocode in Program 5-13 shows an example. In this program, the user specifies both the starting value and the ending value of the numbers displayed in the table. Notice that in line 20 the For loop uses variables to specify both the starting and ending values of the counter variable.

Program 5-13

```
 1 // Variables
 2 Declare Integer counter, square,
 3         lowerLimit, upperLimit
 4
 5 // Get the lower limit.
 6 Display "This program displays numbers and"
 7 Display "their squares. What number should"
 8 Display "I start with?"
 9 Input lowerLimit
10
11 // Get the upper limit.
12 Display "What number should I end with?"
13 Input upperLimit
14
15 // Display table headings.
16 Display "Number", Tab, "Square"
17 Display "---------------------"
18
19 // Display the numbers and their squares.
20 For counter = lowerLimit To upperLimit
21     // Calculate number squared.
22     Set square = counter^2
23
24     // Display number and number squared.
25     Display counter, Tab, square
26 End For
```

Program Output

```
This program displays numbers and
their squares. What number should
I start with?
3 [Enter]
What number should I end with?
7 [Enter]
Number           Square
--------------------
    3               9
    4              16
    5              25
    6              36
    7              49
```

Designing a Count-Controlled While Loop

In most situations, it is best to use the For statement to write a count-controlled loop. Most languages, however, make it possible to use any looping mechanism to create a count-controlled loop. For example, you can create a count-controlled While loop, a count-controlled Do-While loop, or a count-controlled Do-Until loop. Regardless of the type of mechanism that you use, all count-controlled loops perform an initialization, test, and increment operation on a counter variable.

In pseudocode, you can use the following general format to write a count-controlled While loop:

```
① Declare Integer counter = startingValue    ◄──── Initialize a counter variable
                                                    to the starting value.

② While counter <= maxValue    ◄──── Compare the counter to the
                                      maximum value.

       statement
       statement
       statement

③      Set counter = counter + 1    ◄──── Add 1 to the counter variable during
                                          each iteration.
   End While
```

The ①, ②, and ③ callouts show where the initialization, test, and increment actions are performed.

① shows the declaration of an Integer variable that will be used as the counter. The variable is initialized with the appropriate starting value.

② shows where the While loop tests the expression counter <= maxValue. In this general format, maxValue is the maximum value that the counter variable can be set to.

③ shows where 1 is added to the counter variable. In a While loop, the counter variable will not automatically be incremented. You have to explicitly write a statement that performs this action. It's important that you understand how this statement works, so let's take a closer look at it:

```
Set counter = counter + 1
```

This is how the statement would be executed by the computer: First, the computer would get the value of the expression on the right side of the = operator, which is counter + 1. Then, that value would be assigned to the counter variable. The effect of the statement is that 1 is added to the counter variable.

 WARNING! If you forget to increment the counter variable in a count-controlled While loop, the loop will iterate an infinite number of times.

The pseudocode in Program 5-14 shows an example of a count-controlled While loop. This program follows the same logic that you previously saw in Figure 5-13, and displays "Hello world" five times. Figure 5-17 points out where the counter variable's initialization, test, and increment occur in the pseudocode.

Program 5-14

```
 1 // Declare and initialize a counter variable.
 2 Declare Integer counter = 1
 3
 4 // Constant for the maximum value
 5 Constant Integer MAX_VALUE = 5
 6
 7 While counter <= MAX_VALUE
 8    Display "Hello world"
 9    Set counter = counter + 1
10 End While
```

Program Output

```
Hello world
Hello world
Hello world
Hello world
Hello world
```

Figure 5-17 The initialization, test, and increment of the counter variable

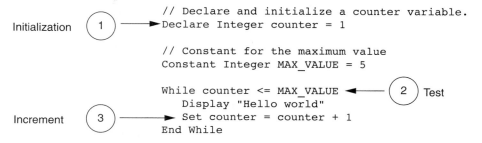

The pseudocode in Program 5-15 shows another example. This program produces the same output that was produced by Program 5-9: the numbers 1 through 10 and their squares. The flowchart that you previously saw in Figure 5-15 shows the logic of this program.

Program 5-15

```
 1 // Variables
 2 Declare Integer counter = 1
 3 Declare Integer square
 4
 5 // Constant for the maximum value
 6 Constant Integer MAX_VALUE = 10
 7
 8 // Display table headings.
 9 Display "Number", Tab, "Square"
10 Display "----------------------"
11
12 // Display the numbers 1 through 10 and
13 // their squares.
14 While counter <= MAX_VALUE
15     // Calculate the square of a number.
16     Set square = counter^2
17
18     // Display the number and its square.
19     Display counter, Tab, square
20
21     // Increment counter.
22     Set counter = counter + 1
23 End While
```

Program Output

```
Number          Square
----------------------
     1              1
     2              4
     3              9
     4             16
     5             25
     6             36
     7             49
     8             64
     9             81
    10            100
```

Incrementing by Values Other Than 1

In Programs 5-14 and 5-15 the counter variable is incremented by 1 during each loop iteration, with a statement such as this:

```
Set counter = counter + 1
```

This statement can be easily modified to increment the counter variable by values other than 1. For example, you could add 2 to the counter variable with the following statement:

```
Set counter = counter + 2
```

The pseudocode in Program 5-16 demonstrates how you can use this statement in a count-controlled While loop. The program displays all of the odd numbers from 1 through 11.

Program 5-16

```
 1 // Declare a counter variable
 2 Declare Integer counter = 1
 3
 4 // Constant for the maximum value
 5 Constant Integer MAX_VALUE = 11
 6
 7 // Display the odd numbers from 1
 8 // through 11.
 9 While counter <= MAX_VALUE
10    Display counter
11    Set counter = counter + 2
12 End While
```

Program Output

```
1
3
5
7
9
11
```

Counting Backward by Decrementing

Previously you saw how a negative step value can be used to decrement the counter variable in a For statement. In a count-controlled While loop, you decrement the counter variable with a statement such as the following:

```
Set counter = counter − 1
```

This statement subtracts one from the counter variable. If the counter variable is set to the value 5 before this statement executes, it will be set to 4 after the statement executes. The pseudocode in Program 5-17 demonstrates how you can use this statement in a While loop. The program counts backward from 10 down to 1.

Program 5-17

```
 1 // Declare a counter variable
 2 Declare Integer counter = 10
 3
 4 // Constant for the minimum value
 5 Constant Integer MIN_VALUE = 1
 6
 7 // Display a count-down.
 8 Display "And the countdown begins..."
```

```
 9 While counter >= MIN_VALUE
10      Display counter
11      Set counter = counter - 1
12 End While
13 Display "Blast off!"
```

Program Output

```
And the countdown begins...
10
9
8
7
6
5
4
3
2
1
Blast off!
```

Let's take a closer look at this program. Notice that line 11 subtracts 1 from the counter variable. Because we are counting backward, we have to reverse many parts of the logic. For example, in line 2 the counter variable must be initialized with the value 10 instead of 1. This is because 10 is the counter's starting value in this program. Also, in line 5 we create a constant to represent the counter's minimum value (which is 1) instead of the maximum value. Because we are counting down, we want the loop to stop when it reaches 1. Finally, notice that we are using the >= relational operator in line 9. In this program we want the loop to iterate as long as the counter is greater than or equal to 1. When the counter becomes less than 1, the loop should stop.

Checkpoint

5.10 What is a counter variable?

5.11 What three actions do count-controlled loops typically perform using the counter variable?

5.12 When you increment a variable, what are you doing? When you decrement a variable, what are you doing?

5.13 Look at the following pseudocode. If it were a real program, what would it display?

```
Declare Integer number = 5
Set number = number + 1
Display number
```

5.14 Look at the following pseudocode. If it were a real program, what would it display?

```
Declare Integer counter
For counter = 1 To 5
   Display counter
End For
```

5.15 Look at the following pseudocode. If it were a real program, what would it display?

```
Declare Integer counter
For counter = 0 To 500 Step 100
   Display counter
End For
```

5.16 Look at the following pseudocode. If it were a real program, what would it display?

```
Declare Integer counter = 1
Constant Integer MAX = 8
While counter <= MAX
    Display counter
    Set counter = counter + 1
End While
```

5.17 Look at the following pseudocode. If it were a real program, what would it display?

```
Declare Integer counter = 1
Constant Integer MAX = 7
While counter <= MAX
    Display counter
    Set counter = counter + 2
End While
```

5.18 Look at the following pseudocode. If it were a real program, what would it display?

```
Declare Integer counter
Constant Integer MIN = 1
While counter = 5 To MIN Step -1
    Display counter
End For
```

5.4 Calculating a Running Total

CONCEPT: A running total is a sum of numbers that accumulates with each iteration of a loop. The variable used to keep the running total is called an accumulator.

Many programming tasks require you to calculate the total of a series of numbers. For example, suppose you are writing a program that calculates a business's total sales for a week. The program would read the sales for each day as input and calculate the total of those numbers.

Programs that calculate the total of a series of numbers typically use two elements:

- A loop that reads each number in the series.
- A variable that accumulates the total of the numbers as they are read.

The variable that is used to accumulate the total of the numbers is called an *accumulator*. It is often said that the loop keeps a *running total* because it accumulates the total as it reads each number in the series. Figure 5-18 shows the general logic of a loop that calculates a running total.

Figure 5-18 Logic for calculating a running total

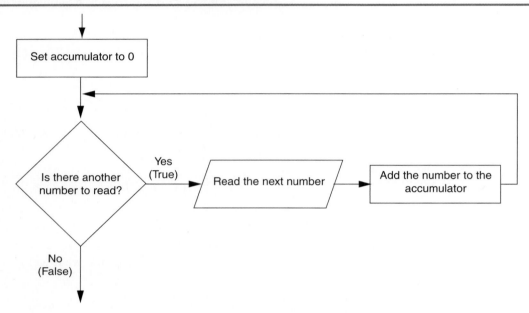

When the loop finishes, the accumulator will contain the total of the numbers that were read by the loop. Notice that the first step in the flowchart is to set the accumulator variable to 0. This is a critical step. Each time the loop reads a number, it adds it to the accumulator. If the accumulator starts with any value other than 0, it will not contain the correct total when the loop finishes.

Let's look at the design of a program that calculates a running total. The pseudocode shown in Program 5-18 allows the user to enter five numbers, and it displays the total of the numbers entered.

Program 5-18

```
 1 // Declare a variable to hold each number
 2 // entered by the user.
 3 Declare Integer number
 4
 5 // Declare an accumulator variable,
 6 // initialized with 0.
 7 Declare Integer total = 0
 8
 9 // Declare a counter variable for the loop.
10 Declare Integer counter
```

```
11
12 // Explain what we are doing.
13 Display "This program calculates the"
14 Display "total of five numbers."
15
16 // Get five numbers and accumulate them.
17 For counter = 1 To 5
18    Display "Enter a number."
19    Input number
20    Set total = total + number
21 End For
22
23 // Display the total of the numbers.
24 Display "The total is ", total
```

Program Output (with Input Shown in Bold)

```
This program calculates the
total of five numbers.
Enter a number.
2 [Enter]
Enter a number.
4 [Enter]
Enter a number.
6 [Enter]
Enter a number.
8 [Enter]
Enter a number.
10 [Enter]
The total is 30
```

First, let's look at the variable declarations. The number variable, declared in line 3, will be used to hold a number entered by the user. The total variable, declared in line 7, is the accumulator. Notice that it is initialized with the value 0. The counter variable, declared in line 10, will be used as a counter by the loop.

The For loop, in lines 17 through 21, does the work of getting the numbers from the user and calculating their total. Line 18 prompts the user to enter a number, and line 19 gets the user's input and stores it in the number variable. Then, the following statement in line 20 adds number to total:

```
Set total = total + number
```

After this statement executes, the value in the number variable will be added to the value in the total variable. When the loop finishes, the total variable will hold the sum of all the numbers that were added to it. This value is displayed in line 24. Figure 5-19 shows a flowchart for the Program 5-18.

Figure 5-19 Flowchart for Program 5-18

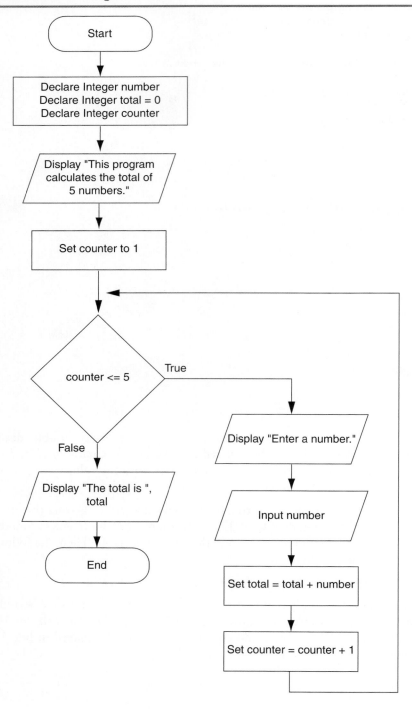

 **Checkpoint**

5.19 A program that calculates the total of a series of numbers typically has what two elements?

5.20 What is an accumulator?

5.21 Should an accumulator be initialized to any specific value? Why or why not?

5.22 Look at the following pseudocode. If it were a real program, what would it display?

```
Declare Integer number1 = 10, number2 = 5
Set number1 = number1 + number2
Display number1
Display number2
```

5.23 Look at the following pseudocode. If it were a real program, what would it display?

```
Declare Integer counter, total = 0
For counter = 1 To 5
    Set total = total + counter
End For
Display total
```

5.5 Sentinels

CONCEPT: A sentinel is a special value that marks the end of a list of values.

Consider the following scenario: You are designing a program that will use a loop to process a long list of values. At the time you are designing the program, you do not know the number of values that will be in the list. In fact, the number of values in the list could be different each time the program is executed. What is the best way to design such a loop? Here are some techniques that you have seen already in this chapter, along with the disadvantages of using them when processing a long list of values:

- Simply ask the user, at the end of each loop iteration, if there is another value to process. If the list of values is long, however, asking this question at the end of each loop iteration might make the program cumbersome for the user.
- Ask the user at the beginning of the program how many items the list contains. This might also inconvenience the user, however. If the list is very long, and the user does not know the number of items in the list, it will require the user to count them.

When processing a long list of values with a loop, perhaps a better technique is to use a sentinel. A *sentinel* is a special value that marks the end of a list of items. When a program reads the sentinel value, it knows it has reached the end of the list, so the loop terminates. For example, suppose a doctor wants a program to calculate the average weight of all her patients. The program might work like this: A loop prompts the user to enter either a patient's weight, or 0 if there are no more weights. When the program reads 0 as a weight, it interprets this as a signal that there are no more weights. The loop ends and the program displays the average weight.

A sentinel value must be unique enough that it will not be mistaken as a regular value in the list. In the example cited above, the doctor (or her medical assistant) enters 0 to signal the end of the list of weights. Because no patient's weight will be 0, this is a good value to use as a sentinel.

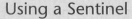

In the Spotlight:
Using a Sentinel

The county tax office calculates the annual taxes on property using the following formula:

$$Property\ Tax = Property\ Value \times 0.0065$$

Every day, a clerk in the tax office gets a list of properties and has to calculate the tax for each property on the list. You have been asked to design a program that the clerk can use to perform these calculations.

In your interview with the tax clerk, you learn that each property is assigned a lot number, and all lot numbers are 1 or greater. You decide to write a loop that uses the number 0 as a sentinel value. During each loop iteration, the program will ask the clerk to enter either a property's lot number, or 0 to end. Program 5-19 shows the pseudocode for the program, and Figure 5-20 shows a flowchart.

Program 5-19

```
 1 Module main()
 2    // Local variable for the lot number
 3    Declare Integer lotNumber
 4
 5    // Get the first lot number.
 6    Display "Enter the property's lot number"
 7    Display "(or enter 0 to end)."
 8    Input lotNumber
 9
10    // Continue processing as long as the user
11    // does not enter lot number 0.
12    While lotNumber ! = 0
13       // Show the tax for the property.
14       Call showTax()
15
```

```
16          // Get the next lot number.
17          Display "Enter the lot number for the"
18          Display "next property (or 0 to end)."
19          Input lotNumber
20      End While
21 End Module
22
23 // The showTax module gets a property's
24 // value and displays its tax.
25 Module showTax()
26      // Local variables
27      Declare Real propertyValue, tax
28
29      // Constant for the tax factor.
30      Constant Real TAX_FACTOR = 0.0065
31
32      // Get the property's value.
33      Display "Enter the property's value."
34      Input propertyValue
35
36      // Calculate the property's tax.
37      Set tax = propertyValue * TAX_FACTOR
38
39      // Display the tax.
40      Display "The property's tax is $", tax
41 End Module
```

Program Output (with Input Shown in Bold)

```
Enter the property's lot number
(or enter 0 to end).
417 [Enter]
Enter the property's value.
100000 [Enter]
The property's tax is $650
Enter the lot number for the
next property(or 0 to end).
692 [Enter]
Enter the property's value.
60000 [Enter]
The property's tax is $390
Enter the lot number for the
next property(or 0 to end).
0 [Enter]
```

Figure 5-20 Flowchart for Program 5-19

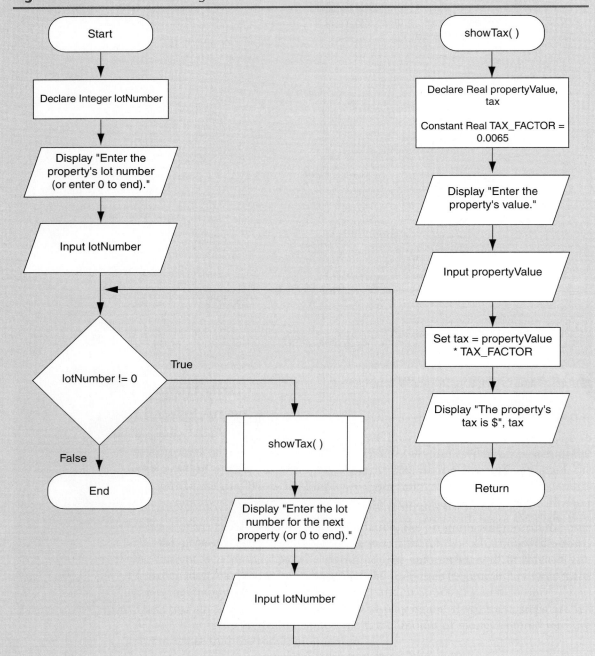

![Checkpoint]

Checkpoint

5.24 Why should you take care to choose a unique value as a sentinel?

5.25 What is a sentinel?

5.6 Nested Loops

CONCEPT: A loop that is inside another loop is called a nested loop.

A nested loop is a loop that is inside another loop. A clock is a good example of something that works like a nested loop. The second hand, minute hand, and hour hand all spin around the face of the clock. The hour hand, however, only makes 1 revolution for every 12 of the minute hand's revolutions. And it takes 60 revolutions of the second hand for the minute hand to make 1 revolution. This means that for every complete revolution of the hour hand, the second hand has revolved 720 times. Here is pseudocode with a loop that partially simulates a digital clock. It displays the seconds from 0 to 59:

```
Declare Integer seconds
For seconds = 0 To 59
    Display seconds
End For
```

We can add a `minutes` variable and nest the loop above inside another loop that cycles through 60 minutes:

```
Declare Integer minutes, seconds
For minutes = 0 To 59
    For seconds = 0 To 59
        Display minutes, ":", seconds
    End For
End For
```

To make the simulated clock complete, another variable and loop can be added to count the hours:

```
Declare Integer hours, minutes, seconds
For hours = 0 To 23
    For minutes = 0 To 59
        For seconds = 0 To 59
            Display hours, ":", minutes, ":", seconds
        End For
    End For
End For
```

If this were a real program, its output would be:

```
0:0:0
0:0:1
0:0:2
```

(The program will count through each second of 24 hours.)

```
23:59:59
```

The innermost loop will iterate 60 times for each iteration of the middle loop. The middle loop will iterate 60 times for each iteration of the outermost loop. When the outermost loop has iterated 24 times, the middle loop will have iterated 1,440 times and the innermost loop will have iterated 86,400 times! Figure 5-21 shows a flowchart for the complete clock simulation program previously shown.

Figure 5-21 Flowchart for a clock simulator

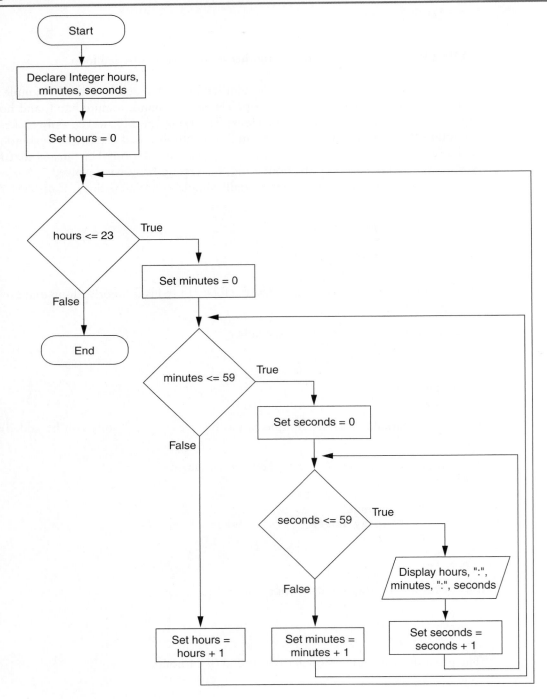

The simulated clock example brings up a few points about nested loops:

- An inner loop goes through all of its iterations for every single iteration of an outer loop.
- Inner loops complete their iterations faster than outer loops.
- To get the total number of iterations of a nested loop, multiply the number of iterations of all the loops.

Review Questions

Multiple Choice

1. A _____-controlled loop uses a true/false condition to control the number of times that it repeats.
   a. Boolean
   b. condition
   c. decision
   d. count

2. A _____-controlled loop repeats a specific number of times.
   a. Boolean
   b. condition
   c. decision
   d. count

3. Each repetition of a loop is known as a(n) _____.
   a. cycle
   b. revolution
   c. orbit
   d. iteration

4. The While loop is a _____ type of loop.
   a. pretest
   b. posttest
   c. prequalified
   d. post iterative

5. The Do-While loop is a _____ type of loop.
   a. pretest
   b. posttest
   c. prequalified
   d. post iterative

6. The For loop is a _____ type of loop.
   a. pretest
   b. posttest
   c. prequalified
   d. post iterative

7. A(n) _____ loop has no way of ending and repeats until the program is interrupted.
   a. indeterminate
   b. interminable
   c. infinite
   d. timeless

8. A _____ loop always executes at least once.
   a. pretest
   b. posttest
   c. condition-controlled
   d. count-controlled

9. A(n) _____ variable keeps a running total.
   a. sentinel
   b. sum
   c. total
   d. accumulator

10. A(n) _____ is a special value that signals when there are no more items from a list of items to be processed. This value cannot be mistaken as an item from the list.
    a. sentinel
    b. flag
    c. signal
    d. accumulator

True or False

1. A condition-controlled loop always repeats a specific number of times.

2. The While loop is a pretest loop.

3. The Do-While loop is a pretest loop.

4. You should not write code that modifies the contents of the counter variable in the body of a For loop.

5. You cannot display the contents of the counter variable in the body of a loop.

6. It is not possible to increment a counter variable by any value other than 1.

7. The following statement decrements the variable x: Set x = x - 1.

8. It is not necessary to initialize accumulator variables.

9. In a nested loop, the inner loop goes through all of its iterations for every single iteration of the outer loop.

10. To calculate the total number of iterations of a nested loop, add the number of iterations of all the loops.

Short Answer

1. Why should you indent the statements in the body of a loop?

2. Describe the difference between pretest loops and posttest loops.

3. What is a condition-controlled loop?

4. What is a count-controlled loop?

5. What three actions do count-controlled loops typically perform using the counter variable?

6. What is an infinite loop? Write the code for an infinite loop.

7. A `For` loop looks like what other loop in a flowchart?

8. Why is it critical that accumulator variables are properly initialized?

9. What is the advantage of using a sentinel?

10. Why must the value chosen for use as a sentinel be carefully selected?

Algorithm Workbench

1. Design a `While` loop that lets the user enter a number. The number should be multiplied by 10, and the result stored in a variable named `product`. The loop should iterate as long as `product` contains a value less than 100.

2. Design a `Do-While` loop that asks the user to enter two numbers. The numbers should be added and the sum displayed. The loop should ask the user if he or she wishes to perform the operation again. If so, the loop should repeat, otherwise it should terminate.

3. Design a `For` loop that displays the following set of numbers:

    0, 10, 20, 30, 40, 50 . . . 1000

4. Design a loop that asks the user to enter a number. The loop should iterate 10 times and keep a running total of the numbers entered.

5. Design a `For` loop that calculates the total of the following series of numbers:

$$\frac{1}{30} + \frac{2}{29} + \frac{3}{28} + \dots \frac{30}{1}$$

6. Design a nested loop that displays 10 rows of # characters. There should be 15 # characters in each row.

7. Convert the `While` loop in the following code to a `Do-While` loop:

```
Declare Integer x = 1
While x > 0
   Display "Enter a number."
   Input x
End While
```

8. Convert the Do-While loop in the following code to a While loop:

```
Declare String sure
Do
    Display "Are you sure you want to quit?"
    Input sure
While sure != "Y" AND sure != "y"
```

9. Convert the following While loop to a For loop:

```
Declare Integer count = 0
While count < 50
    Display "The count is ", count
    Set count = count + 1
End While
```

10. Convert the following For loop to a While loop:

```
Declare Integer count
For count = 1 To 50
    Display count
End For
```

Programming Exercises

VideoNote

The Bug
Collector
Problem

1. **Bug Collector**

   A bug collector collects bugs every day for seven days. Design a program that keeps a running total of the number of bugs collected during the seven days. The loop should ask for the number of bugs collected for each day, and when the loop is finished, the program should display the total number of bugs collected.

2. **Calories Burned**

   Running on a particular treadmill you burn 3.9 calories per minute. Design a program that uses a loop to display the number of calories burned after 10, 15, 20, 25, and 30 minutes.

3. **Budget Analysis**

   Design a program that asks the user to enter the amount that he or she has budgeted for a month. A loop should then prompt the user to enter each of his or her expenses for the month, and keep a running total. When the loop finishes, the program should display the amount that the user is over or under budget.

4. **Sum of Numbers**

   Design a program with a loop that asks the user enter a series of positive numbers. The user should enter a negative number to signal the end of the series. After all the positive numbers have been entered, the program should display their sum.

5. **Tuition Increase**

   At one college, the tuition for a full-time student is $6,000 per semester. It has been announced that the tuition will increase by 2 percent each year for the next five years. Design a program with a loop that displays the projected semester tuition amount for the next five years.

6. **Distance Traveled**

The distance a vehicle travels can be calculated as follows:

$$Distance = Speed \times Time$$

For example, if a train travels 40 miles per hour for three hours, the distance traveled is 120 miles. Design a program that asks the user for the speed of a vehicle (in miles per hour) and how many hours it has traveled. It should then use a loop to display the distance the vehicle has traveled for each hour of that time period. Here is an example of the output:

```
What is the speed of the vehicle in mph? 40 [Enter]
How many hours has it traveled? 3 [Enter]
Hour          Distance Traveled
_____

  1                 40
  2                 80
  3                120
```

7. **Average Rainfall**

Design a program that uses nested loops to collect data and calculate the average rainfall over a period of years. The program should first ask for the number of years. The outer loop will iterate once for each year. The inner loop will iterate twelve times, once for each month. Each iteration of the inner loop will ask the user for the inches of rainfall for that month. After all iterations, the program should display the number of months, the total inches of rainfall, and the average rainfall per month for the entire period.

8. **Celsius to Fahrenheit Table**

Design a program that displays a table of the Celsius temperatures 0 through 20 and their Fahrenheit equivalents. The formula for converting a temperature from Celsius to Fahrenheit is

$$F = \frac{9}{5}C + 32$$

where F is the Fahrenheit temperature and C is the Celsius temperature. Your program must use a loop to display the table.

9. **Pennies for Pay**

Design a program that calculates the amount of money a person would earn over a period of time if his or her salary is one penny the first day, two pennies the second day, and continues to double each day. The program should ask the user for the number of days. Display a table showing what the salary was for each day, and then show the total pay at the end of the period. The output should be displayed in a dollar amount, not the number of pennies.

10. **Largest and Smallest**

Design a program with a loop that lets the user enter a series of numbers. The user should enter –99 to signal the end of the series. After all the numbers have been entered, the program should display the largest and smallest numbers entered.

11. **First and Last**

    Design a program that asks the user for a series of names (in no particular order). After the final person's name has been entered, the program should display the name that is first alphabetically and the name that is last alphabetically. For example, if the user enters the names Kristin, Joel, Adam, Beth, Zeb, and Chris, the program would display Adam and Zeb.

12. **Calculating the Factorial of a Number**

    In mathematics, the notation $n!$ represents the factorial of the nonnegative integer n. The factorial of n is the product of all the nonnegative integers from 1 up through n. For example:

    $$7! = 1 \times 2 \times 3 \times 4 \times 5 \times 6 \times 7 = 5,040$$

    and

    $$4! = 1 \times 2 \times 3 \times 4 = 24$$

    Design a program that asks the user to enter a nonnegative integer and then displays the factorial of that number.

Functions

6.1 Introduction to Functions: Generating Random Numbers

CONCEPT: A *function* is a module that returns a value back to the part of the program that called it. Most programming languages provide a library of prewritten functions that perform commonly needed tasks. In these libraries you typically find a function that generates random numbers.

In Chapter 3 you learned that a module is a group of statements that exist within a program for the purpose of performing a specific task. When you need the module to perform its task, you call the module. This causes the program to execute the statement inside the module.

A *function* is a special type of module. It is like a regular module in the following ways:

- A function is a group of statements that perform a specific task.
- When you want to execute a function, you call it.

When a function finishes, however, it returns a value back to the part of the program that called it. The value that is returned from a function can be used like any other value: it can be assigned to a variable, displayed on the screen, used in a mathematical expression (if it is a number), and so on.

Library Functions

Most programming languages come with a library of functions that have already been written. These functions, known as *library functions*, are built into the programming language, and you can call them any time you need them. Library functions make a programmer's job easier because they perform many of the tasks that programmers commonly need to perform. As you will see in this chapter, there are library functions to manipulate numbers and perform various math operations, to convert data from one type to another, to manipulate strings, and more.

The code for a language's library functions is usually stored in special files. These files are normally placed on your computer when you install a compiler or interpreter. When you call a library function in one of your programs, the compiler or interpreter automatically causes the function to execute, without requiring the function's code to appear in your program. This way, you never have to see the code for a library function—you only need to know the purpose of the library function, the arguments that you must pass to it, and what type of data it returns.

Because you do not see the internal workings of library functions, many programmers think of them as *black boxes*. The term "black box" is used to describe any mechanism that accepts input, performs some operation that cannot be seen on the input, and produces output. Figure 6-1 illustrates this idea.

Figure 6-1 A library function viewed as a black box

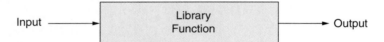

This section demonstrates how functions work by looking at a library function that generates random numbers. Most programming languages provide such a function, and we will look at some interesting programs that can be written with it. In the next section you will learn to write your own functions. The last section in this chapter comes back to the topic of library functions and looks at several other useful functions that programming languages commonly provide.

Using the `random` Function

Most programming languages provide a library function that generates random numbers. This chapter uses the `random` function for this purpose in the pseudocode. Random numbers are useful for lots of different programming tasks. The following are just a few examples:

- Random numbers are commonly used in games. For example, computer games that let the player roll dice use random numbers to represent the values of the dice. Programs that show cards being drawn from a shuffled deck use random numbers to represent the face values of the cards.
- Random numbers are useful in simulation programs. In some simulations, the computer must randomly decide how a person, animal, insect, or other living being will behave. Formulas can be constructed in which a random number is used to determine various actions and events that take place in the program.

- Random numbers are useful in statistical programs that must randomly select data for analysis.
- Random numbers are commonly used in computer security to encrypt sensitive data.

The following pseudocode statement shows an example of how you might call the random function. Assume that `number` is an `Integer` variable.

```
Set number = random(1, 100)
```

The part of the statement that reads `random(1, 100)` is a call to the `random` function. Notice that two arguments appear inside the parentheses: 1 and 100. These arguments tell the function to give a random number in the range of 1 through 100. Figure 6-2 illustrates this part of the statement.

Figure 6-2 A statement that calls the `random` function

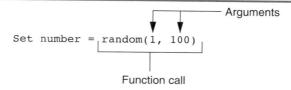

Notice that the call to the `random` function appears on the right side of an = operator. When the function is called, it will generate a random number in the range of 1 through 100 and then *return* that number. The number that is returned will be assigned to the `number` variable, as shown in Figure 6-3.

Figure 6-3 The `random` function returns a value

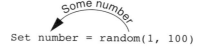

A random number in the range of
1 through 100 will be assigned to
the `number` variable.

Program 6-1 shows the pseudocode for a complete program that uses the `random` function. The statement in line 2 generates a random number in the range of 1 through 10 and assigns it to the `number` variable. (The program output shows that the number 7 was generated, but this value is arbitrary. If this were an actual program, it could display any number between 1 and 10.)

Program 6-1

```
1 Declare Integer number
2 Set number = random(1, 10)
3 Display number
```

Program Output

```
7
```

NOTE: The way that you set up a program to work with library functions differs among programming languages. In some languages you don't have to do anything special to call library functions. That's the approach we take in our pseudocode. In other languages, however, you may have to write a statement near the top of a program indicating that it will access a particular library function.

The pseudocode in Program 6-2 shows another example. This program uses a `For` loop that iterates five times. Inside the loop, the statement in line 9 calls the `random` function to generate a random number in the range of 1 through 100.

Program 6-2

```
 1 // Declare variables
 2 Declare Integer number, counter
 3
 4 // The following loop displays
 5 // five random numbers.
 6 For counter = 1 To 5
 7    // Get a random number in the range of
 8    // 1 through 100 and assign it to number.
 9    Set number = random(1, 100)
10
11    // Display the number.
12    Display number
13 End For
```

Program Output

```
89
7
16
41
12
```

The pseudocode in both Programs 6-1 and 6-2 calls the `random` function and assigns its return value to the `number` variable. If you just want to display a random number, it is not necessary to assign the `random` number to a variable. You can send the `random` function's return value directly to the `Display` statement, as shown here:

```
Display random(1, 10)
```

When this statement executes, the `random` function is called. The function generates a random number in the range of 1 through 10. That value is returned and then sent to the `Display` statement. As a result, a random number in the range of 1 through 10 will be displayed. Figure 6-4 illustrates this.

The pseudocode in Program 6-3 shows how you could simplify Program 6-2. This program also displays five random numbers, but this program does not use a variable to hold those numbers. The `random` function's return value is sent directly to the `Display` statement in line 4.

Figure 6-4 Displaying a random number

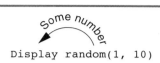

Display random(1, 10)

A random number in the range of
1 through 10 will be displayed.

Program 6-3

```
1 // Counter variable
2 Declare Integer counter
3
4 // This loop displays five random numbers.
5 For counter = 1 To 5
6     Display random(1, 100)
7 End For
```

Program Output

```
32
79
6
12
98
```

In the Spotlight:

Using Random Numbers

Dr. Kimura teaches an introductory statistics class, and has asked you to write a program that he can use in class to simulate the rolling of dice. The program should randomly generate two numbers in the range of 1 through 6 and display them. In your interview with Dr. Kimura, you learn that he would like to use the program to simulate several rolls of the dice, one after the other. You decide to write a loop that simulates one roll of the dice, and then asks the user if another roll should be performed. As long as the user answers "y" for yes, the loop will repeat. Program 6-4 shows the pseudocode for the program, and Figure 6-5 shows the flowchart.

Program 6-4

```
 1 // Declare a variable to control the
 2 // loop iterations.
 3 Declare String again
 4
 5 Do
 6     // Roll the dice.
 7     Display "Rolling the dice..."
 8     Display "Their values are:"
 9     Display random(1, 6)
10     Display random(1, 6)
```

```
11
12    // Do this again?
13    Display "Want to roll them again? (y = yes)"
14    Input again
15 While again == "y" OR again == "Y"
```

Program Output with Input Shown in Bold

```
Rolling the dice...
Their values are:
2
6
Want to roll them again? (y = yes)
y [Enter]
Rolling the dice...
Their values are:
4
1
Want to roll them again? (y = yes)
y [Enter]
Rolling the dice...
Their values are:
3
3
Want to roll them again? (y = yes)
n [Enter]
```

Figure 6-5 Flowchart for Program 6-4

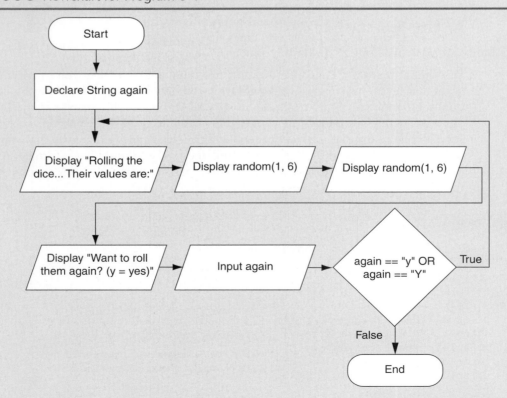

The `random` function returns an integer value, so you can write a call to the function anywhere that you can write an integer value. You have already seen examples where the function's return value is assigned to a variable and where the function's return value is sent to the `Display` statement. To further illustrate the point, here is a statement that uses the `random` function in a math expression:

```
Set x = random(1, 10) * 2
```

In this statement, a random number in the range of 1 through 10 is generated and then multiplied by 2. The result is assigned to the x variable. You can also test the return value of the function with an `If-Then` statement, as demonstrated in the following In the Spotlight section.

In the Spotlight:
Using Random Numbers to
Represent Other Values

Dr. Kimura was so happy with the dice rolling simulator that you wrote for him, he has asked you to write one more program. He would like a program that he can use to simulate ten coin flips, one after the other. Each time the program simulates a coin flip, it should randomly display either "Heads" or "Tails."

You decide that you can simulate the flipping of a coin by randomly generating a number in the range of 1 through 2. You will design a decision structure that displays "Heads" if the random number is 1, or "Tails" otherwise. Program 6-5 shows the pseudocode for the program, and Figure 6-6 shows the flowchart.

Program 6-5

```
 1 // Declare a counter variable.
 2 Declare Integer counter
 3
 4 // Constant for the number of flips.
 5 Constant Integer NUM_FLIPS = 10
 6
 7 For counter = 1 To NUM_FLIPS
 8     // Simulate the coin flip.
 9     If random(1, 2) == 1 Then
10         Display "Heads"
11     Else
12         Display "Tails"
13     End If
14 End For
```

Program Output

```
Tails
Tails
Heads
Tails
```

```
Heads
Heads
Heads
Tails
Heads
Tails
```

Figure 6-6 Flowchart for Program 6-5

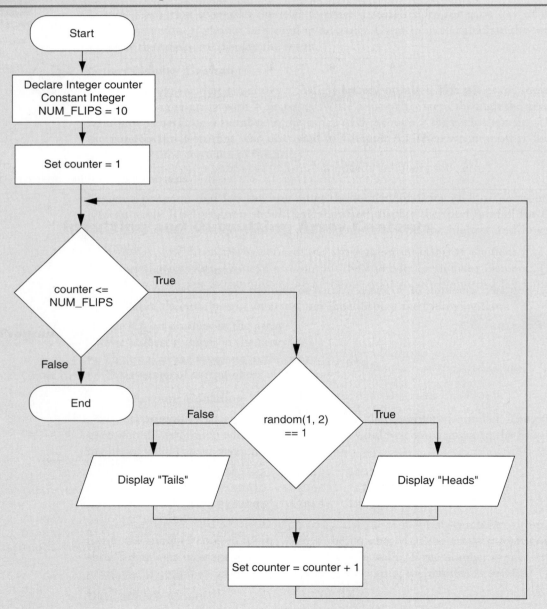

Checkpoint

6.1 How does a function differ from a module?

6.2 What is a library function?

6.3 Why are library functions like "black boxes"?

6.4 In pseudocode, what does the following statement do?
```
Set x = random(1, 100)
```

6.5 In pseudocode, what does the following statement do?
```
Display random(1, 20)
```

6.2 Writing Your Own Functions

CONCEPT: Most programming languages allow you to write your own functions. When you write a function, you are essentially writing a module that can send a value back to the part of the program that called it.

Recall from Chapter 3 that when you create a module you write its definition. Functions are defined in a manner similar to modules. The following are the important characteristics of a function definition.

VideoNote

Writing a
Function

- The first line of a function definition, the *function header,* specifies the data type of the value that is returned from the function, the name of the function, and any parameter variables used by the function to accept arguments.
- Following the function header is the *function body,* which is comprised of one or more statements that are executed when the function is called.
- One of the statements in the function body must be a `Return` statement. A `Return` statement specifies the value that is returned from the function when the function ends.

Here is the general format that we will use for writing functions in pseudocode:

```
Function DataType FunctionName(ParameterList)
    statement
    statement
    etc.                        A function must have a Return statement. This causes a
    Return value         ◀───  value to be sent back to the part of the program that called
End Function                   the function.
```

The first line in this pseudocode, the function header, begins with the word `Function` and is followed by these items:

- `DataType` is the data type of the value that the function returns. For example, if the function returns an integer, the word `Integer` will appear here. If the function returns a real number, the word `Real` will appear here. Likewise, if the function returns a string, the word `String` will appear here.

- *FunctionName* is the name of the function. As with modules, you should give a function a name that describes what the function does. In most languages you follow the same rules for naming functions that you follow for naming modules and variables.
- An optional parameter list appears inside a set of parentheses. If the function does not accept arguments, then an empty set of parentheses will appear.

On the line after the function header, one or more statements will appear. These statements, the function's body, are performed any time the function is executed. One of the statements in the body must be a Return statement, which takes the following form:

```
Return value
```

The *value* that follows the word Return is the value that the function will send back to the part of the program that called the function. This can be any value, variable, or expression that has a value (such as a math expression). The value that is returned must be of the same data type as that specified in the function header. Otherwise, an error will occur.

The last line of the definition, after the body, reads End Function. This line marks the end of the function definition.

Here is an example of a function written in pseudocode:

```
Function Integer sum(Integer num1, Integer num2)
   Declare Integer result
   Set result = num1 + num2
   Return result
End Function
```

Figure 6-7 illustrates the various parts of the function header. Notice that the function returns an Integer, the function's name is sum, and the function has two Integer parameters, named num1 and num2.

Figure 6-7 Parts of the function header

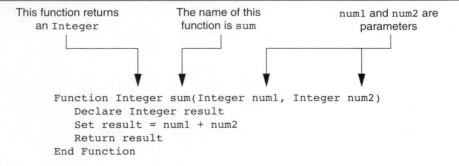

The purpose of this function is to accept two integer values as arguments and return their sum. Let's look at the body of the function to see how it works. The first statement, a variable declaration, declares a local Integer variable named result. The next statement assigns the value of num1 + num2 to the result variable. Next, the Return statement executes, which causes the function to end execution and sends the value in the result variable back to the part of the program that called the function.

Program 6-6 shows a complete pseudocode program that uses the function.

Program 6-6

```
 1 Module main()
 2     // Local variables
 3     Declare Integer firstAge, secondAge, total
 4
 5     // Get the user's age and the user's
 6     // best friend's age.
 7     Display "Enter your age."
 8     Input firstAge
 9     Display "Enter your best friend's age."
10     Input secondAge
11
12     // Get the sum of both ages.
13     Set total = sum(firstAge, secondAge)
14
15     // Display the sum.
16     Display "Together you are ", total, " years old."
17 End Module
18
19 // The sum function accepts two Integer arguments and
20 // returns the sum of those arguments as an Integer.
21 Function Integer sum(Integer num1, Integer num2)
22     Declare Integer result
23     Set result = num1 + num2
24     Return result
25 End Function
```

Program Output (with Input Shown in Bold)

```
Enter your age.
22 [Enter]
Enter your best friend's age.
24 [Enter]
Together you are 46 years old.
```

In the main module, the program gets two integer values from the user and stores them in the firstAge and secondAge variables. The statement in line 13 calls the sum function, passing firstAge and secondAge as arguments. The value that is returned from the sum function is assigned to the total variable. In this case, the function will return 46. Figure 6-8 shows how the arguments are passed into the function, and how a value is returned back from the function.

Figure 6-8 Arguments are passed to the sum function and a value is returned

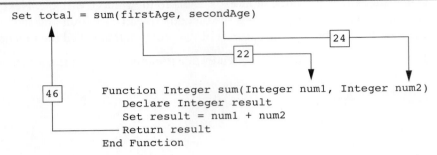

Flowcharting a Function

When creating a flowchart for a program that has functions, you draw a separate flowchart for each function. In a flowchart for a function, the starting terminal symbol usually shows the name of the function, along with any parameters that the function has. The ending terminal symbol reads *Return,* followed by the value or expression that is being returned. Figure 6-9 shows the flowchart for the sum function in Program 6-6.

Figure 6-9 Flowchart for the sum function

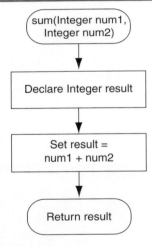

Making the Most of the Return Statement

Look again at the sum function presented in Program 6-6:

```
Function Integer sum(Integer num1, Integer num2)
   Declare Integer result
   Set result = num1 + num2
   Return result
End Function
```

Notice that three things happen inside this function: (1) a local variable, result, is declared, (2) the value of the expression num1 + num2 is assigned to the result variable, and (3) the value of the result variable is returned.

Although this function does what it sets out to do, it can be simplified. Because the Return statement can return the value of an expression, you can eliminate the result variable and rewrite the function as:

```
Function Integer sum(Integer num1, Integer num2)
   Return num1 + num2
End Function
```

This version of the function does not store the value of num1 + num2 in a variable. Instead, it takes advantage of the fact that the Return statement can return the value of an expression. This version of the function does the same thing as the previous version, but in only one step.

> **NOTE:** In most programming languages you can pass as many arguments into a function as you need, but you can return only one value from a function.

How to Use Functions

Most programming languages allow you to create both modules and functions. Functions provide many of the same benefits as modules: they simplify code, reduce duplication, enhance your ability to test code, increase the speed of development, and ease the facilitation of teamwork.

Because functions return a value, they can be useful in specific situations. For example, you can use a function to prompt the user for input, and then it can return the value entered by the user. Suppose you've been asked to design a program that calculates the sale price of an item in a retail business. To do that, the program would need to get the item's regular price from the user. Here is a function you could define for that purpose:

```
Function Real getRegularPrice()
   // Local variable to hold the price.
   Declare Real price

   // Get the regular price.
   Display "Enter the item's regular price."
   Input price

   // Return the regular price.
   Return price
End Function
```

Then, elsewhere in the program, you could call that function, as shown here:

```
   // Get the item's regular price.
   Set regularPrice = getRegularPrice()
```

When this statement executes, the getRegularPrice function is called, which gets a value from the user and returns it. That value is then assigned to the regularPrice variable.

You can also use functions to simplify complex mathematical expressions. For example, calculating the sale price of an item seems like it would be a simple task: you calculate the discount and subtract it from the regular price. In a program, however, a statement that performs this calculation is not that straightforward, as shown in the following example. (Assume DISCOUNT_PERCENTAGE is a global constant that is defined in the program, and it specifies the percentage of the discount.)

```
Set salePrice = regularPrice —
    (regularPrice * DISCOUNT_PERCENTAGE)
```

This statement isn't easy to understand because it performs so many steps: it calculates the discount amount, subtracts that value from regularPrice, and assigns the result to salePrice. You could simplify the statement by breaking out part of the math expression and placing it in a function. Here is a function named discount that accepts an item's price as an argument and returns the amount of the discount:

```
Function Real discount(Real price)
    Return price * DISCOUNT_PERCENTAGE
End Function
```

You could then call the function in your calculation:

```
Set salePrice = regularPrice — discount(regularPrice)
```

This statement is easier to read than the one previously shown, and it is clearer that the discount is being subtracted from the regular price. The pseudocode in Program 6-7 shows the complete sale price calculating program using the functions just described.

Program 6-7

```
 1 // Global constant for the discount percentage.
 2 Constant Real DISCOUNT_PERCENTAGE = 0.20
 3
 4 // The main module is the program's starting point.
 5 Module main()
 6     // Local variables to hold regular and sale prices.
 7     Declare Real regularPrice, salePrice
 8
 9     // Get the item's regular price.
10     Set regularPrice = getRegularPrice()
11
12     // Calculate the sale price.
13     Set salePrice = regularPrice - discount(regularPrice)
14
15     // Display the sale price.
16     Display "The sale price is $", salePrice
17 End Module
18
19 // The getRegularPrice function prompts the
20 // user to enter an item's regular price and
21 // returns that value as a Real.
22 Function Real getRegularPrice()
23     // Local variable to hold the price.
24     Declare Real price
25
```

```
26   // Get the regular price.
27      Display "Enter the item's regular price."
28      Input price
29
30      // Return the regular price.
31      Return price
32 End Function
33
34 // The discount function accepts an item's price
35 // as an argument and returns the amount of the
36 // discount specified by DISCOUNT_PERCENTAGE.
37 Function Real discount(Real price)
38      Return price * DISCOUNT_PERCENTAGE
39 End Function
```

Program Output (with Input Shown in Bold)

```
Enter the item's regular price.
100.00 [Enter]
The sale price is $80
```

Using IPO Charts

An IPO chart is a simple but effective tool that programmers sometimes use while designing functions. IPO stands for *input, processing,* and *output,* and an *IPO chart* describes the input, processing, and output of a function. These items are usually laid out in columns: The input column shows a description of the data that is passed to the function as arguments, the processing column shows a description of the process that the function performs, and the output column describes the data that is returned from the function. For example, Figure 6-10 shows IPO charts for the getRegularPrice and discount functions that you saw in Program 6-7.

Figure 6-10 IPO charts for the getRegularPrice and discount functions

IPO Chart for the getRegularPrice Function		
Input	Processing	Output
None	Prompts the user to enter an item's regular price	The item's regular price, as a Real

IPO Chart for the discount Function		
Input	Processing	Output
An item's regular price	Calculates an item's discount by multiplying the regular price by the global constant DISCOUNT_PERCENTAGE	The item's discount, as a Real

Notice that the IPO charts provide only brief descriptions of a function's input, processing, and output, but do not show the specific steps taken in a function. In many cases, however, IPO charts include sufficient information so that they can be used instead of a flowchart. The decision of whether to use an IPO chart, a flowchart, or both is often left to the programmer's personal preference.

In the Spotlight:
Modularizing with Functions

Hal owns a business named Make Your Own Music, which sells guitars, drums, banjos, synthesizers, and many other musical instruments. Hal's sales staff works strictly on commission. At the end of the month, each salesperson's commission is calculated according to Table 6-1.

Table 6-1 Sales Commission Rates

Sales This Month	Commission Rate
Less than $10,000.00	10%
$10,000.00–14,999.99	12%
$15,000.00–17,999.99	14%
$18,000.00–21,999.99	16%
$22,000 or more	18%

For example, a salesperson with $16,000 in monthly sales will earn a 14 percent commission ($2,240). Another salesperson with $20,000 in monthly sales will earn a 16 percent commission ($3,200). A person with $30,000 in sales will earn an 18 percent commission ($5,400).

Because the staff gets paid once per month, Hal allows each employee to take up to $2,000 per month in advance. When sales commissions are calculated, the amount of each employee's advanced pay is subtracted from the commission. If any salesperson's commissions are less than the amount of their advance, they must reimburse Hal for the difference. To calculate a salesperson's monthly pay, Hal uses the following formula:

$$Pay = Sales \times Commission\ rate - Advanced\ pay$$

Hal has asked you to write a program that makes this calculation for him. The following general algorithm outlines the steps the program must take:

1. Get the salesperson's monthly sales.
2. Get the amount of advanced pay.
3. Use the amount of monthly sales to determine the commission rate.
4. Calculate the salesperson's pay using the formula previously shown. If the amount is negative, indicate that the salesperson must reimburse the company.

Program 6-8 shows the pseudocode for the program, which is modularized with numerous functions. Rather than presenting the entire program at once, let's first examine the main module and then each function separately. Here is the main module:

Program 6-8	Commission rate program: `main` module

```
1 Module main()
2     // Local variables
3     Declare Real sales, commissionRate, advancedPay
4
5     // Get the amount of sales.
6     Set sales = getSales()
7
8     // Get the amount of advanced pay.
9     Set advancedPay = getAdvancedPay()
10
11    // Determine the commission rate.
12    Set commissionRate = determineCommissionRate(sales)
13
14    // Calculate the pay.
15    Set pay = sales * commissionRate - advancedPay
16
17    // Display the amount of pay.
18    Display "The pay is $", pay
19
20    // Determine whether the pay is negative.
21    If pay < 0 Then
22        Display "The salesperson must reimburse"
23        Display "the company."
24    End If
25 End Module
26
```

Line 3 declares the variables to hold the sales, the commission rate, and the amount of advanced pay. Line 6 calls the `getSales` function, which gets the amount of sales from the user and returns that value. The value that is returned from the function is assigned to the `sales` variable. Line 9 calls the `getAdvancedPay` function, which gets the amount of advanced pay from the user and returns that value. The value that is returned from the function is assigned to the `advancedPay` variable.

Line 12 calls the `determineCommissionRate` function, passing `sales` as an argument. This function returns the rate of commission for the amount of sales. That value is assigned to the `commissionRate` variable. Line 15 calculates the amount of pay, and then line 18 displays that amount. The `If-Then` statement in lines 21 through 24 determines whether the pay is negative, and if so, displays a message indicating that the salesperson must reimburse the company. Figure 6-11 shows a flowchart for the main module.

Figure 6-11 Flowchart for the `main` module

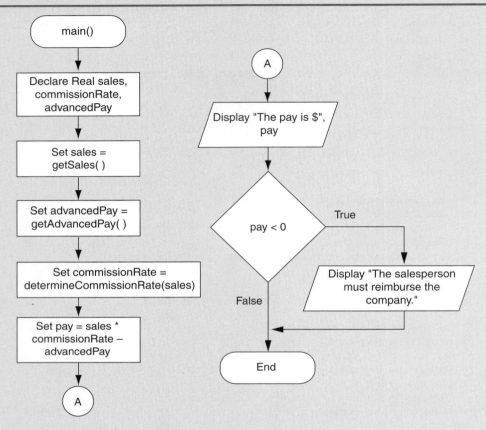

The `getSales` function definition is next.

Program 6-8	**Commission rate program (continued):** `getSales` **function**

```
27 // The getSales function gets a salesperson's
28 // monthly sales from the user and returns
29 // that value as a Real.
30 Function Real getSales()
31    // Local variable to hold the monthly sales.
32    Declare Real monthlySales
33
34    // Get the amount of monthly sales.
35    Display "Enter the salesperson's monthly sales."
36    Input monthlySales
37
38    // Return the amount of monthly sales.
39    Return monthlySales
40 End Function
41
```

The purpose of the getSales function is to prompt the user to enter the amount of sales for a salesperson and return that amount. A local variable named monthlySales is declared in line 32. Line 35 tells the user to enter the sales, and line 36 gets the user's input and stores it in the local monthlySales variable. Line 39 returns the amount in the monthlySales variable. Figure 6-12 shows a flowchart for this function.

Figure 6-12 Flowchart for the getSales function

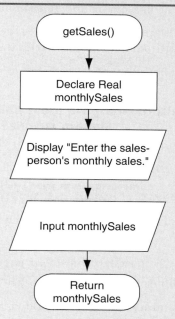

Next is the definition of the getAdvancedPay function.

Program 6-8	**Commission rate program (continued): getAdvancedPay function**

```
42 // The getAdvancedPay function gets the amount of
43 // advanced pay given to the salesperson and
44 // returns that amount as a Real.
45 Function Real getAdvancedPay()
46    // Local variable to hold the advanced pay.
47    Declare Real advanced
48
49    // Get the amount of advanced pay.
50    Display "Enter the amount of advanced pay, or"
51    Display "0 if no advanced pay was given."
52    Input advanced
53
54    // Return the advanced pay.
55    Return advanced
56 End Function
57
```

The purpose of the `getAdvancedPay` function is to prompt the user to enter the amount of advanced pay for a salesperson and return that amount. A local variable named `advanced` is declared in line 47. Lines 50 and 51 tell the user to enter the amount of advanced pay (or 0 if none was given), and line 52 gets the user's input and stores it in the local `advanced` variable. Line 55 returns the amount in the `advanced` variable. Figure 6-13 shows a flowchart for this function.

Figure 6-13 Flowchart for the `getAdvancedPay` function

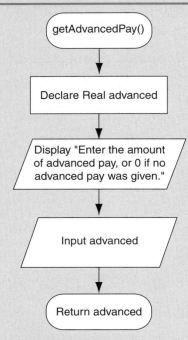

Defining the `determineCommissionRate` function comes next.

Program 6-8	**Commission rate program (continued):** `determineCommissionRate` **function**

```
58 // The determineCommissionRate function accepts the
59 // amount of sales as an argument and returns the
60 // commission rate as a Real.
61 Function Real determineCommissionRate(Real sales)
62     // Local variable to hold commission rate.
63     Declare Real rate
64
65     // Determine the commission rate.
66     If sales < 10000.00 Then
67         Set rate = 0.10
68     Else If sales >= 10000.00 AND sales <= 14999.99 Then
69         Set rate = 0.12
70     Else If sales >= 15000.00 AND sales <= 17999.99 Then
71         Set rate = 0.14
72     Else If sales >= 18000.00 AND sales <= 21999.99 Then
73         Set rate = 0.16
```

```
74      Else
75         Set rate = 0.18
76      End If
77
78      // Return the commission rate.
79      Return rate
80 End Function
```

The `determineCommissionRate` function accepts the amount of sales as an argument, and it returns the applicable commission rate for that amount of sales. Line 63 declares a local variable named `rate` that will hold the commission rate. The `If-Then-Else If` statement in lines 66 through 76 tests the `sales` parameter and assigns the correct value to the local `rate` variable. Line 79 returns the value in the local `rate` variable. Figure 6-14 shows a flowchart for this function.

Figure 6-14 Flowchart for the `determineCommissionRate` function

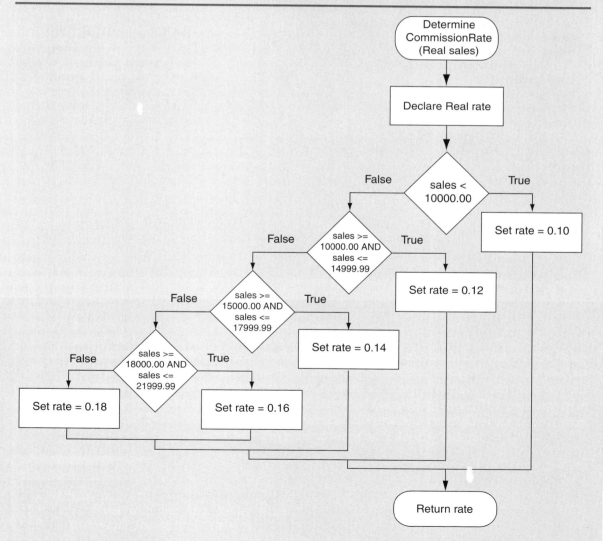

Program Output (with Input Shown in Bold)

Enter the salesperson's monthly sales.
14650.00 [Enter]
Enter the amount of advanced pay, or
0 if no advanced pay was given.
1000.00 [Enter]
The pay is $758.00

Program Output (with Input Shown in Bold)

Enter the salesperson's monthly sales.
9000.00 [Enter]
Enter the amount of advanced pay, or
0 if no advanced pay was given.
0 [Enter]
The pay is $900.00

Program Output (with Input Shown in Bold)

Enter the salesperson's monthly sales.
12000.00 [Enter]
Enter the amount of advanced pay, or
0 if no advanced pay was given.
2000.00 [Enter]
The pay is $-560
The salesperson must reimburse
the company.

Returning Strings

So far you've seen examples of functions that return numbers. Most programming languages also allow you to write functions that return strings. For example, the following pseudocode function prompts the user to enter his or her name, and then returns the string that the user entered.

```
Function String getName()
   // Local variable to hold the user's name.
   Declare String name

   // Get the user's name.
   Display "Enter your name."
   Input name

   // Return the name.
   Return name
End Function
```

Returning Boolean Values

Most languages also allow you to write *Boolean functions*, which return either True or False. You can use a Boolean function to test a condition, and then return either True or False to indicate whether the condition exists. Boolean functions are useful for simplifying complex conditions that are tested in decision and repetition structures.

For example, suppose you are designing a program that will ask the user to enter a number, and then determine whether that number is even or odd. The following pseudocode shows how you can make that determination. Assume `number` is an `Integer` variable containing the number entered by the user.

```
If number MOD 2 == 0 Then
    Display "The number is even."
Else
    Display "The number is odd."
End If
```

The meaning of the Boolean expression being tested by this `If-Then` statement isn't clear, so let's take a closer look at it:

```
number MOD 2 == 0
```

This expression uses the `MOD` operator, which was introduced in Chapter 2. Recall that the `MOD` operator divides two integers and returns the remainder of the division. So, this pseudocode is saying, "If the remainder of `number` divided by 2 is equal to 0, then display a message indicating the number is even, or else display a message indicating the number is odd."

Because dividing an even number by 2 will always give a remainder of 0, this logic will work. The pseudocode would be easier to understand, however, if you could somehow rewrite it to say, "If the number is even, then display a message indicating it is even, or else display a message indicating it is odd." As it turns out, this can be done with a Boolean function. In this example, you could design a Boolean function named `isEven` that accepts a number as an argument and returns `True` if the number is even, or `False` otherwise. The following is the pseudocode for such a function.

```
Function Boolean isEven(Integer number)
    // Local variable to hold True or False.
    Declare Boolean status

    // Determine whether number is even. If it is, set
    // status to True. Otherwise, set status to False.
    If number MOD 2 == 0 Then
       Set status = True
    Else
       Set status = False
    End If

    // Return the value in the status variable.
    Return status
End Function
```

Then you can rewrite the `If-Then` statement so it calls the `isEven` function to determine whether number is even.

```
If isEven(number) Then
   Display "The number is even."
Else
   Display "The number is odd."
End If
```

Not only is this logic easier to understand, but now you have a function that you can call in the program anytime you need to test a number to determine whether it is even.

Checkpoint

6.6 What is the purpose of the `Return` statement in a function?

6.7 Look at the following pseudocode function definition:

```
Function Integer doSomething(Integer number)
    Return number * 2
End Function
```

a. What is the name of the function?

b. What type of data does the function return?

c. Given the function definition, what will the following statement display?

```
Display doSomething (10)
```

6.8 What is an IPO chart?

6.9 What is a Boolean function?

6.3 More Library Functions

> **NOTE:** The library functions that we present in this chapter are generic versions of the ones that you will find in most programming languages. In this book, the names of the functions, the arguments that they accept, and their behavior might differ slightly from the way they work in actual programming languages.

Mathematical Functions

Most programming languages provide several mathematical library functions. These functions typically accept one or more values as arguments, perform a mathematical operation using the arguments, and return the result. For example, two common mathematical functions are `sqrt` and `pow`. Let's take a closer look at each.

The `sqrt` Function

The `sqrt` function accepts an argument and returns the square root of the argument. Here is an example of how it is used:

```
Set result = sqrt(16)
```

This statement calls the `sqrt` function, passing 16 as an argument. The function returns the square root of 16, which is then assigned to the `result` variable. The pseudocode in Program 6-9 demonstrates the `sqrt` function.

Program 6-9

```
 1 // Variable declarations
 2 Declare Integer number
 3 Declare Real squareRoot
 4
 5 // Get a number.
 6 Display "Enter a number."
 7 Input number
 8
 9 // Calculate and display its square root.
10 Set squareRoot = sqrt(number)
11 Display "The square root of that number is ", squareRoot
```

Program Output (with Input Shown in Bold)

```
Enter a number.
25 [Enter]
The square root of that number is 5
```

The pseudocode in Program 6-10 finds the hypotenuse of a right triangle. The program uses the following formula, which you might recall from geometry class:

$$c = \sqrt{a^2 + b^2}$$

In the formula, c is the length of the hypotenuse, and a and b are the lengths of the other sides of the triangle.

Program 6-10

```
 1 // Variable declarations
 2 Declare Real a, b, c
 3
 4 // Get the length of side A.
 5 Display "Enter the length of side A."
 6 Input a
 7
 8 // Get the length of side B.
 9 Display "Enter the length of side B."
10 Input b
11
12 // Calculate the length of the hypotenuse.
13 Set c = sqrt(a^2 + b^2)
14
15 // Display the length of the hypotenuse.
16 Display "The length of the hypotenuse is ", c
```

Program Output (with Input Shown in Bold)

```
Enter the length of side A: 5.0 [Enter]
Enter the length of side B: 12.0 [Enter]
The length of the hypotenuse is 13
```

Take a closer look at line 13:

```
Set c = sqrt(a^2 + b^2)
```

The statement works like this: The value of the expression `a^2 + b^2` is calculated, and that value is passed as an argument to the `sqrt` function. The `sqrt` function returns the square root of the argument, which is then assigned to the variable c.

The pow Function

Another common mathematical function is the `pow` function. The purpose of the `pow` function is to raise a number to a power. In a nutshell, it does the same thing that we have been using the ^ operator for. Some programming languages, however, do not have an operator that raises a number to a power. Instead, they use a function such as `pow`. Here is an example of how the `pow` function is used:

```
Set area = pow(4, 2)
```

This statement calls the `pow` function, passing 4 and 2 as arguments. The function returns the value of 4 raised to the power of 2, which is assigned to the `area` variable.

Other Common Mathematical Functions

In addition to `sqrt` and `pow`, Table 6-2 describes several other mathematical functions that most programming languages provide.

Table 6-2 Other common mathematical functions

Function Name	Description and Example Usage
abs	Returns the absolute value of the argument.
	Example: After the following statement executes, the variable y will contain the absolute value of the value in x. The variable x will remain unchanged.
	`y = abs(x)`
cos	Returns the cosine of the argument. The argument should be an angle expressed in radians.
	Example: After the following statement executes, the variable y will contain the cosine of the angle stored in the variable x. The variable x will remain unchanged.
	`y = cos(x)`
round	Accepts a real number as an argument and returns the value of the argument rounded to the nearest integer. For example, `round(3.5)` will return 4, and `round(3.2)` will return 3.
	Example: After the following statement executes, the variable y will contain the value of the variable x rounded to the nearest integer. The variable x will remain unchanged.
	`y = round(x)`

Table 6-2 Other common mathematical functions (continued)

Function Name	Description and Example Usage
sin	Returns the sine of the argument. The argument should be an angle expressed in radians. *Example*: After the following statement executes, the variable y will contain the sine of the angle stored in the variable x. The variable x will remain unchanged. `y = sin(x)`
tan	Returns the tangent of the argument. The argument should be an angle expressed in radians. *Example*: After the following statement executes, the variable y will contain the tangent of the angle stored in the variable x. The variable x will remain unchanged. `y = tan(x)`

Data Type Conversion Functions

Most programming languages provide library functions that convert values from one data type to another. For example, most languages provide a function that converts a real number to an integer, as well as a function that converts an integer to a real number. In this book's pseudocode, we will use the toInteger function to convert a real number to an integer, and the toReal function to convert an integer to a real number. These functions are described in Table 6-3.

Table 6-3 Data type conversion functions

Function	Description and Example Usage

toInteger	The toInteger function accepts a real number as its argument and returns that number converted to an integer. If the real number has a fractional part, the fractional part will be thrown away. For example, the function call toInteger(2.5) will return 2.
	
	Example: If the following were actual code, the variable i would contain the value 2 after these statements execute.
	
	`Declare Integer i`
	`Declare Real r = 2.5`
	`Set i = toInteger(r)`

toReal	The toReal function accepts an integer number as its argument and returns that number converted to a real number.
	
	Example: If the following were actual code, the variable r would contain the value 7.0 after these statements execute.
	
	`Declare Integer i = 7`
	`Declare Real r`
	`Set r = toReal(i)`

In many languages, an error will occur if you try to assign a value of one data type to a variable of another data type. For example, look at the following pseudocode:

```
Declare Integer number
Set number = 6.17  ◄————— This will cause an error in many languages!
```

The first statement declares an `Integer` variable named `number`. The second statement attempts to assign a real number, 6.17, to the variable. In most programming languages this will cause an error because an integer variable cannot hold fractional values. The error that will result is sometimes referred to as a *type mismatch error.*

> **NOTE:** Most languages let you assign an integer value to a real variable without causing an error because doing so does not cause a loss of data. Functions for converting integers to real numbers still exist in case you need to explicitly perform this type of conversion.

Sometimes you might write code that causes a type mismatch error without realizing it. For example, look at the pseudocode in Program 6-11. This program calculates the number of people who can be served with a given amount of lemonade.

Program 6-11

```
 1 // Declare a variable to hold the number
 2 // of ounces of lemonade available.
 3 Declare Real ounces
 4
 5 // Declare a variable to hold the number
 6 // of people who we can serve.
 7 Declare Integer numberOfPeople
 8
 9 // Constant for the number of ounces per person.
10 Constant Integer OUNCES_PER_PERSON = 8
11
12 // Get the number of ounces of lemonade available.
13 Display "How many ounces of lemonade do you have?"
14 Input ounces
15
16 // Calculate the number of people who can be served.
17 Set numberOfPeople = ounces / OUNCES_PER_PERSON  ◄————— Error!
18
19 // Display the number of people who can be served.
20 Display "You can serve ", numberOfPeople, " people."
```

The ounces variable, declared in line 3, will hold the number of ounces of lemonade that are available, and the `numberOfPeople` variable, declared in line 7, will hold the number of people who can be served. In line 10, the `OUNCES_PER_PERSON` constant is initialized with the value 8. This indicates that each person consumes 8 ounces of lemonade.

After the number of ounces of lemonade are entered and stored in the ounces variable (in line 14), the statement in line 17 attempts to calculate the number of people who can be served. But there is a problem with this statement: numberOfPeople is an Integer variable, and the math expression ounces / OUNCES_PER_PERSON will most likely result in a real number. (For example, if ounces is set to 12, the result will be 1.5.) When the statement attempts to assign the result of the math expression to numberOfPeople, an error will result.

At first, you might decide to simply change the data type of the numberOfPeople variable to Real. That would fix the error, but it wouldn't make sense to use a Real variable to hold the number of people. After all, you can't serve fractional people at your lemonade stand! A better solution is to convert the result of the math expression ounces / OUNCES_PER_PERSON to an integer, and then assign that integer to the numberOfPeople variable. This is the approach taken in Program 6-12.

Program 6-12

```
 1 // Declare a variable to hold the number
 2 // of ounces of lemonade available.
 3 Declare Real ounces
 4
 5 // Declare a variable to hold the number
 6 // of people who we can serve.
 7 Declare Integer numberOfPeople
 8
 9 // Constant for the number of ounces per person.
10 Constant Integer OUNCES_PER_PERSON = 8
11
12 // Get the number of ounces of lemonade available.
13 Display "How many ounces of lemonade do you have?"
14 Input ounces
15
16 // Calculate the number of people who can be served.
17 Set numberOfPeople = toInteger(ounces / OUNCES_PER_PERSON)
18
19 // Display the number of people who can be served.
20 Display "You can serve ", numberOfPeople, " people."
```

Program Output (with Input Shown in Bold)

```
How many ounces of lemonade do you have?
165 [Enter]
You can serve 20 people.
```

In this version of the program, line 17 has been rewritten as follows:

```
Set numberOfPeople = toInteger(ounces / OUNCES_PER_PERSON)
```

Let's see how this statement worked in the sample running of the program. When this statement executes, the math expression ounces / OUNCES_PER_PERSON is evaluated. The user entered 165 into the ounces variable, so this expression gives us the value 20.625. This value is then passed as an argument to the toInteger function. The toInteger function throws away the .625 part of the number and returns the integer 20. The integer 20 is then assigned to the numberOfPeople variable.

The `toInteger` function always throws away the fractional part of its argument. In this particular program it is acceptable to do this because you are calculating the number of people you can serve with the amount of available lemonade. Any fractional part that remains represents an amount of leftover lemonade that is not a full serving.

Formatting Functions

Most programming languages provide one or more functions that format numbers in some way. A common use of formatting functions is to format numbers as currency amounts. In this book we will use a function named `currencyFormat` that accepts a `Real` number as an argument and returns a string containing the number formatted as a currency amount. The following pseudocode shows an example of how the `currencyFormat` function can be used.

```
Declare Real amount = 6450.879
Display currencyFormat(amount)
```

If this pseudocode were an actual program it would display:

```
$6,450.88
```

Notice that the function displays a currency symbol (in this case a dollar sign), inserts commas where necessary, and rounds the number to two decimal places.

NOTE: Many programming languages today support *localization,* which means they can be configured for a specific country. In these languages a function such as `currencyFormat` would display the correct currency symbol for the country that the program is localized for.

String Functions

Many types of programs work extensively with strings. For example, text editors like Notepad and word processors like Microsoft Word work almost entirely with strings. Web browsers also work heavily with strings. When a Web browser loads a Web page, it reads formatting instructions that are written into the text of the Web page.

Most programming languages provide several library functions for working with strings. This section discusses the most commonly supported string functions.

The `length` Function

The `length` function returns the length of a string. It accepts a string as its argument and returns the number of characters in the string (the string's length). The value that is returned is an integer. The following pseudocode shows how the `length` function might be used. In this program segment, the length of a password is checked to make sure it is at least six characters long.

```
Display "Enter your new password."
Input password
If length(password) < 6 Then
    Display "The password must be at least six characters long."
End If
```

The append **Function**

The append function accepts two strings as arguments, which we will refer to as *string1* and *string2*. It returns a third string that is created by appending string2 to the end of string1. After the function executes, string1 and string2 will remain unchanged. The following pseudocode shows an example of its usage:

```
Declare String lastName = "Conway"
Declare String salutation = "Mr. "
Declare String properName
Set properName = append(salutation, lastName)
Display properName
```

If this pseudocode were an actual program, it would display:

```
Mr. Conway
```

> **NOTE:** The process of appending one string to the end of another string is called *concatenation*.

The toUpper **and** toLower **Functions**

The toUpper and toLower functions convert the case of the alphabetic characters in a string. The toUpper function accepts a string as an argument and returns a string that is a copy of the argument, but with all characters converted to uppercase. Any character that is already uppercase or is not an alphabetic letter is left unchanged. The following pseudocode shows an example of its usage:

```
Declare String str = "Hello World!"
Display toUpper(str)
```

If this pseudocode were an actual program, it would display:

```
HELLO WORLD!
```

The toLower function accepts a string as an argument and returns a string that is a copy of the argument, but with all characters converted to lowercase. Any character that is already lowercase or is not an alphabetic letter is left unchanged. The following pseudocode shows an example of its usage:

```
Declare String str = "WARNING!"
Display toLower(str)
```

If this pseudocode were an actual program, it would display:

```
warning!
```

The toUpper and toLower functions are useful for making case-insensitive string comparisons. Normally, string comparisons are *case-sensitive,* which means that the uppercase characters are distinguished from the lowercase characters. For example, in a case-sensitive comparison the string "hello" is not the same as the strings "HELLO" or "Hello" because the case of the characters is different. Sometimes it is more convenient to perform a *case-insensitive* comparison, in which the case of the characters is ignored. In a case-insensitive comparison, the string "hello" is considered the same as "HELLO" and "Hello".

For example, look at the following pseudocode:

```
Declare String again
Do
    Display "Hello!"
    Display "Do you want to see that again? (Y = Yes)"
    Input again
While toUpper(again) == "Y"
```

The loop displays "Hello!" and then prompts the user to enter "Y" to see it again. The expression toUpper(again) == "Y" will be true if the user enters either "y" or "Y." Similar results can be achieved by using the toLower function, as shown here:

```
Declare String again
Do
    Display "Hello!"
    Display "Do you want to see that again? (Y = Yes)"
    Input again
While toLower(again) == "y"
```

The substring Function

This function returns a *substring*, which is a string within a string. The substring function typically accepts three arguments: (1) a string that you want to extract a substring from, (2) the beginning position of the substring, and (3) the ending position of the substring.

Each character in a string is identified by its position number. The first character in a string is at position 0, the second character is at position 1, and so forth. In the sample pseudocode below, the substring function returns the substring in positions 5 through 7 of the string "New York City".

```
Declare String str = "New York City"
Declare String search
Set search = substring(str, 5, 7)
Display search
```

If this pseudocode were an actual program, it would display:

```
ork
```

The substring function can also be used to extract individual characters from a string. For example, look at the following pseudocode:

```
Declare String name = "Kevin"
Display substring(name, 2, 2)
```

This code will display:

```
v
```

The function call substring(name, 2, 2) will return the substring that begins and ends at position 2. In this case, that's the substring "v". The pseudocode in Program 6-13 shows another example. This program prompts the user to enter a string, and then it counts the number of times the letter "T" appears in the string.

Program 6-13

```
 1 // Declare a variable to hold a string.
 2 Declare String str
 3
 4 // Declare a variable to hold the number
 5 // of Ts in a string.
 6 Declare Integer numTs = 0
 7
 8 // Declare a counter variable.
 9 Declare Integer counter
10
11 // Get a sentence from the user.
12 Display "Enter a string."
13 Input str
14
15 // Count the number of Ts in the string.
16 For counter = 0 To length(str)
17    If substring(str, counter, counter) == "T" Then
18       numTs = numTs + 1
19    End If
20 End For
21
22 // Display the number of Ts.
23 Display "That string contains ", numTs
24 Display "instances of the letter T."
```

Program Output (with Input Shown in Bold)

```
Enter a string.
```
Ten Times I Told You To STOP![Enter]
```
That string contains 5
instances of the letter T.
```

The contains Function

The contains function accepts two strings as arguments. It returns True if the first string contains the second string; otherwise, the function returns False. For example, the following pseudocode determines whether the string "four score and seven years ago" contains the string "seven":

```
Declare string1 = "four score and seven years ago"
Declare string2 = "seven"
If contains(string1, string2) Then
   Display string2, " appears in the string."
Else
   Display string2, " does not appear in the string."
End If
```

If this were actual code in a program, it would display "seven appears in the string."

The stringToInteger and stringToReal Functions

Strings are sequences of characters, and are meant to hold text items such as names, addresses, descriptions, and so on. You can also store numbers as strings. In a program, any time you put quotation marks around a number, it becomes a string instead of a number. For example, the following pseudocode declares a String variable named interestRate and initializes it with the string "4.3":

```
Declare String interestRate = "4.3"
```

Problems can arise when you store numbers as strings, however. Most of the things that you do with numbers, such as arithmetic and numeric comparisons, cannot be done with strings. Those types of operations can be done only with numeric data such as Integers and Reals.

Some programs must read data from a source that can provide input only as strings. This commonly happens with programs that read data from files. In addition, some programming languages allow you to read keyboard input only as strings. In these situations, numbers that are read as input initially come into the program as strings and then have to be converted to a numeric data type.

Most programming languages provide library functions that convert strings to numbers. The following pseudocode examples use the stringToInteger and stringToReal functions for this purpose. The stringToInteger function accepts a string as an argument, converts it to an Integer, and returns the Integer value. For example, suppose a program has a String variable named str, and an integer value has been stored as a string in this variable. The following statement converts the contents of the str variable to an Integer and stores it in the intNumber variable.

```
Set intNumber = stringToInteger(str)
```

The stringToReal function works the same way, but it converts a string to a Real. For example, suppose a real number has been stored as a string in the String variable named str. The following statement converts the contents of the str variable to a Real and stores it in the realNumber variable.

```
Set realNumber = stringToReal(str)
```

When you use a function such as these, there is always the possibility of an error. For example, look at the following pseudocode:

```
Set intNumber = stringToInteger("123abc")
```

Obviously, the string "123abc" cannot be converted to an Integer because it contains alphabetic characters. Here is another example that will cause an error:

```
Set realNumber = stringToReal("3.14.159")
```

The string "3.14.159" cannot be converted to a Real because it has two decimal points. Exactly what happens when these errors occur depends on the programming language.

The isInteger and isReal Functions

To help prevent errors when converting strings to numbers, many programming languages provide library functions that test a string and then return either True or False indicating whether the string can successfully be converted to a number. The following pseudocode examples use the isInteger function to determine whether a string can be converted to an Integer, and the isReal function to determine whether a string can be converted to a Real. The following example uses the isInteger function. Assume str is a String and intNumber is an Integer.

```
If isInteger(str) Then
    Set intNumber = stringToInteger(str)
Else
    Display "Invalid data"
End If
```

The isReal function works the same way, as shown in the following example (assume str is a String and realNumber is an Integer).

```
If isReal(str) Then
    Set realNumber = stringToReal(str)
Else
    Display "Invalid data"
End If
```

Review Questions

Multiple Choice

1. This is a prewritten function that is built into a programming language.
   a. standard function
   b. library function
   c. custom function
   d. cafeteria function

2. This term describes any mechanism that accepts input, performs some operation that cannot be seen on the input, and produces output.
   a. glass box
   b. white box
   c. opaque box
   d. black box

3. This part of a function definition specifies the data type of the value that the function returns.
   a. header
   b. footer
   c. body
   d. Return statement

4. This part of a function definition is comprised of one or more statements that are executed when the function is called.
   a. header
   b. footer
   c. body
   d. Return statement

5. This statement causes a function to end and sends a value back to the part of the program that called the function.

   a. `End`
   b. `Send`
   c. `Exit`
   d. `Return`

6. This is a design tool that describes the input, processing, and output of a function.

   a. hierarchy chart
   b. IPO chart
   c. datagram chart
   d. data processing chart

7. This type of function returns either `True` or `False`.

   a. Binary
   b. `TrueFalse`
   c. Boolean
   d. logical

8. This is an example of a data type conversion function.

   a. `sqrt`
   b. `toReal`
   c. `substring`
   d. `isNumeric`

9. This type of error occurs when you try to assign a value of one data type to a variable of another data type.

   a. type mismatch error
   b. Boolean logic error
   c. relational error
   d. bit conversion error

10. This is a string inside of another string.

    a. substring
    b. inner string
    c. mini string
    d. component string

True or False

1. The code for a library function must appear in a program in order for the program to call the library function.

2. Complex mathematical expressions can sometimes be simplified by breaking out part of the expression and putting it in a function.

3. In many languages it is an error to assign a real number to an integer variable.

4. In some languages you must use a library function to raise a number to a power.

5. In a case-sensitive comparison, the strings `"yoda"` and `"YODA"` are equivalent.

Short Answer

1. What is the difference between a module and a function?

2. What three characteristics of a function are described in an IPO chart?

3. When a conversion function is used to convert a real number to an integer, what usually happens to the real number's fractional part?

4. What is a substring?

5. What is the purpose of the `stringToInteger` and `stringToReal` functions described in this chapter?

6. What is the purpose of the `isInteger` and `isReal` functions described in this chapter?

Algorithm Workbench

1. As shown in this chapter, write a pseudocode statement that generates a random number in the range of 1 through 100 and assigns it to a variable named `rand`.

2. The following pseudocode statement calls a function named `half`, which returns a value that is half that of the argument. (Assume both the `result` and `number` variables are `Real`.) Write pseudocode for the function.
   ```
   Set result = half(number)
   ```

3. A pseudocode program contains the following function definition:
   ```
   Function Integer cube(Integer num)
       Return num * num * num
   End Function
   ```
   Write a statement that passes the value 4 to this function and assigns its return value to the variable `result`.

4. Design a function named `timesTen` that accepts an `Integer` argument. When the function is called, it should return the value of its argument multiplied times 10.

5. Design a function named `getFirstName` that asks the user to enter his or her first name, and returns it.

6. Assume that a program has two `String` variables named `str1` and `str2`. Write a pseudocode statement that assigns an all uppercase version of `str1` to the `str2` variable.

Programming Exercises

VideoNote

The Rectangle Area Problem

1. **Rectangle Area**

   The area of a rectangle is calculated according to the following formula:

   $$area = width \times length$$

   Design a function that accepts a rectangle's width and length as arguments and returns the rectangle's area. Use the function in a program that prompts the user to enter the rectangle's width and length, and then displays the rectangle's area.

2. **Feet to Inches**

   One foot equals 12 inches. Design a function named `feetToInches` that accepts a number of feet as an argument, and returns the number of inches in that many feet. Use the function in a program that prompts the user to enter a number of feet and then displays the number of inches in that many feet.

3. **Math Quiz**

   Design a program that gives simple math quizzes. The program should display two random numbers that are to be added, such as:

   ```
     247
   + 129
   ```

   The program should allow the student to enter the answer. If the answer is correct, a message of congratulations should be displayed. If the answer is incorrect, a message showing the correct answer should be displayed.

4. **Maximum of Two Values**

   Design a function named `max` that accepts two integer values as arguments and returns the value that is the greater of the two. For example, if 7 and 12 are passed as arguments to the function, the function should return 12. Use the function in a program that prompts the user to enter two integer values. The program should display the value that is the greater of the two.

5. **Falling Distance**

   When an object is falling because of gravity, the following formula can be used to determine the distance the object falls in a specific time period:

   $$d = \frac{1}{2}gt^2$$

   The variables in the formula are as follows: d is the distance in meters, g is 9.8, and t is the amount of time, in seconds, that the object has been falling.

   Design a function named `fallingDistance` that accepts an object's falling time (in seconds) as an argument. The function should return the distance, in meters, that the object has fallen during that time interval. Design a program that calls the function in a loop that passes the values 1 through 10 as arguments and displays the return value.

6. **Kinetic Energy**

   In physics, an object that is in motion is said to have kinetic energy. The following formula can be used to determine a moving object's kinetic energy:

   $$KE = \frac{1}{2}mv^2$$

   The variables in the formula are as follows: KE is the kinetic energy, m is the object's mass in kilograms, and v is the object's velocity, in meters per second.

   Design a function named `kineticEnergy` that accepts an object's mass (in kilograms) and velocity (in meters per second) as arguments. The function should return the amount of kinetic energy that the object has. Design a program that asks the user to enter values for mass and velocity, and then calls the `kineticEnergy` function to get the object's kinetic energy.

7. **Test Average and Grade**

   Write a program that asks the user to enter five test scores. The program should display a letter grade for each score and the average test score. Design the following functions in the program:

   - `calcAverage`—This function should accept five test scores as arguments and return the average of the scores.
   - `determineGrade`—This function should accept a test score as an argument and return a letter grade for the score (as a `String`), based on the following grading scale:

Score	Letter Grade
90–100	A
80–89	B
70–79	C
60–69	D
Below 60	F

8. **Odd/Even Counter**

   In this chapter you saw an example of how to design an algorithm that determines whether a number is even or odd (see *Returning Boolean Values* in Section 6.2). Design a program that generates 100 random numbers, and keeps a count of how many of those random numbers are even and how many are odd.

9. **Prime Numbers**

   A prime number is a number that is only evenly divisible by itself and 1. For example, the number 5 is prime because it can only be evenly divided by 1 and 5. The number 6, however, is not prime because it can be divided evenly by 1, 2, 3, and 6.

   Design a Boolean function named `isPrime` which takes an integer as an argument and returns `True` if the argument is a prime number, or `False` otherwise. Use the function in a program that prompts the user to enter a number and then displays a message indicating whether the number is prime.

> **TIP:** Recall that the MOD operator divides one number by another and returns the remainder of the division. In an expression such as num1 MOD num2, the MOD operator will return 0 if num1 is evenly divisible by num2.

10. **Prime Number List**

    This exercise assumes you have already designed the `isPrime` function in Programming Exercise 9. Design another program that displays all of the prime numbers from 1 through 100. The program should have a loop that calls the `isPrime` function.

11. **Rock, Paper, Scissors Game**

    Design a program that lets the user play the game of Rock, Paper, Scissors against the computer. The program should work as follows:

(1) When the program begins, a random number in the range of 1 through 3 is generated. If the number is 1, then the computer has chosen rock. If the number is 2, then the computer has chosen paper. If the number is 3, then the computer has chosen scissors. (Don't display the computer's choice yet.)

(2) The user enters his or her choice of "rock," "paper," or "scissors" at the keyboard.

(3) The computer's choice is displayed.

(4) The program should display a message indicating whether the user or the computer was the winner. A winner is selected according to the following rules:

- If one player chooses rock and the other player chooses scissors, then rock wins. (The rock smashes the scissors.)
- If one player chooses scissors and the other player chooses paper, then scissors wins. (Scissors cuts paper.)
- If one player chooses paper and the other player chooses rock, then paper wins. (Paper wraps rock.)
- If both players make the same choice, the game must be played again to determine the winner.

12. Slot Machine Simulation

A slot machine is a gambling device that the user inserts money into and then pulls a lever (or presses a button). The slot machine then displays a set of random images. If two or more of the images match, the user wins an amount of money, which the slot machine dispenses back to the user.

Design a program that simulates a slot machine. When the program runs, it should do the following:

- Ask the user to enter the amount of money he or she wants to insert into the slot machine.
- Instead of displaying images, the program will randomly select a word from the following list:

  Cherries, Oranges, Plums, Bells, Melons, Bars

  The program will select and display a word from this list three times.
- If none of the randomly selected words match, the program will inform the user that he or she has won $0. If two of the words match, the program will inform the user that he or she has won two times the amount entered. If three of the words match, the program will inform the user that he or she has won three times the amount entered.
- The program will ask if the user wants to play again. If so, these steps are repeated. If not, the program displays the total amount of money entered into the slot machine and the total amount won.

CHAPTER

7 Input Validation

TOPICS

7.1 Garbage In, Garbage Out   7.3 Defensive Programming
7.2 The Input Validation Loop

7.1 Garbage In, Garbage Out

CONCEPT: If a program reads bad data as input, it will produce bad data as output. Programs should be designed to reject bad data that is given as input.

One of the most famous sayings among computer programmers is "garbage in, garbage out." This saying, sometimes abbreviated as *GIGO*, refers to the fact that computers cannot tell the difference between good data and bad data. If a user provides bad data as input to a program, the program will process that bad data and, as a result, will produce bad data as output. For example, look at the pseudocode for the payroll program in Program 7-1 and notice what happens in the sample run when the user gives bad data as input.

Program 7-1

```
1 // Variables to hold the hours worked, the
2 // hourly pay rate, and the gross pay.
3 Declare Real hours, payRate, grossPay
4
5 // Get the number of hours worked.
6 Display "Enter the number of hours worked."
7 Input hours
8
9 // Get the hourly pay rate.
10 Display "Enter the hourly pay rate."
```

257

```
11 Input payRate
12
13 // Calculate the gross pay.
14 Set grossPay = hours * payRate
15
16 // Display the gross pay.
17 Display "The gross pay is ", currencyFormat(grossPay)
```

Program Output (with Input Shown in Bold)

```
Enter the number of hours worked.
400 [Enter]
Enter the hourly pay rate.
20 [Enter]
The gross pay is $8,000.00
```

Did you spot the bad data that was provided as input? The person receiving the paycheck will be pleasantly surprised, because in the sample run the payroll clerk entered 400 as the number of hours worked. The clerk probably meant to enter 40, because there are not 400 hours in a week. The computer, however, is unaware of this fact, and the program processed the bad data just as if it were good data. Can you think of other types of input that can be given to this program that will result in bad output? One example is a negative number entered for the hours worked; another is an invalid hourly pay rate.

Sometimes stories are reported in the news about computer errors that mistakenly cause people to be charged thousands of dollars for small purchases or to receive large tax refunds that they were not entitled to. These "computer errors" are rarely caused by the computer, however; they are more commonly caused by software bugs or bad data that was read into a program as input.

The integrity of a program's output is only as good as the integrity of its input. For this reason, you should design your programs in such a way that bad input is never accepted. When input is given to a program, it should be inspected before it is processed. If the input is invalid, the program should discard it and prompt the user to enter the correct data. This process is known as *input validation*. This chapter discusses techniques that you can use to validate data before it is processed.

 Checkpoint

7.1 What does the phrase "garbage in, garbage out" mean?

7.2 Give a general description of the input validation process.

 7.2 The Input Validation Loop

CONCEPT: Input validation is commonly done with a loop that iterates as long as an input variable contains bad data.

Figure 7-1 shows a common technique for validating an item of input. In this technique, the input is read, and then a pretest loop is executed. If the input data is invalid, the body of the loop executes. The loop displays an error message so the user will know that the input was invalid, and then the loop reads the new input. The loop repeats as long as the input is invalid.

Figure 7-1 Logic containing an input validation loop

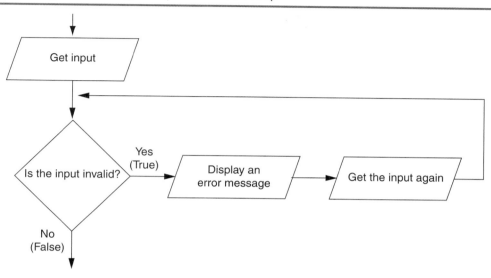

Notice that the flowchart in Figure 7-1 reads input in two places: first just before the loop and then inside the loop. The first input operation—just before the loop—is called a *priming read*, and its purpose is to get the first input value that will be tested by the validation loop. If that value is invalid, the loop will perform subsequent input operations.

Let's consider an example. Suppose you are designing a program that reads a test score and you want to make sure the user does not enter a value less than 0. The following pseudocode shows how you can use an input validation loop to reject any input value that is less than 0.

VideoNote

The Input
Validation
Loop

```
// Get a test score.
Display "Enter a test score."
Input score

// Make sure it is not less than 0.
While score < 0
    Display "ERROR: The score cannot be less than 0."
    Display "Enter the correct score."
    Input score
End While
```

This pseudocode first prompts the user to enter a test score (this is the priming read), and then the `While` loop executes. Recall from Chapter 5 that the `While` loop is a pretest loop, which means it tests the expression `score < 0` before performing an iteration. If the user entered a valid test score, this expression will be false and the loop will not iterate. If the test score is invalid, however, the expression will be true and the statements in the body of the loop will execute. The loop displays an error message and prompts the user to enter the correct test score. The loop will continue to iterate until the user enters a valid test score.

NOTE: An input validation loop, such as the one in Figure 7-1, is sometimes called an *error trap* or an *error handler*.

This pseudocode only rejects negative test scores. What if you also want to reject any test scores that are greater than 100? You can modify the input validation loop so it uses a compound Boolean expression, as shown next.

```
// Get a test score.
Display "Enter a test score."
Input score
// Validate the test score.
While score < 0 OR score > 100
    Display "ERROR: The score cannot be less than 0"
    Display "or greater than 100."
    Display "Enter the correct score."
    Input score
End While
```

The loop in this pseudocode determines whether score is less than 0 or greater than 100. If either is true, an error message is displayed and the user is prompted to enter a correct score.

NOTE: This pseudocode used the OR operator to determine whether score was outside the range. Think about what would happen if this Boolean expression used the AND operator instead:

```
score < 0 AND score > 100
```

This expression would never be true because it is impossible for a number to be less than 0 AND greater than 100!

In the Spotlight:

Designing an Input Validation Loop

In Chapter 5 you saw a program that your friend Samantha can use to calculate the retail price of an item in her import business (see Program 5-6 in Chapter 5). Samantha has encountered a problem when using the program, however. Some of the items that she sells have a wholesale cost of 50 cents, which she enters into the program as 0.50. Because the 0 key is next to the key for the negative sign, she sometimes accidentally enters a negative number. She has asked you to revise the program so it will not allow a negative number to be entered for the wholesale cost.

You decide to add an input validation loop to the showRetail module that rejects any negative numbers that are entered into the wholesale variable. Program 7-2 shows the new pseudocode, with the new input validation code shown in lines 28–33.

Figure 7-2 shows a new flowchart for the showRetail module.

Program 7-2

```
1 Module main()
2    // Local variable
```

```
 3      Declare String doAnother
 4
 5      Do
 6          // Calculate and display a retail price.
 7          Call showRetail()
 8
 9          // Do this again?
10          Display "Do you have another item? (Enter y for yes)"
11          Input doAnother
12      While doAnother == "y" OR doAnother == "Y"
13 End Module
14
15 // The showRetail module gets an item's wholesale cost
16 // from the user and displays its retail price.
17 Module showRetail()
18      // Local variables
19      Declare Real wholesale, retail
20
21      // Constant for the markup percentage
22      Constant Real MARKUP = 2.50
23
24      // Get the wholesale cost.
25      Display "Enter an item's wholesale cost."
26      Input wholesale
27
28      // Validate the wholesale cost.
29      While wholesale < 0
30          Display "The cost cannot be negative. Please"
31          Display "enter the correct wholesale cost."
32          Input wholesale
33      End While
34
35      // Calculate the retail price.
36      Set retail = wholesale * MARKUP
37
38      // Display the retail price.
39      Display "The retail price is $", retail
40 End Module
```

Program Output (with Input Shown in Bold)

```
Enter an item's wholesale cost.
```
−0.50 [Enter]
```
The cost cannot be negative. Please
enter the correct wholesale cost.
```
0.50 [Enter]
```
The retail price is $1.25
Do you have another item? (Enter y for yes)
```
n [Enter]

Figure 7-2 Flowchart for the showRetail module

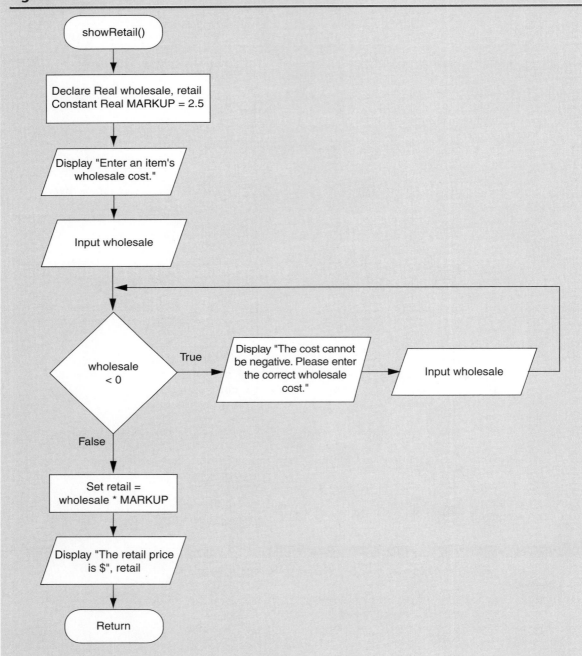

Using a Posttest Loop to Validate Input

You might be wondering if you could use a posttest loop to validate input instead of using the priming read. For example, the pseudocode to get a test score and validate it could be written as follows with a Do-While loop.

```
Do
    Display "Enter a test score."
    Input score
While score < 0 OR score > 100
```

Although this logic will work, it does not display an error message when the user enters an invalid value—it simply repeats the original prompt each time the loop iterates. This might be confusing to the user, so it is usually better to have a priming read followed by a pretest validation loop.

Writing Validation Functions

The input validation examples shown so far have been simple and straightforward. You have seen how to write validation loops that reject both negative numbers and numbers that are outside of a range. However, input validation can sometimes be more complex than these examples.

For instance, suppose you are designing a program that prompts the user to enter a product model number and should only accept the values 100, 200, and 300. You could design the input algorithm as shown next.

```
// Get the model number.
Display "Enter the model number."
Input model

While model != 100 AND model != 200 AND model != 300
    Display "The valid model numbers are 100, 200 and 300."
    Display "Enter a valid model number."
    Input model
End While
```

The validation loop uses a long compound Boolean expression that will iterate as long as model does not equal 100 AND model does not equal 200 AND model does not equal 300. Although this logic will work, you can simplify the validation loop by writing a Boolean function to test the model variable and then calling that function in the loop. For example, suppose you pass the model variable to a function you write named isInvalid. The function returns True if model is invalid, or False otherwise. You could rewrite the validation loop as follows:

```
// Get the model number.
Display "Enter the model number."
Input model

While isInvalid(model)
    Display "The valid model numbers are 100, 200 and 300."
    Display "Enter a valid model number."
    Input model
End While
```

This makes the loop easier to read. It is evident now that the loop iterates as long as model is invalid. The following pseudocode shows how you might design the isInvalid function. It accepts a model number as an argument, and if the argument is not 100 AND the argument is not 200 AND the argument is not 300, the function returns True to indicate that it is invalid. Otherwise, the function returns False.

```
Function Boolean isInvalid(Integer model)
    // A local variable to hold True or False.
    Declare Boolean status

    // If the model number is invalid, set status to True.
    // Otherwise, set status to False.
    If model != 100 AND model != 200 AND model != 300 Then
        Set status = True
    Else
        Set status = False
    End If

    // Return the test status.
    Return status
End Function
```

Validating String Input

In some programs you must validate string input. For example, suppose you are designing a program that asks a yes/no question, and you want to make sure that only the strings "yes" or "no" are accepted as valid input. The following pseudocode shows how this might be done.

```
// Get the answer to the question.
Display "Is your supervisor an effective leader?"
Input answer
// Validate the input.
While answer != "yes" AND answer != "no"
    Display "Please answer yes or no. Is your supervisor an"
    Display "effective leader?"
    Input answer
End While
```

This input validation loop rejects any input except the strings "yes" and "no". This particular design might be too rigid, however; as it is written, the loop performs a case-sensitive comparison. This means that strings such as "YES", "NO", "Yes", and "NO" will be rejected. To make the program more convenient for users, the program should accept "yes" and "no" written in any combination of upper- or lowercase letters. Recall from Chapter 6 that library functions such as toUpper and toLower can help make case-insensitive string comparisons. The following pseudocode shows an example using the toLower function.

```
// Get the answer to the question.
Display "Is your supervisor an effective leader?"
Input answer
// Validate the input.
While toLower(answer) != "yes" AND toLower(answer) != "no"
    Display "Please answer yes or no. Is your supervisor an"
    Display "effective leader?"
    Input answer
End While
```

Sometimes the length of a string plays a role in the string's validity. For example, you have probably used a Web site or other system that required you to set up a password. Some systems require that passwords have a minimum number of characters.

To check the length of a string, you use the `length` function discussed in Chapter 6. In the following pseudocode, the `length` function is used to make sure a password is at least six characters long.

```
// Get the new password.
Display "Enter your new password."
Input password
// Validate the length of the password.
While length(password) < 6
   Display "The password must be at least six"
   Display "characters long. Enter your new password."
   Input password
End While
```

Checkpoint

7.3 Describe the steps that are generally taken when an input validation loop is used to validate data.

7.4 What is a priming read? What is its purpose?

7.5 If the input that is read by the priming read is valid, how many times will the input validation loop iterate?

7.3 Defensive Programming

CONCEPT: Input validation is part of the practice of defensive programming. Thorough input validation anticipates both obvious and unobvious errors.

Defensive programming is the practice of anticipating errors that can happen while a program is running, and designing the program to avoid those errors. All of the input validation algorithms examined in this chapter are examples of defensive programming.

Some types of input errors are obvious and easily handled. For example, you should make sure that negative numbers are not entered for items such as prices and test scores. Some types of input errors are not so obvious, however. One example of such an error is reading *empty input,* which happens when an input operation attempts to read data, but there is no data to read. This occurs when an `Input` statement executes and the user simply presses the Enter key without typing a value. Although different programming languages handle the problem of empty input in different ways, there is often a way to determine whether an input operation failed to read data.

Another often overlooked type of error is the entry of the wrong type of data. This happens, for example, when a program attempts to read an integer but the user enters a real number or a string. Most programming languages provide library functions that you can use to avoid this type of error. Quite often you will find functions similar to the `isInteger` and `isReal` functions discussed in Chapter 6. To use these functions in an input validation algorithm, you typically follow these steps:

1. Read the input as a string.
2. Determine whether the string can be converted to the desired data type.

3. If the string can be converted, convert it and continue processing; otherwise, display an error message and attempt to read the data again.

Thorough input validation also requires that you check for accurate data. Even when the user provides the right type of data, it might not be accurate. Consider the following examples:

- When the user enters a U.S. address, the state abbreviation should be checked to make sure it is a two-character string and also a valid U.S. Postal Service abbreviation. For example, there is no U.S. state with the abbreviation NW. Similar validations can be performed on international addresses. For example, Canadian province abbreviations are two-character strings.
- When the user enters a U.S. address, the value entered as the ZIP code should be checked to verify that it is both in the correct format (a 5- or 9-digit number) and a valid U.S. Postal Service ZIP code. For example, 99999 is not currently a valid U.S. ZIP code. In addition, ZIP codes should be valid for the state that is entered. (Databases of valid ZIP codes are readily available for a small fee. Programmers usually purchase one of these and use it in the validation process.)
- Hourly wages and salary amounts should be checked to make sure they are numeric values and within the range of allowable wages established by the company.
- Dates should be checked for validity. For example, the date February 29 should be accepted only in leap years, and invalid dates such as February 30 should never be accepted.
- Time measurements should also be checked for validity. For example, there are 168 hours in a week, so a payroll program should verify that no value greater than 168 is entered for the number of hours worked in a week.
- Reasonableness should also be considered when validating data. Even though there are 168 hours in a week, it is improbable that any employee ever works 24 hours a day, 7 days a week. Dates should also be checked for reasonableness. For example, a birth date can't be in the future and a person, based on birth year, probably isn't 150 years old. When unreasonable data is entered, the program should at least ask the user to confirm that he or she intended to enter it.

Review Questions

Multiple Choice

1. GIGO stands for
   a. great input, great output
   b. garbage in, garbage out
   c. GIGahertz Output
   d. GIGabyte Operation

2. The integrity of a program's output is only as good as the integrity of the program's
   a. compiler
   b. programming language
   c. input
   d. debugger

3. The input operation that appears just before a validation loop is known as the

    a. prevalidation read
    b. primordial read
    c. initialization read
    d. priming read

4. Validation loops are also known as

    a. error traps
    b. doomsday loops
    c. error avoidance loops
    d. defensive programming loops

5. The term "empty input" describes what happens when

    a. the user presses the [Spacebar] and then the [Enter] key
    b. an input operation attempts to read data, but there is no data to read
    c. the user enters 0 when 0 is an invalid value
    d. the user enters any invalid data as input

True or False

1. The process of input validation works like this: When the user of a program enters invalid data, the program should ask the user, "Are you sure you meant to enter that?" If the user answers "yes," the program should accept the data.

2. The priming read appears inside the validation loop.

3. The approach of using a posttest validation loop shown in this chapter requires a priming read.

Short Answer

1. What does the phrase "garbage in, garbage out" mean?

2. Give a general description of the input validation process.

3. What is the purpose of the priming read?

4. In this chapter you saw how a posttest loop can be used in input validation, as an alternative to the priming read followed by a pretest loop. Why is it typically not best to use a posttest loop approach?

Algorithm Workbench

1. Design an algorithm that prompts the user to enter a positive nonzero number and validates the input.

2. Design an algorithm that prompts the user to enter a number in the range of 1 through 100 and validates the input.

3. Design an algorithm that prompts the user to enter "yes" or "no" and validates the input. (Use a case-insensitive comparison.)

4. Design an algorithm that prompts the user to enter a number that is greater than 99 and validates the input.

5. Design an algorithm that prompts the user to enter a secret word. The secret word should be at least 8 characters long. Validate the input.

VideoNote

The Payroll Program with Input Validation Problem

Programming Exercises

1. **Payroll Program with Input Validation**

   Design a payroll program that prompts the user to enter an employee's hourly pay rate and the number of hours worked. Validate the user's input so that only pay rates in the range of $7.50 through $18.25 and hours in the range of 0 through 40 are accepted. The program should display the employee's gross pay.

2. **Theater Seating Revenue with Input Validation**

   A dramatic theater has three seating sections, and it charges the following prices for tickets in each section: section A seats cost $20 each, section B seats cost $15 each, and section C seats cost $10 each. The theater has 300 seats in section A, 500 seats in section B, and 200 seats in section C. Design a program that asks for the number of tickets sold in each section and then displays the amount of income generated from ticket sales. The program should validate the numbers that are entered for each section.

3. **Fat Gram Calculator**

   Design a program that asks for the number of fat grams and calories in a food item. Validate the input as follows:

   - Make sure the number of fat grams and calories are not less than 0.
   - According to nutritional formulas, the number of calories cannot exceed *fat grams* $\times$ 9. Make sure that the number of calories entered is not greater than *fat grams* $\times$ 9.

   Once correct data has been entered, the program should calculate and display the percentage of calories that come from fat. Use the following formula:

   Percentage of calories from fat = (fat grams $\times$ 9) $\div$ calories

   Some nutritionists classify a food as "low fat" if less than 30 percent of its calories come from fat. If the results of this formula are less than 0.3, the program should display a message indicating the food is low in fat.

4. **Speeding Violation Calculator**

   Design a program that calculates and displays the number of miles per hour over the speed limit that a speeding driver was doing. The program should ask for the speed limit and the driver's speed. Validate the input as follows:

   - The speed limit should be at least 20, but not greater than 70.
   - The driver's speed should be at least the value entered for the speed limit (otherwise the driver was not speeding).

   Once correct data has been entered, the program should calculate and display the number of miles per hour over the speed limit that the driver was doing.

5. **Rock, Paper, Scissors Modification**

   Programming Exercise 11 in Chapter 6 asked you to design a program that plays the rock, paper, scissors game. In the program, the user enters one of the three strings—"rock", "paper", or "scissors"—at the keyboard. Add input validation (with a case-insensitive comparison) to make sure the user enters one of those strings only.

8 Arrays

8.1 Array Basics

CONCEPT: An array allows you to store a group of items of the same data type together in memory. Processing a large number of items in an array is usually easier than processing a large number of items stored in separate variables.

In the programs you have designed so far, you have used variables to store data in memory. In most programming languages, the simplest way to store a value in memory is to store it in a variable. Variables work well in many situations, but they have limitations. For example, they can hold only one value at a time. Consider the following pseudocode variable declaration:

```
Declare Integer number = 99
```

This pseudocode statement declares an `Integer` variable named `number`, initialized with the value 99. Consider what happens if the following statement appears later in the program:

```
Set number = 5
```

This statement assigns the value 5 to `number`, replacing the value 99 that was previously stored there. Because `number` is an ordinary variable, it can hold only one value at a time.

Because variables hold only a single value, they can be cumbersome in programs that process lists of data. For example, suppose you are asked to design a program that holds the names of 50 employees. Imagine declaring 50 variables to hold all of those names:

```
Declare String employee1
Declare String employee2
Declare String employee3
and so on . . .
Declare String employee50
```

Then, imagine designing the code to input all 50 names:

```
// Get the first employee name.
Display "Enter the name of employee 1."
Input employee1

// Get the second employee name.
Display "Enter the name of employee 2."
Input employee2

// Get the third employee name.
Display "Enter the name of employee 3."
Input employee3

and so on . . .

// Get the fiftieth employee name.
Display "Enter the name of employee 50."
Input employee50
```

As you can see, variables are not well-suited for storing and processing lists of data. Each variable is a separate item that must be declared and individually processed. Fortunately, most programming languages allow you to create *arrays*, which are specifically designed for storing and processing lists of data. Like a variable, an array is a named storage location in memory. Unlike a variable, an array can hold a group of values. All of the values in an array must be the same data type. You can have an array of `Integers`, an array of `Reals`, or an array of `Strings`, but you cannot store a mixture of data types in an array. The following example shows how we will declare an array in pseudocode:

```
Declare Integer units[10]
```

Notice that this statement looks like a regular `Integer` variable declaration except for the number inside the brackets. The number inside the brackets, called a *size declarator*, specifies the number of values that the array can hold. This pseudocode statement declares an array named `units` that can hold 10 integer values. In most programming languages, an array size declarator must be a nonnegative integer. Here is another example:

```
Declare Real salesAmounts[7]
```

This statement declares an array named `salesAmounts` that can hold 7 real numbers. The following pseudocode shows one more example. This statement declares an array that can hold 50 strings. The name of the array is `names`.

```
Declare String names[50]
```

In most languages, an array's size cannot be changed while the program is running. If you have written a program that uses an array and then find that you must change the array's size, you have to change the array's size declarator in the source code. Then you must recompile the program (or rerun the program if you are using an interpreted language) with the new size declarator. To make array sizes easier to maintain, many programmers prefer to use named constants as array size declarators. Here is an example:

```
Constant Integer SIZE = 10
Declare Integer units[SIZE]
```

As you will see later in this chapter, many array processing techniques require you to refer to the array's size. When you use a named constant as an array's size declarator, you can use the constant to refer to the size of the array in your algorithms. If you ever need to modify the program so the array is a different size, you need only to change the value of the named constant.

Array Elements and Subscripts

The storage locations in an array are known as *elements*. In memory, an array's elements are usually located in consecutive memory locations. Each element in an array is assigned a unique number known as a *subscript*. Subscripts are used to identify specific elements in an array. In most languages, the first element is assigned the subscript 0, the second element is assigned the subscript 1, and so forth. For example, suppose a pseudocode program has the following declarations:

```
Constant Integer SIZE = 5
Declare Integer numbers[SIZE]
```

As shown in Figure 8-1, the numbers array has five elements. The elements are assigned the subscripts 0 through 4. (Because subscript numbering starts at zero, the subscript of the last element in an array is one less than the total number of elements in the array.)

Figure 8-1 Array subscripts

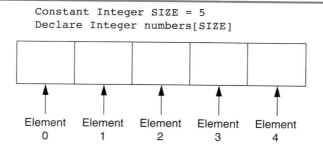

Assigning Values to Array Elements

You access the individual elements in an array by using their subscripts. For example, assuming numbers is the Integer array just described, the following pseudocode assigns the values to each of its five elements.

```
Set numbers[0] = 20
Set numbers[1] = 30
Set numbers[2] = 40
Set numbers[3] = 50
Set numbers[4] = 60
```

This pseudocode assigns the value 20 to element 0, the value 30 to element 1, and so forth. Figure 8-2 shows the contents of the array after these statements execute.

Figure 8-2 Values assigned to each element

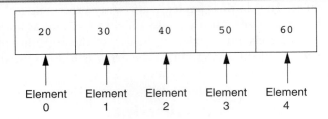

NOTE: The expression numbers[0] is pronounced "numbers sub zero."

Inputting and Outputting Array Contents

You can read values from the keyboard and store them in an array element just as you can a regular variable. You can also output the contents of an array element. The pseudocode in Program 8-1 shows an array being used to store and display values entered by the user.

Program 8-1

```
 1 // Create a constant for the number of employees.
 2 Constant Integer SIZE = 3
 3
 4 // Declare an array to hold the number of hours
 5 // worked by each employee.
 6 Declare Integer hours[SIZE]
 7
 8 // Get the hours worked by employee 1.
 9 Display "Enter the hours worked by employee 1."
10 Input hours[0]
11
12 // Get the hours worked by employee 2.
13 Display "Enter the hours worked by employee 2."
14 Input hours[1]
15
16 // Get the hours worked by employee 3.
17 Display "Enter the hours worked by employee 3."
18 Input hours[2]
19
```

```
20 // Display the values entered.
21 Display "The hours you entered are:"
22 Display hours[0]
23 Display hours[1]
24 Display hours[2]
```

Program Output (with Input Shown in Bold)

```
Enter the hours worked by employee 1.
40 [Enter]
Enter the hours worked by employee 2.
20 [Enter]
Enter the hours worked by employee 3.
15 [Enter]
The hours you entered are:
40
20
15
```

Let's take a closer look at the program. A named constant, SIZE, is declared in line 2 and initialized with the value 3. Then, an Integer array named hours is declared in line 6. The SIZE constant is used as the array size declarator, so the hours array will have 3 elements. The Input statements in lines 10, 14, and 18 read values from the keyboard and store those values in the elements of the hours array. Then, the Display statements in lines 22 through 24 output the values stored in each array element.

In the sample running of the program, the user entered the values 40, 20, and 15, which were stored in the hours array. Figure 8-3 shows the contents of the array after these values are stored in it.

Figure 8-3 Contents of the hours array

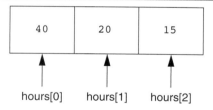

Using a Loop to Step Through an Array

VideoNote
Using a Loop to Step Through an Array

Most programming languages allow you to store a number in a variable and then use that variable as a subscript. This makes it possible to use a loop to step through an entire array, performing the same operation on each element. For example, look at the pseudocode in Program 8-2.

Program 8-2

```
 1 // Declare an Integer array with 10 elements.
 2 Declare Integer series[10]
 3
 4 // Declare a variable to use in the loop.
 5 Declare Integer index
 6
 7 // Set each array element to 100.
 8 For index = 0 To 9
 9    Set series[index] = 100
10 End For
```

In line 2, an Integer array named series is declared with 10 elements, and in line 5 an Integer variable named index is declared. The index variable is used as a counter in the For loop that appears in lines 8 through 10. In the loop, the index variable takes on the values 0 through 9. The first time the loop iterates, index is set to 0, so the statement in line 9 causes the array element series[0] to be set to 100. The second time the loop iterates, index is set to 1, so the array element series[1] is set to 100. This continues until the last loop iteration, in which series[9] is set to 100.

Let's look at another example. Program 8-1 could be simplified by using two For loops: one for inputting the values into the array and the other for displaying the contents of the array. This is shown in Program 8-3.

Program 8-3

```
 1 // Create a constant for the size of the array.
 2 Constant Integer SIZE = 3
 3
 4 // Declare an array to hold the number of hours
 5 // worked by each employee.
 6 Declare Integer hours[SIZE]
 7
 8 // Declare a variable to use in the loops.
 9 Declare Integer index
10
11 // Get the hours for each employee.
12 For index = 0 To SIZE - 1
13    Display "Enter the hours worked by"
14    Display "employee number ", index + 1
15    Input hours[index]
16 End For
17
18 // Display the values entered.
19 For index = 0 To SIZE - 1
20    Display hours[index]
21 End For
```

Program Output (with Input Shown in Bold)

```
Enter the hours worked by
employee 1.
40 [Enter]
Enter the hours worked by
employee 2.
20 [Enter]
Enter the hours worked by
employee 3.
15 [Enter]
The hours you entered are:
40
20
15
```

Let's take a closer look at the first For loop, which appears in lines 12 through 16. Here is the first line of the loop:

```
For index = 0 To SIZE - 1
```

This specifies that the index variable will be assigned the values 0 through 2 as the loop executes. Why did we use the expression SIZE − 1 as the ending value for the index variable? Remember, the subscript of the last element in an array is one less than the size of the array. In this case, the subscript of the last element of the hours array is 2, which is the value of the expression SIZE − 1.

Notice that inside the loop, in line 15, the index variable is used as a subscript:

```
Input hours[index]
```

During the loop's first iteration, the index variable will be set to 0, so the user's input is stored in hours[0]. During the next iteration, the user's input is stored in hours[1]. Then, during the last iteration the user's input is stored in hours[2]. Notice that the loop correctly starts and ends the index variable with valid subscript values (0 through 2).

There is one last thing to point out about Program 8-3. This program reads the number of hours worked by three employees referred to as "employee 1," "employee 2," and "employee 3." Here are the Display statements that appear inside the first For loop, in lines 13 and 14:

```
Display "Enter the hours worked by"
Display "employee number ", index + 1
```

Notice that the second Display statement uses the expression index + 1 to display the employee number. What do you think would happen if we left out the + 1 part of the expression, and the statements were written like this?

```
Display "Enter the hours worked by"
Display "employee number ", index
```

Because the index variable is assigned the values 0, 1, and 2 as the loop runs, these statements would cause the program to refer to the employees as "employee 0," "employee 1," and "employee 2." Most people find it unnatural to start with 0 when counting people or things, so we used the expression `index + 1` to start the employee numbers at 1.

Processing the Elements of an Array

Processing array elements is no different than processing other variables. In the previous programs you saw how you can assign values to array elements, store input in array elements, and display the contents of array elements. The following *In the Spotlight* section shows how array elements can be used in math expressions.

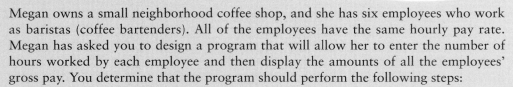

In the Spotlight:
Using Array Elements in a Math Expression

Megan owns a small neighborhood coffee shop, and she has six employees who work as baristas (coffee bartenders). All of the employees have the same hourly pay rate. Megan has asked you to design a program that will allow her to enter the number of hours worked by each employee and then display the amounts of all the employees' gross pay. You determine that the program should perform the following steps:

1. For each employee: get the number of hours worked and store it in an array element.
2. For each array element: use the value stored in the element to calculate an employee's gross pay. Display the amount of the gross pay.

Program 8-4 shows the pseudocode for the program, and Figure 8-4 shows a flowchart.

Program 8-4

```
 1 // Constant for the size of the array.
 2 Constant Integer SIZE = 6
 3
 4 // Array to hold each employee's hours.
 5 Declare Real hours[SIZE]
 6
 7 // Variable to hold the hourly pay rate.
 8 Declare Real payRate
 9
10 // Variable to hold a gross pay amount.
11 Declare Real grossPay
12
13 // Variable to use as a loop counter.
14 Declare Integer index
15
16 // Get each employee's hours worked.
17 For index = 0 To SIZE - 1
18     Display "Enter the hours worked by"
19     Display "employee ", index + 1
20     Input hours[index]
21 End For
22
```

```
23 // Get the hourly pay rate.
24 Display "Enter the hourly pay rate."
25 Input payRate
26
27 // Display each employee's gross pay.
28 Display "Here is each employee's gross pay."
29 For index = 0 To SIZE - 1
30    Set grossPay = hours[index] * payRate
31    Display "Employee ", index + 1, ": $",
32            currencyFormat(grossPay)
33 End For
```

Program Output (with Input Shown in Bold)

```
Enter the hours worked by employee 1.
10 [Enter]
Enter the hours worked by employee 2.
20 [Enter]
Enter the hours worked by employee 3.
15 [Enter]
Enter the hours worked by employee 4.
40 [Enter]
Enter the hours worked by employee 5.
20 [Enter]
Enter the hours worked by employee 6.
18 [Enter]
Enter the hourly pay rate.
12.75 [Enter]
Here is each employee's gross pay.
Employee 1: $127.50
Employee 2: $255.00
Employee 3: $191.25
Employee 4: $510.00
Employee 5: $255.00
Employee 6: $229.50
```

NOTE: Suppose Megan's business increases and she has to hire two additional baristas. This would require you to change the program so it processes 8 employees instead of 6. Because you used a named constant for the array size, this is a simple modification—you just have to change the statement in line 2 to read:

```
Constant Integer SIZE = 8
```

Because the SIZE constant is used as the array size declarator in line 5, the size of the hours array will automatically become 8. Also, because you used the SIZE constant to control the loop iterations in lines 17 and 29, the loops will automatically iterate 8 times, once for each employee.

Imagine how much more difficult this modification would be if you had not used a named constant to specify the array size. You would have to change each individual statement in the program that refers to the array size. Not only would this require more work, but it would open the possibility for errors. If you overlooked only one of the statements that refer to the array size, a bug would occur.

Figure 8-4 Flowchart for Program 8-4

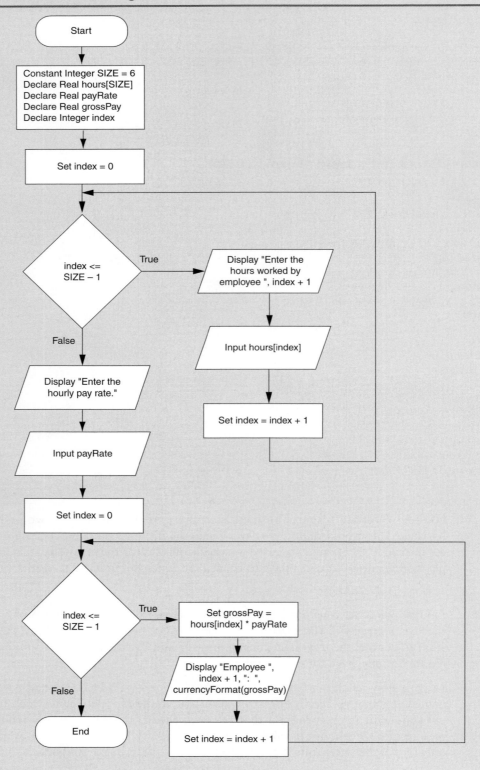

TIP: Programs 8-1, 8-3, and 8-4 show how values can be read from the keyboard into array elements. When a large amount of data is stored in an array, it is usually read from another source, such as a file on the computer's disk drive. In Chapter 10 you will learn how to read data from a file and store it in an array.

Array Initialization

Most languages allow you to initialize an array with values when you declare it. In this book's pseudocode, we will initialize arrays in the following manner:

```
Constant Integer SIZE = 5
Declare Integer numbers[SIZE] = 10, 20, 30, 40, 50
```

The series of values separated with commas is called an *initialization list*. These values are stored in the array elements in the order they appear in the list. (The first value, 10, is stored in `numbers[0]`, the second value, 20, is stored in `numbers[1]`, and so forth.) Here is another example:

```
Constant Integer SIZE = 7
Declare String days[SIZE] = "Sunday", "Monday", "Tuesday",
                            "Wednesday", "Thursday", "Friday",
                            "Saturday"
```

This pseudocode declares `days` as an array of 7 `Strings`, and initializes `days[0]` with `"Sunday"`, `days[1]` with `"Monday"`, and so forth.

Array Bounds Checking

Most programming languages perform *array bounds checking*, which means they do not allow a program to use an invalid array subscript. For example, look at the following pseudocode:

```
// Create an array.
Constant Integer SIZE = 5
Declare Integer numbers[SIZE]

// ERROR! This statement uses an invalid subscript!
Set numbers[5] = 99
```

This pseudocode declares an array with 5 elements. The subscripts for the array's elements are 0 through 4. The last statement will cause an error in most languages because it attempts to assign a value in `numbers[5]`, a nonexistent element.

NOTE: Array bounds checking typically happens at runtime, which is while the program is running.

Watch for Off-By-One Errors

Because array subscripts start at 0 rather than 1, you have to be careful not to perform an off-by-one error. An *off-by-one error* occurs when a loop iterates one time too many or one time too few. For example, look at the following pseudocode:

```
// This code has an off-by-one error.
Constant Integer SIZE = 100;
Declare Integer numbers[SIZE]
Declare Integer index
For index = 1 To SIZE - 1
    Set numbers[index] = 0
End For
```

The intent of this pseudocode is to create an array of integers with 100 elements, and store the value 0 in each element. However, this code has an off-by-one error. The loop uses its counter variable, index, as a subscript with the numbers array. During the loop's execution, the index variable takes on the values 1 through 99, when it should take on the values 0 through 99. As a result, the first element, which is at subscript 0, is skipped.

Assuming numbers is the same array as previously declared, the following loop also performs an off-by-one error. This loop correctly starts with the subscript 0, but it iterates one too many times, ending with the subscript 100:

```
// ERROR!
For index = 0 To SIZE
    Set numbers[index] = 0
End For
```

Because the last subscript in this array is 99, this loop will cause a bounds-checking error.

Partially Filled Arrays

Sometimes you need to store a series of items in an array, but you do not know the number of items in the series. As a result, you do not know the exact number of elements needed for the array. One solution is to make the array large enough to hold the largest possible number of items. This can lead to another problem, however. If the actual number of items stored in the array is less than the number of elements, the array will be only partially filled. When you process a partially filled array, you must only process the elements that contain valid data items.

A partially filled array is normally used with an accompanying integer variable that holds the number of items that are actually stored in the array. If the array is empty, then 0 is stored in this variable because there are no items in the array. Each time an item is added to the array, the variable is incremented. When code steps through the array's elements, the value of this variable is used instead of the array's size to determine the maximum subscript. Program 8-5 shows a demonstration.

Program 8-5

```
1 // Declare a constant for the array size.
2 Constant Integer SIZE = 100
3
4 // Declare an array to hold integer values.
5 Declare Integer values[SIZE]
6
7 // Declare an Integer variable to hold the number of items
```

```
 8  // that are actually stored in the array.
 9  Declare Integer count = 0
10
11  // Declare an Integer variable to hold the user's input.
12  Declare Integer number
13
14  // Declare a variable to step through the array.
15  Declare Integer index
16
17  // Prompt the user to enter a number. If the user enters the
18  // sentinel value -1 we will stop accepting input.
19  Display "Enter a number or -1 to quit."
20  Input number
21
22  // If the input is not -1 and the array is not
23  // full, process the input.
24  While (number != -1 AND count < SIZE)
25     // Store the input in the array.
26     Set values[count] = number
27
28     // Increment count.
29     count = count + 1
30
31     // Prompt the user for the next number.
32     Display "Enter a number or -1 to quit."
33     Input number
34  End While
35
36  // Display the values stored in the array.
37  Display "Here are the values you entered:"
38  For index = 0 To count - 1
39     Display values[index]
40  End For
```

Program Output (With Input Shown in Bold)

```
Enter a number or -1 to quit.
2 [Enter]
Enter a number or -1 to quit.
4 [Enter]
Enter a number or -1 to quit.
6 [Enter]
Enter a number or -1 to quit.
-1 [Enter]
Here are the numbers you entered:
2
4
6
```

Let's examine the pseudocode in detail. Line 2 declares a constant, SIZE, initialized with the value 100. Line 5 declares an Integer array named values, using SIZE as the size declarator. As a result, the values array will have 100 elements. Line 9 declares an Integer variable named count, which will hold the number of items that are stored in the values array. Notice that count is initialized with 0 because there are no values stored in the array. Line 12 declares an `Integer` variable named `number` that will hold values entered by the user, and line 15 declares an `Integer` variable named `index` that will be used in a loop to step through the array, displaying its elements.

Line 19 prompts the user to enter a number or −1 to quit. This program uses the value −1 as a sentinel value. When the user enters −1, the program will stop reading input. Line 20 reads the user's input and stores it in the `number` variable. A `While` loop begins in line 24. The loop iterates as long as `number` is not −1 and `count` is less than the size of the array. Inside the loop, in line 26 the `numbers` variable is assigned to `values[count]`, and in line 29 the `count` variable is incremented. (Each time a number is assigned to an array element, the `count` variable is incremented. As a result, the `count` variable will hold the number of items that are stored in the array.) Then, line 32 prompts the user to enter another number (or −1 to quit) and line 33 reads the user's input into the `number` variable. The loop then starts over.

When the user enters −1, or `count` reaches the size of the array, the `While` loop stops. The `For` loop that begins in line 38 displays all of the items that are stored in the array. Rather than stepping through all of the elements in the array, however, the loop steps only through the elements that contain values. Notice that the `index` variable's starting value is 0, and its ending value is `count` −1. By setting the ending value to `count` − 1 rather than `SIZE` − 1, the loop will stop when the element containing the last valid value has been displayed, not when the end of the array has been reached.

Optional Topic: The `For Each` Loop

Several programming languages provide a specialized version of the `For` loop that is known as the `For Each` loop. The *For Each* loop can simplify array processing when your task is simply to step through an array, retrieving the value of each element. The `For Each` loop is typically used in the following general format:

```
For Each var In array
    statement
    statement
    statement
    etc.
End For
```

In the general format, *var* is the name of a variable and *array* is the name of an array. The loop will iterate once for every element in the array. Each time the loop iterates, it copies an array element to the *var* variable. For example, the first time the loop iterates, *var* will contain the value of *array*[0], the second time the loop iterates *var* will contain the value of *array*[1], and so forth. This continues until the loop has stepped through all of the elements in the array. For example, suppose we have the following declarations:

```
Constant Integer SIZE = 5
Declare Integer numbers[SIZE] = 5, 10, 15, 20, 25
Declare Integer num
```

The following `For Each` loop can be used to display all of the values stored in the numbers array:

```
For Each num In numbers
    Display num
End For
```

NOTE: The For Each loop is not available in all languages, so we will continue to use the regular For loop in our example programs.

 Checkpoint

8.1 Can you store a mixture of data types in an array?

8.2 What is an array size declarator?

8.3 In most languages, can the size of an array be changed while the program is running?

8.4 What is an array element?

8.5 What is a subscript?

8.6 What is usually the first subscript in an array?

8.7 Look at the following pseudocode and answer questions a through d.
```
Constant Integer SIZE = 7
Declare Real numbers[SIZE]
```
a. What is the name of the array that is being declared?

b. What is the size of the array?

c. What data type are the array elements?

d. What is the subscript of the last element in the array?

8.8 What does "array bounds checking" mean?

8.9 What is an off-by-one error?

 8.2 **Sequentially Searching an Array**

CONCEPT: The sequential search algorithm is a simple technique for finding an item in an array. It steps through the array, beginning at the first element, and compares each element to the item being searched for. The search stops when the item is found or the end of the array is reached.

Programs commonly need to search for data that is stored in an array. Various techniques known as *search algorithms* have been developed to locate a specific item in a larger collection of data, such as an array. This section shows you how to use the simplest of all search algorithms—the sequential search. The *sequential search algorithm* uses a loop to sequentially step through an array, starting with the first element. It compares each element with the value being searched for and stops when the value is found or the end of the array is encountered. If the value being searched for is not in the array, the algorithm unsuccessfully searches to the end of the array.

Figure 8-5 shows the general logic of the sequential search algorithm. Here is a summary of the data items in the figure:

- `array` is the array being searched.
- `searchValue` is the value that the algorithm is searching for.
- `found` is a Boolean variable that is used as a flag. Setting `found` to `False` indicates that `searchValue` has not been found. Setting `found` to `True` indicates that `searchValue` has been found.
- `index` is an `Integer` variable used as a loop counter.

When the algorithm finishes, the `found` variable will be set to `True` if the *searchValue* was found in the array. When this is the case, the `index` variable will be set to the

Figure 8-5 Sequential search logic

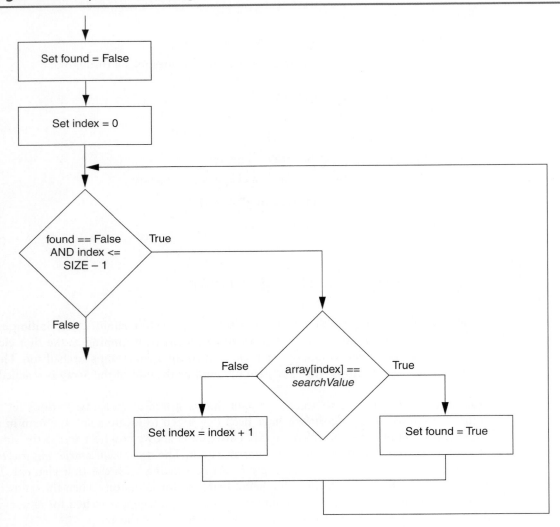

subscript of the element containing the *searchValue*. If the *searchValue* was not found in the array, found will be set to False. The following shows how you can express this logic in pseudocode:

```
Set found = False
Set index = 0
While found == False AND index <= SIZE − 1
    If array[index] == searchValue Then
        Set found = True
    Else
        Set index = index + 1
    End If
End While
```

The pseudocode in Program 8-6 demonstrates how to implement the sequential search in a program. This program has an array that holds test scores. It sequentially searches the array for a score of 100. If a score of 100 is found, the program displays the test number.

Program 8-6

```
 1 // Constant for the array size.
 2 Constant Integer SIZE = 10
 3
 4 // Declare an array to hold test scores.
 5 Declare Integer scores[SIZE] = 87, 75, 98, 100, 82,
 6                                72, 88, 92, 60, 78
 7
 8 // Declare a Boolean variable to act as a flag.
 9 Declare Boolean found
10
11 // Declare a variable to use as a loop counter.
12 Declare Integer index
13
14 // The flag must initially be set to False.
15 Set found = False
16
17 // Set the counter variable to 0.
18 Set index = 0
19
20 // Step through the array searching for a
21 // score equal to 100.
22 While found == False AND index <= SIZE - 1
23    If scores[index] == 100 Then
24       Set found = True
25    Else
26       Set index = index + 1
27    End If
28 End While
29
```

```
30 // Display the search results.
31 If found Then
32     Display "You earned 100 on test number ", index + 1
33 Else
34     Display "You did not earn 100 on any test."
35 End If
```

Program Output

```
You earned 100 on test number 4
```

Searching a String Array

Program 8-6 demonstrates how to use the sequential search algorithm to find a specific number in an Integer array. As shown in Program 8-7, you can also use the algorithm to find a string in a String array.

Program 8-7

```
 1 // Declare a constant for the array size.
 2 Constant Integer SIZE = 6
 3
 4 // Declare a String array initialized with values.
 5 Declare String names[SIZE] = "Ava Fischer", "Chris Rich",
 6                              "Gordon Pike", "Matt Hoyle",
 7                              "Rose Harrison", "Giovanni Ricci"
 8
 9 // Declare a variable to hold the search value.
10 Declare String searchValue
11
12 // Declare a Boolean variable to act as a flag.
13 Declare Boolean found
14
15 // Declare a counter variable for the array.
16 Declare Integer index
17
18 // The flag must initially be set to False.
19 Set found = False
20
21 // Set the counter variable to 0.
22 Set index = 0
23
24 // Get the string to search for.
25 Display "Enter a name to search for in the array."
26 Input searchValue
27
28 // Step through the array searching for
29 // the specified name.
30 While found == False AND index <= SIZE - 1
31     If names[index] == searchValue Then
```

```
32          Set found = True
33      Else
34          Set index = index + 1
35      End If
36 End While
37
38 // Display the search results.
39 If found Then
40      Display "That name was found at subscript ", index
41 Else
42      Display "That name was not found in the array."
43 End If
```

Program Output (with Input Shown in Bold)

Enter a name to search for in the array.
Matt Hoyle [Enter]
That name was found at subscript 3

Program Output (with Input Shown in Bold)

Enter a name to search for in the array.
Matt [Enter]
That name was not found in the array.

This program finds a string in the array only if the user types the complete string, exactly as it appears in the array. For example, in the first sample run the user enters "Matt Hoyle" as the search string and the program locates it at subscript 3. But, in the second sample run the user enters "Matt" and the program reports that the name was not found in the array. This is because the string "Matt" is not equal to the string "Matt Hoyle".

Often, programs must be designed to search for partial string matches. Most languages provide a library function that can determine whether a string partially matches another string. In pseudocode you can use the contains function to implement this. Recall from Chapter 6 that the contains function accepts two strings as arguments, and it returns True if the first string contains the second string; otherwise, the function returns False. The pseudocode in Program 8-8 shows how you can modify Program 8-7 to use the contains function. This version of the program will find strings in the array that partially match the string entered by the user.

Program 8-8

```
1 // Declare a constant for the array size.
2 Constant Integer SIZE = 6
3
4 // Declare a String array initialized with values.
5 Declare String names[SIZE] = "Ava Fischer", "Chris Rich",
6                              "Gordon Pike", "Matt Hoyle",
7                              "Rose Harrison", "Giovanni Ricci"
```

```
 8
 9 // Declare a variable to hold the search value.
10 Declare String searchValue
11
12 // Declare a Boolean variable to act as a flag.
13 Declare Boolean found
14
15 // Declare a counter variable for the array.
16 Declare Integer index
17
18 // The flag must initially be set to False.
19 Set found = False
20
21 // Set the counter variable to 0.
22 Set index = 0
23
24 // Get the string to search for.
25 Display "Enter a name to search for in the array."
26 Input searchValue
27
28 // Step through the array searching for
29 // the specified name.
30 While found == False AND index <= SIZE - 1
31    If contains(names[index], searchValue) Then
32       Set found = True
33    Else
34       Set index = index + 1
35    End If
36 End While
37
38 // Display the search results.
39 If found Then
40    Display "That name matches the following element:"
41    Display names[index]
41 Else
42    Display "That name was not found in the array."
43 End If
```

Program Output (with Input Shown in Bold)

Enter a name to search for in the array.
Matt [Enter]
That name matches the following element:
Matt Hoyle

 **Checkpoint**

8.10   What is a search algorithm?

8.11   Which array element does the sequential search algorithm first look at?

8.12   What does the loop do in the sequential search algorithm? What happens
       when the value being searched for is found?

8.13 How many elements does the sequential search algorithm look at in the case that the search value is not found in the array?

8.14 How do you look for a partial string match when searching an array of strings for a value?

8.3 Processing the Contents of an Array

In this chapter you've seen several examples of how loops are used to step through the elements of an array. There are many operations that you can perform on an array using a loop, and this section examines several such algorithms.

Totaling the Values in an Array

To calculate the total of the values in an array, you use a loop with an accumulator variable. The loop steps through the array, adding the value of each array element to the accumulator. Figure 8-6 shows the logic of the algorithm. In the algorithm `total` is an accumulator variable, `index` is a loop counter, and `array` is an array containing numeric values.

Figure 8-6 Algorithm for totaling the values in an array

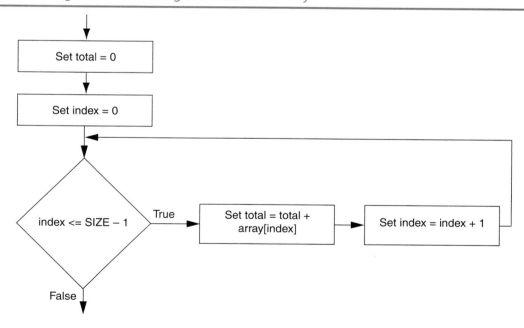

The pseudocode in Program 8-9 demonstrates the algorithm with an `Integer` array named `numbers`.

Program 8-9

```
 1 // Declare a constant for the array size.
 2 Constant Integer SIZE = 5
 3
 4 // Declare an array initialized with values.
 5 Declare Integer numbers[SIZE] = 2, 4, 6, 8, 10
 6
 7 // Declare and initialize an accumulator variable.
 8 Declare Integer total = 0
 9
10 // Declare a counter variable for the loop.
11 Declare Integer index
12
13 // Calculate the total of the array elements.
14 For index = 0 To SIZE - 1
15     Set total = total + numbers[index]
16 End For
17
18 // Display the sum of the array elements.
19 Display "The sum of the array elements is ", total
```

Program Output

```
The sum of the array elements is 30
```

Averaging the Values in an Array

The first step in calculating the average of the values in an array is to get the total of the values. You saw how to do that with a loop in the preceding section. The second step is to divide the total by the number of elements in the array. The pseudocode in Program 8-10 demonstrates the algorithm.

Program 8-10

```
 1 // Declare a constant for the array size.
 2 Constant Integer SIZE = 5
 3
 4 // Declare an array initialized with values.
 5 Declare Real scores[SIZE] = 2.5, 8.3, 6.5, 4.0, 5.2
 6
 7 // Declare and initialize an accumulator variable.
 8 Declare Real total = 0
 9
10 // Declare a variable to hold the average.
11 Declare Real average
12
13 // Declare a counter variable for the loop.
```

```
14 Declare Integer index
15
16 // Calculate the total of the array elements.
17 For index = 0 To SIZE - 1
18     Set total = total + numbers[index]
19 End For
20
21 // Calculate the average of the array elements.
22  Set average = total / SIZE
23
24 // Display the average of the array elements.
25 Display "The average of the array elements is ", average
```

Program Output

```
The average of the array elements is 5.3
```

Finding the Highest Value in an Array

Some programming tasks require you to find the highest value in a set of data. Examples include programs that report the highest sales amount for a given time period, the highest test score in a set of test scores, the highest temperature for a given set of days, and so forth.

The algorithm for finding the highest value in an array works like this: You create a variable to hold the highest value (the following examples name this variable highest). Then, you assign the value at element 0 to the highest variable. Next, you use a loop to step through the rest of the array elements, beginning at element 1. Each time the loop iterates, it compares an array element to the highest variable. If the array element is greater than the highest variable, then the value in the array element is assigned to the highest variable. When the loop finishes, the highest variable will contain the highest value in the array. The flowchart in Figure 8-7 illustrates this logic. The pseudocode in Program 8-11 shows a simple demonstration of the algorithm.

Program 8-11

```
1 // Declare a constant for the array size.
2 Constant Integer SIZE = 5
3
4 // Declare an array initialized with values.
5 Declare Integer numbers[SIZE] = 8, 1, 12, 6, 2
6
7 // Declare a counter variable for the array.
8 Declare Integer index
9
10 // Declare a variable to hold the highest value.
11 Declare Integer highest
12
13 // Assign the first element to highest.
14 Set highest = numbers[0]
15
```

```
16 // Step through the rest of the array,
17 // beginning at element 1. When a value
18 // greater than highest is found, assign
19 // that value to highest.
20 For index = 1 To SIZE - 1
21    If numbers[index] > highest Then
22       Set highest = numbers[index]
23    End If
24 End For
25
26 // Display the highest value.
27 Display "The highest value in the array is ", highest
```

Program Output

```
The highest value in the array is 12
```

Figure 8-7 Flowchart for finding the highest value in an array

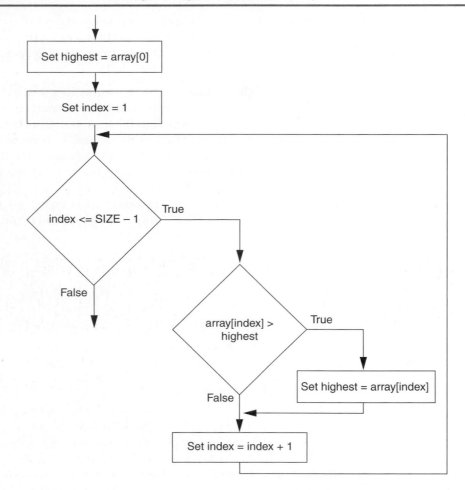

Finding the Lowest Value in an Array

In some programs you are more interested in finding the lowest value than the highest value in a set of data. For example, suppose you are designing a program that stores several players' golf scores in an array and you need to find the best score. In golf, the lower the score the better, so you would need an algorithm that finds the lowest value in the array.

The algorithm for finding the lowest value in an array is very similar to the algorithm for finding the highest score. It works like this: You create a variable to hold the lowest value (the following examples name this variable `lowest`). Then, you assign the value at element 0 to the `lowest` variable. Next, you use a loop to step through the rest of the array elements, beginning at element 1. Each time the loop iterates, it compares an array element to the `lowest` variable. If the array element is less than the `lowest` variable, then the value in the array element is assigned to the `lowest` variable. When the loop finishes, the `lowest` variable will contain the lowest value in the array. The flowchart in Figure 8-8 illustrates this logic. The pseudocode in Program 8-12 shows a simple demonstration of the algorithm.

Figure 8-8 Flowchart for finding the lowest value in an array

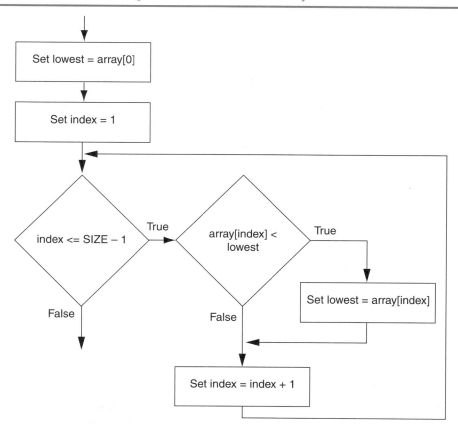

Program 8-12

```
 1 // Declare a constant for the array size.
 2 Constant Integer SIZE = 5
 3
 4 // Declare an array initialized with values.
 5 Declare Integer numbers[SIZE] = 8, 1, 12, 6, 2
 6
 7 // Declare a counter variable for the array.
 8 Declare Integer index
 9
10 // Declare a variable to hold the lowest value.
11 Declare Integer lowest
12
13 // Assign the first element to lowest.
14 Set lowest = numbers[0]
15
16 // Step through the rest of the array,
17 // beginning at element 1. When a value
18 // less than lowest is found, assign
19 // that value to lowest.
20 For index = 1 To SIZE - 1
21    If numbers[index] < lowest Then
22       Set lowest = numbers[index]
23    End If
24 End For
25
26 // Display the lowest value.
27 Display "The lowest value in the array is ", lowest
```

Program Output

```
The lowest value in the array is 1
```

Copying an Array

In most programming languages, if you need to copy the contents of one array to another you have to assign the individual elements of the array that you are copying to the elements of the other array. Usually, this is best done with a loop. For example, look at the following pseudocode:

```
Constant Integer SIZE = 5
Declare Integer firstArray[SIZE] = 100, 200, 300, 400, 500
Declare Integer secondArray[SIZE]
```

Suppose you want to copy the values in firstArray to secondArray. The following pseudocode assigns each element of firstArray to the corresponding element in secondArray.

```
Declare Integer index
For index = 0 To SIZE — 1
   Set secondArray[index] = firstArray[index]
End For
```

Passing an Array as an Argument to a Module or Function

Most languages allow you to pass an array as an argument to a module or a function. This gives you the ability to modularize many of the operations that you perform on an array. Passing an array as an argument typically requires that you pass two arguments: (1) the array itself, and (2) an integer that specifies the number of elements in the array. The pseudocode in Program 8-13 shows an example of a function that accepts an Integer array as an argument. The function returns the total of the array's elements.

Program 8-13

```
 1 Module main()
 2    // A constant for the array size.
 3    Constant Integer SIZE = 5
 4
 5    // An array initialized with values.
 6    Declare Integer numbers[SIZE] = 2, 4, 6, 8, 10
 7
 8    // A variable to hold the sum of the elements.
 9    Declare Integer sum
10
11    // Get the sum of the elements.
12    Set sum = getTotal(numbers, SIZE)
13
14    // Display the sum of the array elements.
15    Display "The sum of the array elements is ", sum
16 End Module
17
18 // The getTotal function accepts an Integer array and the
19 // array's size as arguments. It returns the total of the
20 // array elements.
21 Function Integer getTotal(Integer array[], Integer arraySize)
22    // Loop counter
23    Declare Integer index
24
25    // Accumulator, initialized to 0
26    Declare Integer total = 0
27
28    // Calculate the total of the array elements.
29    For index = 0 To arraySize - 1
30       Set total = total + array[index]
31    End For
32
33    // Return the total.
34    Return total
35 End Function
```

Program Output

```
The sum of the array elements is 30
```

In the `main` module, an `Integer` array is declared in line 6 and initialized with five values. In line 12, the following statement calls the `getTotal` function and assigns its return value to the `sum` variable:

```
Set sum = getTotal(numbers, SIZE)
```

This statement passes two arguments to the `getTotal` function: the `numbers` array and the value of the `SIZE` constant. Here is the first line of the `getTotal` function, which appears in line 21:

```
Function Integer getTotal(Integer array[], Integer arraySize)
```

Notice that the function has the following two parameters.

- `Integer array[]`—This parameter accepts an array of `Integers` as an argument.
- `Integer arraySize`—This parameter accepts an `Integer` that specifies the number of elements in the array.

When the function is called in line 12, it passes the `numbers` array into the `array` parameter, and the value of the `SIZE` constant into the `arraySize` parameter. This is shown in Figure 8-9. The function then calculates the total of the values in `array` and returns that value.

Figure 8-9

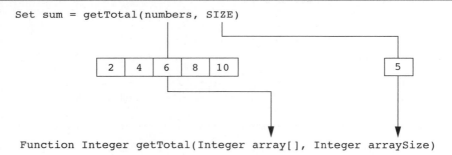

In the Spotlight:
Processing an Array

Dr. LaClaire gives four exams during the semester in her chemistry class. At the end of the semester she drops each student's lowest test score before averaging the scores. She has asked you to design a program that will read a student's four test scores as input, and calculate the average with the lowest score dropped. Here is the algorithm that you developed:

1. Read the student's four test scores.
2. Calculate the total of the scores.
3. Find the lowest score.
4. Subtract the lowest score from the total. This gives the adjusted total.
5. Divide the adjusted total by 3. This is the average.
6. Display the average.

Program 8-14 shows the pseudocode for the program, which is modularized. Rather than presenting the entire program at once, let's first examine the main module, and then each additional module and function separately. Here is the main module:

Program 8-14	**Score calculation program: main module**

```
 1 Module main()
 2    // Constant for the array size.
 3    Constant Integer SIZE = 4
 4
 5    // Array to hold test scores.
 6    Declare Real testScores[SIZE]
 7
 8    // Variable to hold the total of scores.
 9    Declare Real total
10
11    // Variable to hold the lowest score.
12    Declare Real lowestScore
13
14    // Variable to hold the average score.
15    Declare Real average
16
17    // Get the test scores from the user.
18    Call getTestScores(testScores, SIZE)
19
20    // Get the total of the test scores.
21    Set total = getTotal(testScores, SIZE)
22
23    // Get the lowest test score.
24    Set lowestScore = getLowest(testScores, SIZE)
25
26    // Subtract the lowest score from the total.
27    Set total = total - lowestScore
28
29    // Calculate the average. Divide by 3
30    // because the lowest score was dropped.
31    Set average = total / (SIZE - 1)
32
33    // Display the average.
34    Display "The average with the lowest score"
35    Display "dropped is ", average
36 End Module
37
```

Lines 3 through 15 declare the following items:

- SIZE, a constant that is used as an array size declarator
- testScores, a Real array to hold the test scores
- total, a Real variable that will hold the test score totals
- lowestScore, a Real variable that will hold the lowest test score
- average, a Real variable that will hold the average of the test scores

Line 18 calls the `getTestScores` module, passing the `testScores` array and the value of the `SIZE` constant as arguments. As you will see in a moment, the `testScores` array is passed by reference. The module gets the test scores from the user and stores them in the array.

Line 21 calls the `getTotal` module, passing the `testScores` array and the value of the `SIZE` constant as arguments. The function returns the total of the values in the array. This value is assigned to the `total` variable.

Line 24 calls the `getLowest` function, passing the `testScores` array and the value of the `SIZE` constant as arguments. The function returns the lowest value in the array. This value is assigned to the `lowestScore` variable.

Line 27 subtracts the lowest test score from the `total` variable. Then, line 31 calculates the average by dividing `total` by `SIZE − 1`. (The program divides by `SIZE − 1` because the lowest test score was dropped.) Lines 34 and 35 display the average. Figure 8-10 shows a flowchart for the `main` module.

Figure 8-10 Flowchart for the `main` module

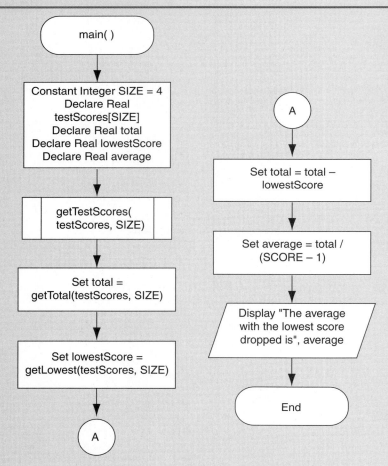

Next is the `getTestScores` module definition.

Program 8-14	**Score calculation program (continued): getTestScores module**

```
38 // The getTestScores module accepts an array (by reference)
39 // and its size as arguments. It prompts the user to enter
40 // test scores, which are stored in the array.
41 Module getTestScores(Real Ref scores[], Integer arraySize)
42    // Loop counter
43    Declare Integer index
44
45    // Get each test score.
46    For index = 0 To arraySize - 1
47       Display "Enter test score number ", index + 1
48       Input scores[index]
49    End For
50 End Module
51
```

The getTestScores module has two parameters:

- scores[]—A Real array is passed by reference into this parameter.
- arraySize—An Integer specifying the size of the array is passed into this parameter.

The purpose of this module is to get a student's test scores from the user and store them in the array that is passed as an argument into the scores[] parameter. Figure 8-11 shows a flowchart for this module.

The getTotal function definition appears next.

Program 8-14	**Score calculation program (continued): getTotal function**

```
52 // The getTotal function accepts a Real array and its
53 // size as arguments. It returns the total of the
54 // array elements.
55 Function Real getTotal(Real array[], Integer arraySize)
56    // Loop counter
57    Declare Integer index
58
59    // Accumulator, initialized to 0
60    Declare Real total = 0
61
62    // Calculate the total of the array elements.
63    For index = 0 To arraySize - 1
64       Set total = total + array[index]
65    End For
66
67    // Return the total.
68    Return total
69 End Function
70
```

The `getTotal` function has two parameters:

- `array[ ]`—A `Real` array
- `arraySize`—An `Integer` specifying the size of the array

This function returns the total of the values in the array that is passed as an argument into the `array[ ]` parameter. Figure 8-12 shows a flowchart for this module.

Figure 8-11 Flowchart for the `getTestScores` module

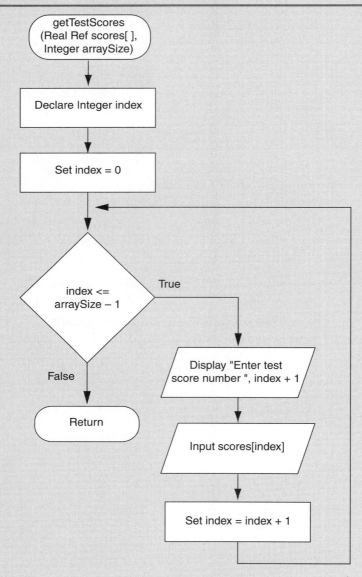

Figure 8-12 Flowchart for the `getTotal` function

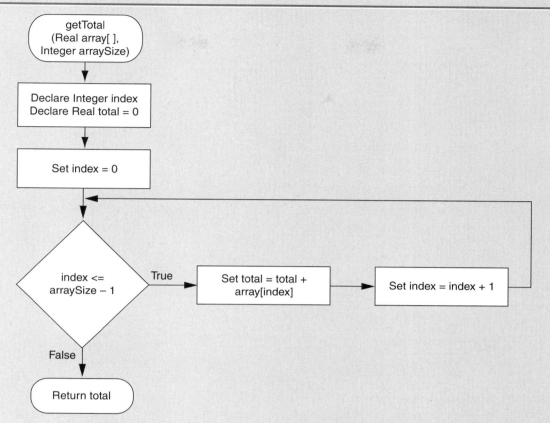

The program continues by defining the `getLowest` function.

Program 8-14	**Score calculation program (continued): `getLowest` function**

```
71 // The getLowest function accepts a Real array and its
72 // size as arguments and returns the lowest value in
73 // the array.
74 Function Real getLowest(Real array[], Integer arraySize)
75     // Variable to hold the lowest value.
76     Declare Real lowest
77
78     // Loop counter
79     Declare Integer index
80
81     // Get the first element of the array.
82     Set lowest = array[0]
83
84     // Step through the rest of the array. When a value
85     // less than lowest is found, assign it to lowest.
86     For index = 0 To arraySize - 1
87         If array[index] < lowest Then
```

```
88              Set lowest = array[index]
89          End If
90      End For
91
92      // Return the lowest value.
93      Return lowest
94 End Function
```

The `getlowest` function has two parameters:

- `array[]`—A Real array
- `arraySize`—An Integer specifying the size of the array

This function returns the lowest value in the array that is passed as an argument into the `array[]` parameter. Figure 8-13 shows a flowchart for this module.

Figure 8-13 Flowchart for the `getLowest` function

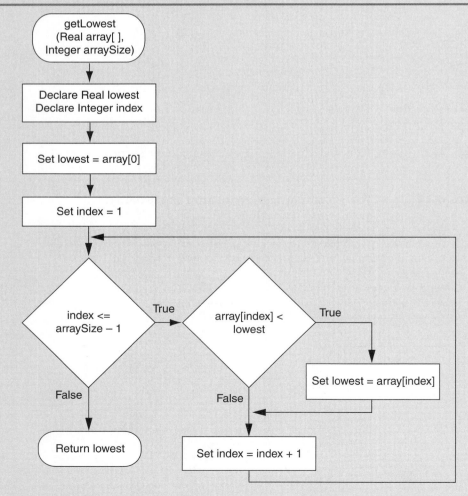

Program Output (with Input Shown in Bold)

```
Enter test score number 1.
92 [Enter]
Enter test score number 2.
67 [Enter]
Enter test score number 3.
75 [Enter]
Enter test score number 4.
88 [Enter]
The average with the lowest score dropped is 85
```

 Checkpoint

8.15 Briefly describe how you calculate the total of the values in an array.

8.16 Briefly describe how you get the average of the values in an array.

8.17 Describe the algorithm for finding the highest value in an array.

8.18 Describe the algorithm for finding the lowest value in an array.

8.19 How do you copy the contents of one array to another array?

8.4 Parallel Arrays

CONCEPT: By using the same subscript, you can establish relationships between data stored in two or more arrays.

VideoNote

Parallel Arrays

Sometimes it is useful to store related data in two or more arrays. For example, assume you have designed a program with the following array declarations:

```
Constant Integer SIZE = 5
Declare String names[SIZE]
Declare String addresses[SIZE]
```

The names array stores the names of five people, and the addresses array stores the addresses of the same five people. The data for each person is stored in the same relative location in each array. For instance, the first person's name is stored in names[0], and that same person's address is stored in addresses[0]. Figure 8-14 illustrates this.

To access the data, you use the same subscript with both arrays. For example, the loop in the following pseudocode displays each person's name and address:

```
Declare Integer index
For index = 0 To SIZE − 1
   Display names[index]
   Display addresses[index]
End For
```

Figure 8-14 The names and addresses arrays

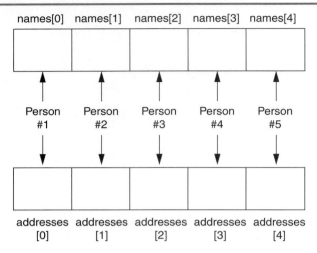

The names and addresses arrays are examples of parallel arrays. *Parallel arrays* are two or more arrays that hold related data, and the related elements in each array are accessed with a common subscript.

In the Spotlight:
Using Parallel Arrays

In this chapter's first *In the Spotlight* section (see Program 8-4), Megan asked you to design a program that allows her to enter the number of hours worked by each of her employees and then displays each employee's gross pay. As it is currently designed, the program refers to the employees as "Employee 1," Employee 2," and so on. Megan has asked you to modify the program so she can enter employees' names along with their hours, and then it should display each employee's name along with his or her gross pay.

Currently, the program has an array named hours that holds each employee's hours worked. You decide to add a parallel array named names that will hold each employee's name. The first employee's data will appear in names[0] and in hours[0], the second employee's data will appear in names[1] and in hours[1], and so on.

Here is the updated algorithm:

1. For each employee:
   a. Get the employee's name and store it in the names array.
   b. Get the employee's number of hours worked and store it in the corresponding element of the hours array.
2. Step through each set of elements in the parallel arrays and display the employee's name and gross pay.

Program 8-15 shows the pseudocode for the revised program, and Figure 8-15 shows a flowchart.

Program 8-15

```
 1 // Constant for the array sizes.
 2 Constant Integer SIZE = 6
 3
 4 // Array to hold each employee's name.
 5 Declare String names[SIZE]
 6
 7 // Array to hold each employee's hours.
 8 Declare Real hours[SIZE]
 9
10 // Variable to hold the hourly pay rate.
11 Declare Real payRate
12
13 // Variable to hold a gross pay amount.
14 Declare Real grossPay
15
16 // Variable to use as a loop counter.
17 Declare Integer index
18
19 // Get each employee's data.
20 For index = 0 To SIZE - 1
21     // Get an employee's name.
22     Display "Enter the name of employee ", index + 1
23     Input names[index]
24
25     // Get the employee's hours.
26     Display "Enter the hours worked by that employee."
27     Input hours[index]
28 End For
29
30 // Get the hourly pay rate.
31 Display "Enter the hourly pay rate."
32 Input payRate
33
34 // Display each employee's gross pay.
35 Display "Here is each employee's gross pay."
36 For index = 0 To SIZE - 1
37     Set grossPay = hours[index] * payRate
38     Display names[index], ": ", currencyFormat(grossPay)
39 End For
```

Program Output (with Input Shown in Bold)

```
Enter the name of employee 1.
Jamie Lynn [Enter]
Enter the hours worked by that employee.
10 [Enter]
Enter the name of employee 2.
Courtney [Enter]
Enter the hours worked by that employee.
20 [Enter]
Enter the name of employee 3.
Ashley [Enter]
Enter the hours worked by that employee.
```

```
15 [Enter]
Enter the name of employee 4.
Brian [Enter]
Enter the hours worked by that employee.
40 [Enter]
Enter the name of employee 5.
Jane [Enter]
Enter the hours worked by that employee.
20 [Enter]
Enter the name of employee 6.
Ian [Enter]
Enter the hours worked by that employee.
18 [Enter]
Enter the hourly pay rate.
12.75 [Enter]
Here is each employee's gross pay.
Jamie Lynn: $127.50
Courtney: $255.00
Ashley: $191.25
Brian: $510.00
Jane: $255.00
Ian: $229.50
```

Figure 8-15 Flowchart for Program 8-15

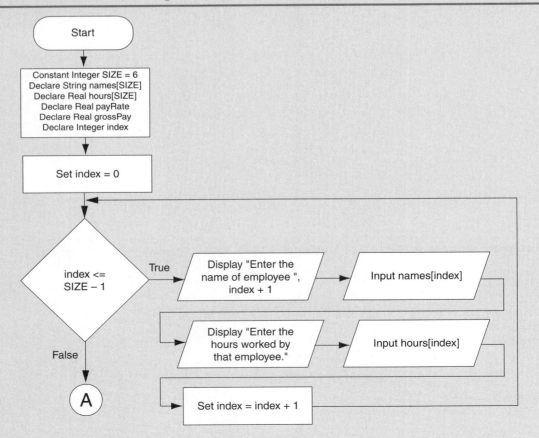

Figure 8-15 (continued)

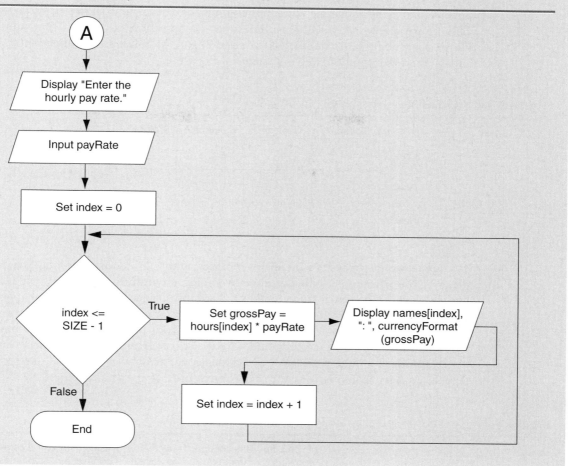

 Checkpoint

8.20 How do you establish a relationship between the data stored in two parallel arrays?

8.21 A program uses two parallel arrays: names and creditScore. The names array holds customer names and the creditScore array holds customer credit scores. If a particular customer's name is stored in names[82], where would that customer's credit score be stored?

8.5 Two-Dimensional Arrays

CONCEPT: A two-dimensional array is like several identical arrays put together. It is useful for storing multiple sets of data.

The arrays that you have studied so far are known as one-dimensional arrays. They are called *one dimensional* because they can only hold one set of data. Two-dimensional arrays, which are also called *2D arrays,* can hold multiple sets of data. Think of a two-dimensional array as having rows and columns of elements, as shown in Figure 8-16. This figure shows a two-dimensional array having three rows and four columns. Notice that the rows are numbered 0, 1, and 2, and the columns are numbered 0, 1, 2, and 3. There is a total of twelve elements in the array.

Figure 8-16 A two-dimensional array

	Column 0	Column 1	Column 2	Column 3
Row 0				
Row 1				
Row 2				

Two-dimensional arrays are useful for working with multiple sets of data. For example, suppose you are designing a grade-averaging program for a teacher. The teacher has six students, and each student takes five exams during the semester. One approach would be to create six one-dimensional arrays, one for each student. Each of these arrays would have five elements, one for each exam score. This approach would be cumbersome, however, because you would have to separately process each of the arrays. A better approach would be to use a two-dimensional array with six rows (one for each student) and five columns (one for each exam score), as shown in Figure 8-17.

Figure 8-17 Two-dimensional array with six rows and five columns

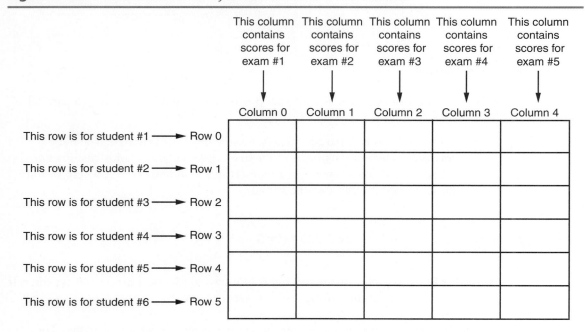

Declaring a Two-Dimensional Array

To declare a two-dimensional array, two size declarators are required: The first one is for the number of rows and the second one is for the number of columns. The following pseudocode shows an example of how to declare a two-dimensional array:

```
Declare Integer values[3][4]
```

This statement declares a two-dimensional Integer array with three rows and four columns. The name of the array is values, and there are a total of twelve elements in the array. As with one-dimensional arrays, it is best to use named constants as the size declarators. Here is an example:

```
Constant Integer ROWS = 3
Constant Integer COLS = 4
Declare Integer values[ROWS][COLS]
```

When processing the data in a two-dimensional array, each element has two subscripts: one for its row and another for its column. In the values array, the elements in row 0 are referenced as follows:

```
values[0][0]
values[0][1]
values[0][2]
values[0][3]
```

The elements in row 1 are as follows:

```
values[1][0]
values[1][1]
values[1][2]
values[1][3]
```

And the elements in row 2 are as follows:

```
values[2][0]
values[2][1]
values[2][2]
values[2][3]
```

Figure 8-18 illustrates the array with the subscripts shown for each element.

Figure 8-18 Subscripts for each element of the values array

	Column 0	Column 1	Column 2	Column 3
Row 0	values[0][0]	values[0][1]	values[0][2]	values[0][3]
Row 1	values[1][0]	values[1][1]	values[1][2]	values[1][3]
Row 2	values[2][0]	values[2][1]	values[2][2]	values[2][3]

Accessing the Elements in a Two-Dimensional Array

To access one of the elements in a two-dimensional array, you must use both subscripts. For example, the following pseudocode statement assigns the number 95 to values[2][1]:

```
Set values[2][1] = 95
```

Programs that process two-dimensional arrays commonly do so with nested loops. The pseudocode in Program 8-16 shows an example. It declares an array with three rows and four columns, prompts the user for values to store in each element, and then displays the values in each element.

Program 8-16

```
 1 // Create a 2D array.
 2 Constant Integer ROWS = 3
 3 Constant Integer COLS = 4
 4 Declare Integer values[ROWS][COLS]
 5
 6 // Counter variables for rows and columns.
 7 Declare Integer row, col
 8
 9 // Get values to store in the array.
10 For row = 0 To ROWS - 1
11     For col = 0 To COLS - 1
12         Display "Enter a number."
13         Input values[row][col]
14     End For
15 End For
16
17 // Display the values in the array.
18 Display "Here are the values you entered."
19 For row = 0 To ROWS - 1
20     For col = 0 To COLS - 1
21         Display values[row][col]
22     End For
23 End For
```

Program Output (with Input Shown in Bold)

Enter a number.
1 [Enter]
Enter a number.
2 [Enter]
Enter a number.
3 [Enter]
Enter a number.
4 [Enter]
Enter a number.
5 [Enter]
Enter a number.
6 [Enter]

```
Here are the values you entered.
1
2
3
4
5
6
```

> **TIP:** Most languages allow you to initialize a two-dimensional array with data when you declare the array. The syntax varies from language to language. Here is an example of how you can initialize a two-dimensional array in pseudocode:
>
> ```
> Declare Integer testScores[3][4] = 88, 72, 90, 92,
>                                     67, 72, 91, 85,
>                                     79, 65, 72, 84
> ```
>
> In this declaration the value 88 is stored in testScores[0][0], the value 72 is stored in testScores[0][1], the value 90 is stored in testScores[0][2], and so forth.

The following *In the Spotlight* section shows another example of a two-dimensional array. This program adds all of the elements of a two-dimensional array to an accumulator.

In the Spotlight:

Using a Two-Dimensional Array

Unique Candy Inc. has three divisions: division 1 (East Coast), division 2 (Midwest), and division 3 (West Coast). The sales manager has asked you to design a program that will read as input each division's sales for each quarter of the year, and then display the total sales for all divisions.

This program requires you to process three sets of data:

- The sales amounts for division 1
- The sales amounts for division 2
- The sales amounts for division 3

Each of these sets of data contains four items:

- The sales for quarter 1
- The sales for quarter 2
- The sales for quarter 3
- The sales for quarter 4

You decide to store the sales amounts in a two-dimensional array. The array will have three rows (one for each division) and four columns (one for each quarter). Figure 8-19 shows how the sales data will be organized in the array.

Figure 8-19 Two-dimensional array to hold sales data

	Column 0	Column 1	Column 2	Column 3
Row 0	sales[0][0] Holds data for division 1, quarter 1	sales[0][1] Holds data for division 1, quarter 2	sales[0][2] Holds data for division 1, quarter 3	sales[0][3] Holds data for division 1, quarter 4
Row 1	sales[1][0] Holds data for division 2, quarter 1	sales[1][1] Holds data for division 2, quarter 2	sales[1][2] Holds data for division 2, quarter 3	sales[1][3] Holds data for division 2, quarter 4
Row 2	sales[2][0] Holds data for division 3, quarter 1	sales[2][1] Holds data for division 3, quarter 2	sales[2][2] Holds data for division 3, quarter 3	sales[2][3] Holds data for division 3, quarter 4

The program will use a pair of nested loops to read the sales amounts. It will then use a pair of nested loops to add all of the array elements to an accumulator variable. Here is an overview of the algorithm:

1. For each division:
   For each quarter:
   Read the amount of sales for the quarter and store it in the array.
2. For each row in the array:
   For each column in the array:
   Add the amount in the column to an accumulator.
3. Display the amount in the accumulator.

Program 8-17 shows the pseudocode for the program.

Program 8-17

```
 1 // Constants for the array sizes.
 2 Constant Integer ROWS = 3
 3 Constant Integer COLS = 4
 4
 5 // An array to hold company sales.
 6 Declare Real sales[ROWS][COLS]
 7
 8 // Counter variables
 9 Declare Integer row, col
10
11 // Accumulator
12 Declare Real total = 0
13
14 // Display instructions.
15 Display "This program calculates the company's"
16 Display "total sales. Enter the quarterly sales"
17 Display "amounts for each division when prompted."
18
19 // Nested loops to fill the array with quarterly
```

```
20  // sales amounts for each division.
21  For row = 0 To ROWS - 1
22     For col = 0 To COLS - 1
23        Display "Division ", row + 1, " quarter ", col + 1
24        Input sales[row][col]
25     End For
26     // Display a blank line.
27     Display
28  End For
29
30  // Nested loops to add all of the array elements.
31  For row = 0 To ROWS - 1
32     For col = 0 To COLS - 1
33        Set total = total + sales[row][col]
34     End For
35  End For
36
37  // Display the total sales.
38  Display "The total company sales are: $",
39            currencyFormat(total)
```

Program Output (with Input Shown in Bold)

This program calculates the company's total sales. Enter the
quarterly sales amounts for each division when prompted.

Division 1 quarter 1
1000.00 [Enter]
Division 1 quarter 2
1100.00 [Enter]
Division 1 quarter 3
1200.00 [Enter]
Division 1 quarter 4
1300.00 [Enter]

Division 2 quarter 1
2000.00 [Enter]
Division 2 quarter 2
2100.00 [Enter]
Division 2 quarter 3
2200.00 [Enter]
Division 2 quarter 4
2300.00 [Enter]

Division 3 quarter 1
3000.00 [Enter]
Division 3 quarter 2
3100.00 [Enter]
Division 3 quarter 3
3200.00 [Enter]
Division 3 quarter 4
3300.00 [Enter]

The total company sales are: $25,800.00

The first set of nested loops appears in lines 21 through 28. This part of the program prompts the user for each quarter's sales amount for each division. Figure 8-20 shows a flowchart for this set of loops.

Figure 8-20 Flowchart for the first nested loops (lines 21 through 28)

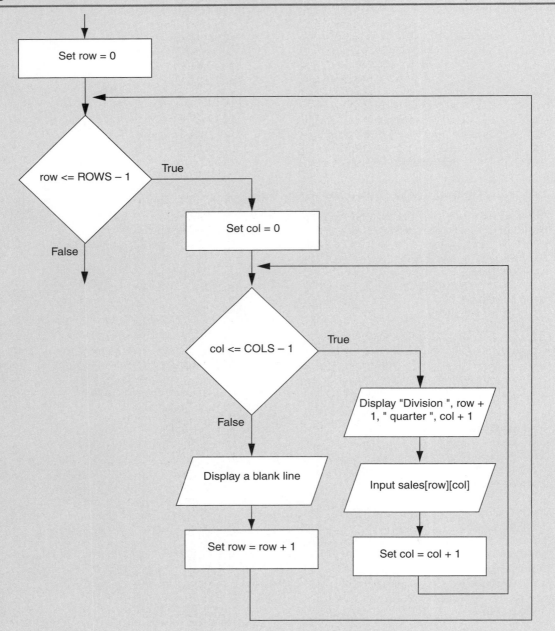

The second set of nested loops appears in lines 31 through 35. This part of the program steps through the `sales` array, adding the value of each element to the `total` variable, which is an accumulator. Figure 8-21 shows a flowchart for this set of loops. After these loops finish running, the `total` variable will contain the total of all the elements in the `sales` array.

Figure 8-21 Flowchart for the second nested loops (lines 31 through 35)

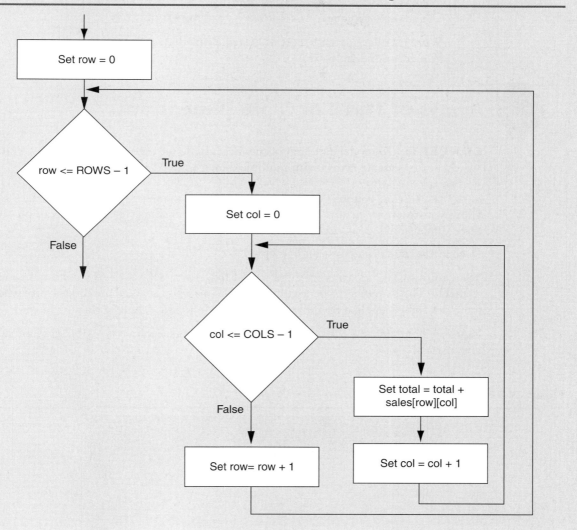

✓ Checkpoint

8.22 How many rows and how many columns are in the following array?

```
Declare Integer points[88][100]
```

8.23 Write a pseudocode statement that assigns the value 100 to the very last element in the points array declared in Checkpoint 8.22.

8.24 Write a pseudocode declaration for a two-dimensional array initialized with the following table of data:

12	24	32	21	42
14	67	87	65	90
19	1	24	12	8

8.25 Assume a program has the following declarations:

```
Constant Integer ROWS = 100
Constant Integer COLS = 50
Declare Integer info[ROWS][COLS]
```

Write pseudocode with a set of nested loops that store the value 99 in each element of the info array.

8.6 Arrays of Three or More Dimensions

CONCEPT: To model data that occurs in multiple sets, most languages allow you to create arrays with multiple dimensions.

In the last section you saw examples of two-dimensional arrays. Most languages also allow you to create arrays with three or more dimensions. Here is an example of a three-dimensional array declaration in pseudocode:

```
Declare Real seats [3][5][8]
```

You can think of this array as three sets of five rows, with each row containing eight elements. The array might be used to store the prices of seats in an auditorium, where there are eight seats in a row, five rows in a section, and a total of three sections.

Figure 8-22 illustrates the concept of a three-dimensional array as "pages" of two-dimensional arrays.

Figure 8-22 A three-dimensional array

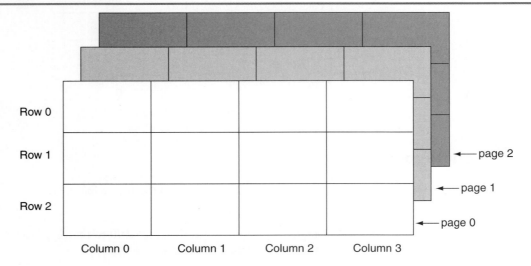

Arrays with more than three dimensions are difficult to visualize, but they can be useful in some programming problems. For example, in a factory warehouse where cases of widgets are stacked on pallets, an array with four dimensions could be used to store a part number for each widget. The four subscripts of each element could represent the pallet number, case number, row number, and column number of each widget. Similarly, an array with five dimensions could be used if there were multiple warehouses.

 ## Checkpoint

8.26 A bookstore keeps books on 50 racks with 10 shelves each. Each shelf holds 25 books. Declare a 3D `string` array to hold the names of all the books in the store. The array's 3 dimensions should represent the racks, shelves, and books in the store.

Review Questions

Multiple Choice

1. This appears in an array declaration and specifies the number of elements in the array.
   a. subscript
   b. size declarator
   c. array name
   d. initialization value

2. To make programs easier to maintain, many programmers use these to specify the size of an array.
   a. real numbers
   b. string expressions
   c. math expressions
   d. named constants

3. This is an individual storage location in an array.
   a. element
   b. bin
   c. cubby hole
   d. size declarator

4. This is a number that identifies a storage location in an array.
   a. element
   b. subscript
   c. size declarator
   d. identifier

5. This is typically the first subscript in an array.
   a. −1
   b. 1
   c. 0
   d. The size of the array minus one

6. This is typically the last subscript in an array.

    a. −1
    b. 99
    c. 0
    d. The size of the array minus one

7. This algorithm uses a loop to step through each element of an array, starting with the first element, searching for a value.

    a. sequential search
    b. step-by-step search
    c. elemental search
    d. binary search

8. Many programming languages perform this, which means they do not allow a program to use an invalid array subscript.

    a. memory checking
    b. bounds checking
    c. type compatibility checking
    d. syntax checking

9. This term describes two or more arrays that hold related data, and the related elements in each array are accessed with a common subscript.

    a. synchronous arrays
    b. asynchronous arrays
    c. parallel arrays
    d. two-dimensional arrays

10. You typically think of a two-dimensional array as containing

    a. lines and statements
    b. chapters and pages
    c. rows and columns
    d. horizontal and vertical elements

True or False

1. You can store a mixture of different data types in an array.

2. In most languages, an array's size cannot be changed while the program is running.

3. Array bounds checking typically occurs while a program is running.

4. You can do many things with arrays, but you cannot pass one as an argument to a module or a function.

5. A declaration for a two-dimensional array requires only one size declarator.

Short Answer

1. What is an off-by-one error?

2. Look at the following pseudocode:

```
Constant Integer SIZE = 10
Declare Integer values[SIZE]
```

a. How many elements does the array have?
b. What is the subscript of the first element in the array?
c. What is the subscript of the last element in the array?

3. Look at the following pseudocode:

```
Constant Integer SIZE = 3
Declare Integer numbers[SIZE] = 1, 2, 3
```

a. What value is stored in `numbers[2]`?
b. What value is stored in `numbers[0]`?

4. A program uses two parallel arrays named `customerNumbers` and `balances`. The `customerNumbers` array holds customer numbers and the `balances` array holds customer account balances. If a particular customer's customer number is stored in `customerNumbers[187]`, where would that customer's account balance be stored?

5. Look at the following pseudocode array declaration:

```
Declare Real sales[8][10]
```

a. How many rows does the array have?
b. How many columns does the array have?
c. How many elements does the array have?
d. Write a pseudocode statement that stores a number in the last column of the last row in the array.

Algorithm Workbench

1. Write a pseudocode declaration for a `String` array initialized with the following strings: `"Einstein"`, `"Newton"`, `"Copernicus"`, and `"Kepler"`.

2. Assume `names` is an `Integer` array with 20 elements. Design a `For` loop that displays each element of the array.

3. Assume the arrays `numberArray1` and `numberArray2` each have 100 elements. Design an algorithm that copies the values in `numberArray1` to `numberArray2`.

4. Draw a flowchart showing the general logic for totaling the values in an array.

5. Draw a flowchart showing the general logic for finding the highest value in an array.

6. Draw a flowchart showing the general logic for finding the lowest value in an array.

7. Assume the following declarations appear in a pseudocode program:

```
Constant Integer SIZE = 100
Declare Integer firstArray[SIZE]
Declare Integer secondArray[SIZE]
```

Also, assume that values have been stored in each element of `firstArray`. Design an algorithm that copies the contents of `firstArray` to `secondArray`.

8. Design an algorithm for a function that accepts an `Integer` array as an argument and returns the total of the values in the array.

9. Write a pseudocode algorithm that uses the For Each loop to display all of the values in the following array:

```
Constant Integer SIZE = 10
Declare Integer values[SIZE] = 1, 2, 3, 4, 5, 6, 7, 8, 9, 10
```

VideoNote

The Total
Sales
Problem

Programming Exercises

1. Total Sales

Design a program that asks the user to enter a store's sales for each day of the week. The amounts should be stored in an array. Use a loop to calculate the total sales for the week and display the result.

2. Lottery Number Generator

Design a program that generates a 7-digit lottery number. The program should have an Integer array with 7 elements. Write a loop that steps through the array, randomly generating a number in the range of 0 through 9 for each element. (Use the random function that was discussed in Chapter 6.) Then write another loop that displays the contents of the array.

3. Rainfall Statistics

Design a program that lets the user enter the total rainfall for each of 12 months into an array. The program should calculate and display the total rainfall for the year, the average monthly rainfall, and the months with the highest and lowest amounts.

4. Number Analysis Program

Design a program that asks the user to enter a series of 20 numbers. The program should store the numbers in an array and then display the following data:

- The lowest number in the array
- The highest number in the array
- The total of the numbers in the array
- The average of the numbers in the array

5. Charge Account Validation

Design a program that asks the user to enter a charge account number. The program should determine whether the number is valid by comparing it to the following list of valid charge account numbers:

5658845	4520125	7895122	8777541	8451277	1302850
8080152	4562555	5552012	5050552	7825877	1250255
1005231	6545231	3852085	7576651	7881200	4581002

These numbers should be stored in an array. Use the sequential search algorithm to locate the number entered by the user. If the number is in the array, the program should display a message indicating the number is valid. If the number is not in the array, the program should display a message indicating the number is invalid.

6. Days of Each Month

Design a program that displays the number of days in each month. The program's output should be similar to this:

```
January has 31 days.
February has 28 days.
March has 31 days.
April has 30 days.
May has 31 days.
June has 30 days.
July has 31 days.
August has 31 days.
September has 30 days.
October has 31 days.
November has 30 days.
December has 31 days.
```

The program should have two parallel arrays: a 12-element `String` array that is initialized with the names of the months, and a 12-element `Integer` array that is initialized with the number of days in each month. To produce the output specified, use a loop to step through the arrays getting the name of a month and the number of days in that month.

7. **Phone Number Lookup**

   Design a program that has two parallel arrays: a `String` array named `people` that is initialized with the names of seven of your friends, and a `String` array named `phoneNumbers` that is initialized with your friends' phone numbers. The program should allow the user to enter a person's name (or part of a person's name). It should then search for that person in the `people` array. If the person is found, it should get that person's phone number from the `phoneNumbers` array and display it. If the person is not found in the `people` array, the program should display a message indicating so.

8. **Payroll**

   Design a program that uses the following parallel arrays:

   - `empId`: An array of seven `Integers` to hold employee identification numbers. The array should be initialized with the following numbers:

     56588   45201   78951   87775   84512   13028   75804
   - `hours`: An array of seven `Integers` to hold the number of hours worked by each employee.
   - `payRate`: An array of seven `Reals` to hold each employee's hourly pay rate.
   - `wages`: An array of seven `Reals` to hold each employee's gross wages.

   The program should relate the data in each array through the subscripts. For example, the number in element 0 of the `hours` array should be the number of hours worked by the employee whose identification number is stored in element 0 of the `empId` array. That same employee's pay rate should be stored in element 0 of the `payRate` array.

   The program should display each employee number and ask the user to enter that employee's hours and pay rate. It should then calculate the gross wages for that employee (hours times pay rate), which should be stored in the `wages` array. After the data has been entered for all the employees, the program should display each employee's identification number and gross wages.

9. **Driver's License Exam**

The local driver's license office has asked you to design a program that grades the written portion of the driver's license exam. The exam has 20 multiple choice questions. Here are the correct answers:

1. B	6. A	11. B	16. C
2. D	7. B	12. C	17. C
3. A	8. A	13. D	18. B
4. A	9. C	14. A	19. D
5. C	10. D	15. D	20. A

Your program should store these correct answers in an array. (Store each question's correct answer in an element of a `String` array.) The program should ask the user to enter the student's answers for each of the 20 questions, which should be stored in another array. After the student's answers have been entered, the program should display a message indicating whether the student passed or failed the exam. (A student must correctly answer 15 of the 20 questions to pass the exam.) It should then display the total number of correctly answered questions, the total number of incorrectly answered questions, and a list showing the question numbers of the incorrectly answered questions.

10. **Tic-Tac-Toe Game**

Design a program that allows two players to play a game of tic-tac-toe. Use a two-dimensional `String` array with three rows and three columns as the game board. Each element of the array should be initialized with an asterisk (*). The program should run a loop that does the following:

a. Displays the contents of the board array.

b. Allows player 1 to select a location on the board for an X. The program should ask the user to enter the row and column number.

c. Allows player 2 to select a location on the board for an O. The program should ask the user to enter the row and column number.

d. Determines whether a player has won or if a tie has occurred. If a player has won, the program should declare that player the winner and end. If a tie has occurred, the program should say so and end.

e. Player 1 wins when there are three Xs in a row on the game board. Player 2 wins when there are three Os in a row on the game board. The winning Xs or Os can appear in a row, in a column, or diagonally across the board. A tie occurs when all of the locations on the board are full, but there is no winner.

CHAPTER

9 Sorting and Searching Arrays

TOPICS

9.1   The Bubble Sort Algorithm   9.3   The Insertion Sort Algorithm

9.2   The Selection Sort Algorithm   9.4   The Binary Search Algorithm

9.1

The Bubble Sort Algorithm

> **CONCEPT:** A sorting algorithm rearranges the contents of an array so they appear in a specific order. The bubble sort is a simple sorting algorithm.

Sorting Algorithms

Many programming tasks require that the data in an array be sorted in some order. Customer lists, for instance, are commonly sorted in alphabetical order, student grades might be sorted from highest to lowest, and product codes could be sorted so all the products of the same color are stored together. To sort the data in an array, the programmer must use an appropriate sorting algorithm. A *sorting algorithm* is a technique for stepping through an array and rearranging its contents in some order.

The data in an array can be sorted in either ascending or descending order. If an array is sorted in *ascending order,* it means the values in the array are stored from lowest to highest. If the values are sorted in *descending order*, they are stored from highest to lowest. This chapter discusses three sorting algorithms that you can use to sort the data in an array: the *bubble sort,* the *selection sort,* and the *insertion sort.* This section examines the bubble sort algorithm.

The Bubble Sort

The bubble sort is an easy way to arrange data in ascending or descending order. It is called the *bubble sort* algorithm because as it makes passes through and compares the elements of the array, certain values "bubble" toward the end of the array with each pass. For example, if you are using the algorithm to sort an array in ascending order, the larger values move toward the end. If you are using the algorithm to sort an array in descending order, the smaller values move toward the end. In this section you will see how the bubble sort algorithm can be used to sort an array in ascending order.

Suppose we have the array shown in Figure 9-1. Let's see how the bubble sort can be used in arranging the array's elements in ascending order.

Figure 9-1 An array

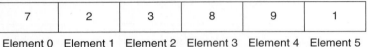

The bubble sort starts by comparing the first two elements in the array. If element 0 is greater than element 1, they are swapped. The array would then appear as shown in Figure 9-2.

Figure 9-2 Elements 0 and 1 are swapped

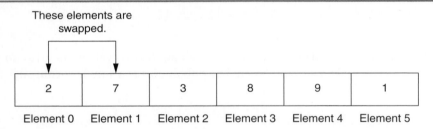

This method is repeated with elements 1 and 2. If element 1 is greater than element 2, they are swapped. The array would then appear as shown in Figure 9-3.

Figure 9-3 Elements 1 and 2 are swapped

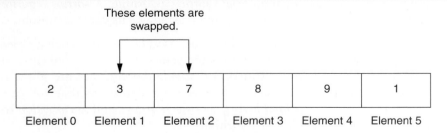

Next, elements 2 and 3 are compared. In this array, these elements are already in the proper order (element 2 is less than element 3), so no values are swapped. As the cycle continues, elements 3 and 4 are compared. Once again, it is not necessary to swap the values because they are already in the proper order.

When elements 4 and 5 are compared, however, they must be swapped because element 4 is greater than element 5. The array now appears as shown in Figure 9-4.

Figure 9-4 Elements 4 and 5 are swapped

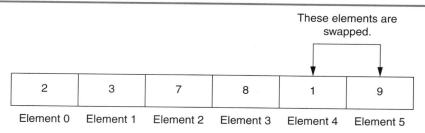

At this point, the entire array has been scanned once, and the largest value, 9, is in the correct position. There are other elements, however, that are not yet in their final positions. So, the algorithm will make another pass through the array, comparing each element with its neighbor. In the next pass it will stop comparing after reaching the next-to-last element because the last element already contains the correct value.

The second pass starts by comparing elements 0 and 1. Because those two are in the proper order, they are not swapped. Elements 1 and 2 are compared next, but once again, they are not swapped. This continues until elements 3 and 4 are compared. Because element 3 is greater than element 4, they are swapped. Element 4 is the last element that is compared during this pass, so this pass stops. The array now appears as shown in Figure 9-5.

Figure 9-5 Elements 3 and 4 are swapped

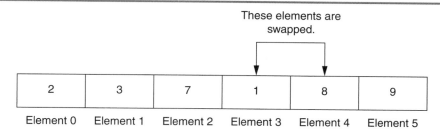

At the end of the second pass, the last two elements in the array contain the correct values. The third pass starts now, comparing each element with its neighbor. The third pass will not involve the last two elements, however, because they have already been sorted. When the third pass is finished, the last three elements will hold the correct values, as shown in Figure 9-6.

Figure 9-6 The array after the third pass

2	3	1	7	8	9
Element 0	Element 1	Element 2	Element 3	Element 4	Element 5

Each time the algorithm makes a pass through the array, the portion of the array that is scanned is decreased in size by one element, and the largest value in the scanned portion of the array is moved to its final position. When all of the passes have been made, the array will appear as shown in Figure 9-7.

Figure 9-7 The array with all elements sorted

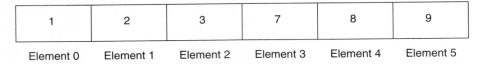

1	2	3	7	8	9
Element 0	Element 1	Element 2	Element 3	Element 4	Element 5

Swapping Array Elements

As you saw in the description of the bubble sort algorithm, certain elements are swapped as the algorithm steps through the array. Let's briefly discuss the process of swapping two items in computer memory. Assume we have the following variable declarations:

```
Declare Integer a = 1
Declare Integer b = 9
```

Suppose we want to swap the values in these variables so the variable a contains 9 and the variable b contains 1. At first, you might think that we only need to assign the variables to each other, like this:

```
// ERROR! The following does NOT swap the variables.
Set a = b
Set b = a
```

To understand why this doesn't work, let's step through the pseudocode. The first statement is Set a = b. This causes the value 9 to be assigned to a. But, what happens to the value 1 that was previously stored in a? Remember, when you assign a new value to a variable, the new value replaces any value that was previously stored in the variable. So, the old value, 1, will be thrown away. Then the next statement is Set b = a. Since the variable a contains 9, this assigns 9 to b. After these statements execute, the variables a and b will both contain the value 9.

To successfully swap the contents of two variables, we need a third variable that can serve as a temporary storage location:

```
Declare Integer temp
```

Then we can perform the following steps to swap the values in the variables a and b:

- Assign the value of a to temp.
- Assign the value of b to a.
- Assign the value of temp to b.

Figure 9-8 shows the contents of these variables as we perform each of these steps. Notice that after the steps are finished, the values in a and b are swapped.

Let's create a module named swap that will swap two items in memory. We will use the module in the bubble sort algorithm. Figure 9-9 shows a flowchart for the swap module. Notice that the module has two reference parameters, a and b. When we call the module, we pass two variables (or array elements) as arguments. When the module is finished, the values of the arguments will be swapped.

Figure 9-8 Swapping the values of a and b

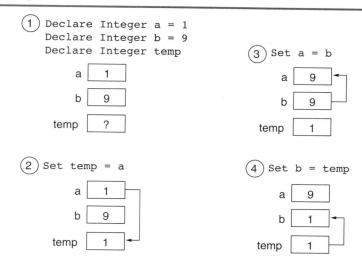

 NOTE: It is critical that we use reference parameters in the swap module, because the module must be able to change the values of the items that are passed to it as arguments.

Figure 9-9 Flowchart for a swap module

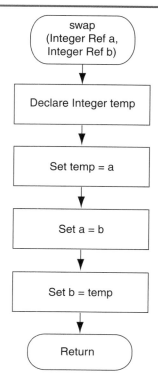

Here is the pseudocode for the swap module:

```
Module swap(Integer Ref a, Integer Ref b)
    // Local variable for temporary storage.
    Declare Integer temp

    // Swap the values in a and b.
    Set temp = a
    Set a = b
    Set b = temp
End Module
```

Of course, this version of the swap module works only with Integer arguments. If we want to swap the contents of other types of variables, we would have to change the data type of the a and b parameters as well as the temp variable.

Designing the Bubble Sort Algorithm

The bubble sort algorithm is usually incorporated into a program as a module. When you need to sort an array, pass the array to the module and it sorts the array. Figure 9-10 shows a flowchart for a bubbleSort module that sorts an array of integers. Program 9-1 shows the pseudocode for the module. (Note that the pseudocode shown in Program 9-1 is only the bubbleSort module and not a complete program.)

Figure 9-10 Flowchart for the bubble sort algorithm

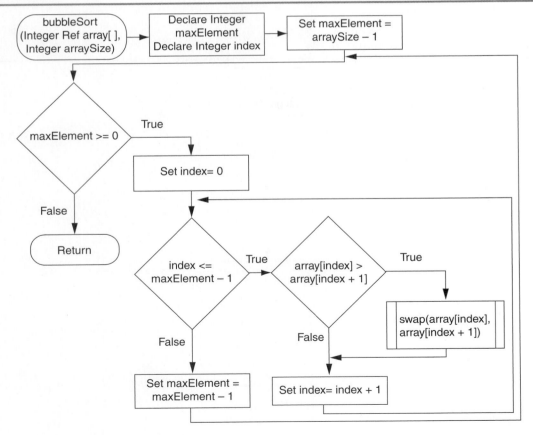

Program 9-1   **bubbleSort module**
(not a complete program)

```
1 Module bubbleSort(Integer Ref array[], Integer arraySize)
2    // The maxElement variable will contain the subscript
3    // of the last element in the array to compare.
4    Declare Integer maxElement
5
6    // The index variable will be used as a counter
7    // in the inner loop.
8    Declare Integer index
9
10   // The outer loop positions maxElement at the last
11   // element to compare during each pass through the
12   // array. Initially maxElement is the index of the
13   // last element in the array. During each iteration,
14   // it is decreased by one.
15   For maxElement = arraySize - 1 To 0 Step -1
16
17      // The inner loop steps through the array, comparing
18      // each element with its neighbor. All of the
19      // elements from index 0 through maxElement are
20      // involved in the comparison. If two elements are
21      // out of order, they are swapped.
22      For index = 0 To maxElement - 1
23
24         // Compare an element with its neighbor and swap
25         // if necessary.
26         If array[index] > array[index + 1] Then
27            Call swap(array[index], array[index + 1])
28         End If
29      End For
30   End For
31 End Module
```

In lines 4 and 8 the following variables are declared:

- The maxElement variable will hold the subscript of the last element that is to be compared to its immediate neighbor.
- The index variable is used as an array subscript in one of the loops.

The module uses two For loops, one nested inside another. The outer loop begins in line 15 as follows:

```
For maxElement = arraySize - 1 To 0 Step -1
```

This loop will iterate once for each element in the array. It causes the maxElement variable to take on all of the array's subscripts, from the highest subscript down to 0. After each iteration, maxElement is decremented by one.

The second loop, which is nested inside the first loop, begins in line 22 as follows:

```
For index = 0 To maxElement - 1
```

This loop iterates once for each of the unsorted array elements. It starts index at 0 and increments it up through maxElement - 1. During each iteration, the comparison in line 26 is performed:

```
If array[index] > array[index + 1] Then
```

This If statement compares the element at array[index] with its neighbor array[index + 1]. If the element's neighbor is greater, then the two are swapped in line 27. (The swap module must also appear in any program that uses the bubbleSort module.) The following *In the Spotlight* section shows how the bubble sort algorithm is used in a complete program.

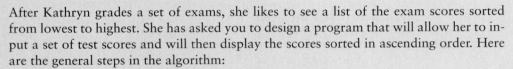

In the Spotlight:
Using the Bubble Sort Algorithm

After Kathryn grades a set of exams, she likes to see a list of the exam scores sorted from lowest to highest. She has asked you to design a program that will allow her to input a set of test scores and will then display the scores sorted in ascending order. Here are the general steps in the algorithm:

1. Get the test scores from the user and store them in an array.
2. Sort the array in ascending order.
3. Display the contents of the array.

For testing purposes, you ask Kathryn if you can first design the program for her smallest class, which has only six students. If she is satisfied with the program, you can modify it to work with her other classes. She agrees with your plan.

Program 9-2 shows the pseudocode for the program, which is modularized. Rather than presenting the entire program at once, we will first examine the main module, and then we will look at the additional modules separately. Here is the main module:

Program 9-2	**Ascending score program: main module**

```
 1 Module main()
 2    // Constant for the array size
 3    Constant Integer SIZE = 6
 4
 5    // Array to hold test scores
 6    Declare Integer testScores[SIZE]
 7
 8    // Get the test scores.
 9    getTestScores(testScores, SIZE)
10
11    // Sort the test scores.
12    bubbleSort(testScores, SIZE)
13
14    // Display the test scores.
15    Display "Here are the test scores"
16    Display "sorted from lowest to highest."
17    showTestScores(testScores, SIZE)
18 End Module
19
```

Line 3 declares a constant, SIZE, that will be used as an array size declarator. The testScores array, which will hold the test scores, is declared in line 6. In line 9 the testScores array and the SIZE constant are passed to the getTestScores module. As you will see in a moment, the testScores array is passed by reference. The module gets the test scores from the user and stores them in the array.

Line 12 passes the testScores array and the SIZE constant to the bubbleSort module. (The array is passed by reference.) When the module finishes, the values in the array will be sorted in ascending order.

Line 17 passes the testScores array and the SIZE constant to the showTestScores module. This module displays the values in the array.

Next is the definition of the getTestScores module, shown here:

Program 9-2   **Ascending score program (continued):**
                         getTestScores module

```
20 // The getTestScores module prompts the user
21 // to enter test scores into the array that is
22 // passed as an argument.
23 Module getTestScores(Integer Ref array[], Integer arraySize)
24     // Counter variable
25     Declare Integer index
26
27     // Get the test scores.
28     For index = 0 to arraySize - 1
29         Display "Enter score number ", index + 1
30         Input array[index]
31     End For
32 End Module
33
```

The getTestScores module has two parameters:

- array[]—An Integer array is passed by reference into this parameter.
- arraySize—An Integer specifying the size of the array is passed into this parameter.

The purpose of this module is to get a student's test scores from the user and store them in the array that is passed as an argument into the array[] parameter.

The definitions of the bubbleSort and swap modules appear next. These modules are the same as presented earlier in this chapter.

Program 9-2   **Ascending score program (continued):**
                         the bubbleSort and swap modules

```
34 // The bubbleSort module accepts an array of Integers
35 // and the array's size as arguments. When the module
36 // is finished, the values in the array will be sorted
37 // in ascending order.
38 Module bubbleSort(Integer Ref array[], Integer arraySize)
```

```
39       // The maxElement variable will contain the subscript
40       // of the last element in the array to compare.
41       Declare Integer maxElement
42
43       // The index variable will be used as a counter
44       // in the inner loop.
45       Declare Integer index
46
47       // The outer loop positions maxElement at the last
48       // element to compare during each pass through the
49       // array. Initially maxElement is the index of the
50       // last element in the array. During each iteration,
51       // it is decreased by one.
52       For maxElement = arraySize - 1 To 0 Step -1
53
54          // The inner loop steps through the array, comparing
55          // each element with its neighbor. All of the
56          // elements from index 0 through maxElement are
57          // involved in the comparison. If two elements are
58          // out of order, they are swapped.
59          For index = 0 To maxElement - 1
60
61             // Compare an element with its neighbor and swap
62             // if necessary.
63             If array[index] > array[index + 1] Then
64                Call swap(array[index], array[index + 1])
65             End If
66          End For
67       End For
68 End Module
69
70 // The swap module accepts two Integer arguments
71 // and swaps their contents.
72 Module swap(Integer Ref a, Integer Ref b)
73    // Local variable for temporary storage.
74    Declare Integer temp
75
76    // Swap the values in a and b.
77    Set temp = a
78    Set a = b
79    Set b = temp
80 End Module
81
```

The definition of the showTestScore module appears next.

Program 9-2   **Ascending score program (continued): the showTestScores module**

```
82 // The showTestScores module displays the contents
83 // of the array that is passed as an argument.
84 Module showTestScores(Integer array[], Integer arraySize)
85    // Counter variable
86    Declare Integer index
```

```
87
88    // Display the test scores.
89    For index = 0 to arraySize - 1
90       Display array[index]
91    End For
92 End Module
```

The `getTestScores` module has two parameters:

- `array[]`—An `Integer` array is passed by reference into this parameter.
- `arraySize`—An `Integer` specifying the size of the array is passed into this parameter.

The purpose of this module is to display the contents of the array that is passed into the array parameter.

Program Output (with Input Shown in Bold)

```
Enter score number 1
88 [Enter]
Enter score number 2
92 [Enter]
Enter score number 3
73 [Enter]
Enter score number 4
69 [Enter]
Enter score number 5
98 [Enter]
Enter score number 6
79 [Enter]
Here are the test scores sorted from lowest to highest.
69
73
79
88
92
98
```

Sorting an Array of Strings

Recall from Chapter 4 that most languages allow you to determine whether one string is greater than, less than, equal to, or not equal to another string. As a result, you can design the bubble sort algorithm to work with an array of strings. This gives you the ability to sort an array of strings in alphabetical (ascending) order. The pseudocode in Program 9-3 shows an example. Notice that this program's version of the `bubbleSort` and `swap` modules have been designed to work with `String` arrays.

Program 9-3

```
1 Module main()
2    // Constant for the array size
3    Constant Integer SIZE = 6
```

```
 4
 5    // An array of strings
 6    Declare String names[SIZE] = "David", "Abe", "Megan",
 7                                 "Beth", "Jeff", "Daisy"
 8
 9    // Loop counter
10    Declare Integer index
11
12    // Display the array in its original order.
13    Display "Original order:"
14    For index = 0 To SIZE - 1
15       Display names[index]
16    End For
17
18    // Sort the names.
19    Call bubbleSort(names, SIZE)
20
21    // Display a blank line.
22    Display
23
24    // Display the sorted array.
25    Display "Sorted order:"
26    For index = 0 To SIZE - 1
27       Display names[index]
28    End For
29 End Module
30
31 // The bubbleSort module accepts an array of Strings
32 // and the array's size as arguments. When the module
33 // is finished, the values in the array will be sorted
34 // in ascending order.
35 Module bubbleSort(String Ref array[], Integer arraySize)
36    // The maxElement variable will contain the subscript
37    // of the last element in the array to compare.
38    Declare Integer maxElement
39
40    // The index variable will be used as a counter
41    // in the inner loop.
42    Declare Integer index
43
44    // The outer loop positions maxElement at the last
45    // element to compare during each pass through the
46    // array. Initially maxElement is the index of the
47    // last element in the array. During each iteration,
48    // it is decreased by one.
49    For maxElement = arraySize - 1 To 0 Step -1
50
51       // The inner loop steps through the array, comparing
52       // each element with its neighbor. All of the
53       // elements from index 0 through maxElement are
54       // involved in the comparison. If two elements are
55       // out of order, they are swapped.
56       For index = 0 To maxElement - 1
57
```

```
58              // Compare an element with its neighbor and swap
59              // if necessary.
60              If array[index] > array[index + 1] Then
61                  Call swap(array[index], array[index + 1])
62              End If
63          End For
64      End For
65 End Module
66
67 // The swap module accepts two String arguments
68 // and swaps their contents.
69 Module swap(String Ref a, String Ref b)
70      // Local variable for temporary storage
71      Declare String temp
72
73      // Swap the values in a and b.
74      Set temp = a
75      Set a = b
76      Set b = temp
77 End Module
```

Program Output (with Input Shown in Bold)

```
Original order:
David
Abe
Megan
Beth
Jeff
Daisy

Sorted order:
Abe
Beth
Daisy
David
Jeff
Megan
```

TIP: All of the algorithms presented in this chapter can be designed to work with strings, as long as the language you are using allows you to compare string values.

Sorting in Descending Order

The bubble sort algorithm can be easily modified to sort an array in descending order, which means that the values will be ordered from highest to lowest. For example, the pseudocode in Program 9-4 is a modified version of Program 9-3. This version sorts the names array in descending order. The only modification to the bubble sort algorithm is in line 60. The comparison has been changed to determine whether array[index] is less than array[index + 1].

Program 9-4

```
 1 Module main()
 2    // Constant for the array size
 3    Constant Integer SIZE = 6
 4
 5    // An array of strings
 6    Declare String names[SIZE] = "David", "Abe", "Megan",
 7                                 "Beth", "Jeff", "Daisy"
 8
 9    // Loop counter
10    Declare Integer index
11
12    // Display the array in its original order.
13    Display "Original order:"
14    For index = 0 To SIZE - 1
15       Display names[index]
16    End For
17
18    // Sort the names.
19    Call bubbleSort(names, SIZE)
20
21    // Display a blank line.
22    Display
23
24    // Display the sorted array.
25    Display "Sorted in descending order:"
26    For index = 0 To SIZE - 1
27       Display names[index]
28    End For
29 End Module
30
31 // The bubbleSort module accepts an array of Strings
32 // and the array's size as arguments. When the module
33 // is finished, the values in the array will be sorted
34 // in descending order.
35 Module bubbleSort(String Ref array[], Integer arraySize)
36    // The maxElement variable will contain the subscript
37    // of the last element in the array to compare.
38    Declare Integer maxElement
39
40    // The index variable will be used as a counter
41    // in the inner loop.
42    Declare Integer index
43
44    // The outer loop positions maxElement at the last
45    // element to compare during each pass through the
46    // array. Initially maxElement is the index of the
47    // last element in the array. During each iteration,
48    // it is decreased by one.
49    For maxElement = arraySize - 1 To 0 Step -1
50
51       // The inner loop steps through the array, comparing
52       // each element with its neighbor. All of the
```

```
53          // elements from index 0 through maxElement are
54          // involved in the comparison. If two elements are
55          // out of order, they are swapped.
56          For index = 0 To maxElement - 1
57
58              // Compare an element with its neighbor and swap
59              // if necessary.
60              If array[index] < array[index + 1] Then
61                  Call swap(array[index], array[index + 1])
62              End If
63          End For
64      End For
65  End Module
66
67  // The swap module accepts two String arguments
68  // and swaps their contents.
69  Module swap(String Ref a, String Ref b)
70      // Local variable for temporary storage
71      Declare String temp
72
73      // Swap the values in a and b.
74      Set temp = a
75      Set a = b
76      Set b = temp
77  End Module
```

Program Output

```
Original order:
David
Abe
Megan
Beth
Jeff
Daisy

Sorted in descending order:
Megan
Jeff
David
Daisy
Beth
Abe
```

9.2 The Selection Sort Algorithm

CONCEPT: The selection sort is a sorting algorithm that is much more efficient than the bubble sort. The selection sort algorithm steps through an array, moving each value to its final sorted position.

The bubble sort algorithm is simple, but it is inefficient because values move by only one element at a time toward their final destination in the array. The *selection sort algorithm* usually performs fewer swaps because it moves items immediately to their final position in the array. The selection sort works like this: The smallest value in the array is located and moved to element 0. Then, the next smallest value is located and moved to element 1. This process continues until all of the elements have been placed in their proper order. Let's see how the selection sort works when arranging the elements of the array in Figure 9-11.

Figure 9-11 Values in an array

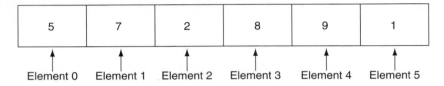

The selection sort scans the array, starting at element 0, and locates the element with the smallest value. Then, the contents of this element are swapped with the contents of element 0. In this example, the 1 stored in element 5 is swapped with the 5 stored in element 0. After the swap, the array appears as shown in Figure 9-12.

Figure 9-12 Values in the array after the first swap

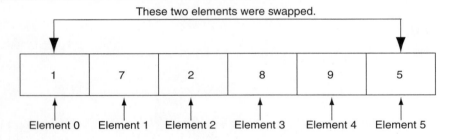

Then, the algorithm repeats the process, but because element 0 already contains the smallest value in the array, it can be left out of the procedure. This time, the algorithm begins the scan at element 1. In this example, the value in element 2 is swapped with the value in element 1. Then, the array appears as shown in Figure 9-13.

Figure 9-13 Values in the array after the second swap

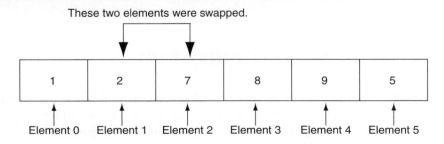

Once again the process is repeated, but this time the scan begins at element 2. The algorithm will find that element 5 contains the next smallest value. This element's value is swapped with that of element 2, causing the array to appear as shown in Figure 9-14.

Figure 9-14 Values in the array after the third swap

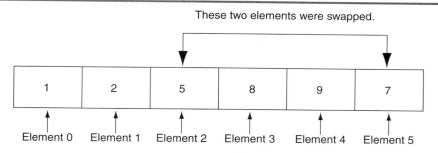

Next, the scanning begins at element 3. Its value is swapped with that of element 5, causing the array to appear as shown in Figure 9-15.

Figure 9-15 Values in the array after the fourth swap

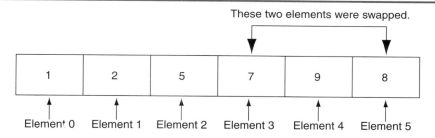

At this point there are only two elements left to sort. The algorithm finds that the value in element 5 is smaller than that of element 4, so the two are swapped. This puts the array in its final arrangement, as shown in Figure 9-16.

Figure 9-16 Values in the array after the fifth swap

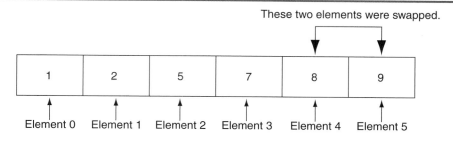

Figure 9-17 shows a flowchart for a module that performs the selection sort algorithm. The module accepts an `Integer` array (passed by reference) and an `Integer` that specifies the array's size. When the module is finished executing, the array will be sorted in ascending order. Program 9-5 shows the `selectionSort` module in pseudocode.

Program 9-5

```
 1 Module main()
 2     // Constant for the array size
 3     Constant Integer SIZE = 6
 4
 5     // An array of Integers
 6     Declare Integer numbers[SIZE] = 4, 6, 1, 3, 5, 2
 7
 8     // Loop counter
 9     Declare Integer index
10
11     // Display the array in its original order.
12     Display "Original order:"
13     For index = 0 To SIZE - 1
14         Display numbers[index]
15     End For
16
17     // Sort the numbers.
18     Call selectionSort(numbers, SIZE)
19
20     // Display a blank line.
21     Display
22
23     // Display the sorted array.
24     Display "Sorted order:"
25     For index = 0 To SIZE - 1
26         Display numbers[index]
27     End For
28 End Module
29
30 // The selectionSort module accepts an array of integers
31 // and the array's size as arguments. When the module is
32 // finished, the values in the array will be sorted in
33 // ascending order.
34 Module selectionSort(Integer Ref array[], Integer arraySize)
35     // startScan will hold the starting position of the scan.
36     Declare Integer startScan
37
38     // minIndex will hold the subscript of the element with
39     // the smallest value found in the scanned area.
40     Declare Integer minIndex
41
42     // minValue will hold the smallest value found in the
43     // scanned area.
44     Declare Integer minValue
45
46     // index is a counter variable used to hold a subscript.
47     Declare Integer index
48
49     // The outer loop iterates once for each element in the
50     // array, except the last element. The startScan variable
51     // marks the position where the scan should begin.
```

```
52      For startScan = 0 To arraySize - 2
53
54         // Assume the first element in the scannable area
55         // is the smallest value.
56         Set minIndex = startScan
57         Set minValue = array[startScan]
58
59         // Scan the array, starting at the 2nd element in
60         // the scannable area. We are looking for the smallest
61         // value in the scannable area.
62         For index = startScan + 1 To arraySize - 1
63            If array[index] < minValue Then
64               Set minValue = array[index]
65               Set minIndex = index
66            End If
67         End For
68
69         // Swap the element with the smallest value
70         // with the first element in the scannable area.
71         Call swap(array[minIndex], array[startScan])
72      End For
73 End Module
74
75 // The swap module accepts two Integer arguments
76 // and swaps their contents.
77 Module swap(Integer Ref a, Integer Ref b)
78      // Local variable for temporary storage
79      Declare Integer temp
80
81      // Swap the values in a and b.
82      Set temp = a
83      Set a = b
84      Set b = temp
85 End Module
```

Program Output

```
Original order:
4
6
1
3
5
2

Sorted order:
1
2
3
4
5
6
```

Figure 9-17 Flowchart for the `selectionSort` module

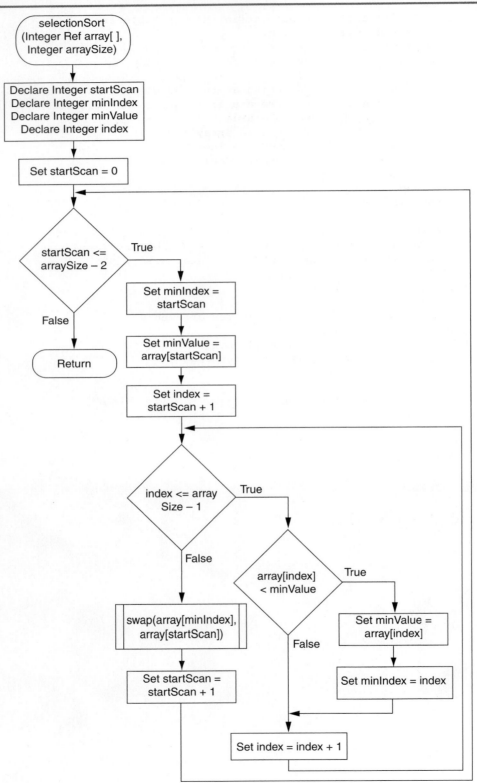

> **NOTE:** You can modify the selectionSort module so it sorts the array in descending order by changing the less than operator in line 63 to a greater than operator, as shown here:
>
> ```
> If array[index] > maxValue Then
> ```
>
> Notice that we have also changed the name of the minValue variable to maxValue, which is more appropriate for a descending order sort. You would need to make this change throughout the module.

9.3 The Insertion Sort Algorithm

CONCEPT: The insertion sort algorithm is also more efficient than the bubble sort algorithm. It sorts the first two elements, which become the sorted part of the array. It then inserts each of the remaining elements, one at a time, into the sorted part of the array at the correct location.

VideoNote

The Insertion Sort Algorithm

The *insertion sort algorithm* is another sorting algorithm that is also more efficient than the bubble sort. The insertion sort begins sorting the first two elements of the array. It simply compares the elements and, if necessary, swaps them so they are in the proper order. This becomes a sorted subset of the array.

Then, the objective is to incorporate the third element of the array into the sorted subset. This is done by inserting the third element of the array into the proper position relative to the first two elements. If the sort needs to shift either of the first two elements to accommodate the third element, it does so. Once it has inserted the third element into the correct position (relative to the first two elements), the first three elements become the sorted subset of the array.

This process continues with the fourth and subsequent elements, until all of the elements have been inserted into their proper positions. Let's look at an example. Suppose we start with the Integer array shown in Figure 9-18. As shown in the figure, the values in the first and second elements are out of order, so they will be swapped.

Figure 9-18 An unsorted array

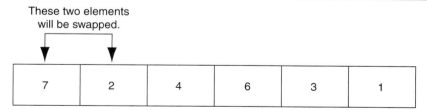

After the swap takes place, the first and second elements will be the sorted subset of the array. The next step is to move the value of the third element so it is in the correct position relative to the first two elements. As shown in Figure 9-19, the value in the third element must be positioned between the values in the first and second elements.

Figure 9-19 The third element must be moved

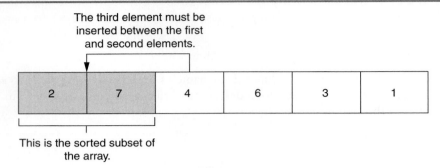

After the value in the third element is moved to its new position, the first three elements become the sorted subset of the array. The next step is to move the value of the fourth element so it is in the correct position relative to the first three elements. As shown in Figure 9-20, the value in the fourth element must be positioned between the values in the second and third elements.

Figure 9-20 The fourth element must be moved

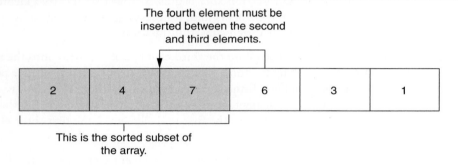

After the value in the fourth element is moved to its new position, the first four elements become the sorted subset of the array. The next step is to move the value of the fifth element so it is in the correct position relative to the first four elements. As shown in Figure 9-21, the value in the fifth element must be positioned between the values in the first and second elements.

Figure 9-21 The fifth element must be moved

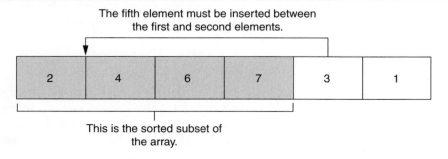

After the value in the fifth element is moved to its new position, the first five elements become the sorted subset of the array. The next step is to move the value of the sixth element so it is in the correct position relative to the first five elements. As shown in Figure 9-22, the value in the sixth element must be moved to the beginning of the array.

Figure 9-22 The sixth element must be moved

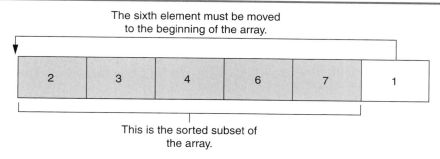

The sixth element is the last element in the array. Once it is moved to its correct position, the entire array is sorted. This is shown in Figure 9-23.

Figure 9-23 All of the elements are in the correct position

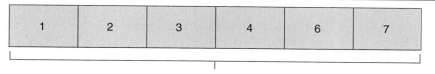

Figure 9-24 shows a flowchart for a module that performs the insertion sort algorithm. The module accepts an Integer array (passed by reference) and an Integer that specifies the array's size. When the module is finished executing, the array will be sorted in ascending order. Program 9-6 shows the insertionSort module in pseudocode.

Program 9-6

```
 1 Module main()
 2    // Constant for the array size
 3    Constant Integer SIZE = 6
 4
 5    // An array of Integers
 6    Declare Integer numbers[SIZE] = 4, 6, 1, 3, 5, 2
 7
 8    // Loop counter
 9    Declare Integer index
10
```

```
11      // Display the array in its original order.
12      Display "Original order:"
13      For index = 0 To SIZE - 1
14          Display numbers[index]
15      End For
16
17      // Sort the numbers.
18      Call insertionSort(numbers, SIZE)
19
20      // Display a blank line.
21      Display
22
23      // Display the sorted array.
24      Display "Sorted order:"
25      For index = 0 To SIZE - 1
26          Display numbers[index]
27      End For
28  End Module
29
30  // The insertionSort module accepts an array of integers
31  // and the array's size as arguments. When the module is
32  // finished, the values in the array will be sorted in
33  // ascending order.
34  Module insertionSort(Integer Ref array[], Integer arraySize)
35      // Loop counter
36      Declare Integer index
37
38      // Variable used to scan through the array.
39      Declare Integer scan
40
41      // Variable to hold the first unsorted value.
42      Declare Integer unsortedValue
43
44      // The outer loop steps the index variable through
45      // each subscript in the array, starting at 1. This
46      // is because element 0 is considered already sorted.
47      For index = 1 To arraySize - 1
48
49          // The first element outside the sorted subset is
50          // array[index]. Store the value of this element
51          // in unsortedValue.
52          Set unsortedValue = array[index]
53
54          // Start scan at the subscript of the first element
55          // outside the sorted subset.
56          Set scan = index
57
58          // Move the first element outside the sorted subset
59          // into its proper position within the sorted subset.
60          While scan > 0 AND array[scan-1] < array[scan]
61              Call swap(array[scan-1], array[scan])
62              Set scan = scan - 1
63          End While
```

```
64
65        // Insert the unsorted value in its proper position
66        // within the sorted subset.
67        Set array[scan] = unsortedValue
68     End For
69 End Module
70
71 // The swap module accepts two Integer arguments
72 // and swaps their contents.
73 Module swap(Integer Ref a, Integer Ref b)
74     // Local variable for temporary storage
75     Declare Integer temp
76
77     // Swap the values in a and b.
78     Set temp = a
79     Set a = b
80     Set b = temp
81 End Module
```

Program Output

```
Original order:
4
6
1
3
5
2

Sorted order:
1
2
3
4
5
6
```

NOTE: You can modify the insertionSort module so it sorts the array in descending order by changing the less than operator in line 60 to a greater than operator, as shown here:

```
While scan > 0 AND array[scan-1] > array[scan]
```

Figure 9-24 Flowchart for the insertionSort module

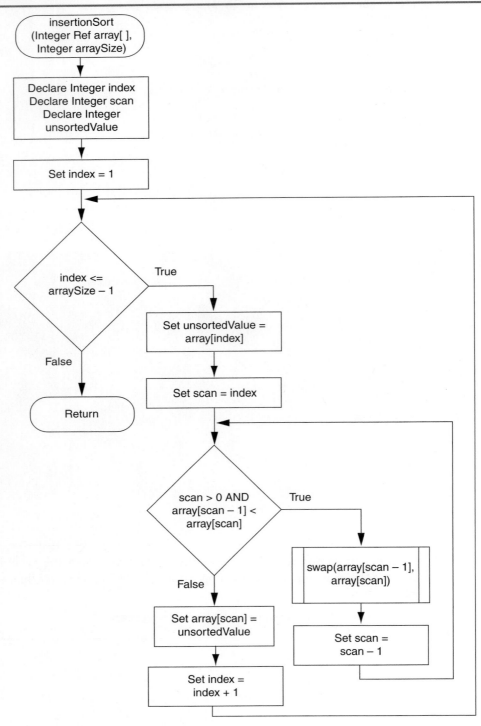

Checkpoint

9.1 Which of the sorting algorithms discussed makes several passes through an array and causes the larger values to move gradually toward the end of the array with each pass?

9.2 One of the sorting algorithms discussed works like this: It begins by sorting the first two elements of the array, which becomes a sorted subset. Then the third element is moved to its correct position relative to the first two elements. At that point the first three elements become the sorted subset. This process continues with the fourth and subsequent elements until the entire array is sorted. Which algorithm is this?

9.3 One of the sorting algorithms discussed works like this: The smallest value in the array is located and moved to element 0. Then the next smallest value is located and moved to element 1. This process continues until all of the elements have been placed in their proper order. Which algorithm is this?

9.4 The Binary Search Algorithm

CONCEPT: The binary search algorithm is much more efficient than the sequential search, which was discussed in Chapter 8. The binary search algorithm locates an item in an array by repeatedly dividing the array in half. Each time it divides the array, it eliminates the half of the array that does not contain the item.

Chapter 8 discussed the sequential search algorithm, which uses a loop to step sequentially through an array, starting with the first element. It compares each element with the value being searched for and stops when the value is found or the end of the array is encountered. If the value being searched for is not in the array, the algorithm unsuccessfully searches to the end of the array.

The advantage of the sequential search is its simplicity: It is very easy to understand and implement. Furthermore, it doesn't require the data in the array to be stored in any particular order. Its disadvantage, however, is its inefficiency. If the array being searched contains 20,000 elements, the algorithm will have to look at all 20,000 elements in order to find a value stored in the last element.

In an average case, an item is just as likely to be found near the beginning of an array as near the end. Typically, for an array of n items, the sequential search will locate an item in $n/2$ attempts. If an array has 50,000 elements, the sequential search will make a comparison with 25,000 of them in a typical case. This is assuming, of course, that the search item is consistently found in the array. ($n/2$ is the average number of comparisons. The maximum number of comparisons is always n.)

When the sequential search fails to locate an item, it must make a comparison with every element in the array. As the number of failed search attempts increases, so does the average number of comparisons. Although the sequential search algorithm is adequate for small arrays, it should not be used on large arrays if speed is important.

The *binary search* is a clever algorithm that is much more efficient than the sequential search. Its only requirement is that the values in the array must be sorted in ascending order. Instead of testing the array's first element, this algorithm starts with the element in the middle. If that element happens to contain the desired value, then the search is over. Otherwise, the value in the middle element is either greater than or less than the value being searched for. If it is greater, then the desired value (if it is in the list) will be found somewhere in the first half of the array. If it is less, then the desired value (again, if it is in the list) will be found somewhere in the last half of the array. In either case, half of the array's elements have been eliminated from further searching.

If the desired value isn't found in the middle element, the procedure is repeated for the half of the array that potentially contains the value. For instance, if the last half of the array is to be searched, the algorithm tests *its* middle element. If the desired value isn't found there, the search is narrowed to the quarter of the array that resides before or after that element. This process continues until the value being searched for is either found or there are no more elements to test.

Figure 9-25 shows a flowchart for a function that performs the binary search algorithm. The function accepts an `Integer` array, an `Integer` value to search the array for, and an `Integer` that specifies the array's size. If the value is found in the array, the function returns the subscript of the element containing the value. If the value is not found in the array, the function returns –1. Program 9-7 shows the `binarySearch` function in pseudocode. Note that the pseudocode shown in Program 9-7 is only the `binarySearch` function and not a complete program.

This algorithm uses three variables to mark positions within the array: `first`, `last`, and `middle`. The `first` and `last` variables mark the boundaries of the portion of the array currently being searched. They are initialized with the subscripts of the array's `first` and `last` elements. The subscript of the element halfway between `first` and `last` is calculated and stored in the `middle` variable. If the element in the middle of the array does not contain the search value, the `first` or `last` variables are adjusted so that only the top or bottom half of the array is searched during the next iteration. This cuts the portion of the array being searched in half each time the loop fails to locate the search value.

Program 9-7   `binarySearch` **function**
                          (not a complete program)

```
 1 // The binarySearch function accepts as arguments an Integer
 2 // array, a value to search the array for, and the size
 3 // of the array. If the value is found in the array, its
 4 // subscript is returned. Otherwise, -1 is returned,
 5 // indicating that the value was not found in the array.
 6 Function Integer binarySearch(Integer array[], Integer value,
 7                         Integer arraySize)
 8    // Variable to hold the subscript of the first element.
 9    Declare Integer first = 0
10
11    // Variable to hold the subscript of the last element.
12    Declare Integer last = arraySize - 1
13
14    // Position of the search value
15    Declare Integer position = -1
16
17    // Flag
18    Declare Boolean found = False
19
20    // Variable to hold the subscript of the midpoint.
21    Declare Integer middle
22
23    While (NOT found) AND (first <= last)
24       // Calculate the midpoint.
25       Set middle = (first + last) / 2
26
27       // See if the value is found at the midpoint...
28       If array[middle] == value Then
29          Set found = True
30          Set position = middle
31
32       // Else, if the value is in the lower half...
33       Else If array[middle] > value Then
34          Set last = middle - 1
35
36       // Else, if the value is in the upper half...
37       Else
38          Set first = middle + 1
39       End If
40    End While
41
42    // Return the position of the item, or -1
43    // if the item was not found.
44    Return position
45 End Function
```

Figure 9-25 Flowchart for the `binarySearch` function

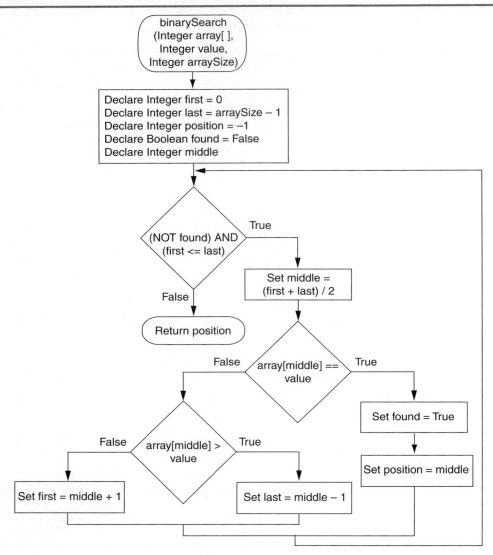

Efficiency of a Binary Search

Obviously, a binary search is much more efficient than a sequential search. Every time a binary search makes a comparison and fails to find the desired item, it eliminates half of the remaining portion of the array that must be searched. For example, consider an array with 1,000 elements. If a binary search fails to find an item on the first attempt, the number of elements that remains to be searched is 500. If the item is not found on the second attempt, the number of elements that remains to be searched is 250. This process continues until the binary search has either located the desired item or determined that it is not in the array. With 1,000 elements this takes no more than 10 comparisons. (Compare this to a sequential search, which would make an average of 500 comparisons!)

In the Spotlight:

Using the Binary Search Algorithm

Constance manages a cooking school that employees six instructors. She has asked you to design a program that she can use to look up an instructor's phone number. You decide to use two parallel arrays: one named names that will hold the instructors' last names, and another named phones that will hold each instructor's phone number. Here is the general algorithm:

1. Get an instructor's last name from the user.
2. Search for the name in the names array.
3. If the name is found, get its subscript. Use the subscript to display the contents of the parallel phones array. If the name is not found, display a message indicating so.

Program 9-8 shows the pseudocode for the program. Note that the array contents are already sorted in ascending order. This is important because the program uses the binary search algorithm to locate a name in the names array.

Program 9-8

```
 1 Module main()
 2    // Constant for array sizes
 3    Constant Integer SIZE = 6
 4
 5    // Array of instructor names, already sorted in
 6    // ascending order.
 7    Declare String names[SIZE] = "Hall", "Harrison",
 8                                 "Hoyle", "Kimura",
 9                                 "Lopez", "Pike"
10
11    // Parallel array of instructor phone numbers.
12    Declare String phones[SIZE] = "555-6783", "555-0199",
13                                  "555-9974", "555-2377",
14                                  "555-7772", "555-1716"
15
16    // Variable to hold the last name to search for.
17    Declare String searchName
18
19    // Variable to hold the subscript of the name.
20    Declare Integer index
21
22    // Variable to control the loop.
23    Declare String again = "Y"
24
25    While (again == "Y" OR again == "y")
26      // Get the name to search for.
27      Display "Enter a last name to search for."
28      Input searchName
29
30      // Search for the last name.
31      index = binarySearch(names, searchName, SIZE)
```

```
32
33        If index ! = -1 Then
34           // Display the phone number.
35           Display "The phone number is ", phones[index]
36        Else
37           // The name was not found in the array.
38           Display searchName, " was not found."
39        End If
40
41        // Search again?
42        Display "Do you want to search again? (Y=Yes, N=No)"
43        Input again
44     End While
45
46 End Module
47
48 // The binarySearch function accepts as arguments a String
49 // array, a value to search the array for, and the size
50 // of the array. If the value is found in the array, its
51 // subscript is returned. Otherwise, -1 is returned,
52 // indicating that the value was not found in the array.
53 Function Integer binarySearch(String array[], String value,
54                             Integer arraySize)
55     // Variable to hold the subscript of the first element.
56     Declare Integer first = 0
57
58     // Variable to hold the subscript of the last element.
59     Declare Integer last = arraySize - 1
60
61     // Position of the search value
62     Declare Integer position = -1
63
64     // Flag
65     Declare Boolean found = False
66
67     // Variable to hold the subscript of the midpoint.
68     Declare Integer middle
69
70     While (NOT found) AND (first <= last)
71        // Calculate the midpoint.
72        Set middle = (first + last) / 2
73
74        // See if the value is found at the midpoint...
75        If array[middle] == value Then
76           Set found = True
77           Set position = middle
78
79        // Else, if the value is in the lower half...
80        Else If array[middle] > value Then
81           Set last = middle - 1
82
83        // Else, if the value is in the upper half...
84        Else
85           Set first = middle + 1
86        End If
87     End While
```

```
88
89     // Return the position of the item, or -1
90     // if the item was not found.
91     Return position
92 End Function
```

Program Output (with Input Shown in Bold)

```
Enter a last name to search for.
Lopez [Enter]
The phone number is 555-7772
Do you want to search again? (Y=Yes, N=No)
Y [Enter]
Enter a last name to search for.
Harrison [Enter]
The phone number is 555-0199
Do you want to search again? (Y=Yes, N=No)
Y [Enter]
Enter a last name to search for.
Lee [Enter]
Lee was not found.
Do you want to search again? (Y=Yes, N=No)
N [Enter]
```

Checkpoint

9.4   Describe the difference between a sequential search and a binary search.

9.5   On average, with an array of 1,000 elements, how many comparisons will a sequential search perform? (Assume the items being searched for are consistently found in the array.)

9.6   With an array of 1,000 elements, what is the maximum number of comparisons a binary search will perform?

Review Questions

Multiple Choice

1. This type of algorithm rearranges the values stored in an array in some particular order.
   a. search algorithm
   b. sorting algorithm
   c. ordering algorithm
   d. selection algorithm

2. If an array is sorted in this order, the values are stored from lowest to highest.
   a. asymptotic
   b. logarithmic
   c. ascending
   d. descending

3. If an array is sorted in this order, the values are stored from highest to lowest.

    a. asymptotic
    b. logarithmic
    c. ascending
    d. descending

4. This algorithm makes several passes through an array and causes the larger values to gradually move toward the end of the array with each pass.

    a. bubble sort
    b. selection sort
    c. insertion sort
    d. sequential sort

5. In this algorithm, the smallest value in the array is located and moved to element 0. Then the next smallest value is located and moved to element 1. This process continues until all of the elements have been placed in their proper order.

    a. bubble sort
    b. selection sort
    c. insertion sort
    d. sequential sort

6. This algorithm begins by sorting the first two elements of the array, which become a sorted subset. Then, the third element is moved to its correct position relative to the first two elements. At that point, the first three elements become the sorted subset. This process continues with the fourth and subsequent elements until the entire array is sorted.

    a. bubble sort
    b. selection sort
    c. insertion sort
    d. sequential sort

7. This search algorithm steps sequentially through an array, comparing each item with the search value.

    a. sequential search
    b. binary search
    c. natural order search
    d. selection search

8. This search algorithm repeatedly divides the portion of an array being searched in half.

    a. sequential search
    b. binary search
    c. natural order search
    d. selection search

9. This search algorithm is adequate for small arrays but not large arrays.

    a. sequential search
    b. binary search
    c. natural order search
    d. selection search

10. This search algorithm requires that the array's contents be sorted.
    a. sequential search
    b. binary search
    c. natural order search
    d. selection search

True or False

1. If data is sorted in ascending order, it means it is ordered from lowest value to highest value.

2. If data is sorted in descending order, it means it is ordered from lowest value to highest value.

3. Regardless of the programming language being used, it is not possible to use the bubble sort algorithm to sort strings.

4. The *average* number of comparisons performed by the sequential search algorithm on an array of *n* elements is *n*/2 (assuming the search values are consistently found).

5. The *maximum* number of comparisons performed by the sequential search algorithm on an array of *n* elements is *n*/2 (assuming the search values are consistently found).

Algorithm Workbench

1. Design a swap module that accepts two arguments of the Real data type and swaps them.

2. What algorithm does the following pseudocode perform?

```
Declare Integer maxElement
Declare Integer index

For maxElement = arraySize - 1 To 0 Step -1
    For index = 0 To maxElement - 1
        If array[index] > array[index + 1] Then
            Call swap(array[index], array[index + 1])
        End If
    End For
End For
```

3. What algorithm does the following pseudocode perform?

```
Declare Integer index
Declare Integer scan
Declare Integer unsortedValue

For index = 1 To arraySize - 1
    Set unsortedValue = array[index]
    Set scan = index

    While scan > 0 AND array[scan-1] < array[scan]
        Call swap(array[scan-1], array[scan])
        Set scan = scan - 1
    End While
```

```
        Set array[scan] = unsortedValue
    End For
```

4. What algorithm does the following pseudocode perform?

```
Declare Integer startScan

Declare Integer minIndex
Declare Integer minValue
Declare Integer index

For startScan = 0 To arraySize - 2
    Set minIndex = startScan
    Set minValue = array[startScan]

    For index = startScan + 1 To arraySize - 1
        If array[index] < minValue
            Set minValue = array[index]
            Set minIndex = index
        End If
    End For

    Call swap(array[minIndex], array[startScan])
End For
```

Short Answer

1. If a sequential search function is searching for a value that is stored in the last element of a 10,000-element array, how many elements will the search code have to read to locate the value?

2. In an average case involving an array of n elements, how many times will a sequential search function have to read the array to locate a specific value?

3. A binary search function is searching for a value that happens to be stored in the middle element of an array. How many times will the function read an element in the array before finding the value?

4. What is the maximum number of comparisons that a binary search function will make when searching for a value in a 1,000-element array?

5. Why is the bubble sort inefficient for large arrays?

6. Why is the selection sort more efficient than the bubble sort on large arrays?

7. List the steps that the selection sort algorithm would make in sorting the following values: 4, 1, 3, 2.

8. List the steps that the insertion sort algorithm would make in sorting the following values: 4, 1, 3, 2.

Programming Exercises

VideoNote
Sorted Golf Scores

1. **Sorted Golf Scores**

Design a program that asks the user to enter 10 golf scores. The scores should be stored in an `Integer` array. Sort the array in ascending order and display its contents.

2. **Sorted Names**

   Design a program that allows the user to enter 20 names into a `String` array. Sort the array in ascending (alphabetical) order and display its contents.

3. **Rainfall Program Modification**

   Recall that Programming Exercise 3 in Chapter 8 asked you to design a program that lets the user enter the total rainfall for each of 12 months into an array. The program should calculate and display the total rainfall for the year, the average monthly rainfall, and the months with the highest and lowest amounts. Enhance the program so it sorts the array in ascending order and displays the values it contains.

4. **Name Search**

   Modify the *Sorted Names* program that you wrote for exercise #2 so it allows you to search the array for a specific name.

5. **Charge Account Validation**

   Recall that Programming Exercise 5 in Chapter 8 asked you to design a program that asks the user to enter a charge account number. The program should determine whether the number is valid by comparing it to a list of valid charge account numbers. Modify the program so it uses the binary search algorithm instead of the sequential search algorithm.

6. **Phone Number Lookup**

   Recall that Programming Exercise 7 in Chapter 8 asked you to design a program with two parallel arrays: a `String` array named `people` and a `String` array named `phoneNumbers`. The program allows you to search for a person's name in the `people` array. If the name is found, it displays that person's phone number. Modify the program so it uses the binary search algorithm instead of the sequential search algorithm.

7. **Search Benchmarks**

   Design an application that has an array of at least 20 integers. It should call a module that uses the sequential search algorithm to locate one of the values. The module should keep a count of the number of comparisons it makes until it finds the value. Then the program should call another module that uses the binary search algorithm to locate the same value. It should also keep a count of the number of comparisons it makes. Display these values on the screen.

8. **Sorting Benchmarks**

   Modify the modules presented in this chapter that perform the bubble sort, selection sort, and insertion sort algorithms on an `Integer` array, such that each module keeps a count of the number of swaps it makes.

   Then, design an application that uses three identical arrays of at least 20 integers. It should call each module on a different array, and display the number of swaps made by each algorithm.

10 Files

10.1 Introduction to File Input and Output

CONCEPT: When a program needs to save data for later use, it writes the data in a file. The data can be read from the file at a later time.

The programs you have designed so far require the user to reenter data each time the program runs, because data that is stored in variables in RAM disappears once the program stops running. If a program is to retain data between the times it runs, it must have a way of saving it. Data is saved in a file, which is usually stored on a computer's disk. Once the data is saved in a file, it will remain there after the program stops running. Data that is stored in a file can be retrieved and used at a later time.

Most of the commercial software packages that you use on a day-to-day basis store data in files. The following are a few examples:

- **Word processors:** Word processing programs are used to write letters, memos, reports, and other documents. The documents are then saved in files so they can be edited and printed.
- **Image editors:** Image editing programs are used to draw graphics and edit images such as the ones that you take with a digital camera. The images that you create or edit with an image editor are saved in files.
- **Spreadsheets:** Spreadsheet programs are used to work with numerical data. Numbers and mathematical formulas can be inserted into the rows and columns of the spreadsheet. The spreadsheet can then be saved in a file for use later.

- **Games:** Many computer games keep data stored in files. For example, some games keep a list of player names with their scores stored in a file. These games typically display the players' names in order of their scores, from highest to lowest. Some games also allow you to save your current game status in a file so you can quit the game and then resume playing it later without having to start from the beginning.
- **Web browsers:** Sometimes when you visit a Web page, the browser stores a small file known as a *cookie* on your computer. Cookies typically contain information about the browsing session, such as the contents of a shopping cart.

Programs that are used in daily business operations rely extensively on files. Payroll programs keep employee data in files, inventory programs keep data about a company's products in files, accounting systems keep data about a company's financial operations in files, and so on.

Programmers usually refer to the process of saving data in a file as "writing data to" the file. When a piece of data is written to a file, it is copied from a variable in RAM to the file. This is illustrated in Figure 10-1. The term *output file* is used to describe a file that data is written to. It is called an output file because the program stores output in it.

Figure 10-1 Writing data to a file

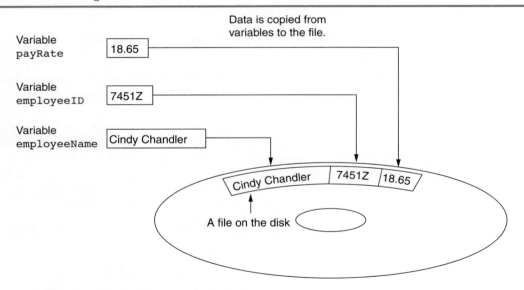

The process of retrieving data from a file is known as "reading data from" the file. When a piece of data is read from a file, it is copied from the file into a variable in RAM. Figure 10-2 illustrates this. The term *input file* is used to describe a file that data is read from. It is called an input file because the program gets input from the file.

Figure 10-2 Reading data from a file

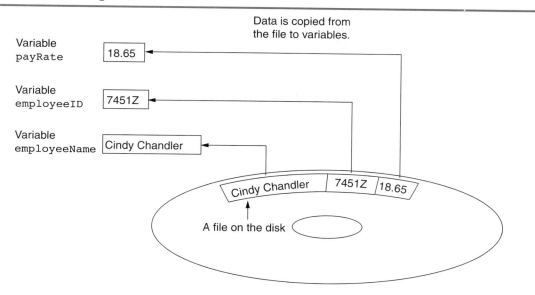

This chapter discusses how to design programs that write data to files and read data from files. There are always three steps that must be taken when a file is used by a program.

1. **Open the file:** Opening a file creates a connection between the file and the program. Opening an output file usually creates the file on the disk and allows the program to write data to it. Opening an input file allows the program to read data from the file.
2. **Process the file:** In this step data is either written to the file (if it is an output file) or read from the file (if it is an input file).
3. **Close the file:** When the program is finished using the file, the file must be closed. Closing a file disconnects the file from the program.

Types of Files

In general, there are two types of files: text and binary. A *text file* contains data that has been encoded as text, using a scheme such as ASCII or Unicode. Even if the file contains numbers, those numbers are stored in the file as a series of characters. As a result, the file may be opened and viewed in a text editor such as Notepad. A *binary file* contains data that has not been converted to text. As a consequence, you cannot view the contents of a binary file with a text editor.

File Access Methods

Most programming languages provide two different ways to access data stored in a file: sequential access and direct access. When you work with a *sequential access file,* you access data from the beginning of the file to the end of the file. If you want to read a piece of data that is stored at the very end of the file, you have to read all of the data that comes before it—you cannot jump directly to the desired data. This is similar to the way cassette tape players work. If you want to listen to the last song on a cassette tape, you have to either fast-forward over all of the songs that come before it or listen to them. There is no way to jump directly to a specific song.

When you work with a *direct access file* (which is also known as a *random access file*), you can jump directly to any piece of data in the file without reading the data that comes before it. This is similar to the way a CD player or an MP3 player works. You can jump directly to any song that you want to listen to.

This chapter focuses on sequential access files. Sequential access files are easy to work with, and you can use them to gain an understanding of basic file operations.

Creating a File and Writing Data to It

Most computer users are accustomed to the fact that files are identified by a filename. For example, when you create a document with a word processor and then save the document in a file, you have to specify a filename. When you use a utility such as Windows Explorer to examine the contents of your disk, you see a list of filenames. Figure 10-3 shows how three files named `cat.jpg`, `notes.txt`, and `resume.doc` might be represented in Windows Explorer.

Figure 10-3 Three files

cat.jpg   notes.txt   resume.doc

Each operating system has its own rules for naming files. Many systems support the use of *filename extensions*, which are short sequences of characters that appear at the end of a filename preceded by a period (which is known as a "dot"). For example, the files depicted in Figure 10-3 have the extensions `.jpg`, `.txt`, and `.doc`. The extension usually indicates the type of data stored in the file. For example, the `.jpg` extension usually indicates that the file contains a graphic image that is compressed according to the JPEG image standard. The `.txt` extension usually indicates that the file contains text. The `.doc` extension usually indicates that the file contains a Microsoft Word document. (In this book we will use the `.dat` extension with all of the files we create in our programs. The `.dat` extension simply stands for "data.")

When writing a program that performs an operation on a file, there are two names that you have to work with in the program's code. The first of these is the filename that identifies the file on the computer's disk. The second is an internal name that is similar to a variable name. In fact, you usually declare a file's internal name in a manner that is similar to declaring a variable. The following example shows how we declare a name for an output file in our pseudocode:

```
Declare OutputFile customerFile
```

This statement declares two things.

- The word `OutputFile` indicates the *mode* in which we will use the file. In our pseudocode, `OutputFile` indicates that we will be writing data to the file.
- The name `customerFile` is the internal name we will use to work with the output file in our code.

Although the syntax for making this declaration varies greatly among programming languages, you typically have to declare both the mode in which you will use a file and the file's internal name before you can work with the file.

The next step is to open the file. In our pseudocode we will use the `Open` statement. Here is an example:

```
Open customerFile "customers.dat"
```

The word `Open` is followed by an internal name that was previously declared, and then a string that contains a filename. After this statement executes, a file named `customers.dat` will be created on the disk, and we will be able to use the internal name `customerFile` to write data to the file.

> **WARNING!** Remember, when you open an output file you are creating the file on the disk. In most languages, if a file with the specified external name already exists when the file is opened, the contents of the existing file will be erased.

Writing Data to a File

Once you have opened an output file you can write data to it. In our pseudocode we will use the `Write` statement to write data to a file. For example,

```
Write customerFile "Charles Pace"
```

writes the string `"Charles Pace"` to the file that is associated with `customerFile`. You can also write the contents of a variable to a file, as shown in the following pseudocode:

```
Declare String name = "Charles Pace"
Write customerFile name
```

The second statement in this pseudocode writes the contents of the `name` variable to the file associated with `customerFile`. (These examples show a string being written to a file, but you can also write numeric values.)

Closing an Output File

Once a program is finished working with a file, it should close the file. Closing a file disconnects the program from the file. In some systems, failure to close an output file can cause a loss of data. This happens because the data that is written to a file is first written to a *buffer,* which is a small "holding section" in memory. When the buffer is full, the computer's operating system writes the buffer's contents to the file. This technique increases the system's performance, because writing data to memory is faster than writing it to a disk. The process of closing an output file forces any unsaved data that remains in the buffer to be written to the file.

In our pseudocode, we will use the `Close` statement to close a file. For example,

```
Close customerFile
```

closes the file that is associated with the name `customerFile`.

Program 10-1 shows the pseudocode for a sample program that opens an output file, writes data to it, and then closes it. Figure 10-4 shows a flowchart for the program. Because the `Write` statements are output operations, they are shown in parallelograms.

Figure 10-4 Flowchart for Program 10-1

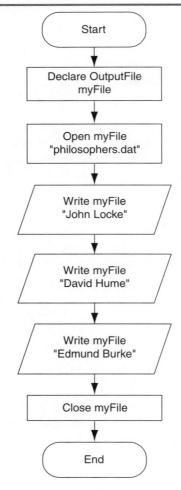

Program 10-1

```
1 // Declare an internal name for an output file.
2 Declare OutputFile myFile
3
4 // Open a file named philosophers.dat on
5 // the disk.
```

```
 6 Open myFile "philosophers.dat"
 7
 8 // Write the names of three philosophers
 9 // to the file.
10 Write myFile "John Locke"
11 Write myFile "David Hume"
12 Write myFile "Edmund Burke"
13
14 // Close the file.
15 Close myFile
```

The statement in line 2 declares the name `myFile` as the internal name for an output file. Line 6 opens the file `philosophers.dat` on the disk and creates an association between the file and the internal name `myFile`. This will allow us to use the name `myFile` to work with the file `philosophers.dat`.

The statements in lines 10 through 12 write three items to the file. Line 10 writes the string `"John Locke"`, line 11 writes the string `"David Hume"`, and line 12 writes the string `"Edmund Burke"`. Line 15 closes the file. If this were an actual program and were executed, the three items shown in Figure 10-5 would be written to the `philosophers.dat` file.

Figure 10-5 Contents of the file `philosophers.dat`

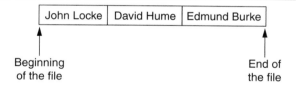

Notice that the items in the file appear in the same order that they were written by the program. "John Locke" is the first item, "David Hume" is the second item, and "Edmund Burke" is the third item. You will see the significance of this when we read data from the file momentarily.

Delimiters and the EOF Marker

Figure 10-5 shows that three items were written to the `philosphers.dat` file. In most programming languages, the actual contents of the file would be more complex than the figure shows. In many languages, a special character known as a delimiter is written to a file after each item. A *delimiter* is simply a predefined character or set of characters that marks the end of each piece of data. The delimiter's purpose is to separate the different items that are stored in a file. The exact character or set of characters that are used as delimiters varies from system to system.

In addition to delimiters, many systems write a special character or set of characters, known as an *end-of-file (EOF) marker,* at the end of a file. The purpose of the EOF marker is to indicate where the file's contents end. The character that is used as the EOF marker also varies among different systems. Figure 10-6 shows the layout of the `philosphers.dat` file, with delimiters and an EOF marker.

Figure 10-6 Contents of the file `philosophers.dat` with delimiters and the EOF marker

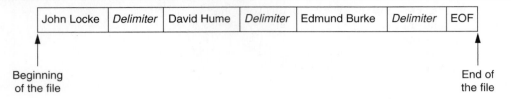

Reading Data from a File

To read data from an input file, you first declare an internal name that you will use to reference the file. In pseudocode we will use a `Declare` statement such as this:

```
Declare InputFile inventoryFile
```

This statement declares two things.

- The word `InputFile` indicates the mode in which we will use the file. In our pseudocode, `InputFile` indicates that we will be reading data from the file.
- The name `inventoryFile` is the internal name we will use to work with the output file in our code.

As previously mentioned, the actual syntax for declaring a file mode and internal name varies greatly among programming languages.

The next step is to open the file. In our pseudocode we will use the `Open` statement. For example, in

```
Open inventoryFile "inventory.dat"
```

the word `Open` is followed by an internal name that was previously declared, and then a string that contains a filename. After this statement executes, the file named `inventory.dat` will be opened, and we will be able to use the internal name `inventoryFile` to read data from the file.

Because we are opening the file for input, it makes sense that the file should already exist. In most systems, an error will occur if you try to open an input file but the file does not exist.

Reading Data

Once you have opened an input file you can read data from it. In our pseudocode we will use the `Read` statement to read a piece of data from a file. The following is an example (assume `itemName` is a variable that has already been declared).

```
Read inventoryFile itemName
```

This statement reads a piece of data from the file that is associated with `inventoryFile`. The piece of data that is read from the file will be stored in the `itemName` variable.

Closing an Input File

As previously mentioned, a program should close a file when it is finished working with it. In our pseudocode, we will use the `Close` statement to close input files, in the same way that we close output files. For example,

```
Close inventoryFile
```

closes the file that is associated with the name `inventoryFile`.

Program 10-2 shows the pseudocode for a program that opens the `philosophers.dat` file that would be created by Program 10-1, reads the three names from the file, closes the file, and then displays the names that were read. Figure 10-7 shows a flowchart for the program. Notice that the `Read` statements are shown in parallelograms.

Figure 10-7 Flowchart for Program 10-2

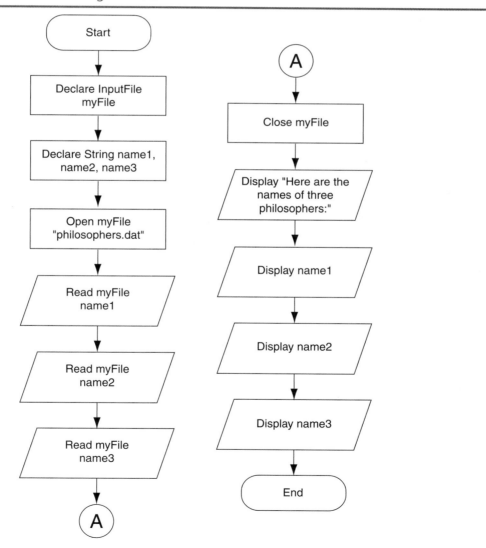

Program 10-2

```
1  // Declare an internal name for an input file.
2  Declare InputFile myFile
3
4  // Declare three variables to hold values
5  // that will be read from the file.
6  Declare String name1, name2, name3
7
8  // Open a file named philosophers.dat on
9  // the disk.
10 Open myFile "philosophers.dat"
11
12 // Read the names of three philosophers
13 // from the file into the variables.
14 Read myFile name1
15 Read myFile name2
16 Read myFile name3
17
18 // Close the file.
19 Close myFile
20
21 // Display the names that were read.
22 Display "Here are the names of three philosophers:"
23 Display name1
24 Display name2
25 Display name3
```

Program Output

```
Here are the names of three philosophers:
John Locke
David Hume
Edmund Burke
```

The statement in line 2 declares the name myFile as the internal name for an input file. Line 6 declares three String variables: name1, name2, and name3. We will use these variables to hold the values read from the file. Line 10 opens the file philosophers.dat on the disk and creates an association between the file and the internal name myFile. This will allow us to use the name myFile to work with the file philosophers.dat.

When a program works with an input file, a special value known as a *read position* is internally maintained for that file. A file's read position marks the location of the next item that will be read from the file. When an input file is opened, its read position is initially set to the first item in the file. After the statement in line 10 executes, the read position for the philosophers.dat file will be positioned as shown in Figure 10-8.

Figure 10-8 Initial read position

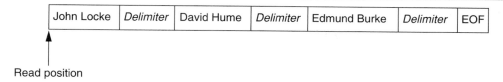

The Read statement in line 14 reads an item from the file's current read position and stores that item in the name1 variable. Once this statement executes, the name1 variable will contain the string "John Locke". In addition, the file's read position will be advanced to the next item in the file, as shown in Figure 10-9.

Figure 10-9 Read position after the first Read statement

Another Read statement appears in line 15. This reads an item from the file's current read position and stores that value in the name2 variable. Once this statement executes, the name2 variable will contain the string "David Hume". The file's read position will be advanced to the next item, as shown in Figure 10-10.

Figure 10-10 Read position after the second Read statement

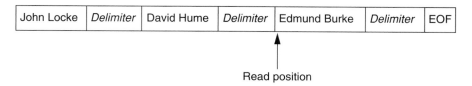

Another Read statement appears in line 16. This reads the next item from the file's current read position and stores that value in the name3 variable. Once this statement executes, the name3 variable will contain the string "Edmund Burke". The file's read position will be advanced to the EOF marker, as shown in Figure 10-11.

Figure 10-11 Read position after the third Read statement

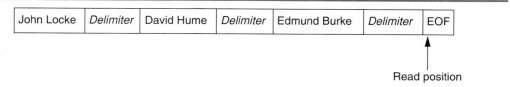

The statement in line 19 closes the file. The Display statements in lines 23 through 25 display the contents of the name1, name2, and name3 variables.

> **NOTE:** Did you notice that Program 10-2 read the items in the `philosophers.dat` file in sequence, from the beginning of the file to the end of the file? Recall from our discussion at the beginning of the chapter that this is the nature of a sequential access file.

Appending Data to an Existing File

In most programming languages, when you open an output file and a file with the specified external name already exists on the disk, the existing file will be erased and a new empty file with the same name will be created. Sometimes you want to preserve an existing file and append new data to its current contents. Appending data to a file means writing new data to the end of the data that already exists in the file.

Most programming languages allow you to open an output file in *append mode*, which means the following:

- If the file already exists, it will not be erased. If the file does not exist, it will be created.
- When data is written to the file, it will be written at the end of the file's current contents.

The syntax for opening an output file in append mode varies greatly from one language to another. In pseudocode we will simply add the word `AppendMode` to the `Declare` statement, as shown here:

```
Declare OutputFile AppendMode myFile
```

This statement declares that we will use the internal name `myFile` to open an output file in append mode. For example, assume the file `friends.dat` exists and contains the following names:

```
Joe
Rose
Greg
Geri
Renee
```

The following pseudocode opens the file and appends additional data to its existing contents.

```
Declare OutputFile AppendMode myFile
Open myFile "friends.dat"
Write myFile "Matt"
Write myFile "Chris"
Write myFile "Suze"
Close myFile
```

After this program runs, the file `friends.dat` will contain the following data:

```
Joe
Rose
Greg
Geri
Renee
```

```
Matt
Chris
Suze
```

Checkpoint

10.1 Where are files normally stored?

10.2 What is an output file?

10.3 What is an input file?

10.4 What three steps must be taken by a program when it uses a file?

10.5 In general, what are the two types of files? What is the difference between these two types of files?

10.6 What are the two types of file access? What is the difference between these two?

10.7 When writing a program that performs an operation on a file, what two file-associated names do you have to work with in your code?

10.8 In most programming languages, if a file already exists what happens to it if you try to open it as an output file?

10.9 What is the purpose of opening a file?

10.10 What is the purpose of closing a file?

10.11 Generally speaking, what is a delimiter? How are delimiters typically used in files?

10.12 In many systems, what is written at the end of a file?

10.13 What is a file's read position? Initially, where is the read position when an input file is opened?

10.14 In what mode do you open a file if you want to write data to it, but you do not want to erase the file's existing contents? When you write data to such a file, to what part of the file is the data written?

10.2 Using Loops to Process Files

CONCEPT: Files usually hold large amounts of data, and programs typically use a loop to process the data in a file.

VideoNote

Using Loops to Process Files

Although some programs use files to store only small amounts of data, files are typically used to hold large collections of data. When a program uses a file to write or read a large amount of data, a loop is typically involved. For example, look at the pseudocode in Program 10-3. This program gets sales amounts for a series of days from the user and stores those amounts in a file named `sales.dat`. The user specifies the number of days of sales data he or she needs to enter. In the sample run of the program, the user enters sales amounts for five days. Figure 10-12 shows the contents of the `sales.dat` file containing the data entered by the user in the sample run. Figure 10-13 shows a flowchart for the program.

Program 10-3

```
 1 // Variable to hold the number of days
 2 Declare Integer numDays
 3
 4 // Counter variable for the loop
 5 Declare Integer counter
 6
 7 // Variable to hold an amount of sales
 8 Declare Real sales
 9
10 // Declare an output file.
11 Declare OutputFile salesFile
12
13 // Get the number of days.
14 Display "For how many days do you have sales?"
15 Input numDays
16
17 // Open a file named sales.dat.
18 Open salesFile "sales.dat"
19
20 // Get the amount of sales for each day and write
21 // it to the file.
22 For counter = 1 To numDays
23    // Get the sales for a day.
24    Display "Enter the sales for day #", counter
25    Input sales
26
27    // Write the amount to the file.
28    Write salesFile sales
29 End For
30
31 // Close the file.
32 Close salesFile
33 Display "Data written to sales.dat."
```

Program Output (with Input Shown in Bold)

```
For how many days do you have sales?
5 [Enter]
Enter the sales for day #1
1000.00 [Enter]
Enter the sales for day #2
2000.00 [Enter]
Enter the sales for day #3
3000.00 [Enter]
Enter the sales for day #4
4000.00 [Enter]
Enter the sales for day #5
5000.00 [Enter]
Data written to sales.dat.
```

Figure 10-12 Contents of the `sales.dat` file

| 1000.00 | Delimiter | 2000.00 | Delimiter | 3000.00 | Delimiter | 4000.00 | Delimiter | 5000.00 | Delimiter | EOF |

Figure 10-13 Flowchart for Program 10-3

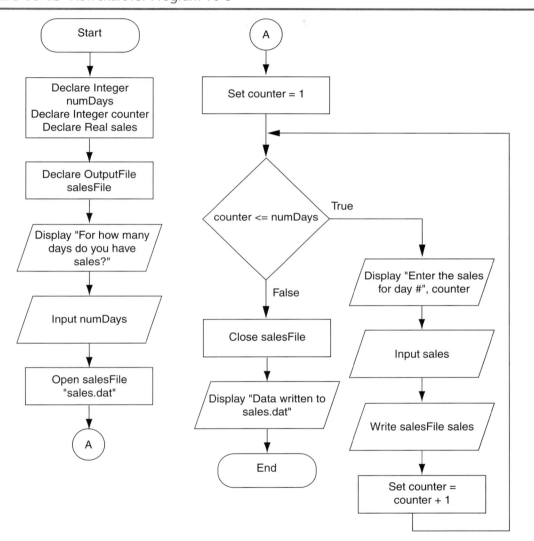

Reading a File with a Loop and Detecting the End of the File

Quite often a program must read the contents of a file without knowing the number of items that are stored in the file. For example, the `sales.dat` file that would be created by Program 10-3 can have any number of items stored in it, because the program asks the user for the number of days that he or she has sales amounts for. If the user enters 5 as the number of days, the program gets 5 sales amounts and stores them in the file. If the user enters 100 as the number of days, the program gets 100 sales amounts and stores them in the file.

This presents a problem if you want to write a program that processes all of the items in the file, regardless of how many there are. For example, suppose you need to write a program that reads all of the amounts in the file and calculates their total. You can use a loop to read the items in the file, but an error will occur if the program tries to read beyond the end of the file. The program needs some way of knowing when the end of the file has been reached so it will not try to read beyond it.

Most programming languages provide a library function for this purpose. In our pseudocode we will use the eof function. Here is the function's general format:

    eof(*internalFileName*)

The eof function accepts a file's internal name as an argument, and returns True if the end of the file has been reached or False if the end of the file has not been reached. The pseudocode in Program 10-4 shows an example of how to use the eof function. This program displays all of the sales amounts in the sales.dat file.

Program 10-4

```
 1 // Declare an input file.
 2 Declare InputFile salesFile
 3
 4 // Declare a variable to hold a sales amount
 5 // that is read from the file.
 6 Declare Real sales
 7
 8 // Open the sales.dat file.
 9 Open salesFile "sales.dat"
10
11 Display "Here are the sales amounts:"
12
13 // Read all of the items in the file
14 // and display them.
15 While NOT eof(salesFile)
16    Read salesFile sales
17    Display currencyFormat(sales)
18 End While
19
20 // Close the file.
21 Close salesFile
```

Program Output

```
Here are the sales amounts:
$1,000.00
$2,000.00
$3,000.00
$4,000.00
$5,000.00
```

Take a closer look at line 15:

```
While NOT eof(salesFile)
```

When you read this pseudocode, you naturally think: *While not at the end of the file...*
This statement could have been written as:

```
While eof(salesFile) == False
```

Although this is logically equivalent, most programmers will prefer to use the NOT
operator as shown in line 15 because it more clearly states the condition that is being
tested. Figure 10-14 shows a flowchart for the program.

Figure 10-14 Flowchart for Program 10-4

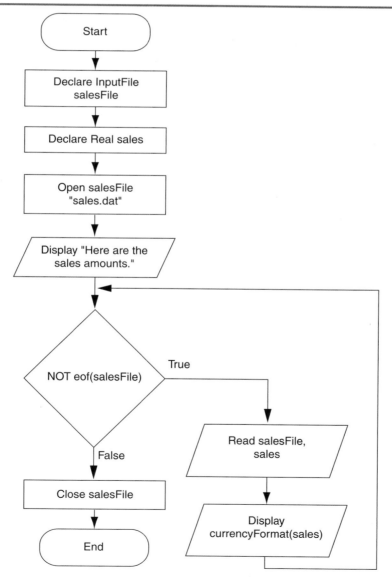

In the Spotlight:
Working with Files

Kevin is a freelance video producer who makes TV commercials for local businesses. When he makes a commercial, he usually films several short videos. Later, he puts these short videos together to make the final commercial. He has asked you to design the following two programs:

1. A program that allows him to enter the running time (in seconds) of each short video in a project. The running times are saved to a file.
2. A program that reads the contents of the file, displays the running times, and then displays the total running time of all the segments.

Here is the general algorithm for the first program:

1. Get the number of videos in the project.
2. Open an output file.
3. For each video in the project:
   Get the video's running time.
   Write the running time to the file.
4. Close the file.

Program 10-5 shows the pseudocode for the first program. Figure 10-15 shows a flowchart.

Program 10-5

```
 1 // Declare an output file.
 2 Declare OutputFile videoFile
 3
 4 // A variable to hold the number of videos.
 5 Declare Integer numVideos
 6
 7 // A variable to hold a video's running time.
 8 Declare Real runningTime
 9
10 // Counter variable for the loop
11 Declare Integer counter
12
13 // Get the number of videos.
14 Display "Enter the number of videos in the project."
15 Input numVideos
16
17 // Open an output file to save the running times.
18 Open videoFile "video_times.dat"
19
20 // Write each video's running times to the file.
21 For counter = 1 To numVideos
22     // Get the running time.
23     Display "Enter the running time for video #", counter
24     Input runningTime
25
26     // Write the running time to the file.
```

```
27     Write videoFile runningTime
28 End For
29
30 // Close the file.
31 Close videoFile
32 Display "The times have been saved to video_times.dat."
```

Program Output (with Input Shown in Bold)

```
Enter the number of videos in the project.
6 [Enter]
Enter the running time for video #1
24.5 [Enter]
Enter the running time for video #2
12.2 [Enter]
Enter the running time for video #3
14.6 [Enter]
Enter the running time for video #4
20.4 [Enter]
Enter the running time for video #5
22.5 [Enter]
Enter the running time for video #6
19.3 [Enter]
The times have been saved to video_times.dat.
```

Figure 10-15 Flowchart for Program 10-5

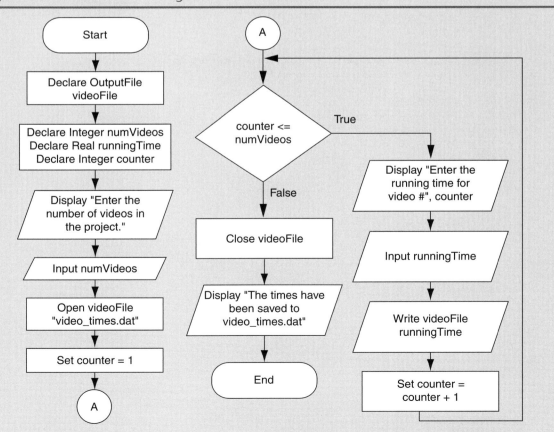

Here is the general algorithm for the second program:

1. Initialize an accumulator to 0.
2. Open the input file.
3. While not at the end of the file:
   Read a value from the file.
   Add the value to the accumulator.
4. Close the file.
5. Display the contents of the accumulator as the total running time.

Program 10-6 shows the pseudocode for the second program. Figure 10-16 shows a flowchart.

Program 10-6

```
 1 // Declare an input file.
 2 Declare InputFile videoFile
 3
 4 // A variable to hold a time
 5 // that is read from the file.
 6 Declare Real runningTime
 7
 8 // Accumulator to hold the total time,
 9 // initialized to 0.
10 Declare Real total = 0
11
12 // Open the video_times.dat file.
13 Open videoFile "video_times.dat"
14
15 Display "Here are the running times, in seconds, of ",
16         "each video in the project:"
17
18 // Read all of the times in the file,
19 // display them, and calculate their total.
20 While NOT eof(videoFile)
21    // Read a time.
22    Read videoFile runningTime
23
24    // Display the time for this video.
25    Display runningTime
26
27    // Add runningTime to total.
28    Set total = total + runningTime
29 End While
30
31 // Close the file.
32 Close videoFile
33
34 // Display the total running time.
35 Display "The total running time of the videos is ",
36         total, " seconds."
```

Program Output

```
Here are the running times, in seconds, of each video in the project:
24.5
12.2
14.6
20.4
22.5
19.3
The total running time of the videos is 113.5 seconds.
```

Figure 10-16 Flowchart for Program 10-6

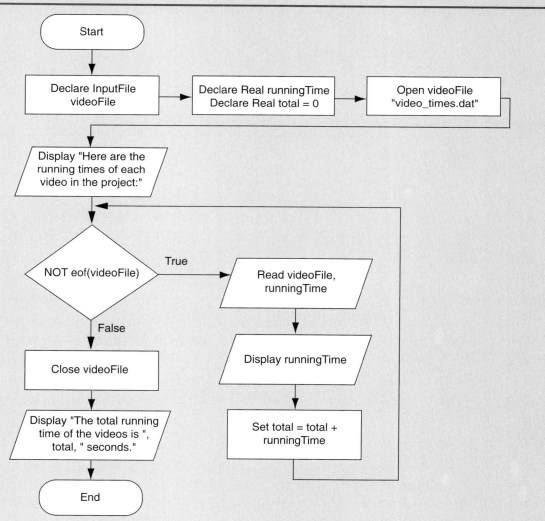

> **NOTE:** The examples that we have used in this book call the `eof` function before performing a `Read` operation. This is a common technique, but in some languages the `eof` function (or its equivalent) must be called *after* a `Read` operation. In these languages a program must perform a priming read just before entering the loop that tests the `eof` function. Figure 10-17 shows the general logic.
>
> For example, assume that `myFile` references an input file that has been opened, and `item` is a variable. The following pseudocode shows how we would use this logic to read and display all of the items in the file:
>
> ```
> // Read the first item in the file.
> Read myFile item
> // Read the remaining items in the file
> // and display them.
> While NOT eof(myFile)
>     Display item
>     Read myFile item
> End While
> ```

Figure 10-17 Using a priming read before testing the `eof` function

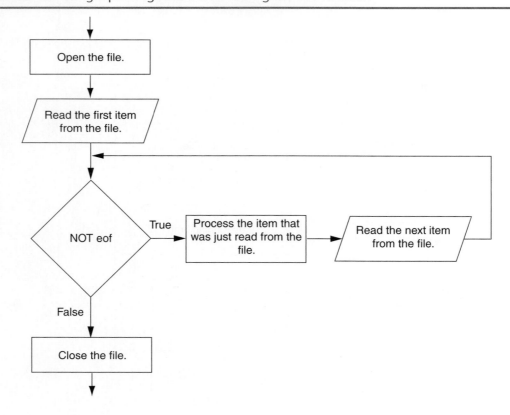

Checkpoint

10.15 Design an algorithm that uses a For loop to write the numbers 1 through 10 to a file.

10.16 What is the purpose of the eof function?

10.17 Is it acceptable for a program to attempt to read beyond the end of a file?

10.18 What would it mean if the expression eof(myFile) returns True?

10.19 Which of the following loops would you use to read all of the items from the file associated with myFile?

```
a. While eof(myFile)
       Read myFile item
   End While
b. While NOT eof(myFile)
       Read myFile item
   End While
```

10.3 Using Files and Arrays

CONCEPT: For some algorithms, files and arrays can be used together effectively. You can easily write a loop that saves the contents of an array to a file, and vice-versa.

Some tasks may require you to save the contents of an array to a file so the data can be used at a later time. Likewise, some situations may require you to read the data from a file into an array. For example, suppose you have a file that contains a set of values that appear in random order and you want to sort the values. One technique for sorting the values in the file would be to read them into an array, perform a sorting algorithm on the array, and then write the values in the array back to the file.

Saving the contents of an array to a file is a straightforward procedure: Open the file and use a loop to step through each element of the array, writing its contents to the file. For example, assume a program declares an array as:

```
Constant Integer SIZE = 5
Declare Integer numbers[SIZE] = 10, 20, 30, 40, 50
```

The following pseudocode opens a file named values.dat and writes the contents of each element of the numbers array to the file:

```
// Counter variable to use in the loop.
Declare Integer index
// Declare an output file.
Declare OutputFile numberFile
// Open the values.dat file.
Open numberFile "values.dat"
```

```
// Write each array element to the file.
For index = 0 To SIZE - 1
    Write numberFile numbers[index]
End For
// Close the file.
Close numberFile
```

Reading the contents of a file into an array is also straightforward: Open the file and use a loop to read each item from the file, storing each item in an array element. The loop should iterate until either the array is filled or the end of the file is reached. For example, assume a program declares an array as:

```
Constant Integer SIZE = 5
Declare Integer numbers[SIZE]
```

The following pseudocode opens a file named values.dat and reads its contents into the numbers array:

```
// Counter variable to use in the loop, initialized
// with 0.
Declare Integer index = 0
// Declare an input file.
Declare InputFile numberFile
// Open the values.dat file.
Open numberFile "values.dat"
// Read the contents of the file into the array.
While (index <= SIZE — 1) AND (NOT eof(numberFile))
    Write numberFile numbers[index]
    Set index = index + 1
End While
// Close the file.
Close numberFile
```

Notice that the While loop tests two conditions. The first condition is index <= SIZE — 1. The purpose of this condition is to prevent the loop from writing beyond the end of the array. When the array is full, the loop will stop. The second condition is NOT eof(numberFile). The purpose of this condition is to prevent the loop from reading beyond the end of the file. When there are no more values to read from the file, the loop will stop.

10.4 Processing Records

CONCEPT: The data that is stored in a file is frequently organized in records. A record is a complete set of data about an item, and a field is an individual piece of data within a record.

When data is written to a file, it is often organized into records and fields. A *record* is a complete set of data that describes one item, and a *field* is a single piece of data within a record. For example, suppose we want to store data about employees in a file. The file will contain a record for each employee. Each record will be a collection of fields, such as name, ID number, and department. This is illustrated in Figure 10-18.

Figure 10-18 Fields in a record

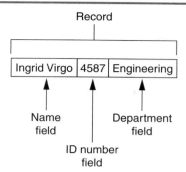

Writing Records

In pseudocode, we will write an entire record using a single Write statement. For example, assume the variables name, idNumber, and department contain data about an employee, and employeeFile is the file we will write the data to. We can write the contents of these variables to the file with the following statement:

```
Write employeeFile name, idNumber, department
```

In the statement we have simply listed the variables, separated by commas, after the file's internal name. The pseudocode in Program 10-7 shows how this statement might be used in a complete program.

Program 10-7

```
 1 // Variables for the fields
 2 Declare String name
 3 Declare Integer idNumber
 4 Declare String department
 5
 6 // A variable for the number of employee records.
 7 Declare Integer numEmployees
 8
 9 // A counter variable for the loop
10 Declare Integer counter
11
12 // Declare an output file.
13 Declare OutputFile employeeFile
14
15 // Get the number of employees.
16 Display "How many employee records do ",
17         "you want to create?"
18 Input numEmployees
19
20 // Open a file named employees.dat.
21 Open employeeFile "employees.dat"
22
23 // Get each employee's data and write it
24 // to the file.
```

```
25 For counter = 1 To numEmployees
26     // Get the employee name.
27     Display "Enter the name of employee #", counter
28     Input name
29
30     // Get the employee ID number.
31     Display "Enter the employee's ID number."
32     Input idNumber
33
34     // Get the employee's department.
35     Display "Enter the employee's department."
36     Input department
37
38     // Write the record to the file.
39     Write employeeFile name, idNumber, department
40
41     // Display a blank line.
42     Display
43 End For
44
45 // Close the file.
46 Close employeeFile
47 Display "Employee records written to employees.dat."
```

Program Output (with Input Shown in Bold)

How many employee records do you want to create?
3 [Enter]
Enter the name of employee #1
Colleen Pickett [Enter]
Enter the employee's ID number.
7311 [Enter]
Enter the employee's department.
Accounting [Enter]

Enter the name of employee #2
Ryan Pryce [Enter]
Enter the employee's ID number.
8996 [Enter]
Enter the employee's department.
Security [Enter]

Enter the name of employee #3
Bonnie Dundee [Enter]
Enter the employee's ID number.
2301 [Enter]
Enter the employee's department.
Marketing [Enter]

Employee records written to employees.dat.

Lines 16 through 18 prompt the user for the number of employee records that he or she wants to create. Inside the loop, the program gets an employee's name, ID number, and department. This data is written to the file in line 39. The loop iterates once for each employee record.

In the sample run of the program, the user enters data for three employees. The table shown in Figure 10-19 shows how you can think of the resulting records that will be written to the file. The file contains three records, one for each employee, and each record has three fields.

Figure 10-19 Records written to the `employees.dat` file

Name	ID Number	Department
Colleen Pickett	7311	Accounting
Ryan Pryce	8996	Security
Bonnie Dundee	2301	Marketing

The way that fields and records are actually organized inside the file, however, varies slightly from language to language. Earlier we mentioned that many systems write a delimiter after each item in a file. Figure 10-20 shows how part of the file's contents might appear with a delimiter after each field.

Figure 10-20 File contents with a delimiter after each field

| Colleen Pickett | *Delimiter* | 7311 | *Delimiter* | Accounting | *Delimiter* | Ryan Pryce | *Delimiter* | 8996 | ... and so forth |

> **NOTE:** When records are created in a file, some systems write one type of delimiter after each field and another type of delimiter after each record.

Reading Records

In pseudocode we will read an entire record from a file using a single `Read` statement. The following statement shows how we can read three values from `employeeFile` into the `name`, `idNumber`, and `department` variables:

```
Read employeeFile name, idNumber, department
```

The pseudocode in Program 10-8 shows a program that reads the records written to the `employees.dat` file by Program 10-7.

Program 10-8

```
 1 // Variables for the fields
 2 Declare String name
 3 Declare Integer idNumber
 4 Declare String department
 5
 6 // Declare an input file.
 7 Declare InputFile employeeFile
 8
 9 // Open a file named employees.dat.
10 Open employeeFile "employees.dat"
```

```
11
12 Display "Here are the employee records."
13
14 // Display the records in the file.
15 While NOT eof(employeeFile)
16    // Read a record from the file.
17    Read employeeFile name, idNumber, department
18
19    // Display the record.
20    Display "Name: ", name
21    Display "ID Number: ", idNumber
22    Display "Department: ", department
23
24    // Display a blank line.
25    Display
26 End For
27
28 // Close the file.
29 Close employeeFile
```

Program Output

```
Here are the employee records.
Name: Colleen Pickett
ID Number: 7311
Department: Accounting

Name: Ryan Pryce
ID Number: 8996
Department: Security

Name: Bonnie Dundee
ID Number: 2301
Department: Marketing
```

Applications that store records in a file typically require more capabilities than simply writing and reading records. In the following *In the Spotlight* sections we will examine algorithms for adding records to a file, searching a file for specific records, modifying a record, and deleting a record.

In the Spotlight:

Adding and Displaying Records

Midnight Coffee Roasters, Inc. is a small company that imports raw coffee beans from around the world and roasts them to create a variety of gourmet coffees. Julie, the owner of the company, has asked you to design a series of programs that she can use to manage her inventory. After speaking with her, you have determined that a file is needed to keep inventory records. Each record should have two fields to hold the following data:

- Description: a string containing the name of the coffee
- Quantity in inventory: the number of pounds in inventory, as a real number

Your first job is to design a program that can be used to add records to the file. Program 10-9 shows the pseudocode, and Figure 10-21 shows a flowchart. Note that the output file is opened in append mode. Each time the program is executed, the new records will be added to the file's existing contents.

Program 10-9

```
1  // Variables for the fields
2  Declare String description
3  Declare Real quantity
4
5  // A variable to control the loop.
6  Declare String another = "Y"
7
8  // Declare an output file in append mode.
9  Declare OutputFile AppendMode coffeeFile
10
11 // Open the file.
12 Open coffeeFile "coffee.dat"
13
14 While toUpper(another) == "Y"
15    // Get the description.
16    Display "Enter the description."
17    Input description
18
19    // Get the quantity on hand.
20    Display "Enter the quantity on hand ",
21           "(in pounds)."
22    Input quantity
23
24    // Append the record to the file.
25    Write coffeeFile description, quantity
26
27    // Determine whether the user wants to enter
28    // another record.
29    Display "Do you want to enter another record? ",
30    Display "(Enter Y for yes, or anything else for no.)"
31    Input another
32
33    // Display a blank line.
34    Display
35 End While
36
37 // Close the file.
38 Close coffeeFile
39 Display "Data appended to coffee.dat."
```

Program Output (with Input Shown in Bold)

```
Enter the description.
Brazilian Dark Roast [Enter]
Enter the quantity on hand (in pounds).
18 [Enter]
Do you want to enter another record?
```

```
(Enter Y for yes, or anything else for no.)
y [Enter]
Enter the description.
Sumatra Medium Roast [Enter]
Enter the quantity on hand (in pounds).
25 [Enter]
Do you want to enter another record?
(Enter Y for yes, or anything else for no.)
n [Enter]
Data appended to coffee.dat.
```

Figure 10-21 Flowchart for Program 10-9

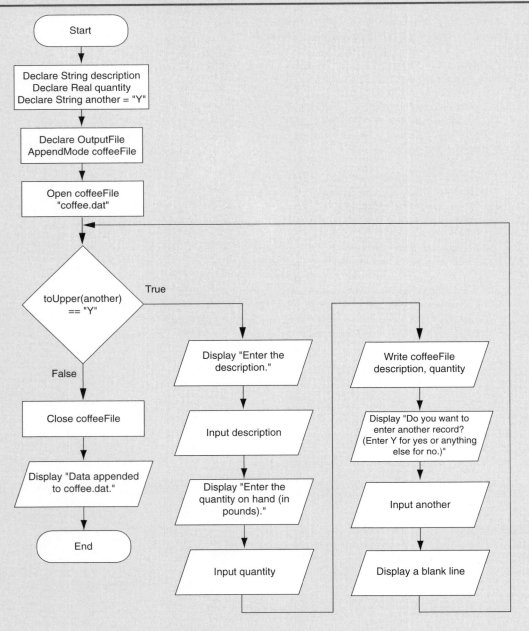

Your next job is to design a program that displays all of the records in the inventory file. Program 10-10 shows the pseudocode and Figure 10-22 shows a flowchart.

Program 10-10

```
1 // Variables for the fields
2 Declare String description
3 Declare Real quantity
4
5 // Declare an input file.
6 Declare InputFile coffeeFile
7
8 // Open the file.
9 Open coffeeFile "coffee.dat"
10
11 While NOT eof(coffeeFile)
12     // Read a record from the file.
13     Read coffeeFile description, quantity
14
15     // Display the record.
16     Display "Description: ", description,
17             "Quantity: ", quantity, " pounds"
18 End While
19
20 // Close the file.
21 Close coffeeFile
```

Program Output

```
Description: Brazilian Dark Roast Quantity: 18 pounds
Description: Sumatra Medium Roast Quantity: 25 pounds
```

Figure 10-22 Flowchart for Program 10-10

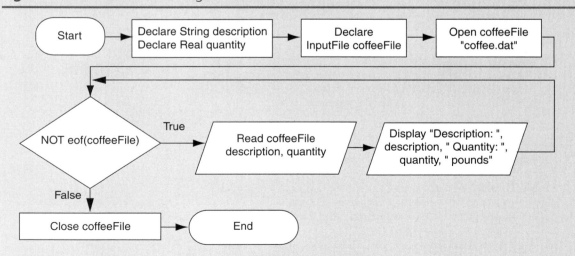

In the Spotlight:

Searching for a Record

Julie has been using the first two programs that you designed for her. She now has several records stored in the `coffee.dat` file, and has asked you to design another program that she can use to search for records. She wants to be able to enter a string and see a list of all the records containing that string in the description field. For example, suppose the file contains the following records:

Description	Quantity
Sumatra Dark Roast	12
Sumatra Medium Roast	30
Sumatra Decaf	20
Sumatra Organic Medium Roast	15

If she enters "Sumatra" as the value to search for, the program should display all of these records. Program 10-11 shows the pseudocode, and Figure 10-23 shows the flowchart for the program.

Notice that line 27 of the pseudocode uses the `contains` function. Recall from Chapter 6 that the `contains` function returns `True` if the first argument, a string, contains the second argument, also a string.

Program 10-11

```
 1  // Variables for the fields
 2  Declare String description
 3  Declare Real quantity
 4
 5  // A variable to hold the search value.
 6  Declare String searchValue
 7
 8  // A Flag to indicate whether the value was found.
 9  Declare Boolean found = False
10
11  // Declare an input file.
12  Declare InputFile coffeeFile
13
14  // Get the value to search for.
15  Display "Enter a value to search for."
16  Input searchValue
17
18  // Open the file.
19  Open coffeeFile "coffee.dat"
20
21  While NOT eof(coffeeFile)
22      // Read a record from the file.
23      Read coffeeFile description, quantity
24
25      // If the record contains the search value,
26      // then display it.
27      If contains(description, searchValue) Then
```

```
28          // Display the record.
29          Display "Description: ", description,
30                   "Quantity: ", quantity, " pounds"
31
32          // Set the found flag to true.
33          Set found = True
34      End If
35 End While
36
37 // If the value was not found in the file,
38 // display a message indicating so.
39 If NOT found Then
40     Display searchValue, " was not found."
41 End If
42
43 // Close the file.
44 Close coffeeFile
```

Program Output (with Input Shown in Bold)

Enter a value to search for.
Sumatra [Enter]
Description: Sumatra Dark Roast Quantity: 12 pounds
Description: Sumatra Medium Roast Quantity: 30 pounds
Description: Sumatra Decaf Quantity: 20 pounds
Description: Sumatra Organic Medium Roast Quantity: 15 pounds

Figure 10-23 Flowchart for Program 10-11

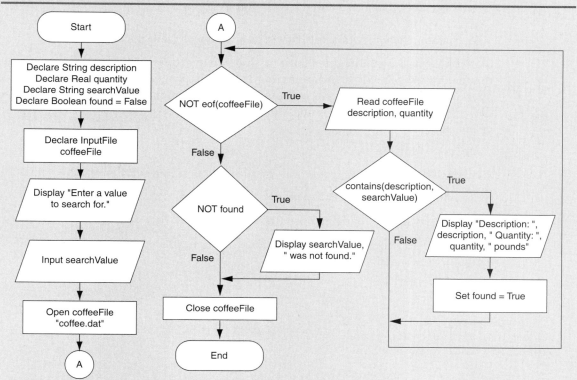

In the Spotlight:
Modifying Records

Julie is very happy with the programs that you have designed so far. Your next job is to design a program that she can use to modify the quantity field in an existing record. This will allow her to keep the records up to date as coffee is sold or more coffee is added to inventory.

To modify a record in a sequential file, you must create a second temporary file. You copy all of the original file's records to the temporary file, but when you get to the record that is to be modified, you do not write its old contents to the temporary file. Instead, you write its new modified values to the temporary file. Then, you finish copying any remaining records from the original file to the temporary file.

The temporary file then takes the place of the original file. You delete the original file and rename the temporary file, giving it the name that the original file had on the computer's disk. Here is the general algorithm for your program:

1. Open the original file for input and create a temporary file for output.
2. Get the description field of the record to be modified and the new value for the quantity field.
3. While not at the end of the original file:
      Read a record.
      If this record's description field matches the description entered, then:
          Write the new data to the temporary file.
      Else write the existing record to the temporary file.
4. Close the original file and the temporary file.
5. Delete the original file.
6. Rename the temporary file, giving it the name of the original file.

Notice that at the end of the algorithm you delete the original file and then rename the temporary file. Most programming languages provide a way to perform these operations. In pseudocode we will use the `Delete` statement to delete a file on the disk. You simply provide a string containing the name of the file that you wish to delete, such as:

```
Delete "coffee.dat"
```

To change the name of a file, we will use the `Rename` statement. For example,

```
Rename "temp.dat", "coffee.dat"
```

indicates that we are changing the name of the file `temp.dat` to `coffee.dat`.

Program 10-12 shows the pseudocode for the program, and Figures 10-24 and 10-25 show the flowchart.

Program 10-12

```
1 // Variables for the fields
2 Declare String description
3 Declare Real quantity
4
```

```
 5 // A variable to hold the search value.
 6 Declare String searchValue
 7
 8 // A variable to hold the new quantity.
 9 Declare Real newQuantity
10
11 // A Flag to indicate whether the value was found.
12 Declare Boolean found = False
13
14 // Declare an input file.
15 Declare InputFile coffeeFile
16
17 // Declare an output file to copy the original
18 // file to.
19 Declare OutputFile tempFile
20
21 // Open the original file.
22 Open coffeeFile "coffee.dat"
23
24 // Open the temporary file.
25 Open tempFile "temp.dat"
26
27 // Get the value to search for.
28 Display "Enter the coffee you wish to update."
29 Input searchValue
30
31 // Get the new quantity.
32 Display "Enter the new quantity."
33 Input newQuantity
34
35 While NOT eof(coffeeFile)
36    // Read a record from the file.
37    Read coffeeFile description, quantity
38
39    // Write either this record to the temporary
40    // file, or the new record if this is the
41    // one that is to be changed.
42    If description == searchValue Then
43       Write tempFile description, newQuantity
44       Set found = True
45    Else
46       Write tempFile description, quantity
47    End If
48 End While
49
50 // Close the original file.
51 Close coffeeFile
52
53 // Close the temporary file.
54 Close tempFile
55
56 // Delete the original file.
57 Delete "coffee.dat"
58
59 // Rename the temporary file.
```

```
60 Rename "temp.dat", "coffee.dat"
61
62 // Indicate whether the operation was successful.
63 If found Then
64    Display "The record was updated."
65 Else
66    Display searchValue, " was not found in the file."
67 End If
```

Program Output (with Input Shown in Bold)

Enter the coffee you wish to update.
Sumatra Medium Roast [Enter]
Enter the new quantity.
18 [Enter]
The record was updated.

Figure 10-24 Flowchart for Program 10-12, part 1

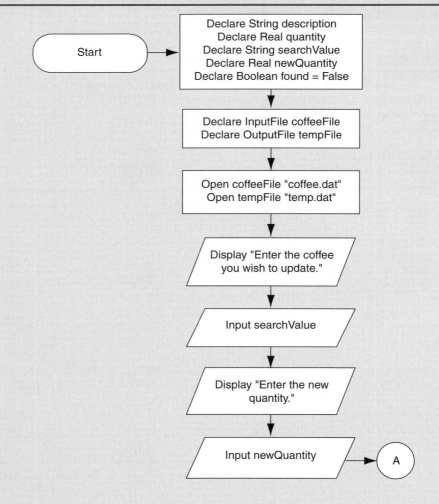

Figure 10-25 Flowchart for Program 10-12, part 2

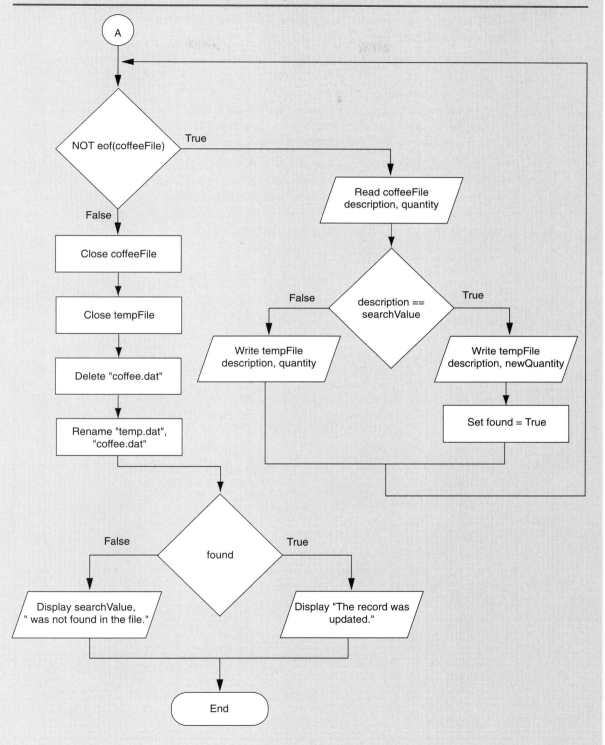

> **TIP:** If you are using a language that does not have built-in statements for deleting and renaming files, you can perform the following steps after closing the original file and the temporary file:
>
> 1. Open the original file for output. (This will erase the contents of the original file.)
> 2. Open the temporary file for input.
> 3. Read each record in the temporary file and then write it to the original file. (This copies all of the records from the temporary file to the original file.)
> 4. Close the original and temporary files.
>
> A disadvantage to using this approach is that the additional steps of copying the temporary file to the original file will slow the program down. Another disadvantage is that the temporary file will remain on the disk. If the temporary file contains a large amount of data, you might need to open it for output once again and then immediately close it. This erases the file's contents.

In the Spotlight:

Deleting Records

Your last task is to write a program that Julie can use to delete records from the `coffee.dat` file. Like the process of modifying a record, the process of deleting a record from a sequential access file requires that you create a second temporary file. You copy all of the original file's records to the temporary file, except for the record that is to be deleted. The temporary file then takes the place of the original file. You delete the original file and rename the temporary file, giving it the name that the original file had on the computer's disk. Here is the general algorithm for your program:

1. Open the original file for input and create a temporary file for output.
2. Get the description field of the record to be deleted.
3. While not at the end of the original file:
    Read a record.
    If this record's description field does not match the description entered, then:
        Write the record to the temporary file.
4. Close the original file and the temporary file.
5. Delete the original file.
6. Rename the temporary file, giving it the name of the original file.

Program 10-13 shows the pseudocode for the program, and Figure 10-26 shows a flowchart.

Program 10-13

```
 1 // Variables for the fields
 2 Declare String description
 3 Declare Real quantity
 4
 5 // A variable to hold the search value.
 6 Declare String searchValue
 7
 8 // Declare an input file.
 9 Declare InputFile coffeeFile
10
11 // Declare an output file to copy the original
12 // file to.
13 Declare OutputFile tempFile
14
15 // Open the files.
16 Open coffeeFile "coffee.dat"
17 Open tempFile "temp.dat"
18
19 // Get the value to search for.
20 Display "Enter the coffee you wish to delete."
21 Input searchValue
22
23 While NOT eof(coffeeFile)
24     // Read a record from the file.
25     Read coffeeFile description, quantity
26
27     // If this is not the record to delete, then
28     // write it to the temporary file.
29     If description != searchValue Then
30         Write tempFile description, quantity
31     End If
32 End While
33
34 // Close the two files.
35 Close coffeeFile
36 Close tempFile
37
38 // Delete the original file.
39 Delete("coffee.dat")
40
41 // Rename the temporary file.
42 Rename "temp.dat", "coffee.dat"
43
44 Display "The file has been updated."
```

Program Output (with Input Shown in Bold)

```
Enter the coffee you wish to delete.
```
Sumatra Organic Medium Roast [Enter]
```
The file has been updated.
```

Figure 10-26 Flowchart for Program 10-13

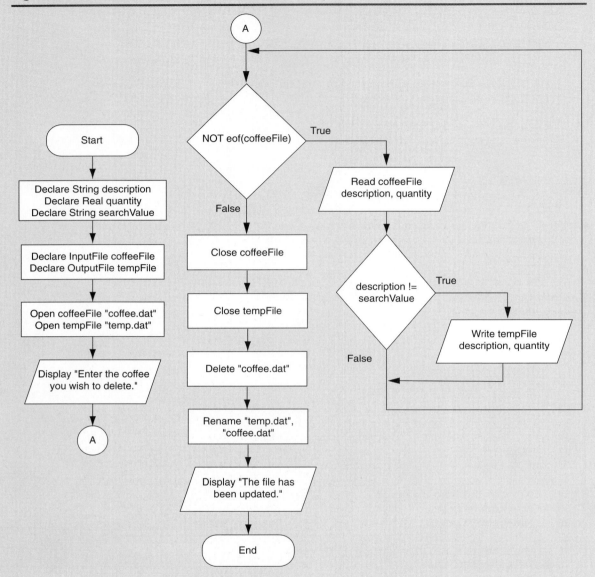

![Flowchart showing:]

Start → Declare String description / Declare Real quantity / Declare String searchValue → Declare InputFile coffeeFile / Declare OutputFile tempFile → Open coffeeFile "coffee.dat" / Open tempFile "temp.dat" → Display "Enter the coffee you wish to delete." → A

A → NOT eof(coffeeFile)
- True → Read coffeeFile description, quantity → description != searchValue
  - True → Write tempFile description, quantity
  - False → (loop back to A)
- False → Close coffeeFile → Close tempFile → Delete "coffee.dat" → Rename "temp.dat", "coffee.dat" → Display "The file has been updated." → End

![Checkpoint icon] **Checkpoint**

10.20 What is a record? What is a field?

10.21 Describe the way that you use a temporary file in a program that modifies a record in a sequential access file.

10.22 Describe the way that you use a temporary file in a program that deletes a record from a sequential file.

10.5 Control Break Logic

CONCEPT: Control break logic interrupts (breaks) a program's regular processing to perform a different action when a control variable's value changes or the variable acquires a specific value. After the action is complete, the program's regular processing resumes.

Sometimes a program that performs an ongoing process must be periodically interrupted so an action can take place. For example, consider a program that displays the contents of a lengthy file in a console output window, as shown in Figure 10-27. Suppose the window displays a maximum of 25 lines of output. If the program displays more items than will fit in the window, some of the items will scroll out of view. To prevent this from happening, the program can keep count of the number of items that have been displayed. When 24 items have been displayed, the program can display a message such as "Press any key to continue…" on the 25th line, and pause its output until the user presses a key. When this happens, the program can resume, pausing each time 24 items have been displayed.

Program 10-14 shows the pseudocode for a program that performs this operation. The program displays the contents of a file named student_names.dat, which contains a list of names. The program's output will be similar to that shown in Figure 10-27.

Figure 10-27 Pausing output after 24 items are displayed

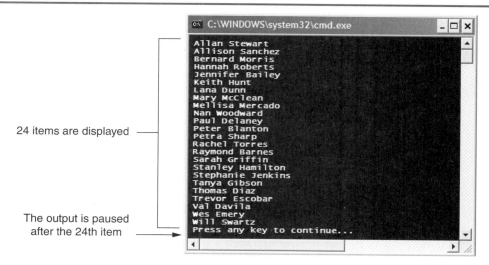

24 items are displayed

The output is paused after the 24th item

Program 10-14

```
1 // A variable for a name read from the file.
2 Declare String name
3
4 // A variable to count lines.
5 Declare Integer lines = 0
6
```

```
 7 // Declare an input file.
 8 Declare InputFile nameFile
 9
10 // Open the file.
11 Open nameFile "student_names.dat"
12
13 While NOT eof(nameFile)
14     // Read a name from the file.
15     Read nameFile name
16
17     // Display the name.
18     Display name
19
20     // Increment the line counter.
21     Set lines = lines + 1
22
23     If lines == 24 Then
24         // Pause output until the user presses a key.
25         Display "Press any key to continue..."
26         Input
27
28         // Reset the line counter.
29         Set lines = 0
30     End If
31 End While
32
33 // Close the file.
34 Close nameFile
```

Notice that the program declares an Integer variable named lines in line 5, and initializes the variable to 0. This variable is used in the loop to keep count of the number of lines that have been displayed. Each time an item is displayed, the variable is incremented in line 21. The If statement in line 23 determines whether the lines variable is equal to 24. If this is true, the message "Press any key to continue..." in line 25 is displayed. In line 26 the Input statement is used to read a key stroke. (We did not store the value of the key in a variable because we are not concerned with knowing which key was pressed—we simply want to pause the program until the user presses a key.) Then, in line 29 we reset the lines variable to 0. This allows the program to display another 24 lines of output before pausing.

Using this type of logic, commonly called *control break* logic, the program performs some ongoing task (such as processing the items in a file), but temporarily interrupts the task when a control variable reaches a specific value or changes its value. When this happens, some other action is performed and then the program resumes its ongoing task.

Control break logic is used often in programs that print reports where data is organized into categories. The next *In the Spotlight* section shows an example of this, and also introduces a new pseudocode statement: Print. We will use the Print statement exactly like we use the Display statement, except the Print statement sends its output to the printer. (The actual process of sending data to a printer varies greatly among systems.)

In the Spotlight:
Using Control Break Logic

Dr. Shephard, the headmaster at Pinebrook Academy, has organized a fundraiser where each student has an opportunity to collect donations. She has asked you to design a program that prints a donation report. The report should show the amounts that each student has collected, the total collected by each student, and the total of all donations.

Dr. Shephard has provided a file, donations.dat, that has all of the data that you will need to generate the report. The file contains a record for each donation. Each record has two fields: one containing the ID number of the student who collected the donation (an integer), and another containing the amount of the donation. The records in the file are already sorted in order of student ID numbers.

Here is an example of how the report should appear:

```
Pinebrook Academy Fundraiser Report

Student ID            Donation Amount
======================================
104                      $250.00
104                      $100.00
104                      $500.00
Total donations for student: $850.00

105                      $100.00
105                      $800.00
105                      $400.00
Total donations for student: $1,300.00

106                      $350.00
106                      $450.00
106                      $200.00
Total donations for student: $1,000.00
Total of all donations: $3,150.00
```

Program 10-15 shows the pseudocode for the program. Let's first look at the main module and the printHeader module:

Program 10-15   **Fundraiser report program:**
                      main and printHeader modules

```
1 Module main()
2    // Print the report header.
3    Call printHeader()
4
5    // Print the details of the report.
6    Call printDetails()
7 End Module
8
9 // The printHeader module prints the report header.
10 Module printHeader()
```

```
11       Print "Pinebrook Academy Fundraiser Report"
12       Print
13       Print "Student ID        Donation Amount"
14       Print "====================================="
15 End Module
16
```

In the `main` module, line 3 calls the `printHeader` module, which prints the report header. Then, line 6 calls the `printDetails` module, which prints the body of the report. The pseudocode for the `printDetails` module follows.

Program 10-15   **Fundraiser report program (continued): `printDetails` module**

```
17 // The printDetails module prints the report details.
18 Module printDetails()
19     // Variables for the fields
20     Declare Integer studentID
21     Declare Real donation
22
23     // Accumulator variables
24     Declare Real studentTotal = 0
25     Declare Real total = 0
26
27     // A variable to use in the control
28     // break logic.
29     Declare Integer currentID
30
31     // Declare an input file and open it.
32     Declare InputFile donationsFile
33     Open donationsFile "donations.dat"
34
35     // Read the first record.
36     Read donationsFile studentID, donation
37
38     // Save the student ID number.
39     Set currentID = studentID
40
41     // Print the report details.
42     While NOT eof(donationsFile)
43         // Check the student ID field to see if
44         // it has changed.
45         If studentID != currentID Then
46             // Print the total for the student,
47             // followed by a blank line.
48             Print "Total donations for student: ",
49                   currencyFormat(studentTotal)
50             Print
51
52             // Save the next student's ID number.
53             Set currentID = studentID
54
55             // Reset the student accumulator.
56             Set studentTotal = 0
```

```
57          End If
58
59          // Print the data for the donation.
60          Print studentID, Tab, currencyFormat(donation)
61
62          // Update the accumulators.
63          Set studentTotal = studentTotal + donation
64          Set total = total + donation
65
66          // Read the next record.
67          Read donationsFile, studentID, donation
68      End While
69
70      // Print the total for the last student.
71      Print "Total donations for student: ",
72          currencyFormat(studentTotal)
73
74      // Print the total of all donations.
75      Print "Total of all donations: ",
76          currencyFormat(total)
77
78      // Close the file.
79      Close donationsFile
80  End Module
```

Let's take a closer look at the printDetails module. Here is a summary of the variable declarations:

- Lines 20 and 21 declare the studentID and donation variables, which will hold the field values for each record read from the file.
- Lines 24 and 25 declare the studentTotal and total variables. The studentTotal is an accumulator that the program will use to calculate the total donations that each student collects. The total variable is an accumulator that will calculate the total of all donations.
- Line 29 declares the currentID variable. This will store the ID number of the student whose donation total is currently being calculated.
- Line 32 declares donationsFile as an internal name associates with the donations.dat file.

Line 33 opens the donations.dat file, and line 36 reads the first record. The values that are read are stored in the studentID and donation variables.

Line 39 assigns the student ID that was read from the file to the currentID variable. The currentID variable will hold the ID of the student whose records are currently being processed.

Line 42 is the beginning of the loop that processes the file. The If statement that appears in lines 45 through 57 contains the control break logic. It tests the control variable, studentID, to determine whether it is *not* equal to currentID. If the two are not equal, then the program has read a record with a student ID that is different from the value stored in currentID. This means it has read the last record for the student whose ID is stored in currentID, so the program momentarily breaks out of the process to display the student's total donations (lines 48 and 49), save the new student ID in currentID (line 53), and reset the studentTotal accumulator (line 56).

Line 60 prints the contents of the current record. Lines 63 and 64 update the accumulator variables. Line 67 reads the next record from the file. Once all the records have been processed, lines 71 and 72 display the total donations for the last student, lines 75 and 76 display the total of all donations, and line 79 closes the file. The report that is printed by the program will appear similar to the sample report previously shown.

NOTE: The logic of this program assumes that the records in the `donations.dat` file are already sorted by student ID. If the records are not sorted by student ID, the sales report will not list all of the donations for each student together.

Figure 10-28 shows a flowchart for the `printDetails` module.

Figure 10-28 Flowchart for the `printDetails` module

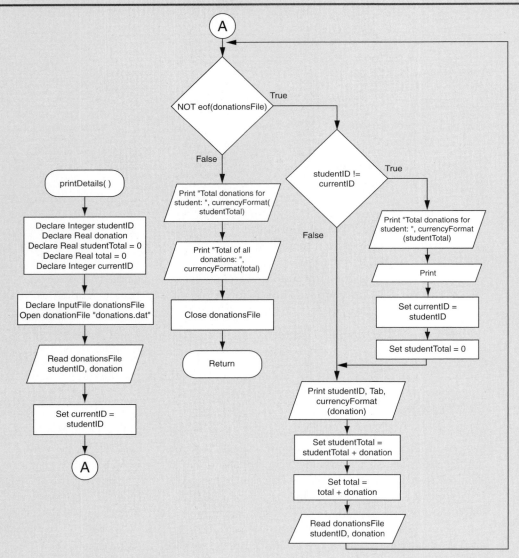

Review Questions

Multiple Choice

1. A file that data is written to is known as a(n)

   a. input file
   b. output file
   c. sequential access file
   d. binary file

2. A file that data is read from is known as a(n)

   a. input file
   b. output file
   c. sequential access file
   d. binary file

3. Before a file can be used by a program, it must be

   a. formatted
   b. encrypted
   c. closed
   d. opened

4. When a program is finished using a file, it should do this.

   a. erase the file
   b. open the file
   c. close the file
   d. encrypt the file

5. The contents of this type of file can be viewed in an editor such as Notepad.

   a. text file
   b. binary file
   c. English file
   d. human-readable file

6. This type of file contains data that has not been converted to text.

   a. text file
   b. binary file
   c. Unicode file
   d. symbolic file

7. When working with this type of file, you access its data from the beginning of the file to the end of the file.

   a. ordered access
   b. binary access
   c. direct access
   d. sequential access

8. When working with this type of file, you can jump directly to any piece of data in the file without reading the data that comes before it.

   a. ordered access
   b. binary access
   c. direct access
   d. sequential access

9. This is a small "holding section" in memory that many systems write data to before writing the data to a file.

   a. buffer
   b. variable
   c. virtual file
   d. temporary file

10. This is a character or set of characters that marks the end of a piece of data.

   a. median value
   b. delimiter
   c. boundary marker
   d. EOF marker

11. This is a character or set of characters that marks the end of a file.

   a. median value
   b. delimiter
   c. boundary marker
   d. EOF marker

12. This marks the location of the next item that will be read from a file.

   a. input position
   b. delimiter
   c. pointer
   d. read position

13. When a file is opened in this mode, data will be written at the end of the file's existing contents.

   a. output mode
   b. append mode
   c. backup mode
   d. read-only mode

14. The expression `NOT eof(myFile)` is equivalent to

   a. `eof(myFile) == True`
   b. `eof(myFile)`
   c. `eof(myFile) == False`
   d. `eof(myFile) < 0`

15. This is a single piece of data within a record.

   a. field
   b. variable
   c. delimiter
   d. subrecord

True or False

1. When working with a sequential access file, you can jump directly to any piece of data in the file without reading the data that comes before it.

2. In most languages, when you open an output file and that file already exists on the disk, the contents of the existing file will be erased.

3. The process of opening a file is only necessary with input files. Output files are automatically opened when data is written to them.

4. The purpose of an EOF marker is to indicate where a field ends. Files typically contain several EOF markers.

5. When an input file is opened, its read position is initially set to the first item in the file.

6. When a file that already exists is opened in append mode, the file's existing contents are erased.

7. In control break logic, the program performs some ongoing task (such as processing the items in a file), but permanently stops the task when a control variable reaches a specific value or changes its value.

Short Answer

1. Describe the three steps that must be taken when a file is used by a program.

2. Why should a program close a file when it's finished using it?

3. What is a file's read position? Where is the read position when a file is first opened for reading?

4. If an existing file is opened in append mode, what happens to the file's existing contents?

5. In most languages, if a file does not exist and a program attempts to open it in append mode, what happens?

6. What is the purpose of the eof function that was discussed in this chapter?

7. What is control break logic?

Algorithm Workbench

1. Design a program that opens an output file with the external name my_name.dat, writes your name to the file, and then closes the file.

2. Design a program that opens the my_name.dat file that was created by the algorithm in question 1, reads your name from the file, displays the name on the screen, and then closes the file.

3. Design an algorithm that does the following: Opens an output file with the external name number_list.dat, uses a loop to write the numbers 1 through 100 to the file, and then closes the file.

4. Design an algorithm that does the following: Opens the `number_list.dat` file that was created by the algorithm created in question 3, reads all of the numbers from the file and displays them, and then closes the file.

5. Modify the algorithm that you designed in question 4 so it adds all of the numbers read from the file and displays their total.

6. Write pseudocode that opens an output file with the external name `number_list.dat`, but does not erase the file's contents if it already exists.

7. A file exists on the disk named `students.dat`. The file contains several records, and each record contains two fields: (1) the student's name, and (2) the student's score for the final exam. Design an algorithm that deletes the record containing "John Perez" as the student name.

8. A file exists on the disk named `students.dat`. The file contains several records, and each record contains two fields: (1) the student's name, and (2) the student's score for the final exam. Design an algorithm that changes Julie Milan's score to 100.

Programming Exercises

VideoNote

File Display

1. **File Display**

   Assume that a file containing a series of integers is named `numbers.dat` and exists on the computer's disk. Design a program that displays all of the numbers in the file.

2. **Item Counter**

   Assume that a file containing a series of names (as strings) is named `names.dat` and exists on the computer's disk. Design a program that displays the number of names that are stored in the file. (*Hint*: Open the file and read every string stored in it. Each time you read a string, increment a counter variable. When you've read all the strings from the file, the counter variable will contain the number of names stored in the file.)

3. **Sum of Numbers**

   Assume that a file containing a series of integers is named `numbers.dat` and exists on the computer's disk. Design a program that reads all of the numbers stored in the file and calculates their total.

4. **Average of Numbers**

   Assume that a file containing a series of integers is named `numbers.dat` and exists on the computer's disk. Design a program that calculates the average of all the numbers stored in the file.

5. **Largest Number**

   Assume that a file containing a series of integers is named `numbers.dat` and exists on the computer's disk. Design a program that determines the largest number stored in the file. (*Hint*: Use a technique similar to the one that was discussed in Chapter 8 for finding the largest value in an array. You do not need to read the file into an array to use this technique, however. It can be adapted for use with a file.)

6. **Golf Scores**

   The Springfork Amateur Golf Club has a tournament every weekend. The club president has asked you to design two programs.

   (1) A program that will read each player's name and golf score as keyboard input, and then save these as records in a file named golf.dat. (Each record will have a field for the player's name and a field for the player's score.)

   (2) A program that reads the records from the golf.dat file and displays them.

7. **Best Golf Score**

   Modify program #2 that you wrote for Programming Exercise 6 so it also displays the name of the player with the best (lowest) golf score. (*Hint*: Use a technique similar to the one that was discussed in Chapter 8 for finding the lowest value in an array. You do not need to read the file into an array to use this technique, however. It can be adapted for use with a file.)

8. **Sales Report**

   Brewster's Used Cars, Inc. employs several salespeople. Brewster, the owner of the company, has provided a file that contains sales records for each salesperson for the past month. Each record in the file contains the following two fields:

   - The salesperson's ID number, as an integer
   - The amount of a sale, as a real number

   The records are already sorted by salesperson ID. Brewster wants you to design a program that prints a sales report. The report should show each salesperson's sales and the total sales for that salesperson. The report should also show the total sales for all salespeople for the month. Here is an example of how the sales report should appear:

```
Brewster's Used Cars, Inc.
Sales Report

Salesperson ID            Sale Amount
======================================
100                       $10,000.00
100                       $12,000.00
100                       $5,000.00
Total sales for this salesperson: $27,000.00

101                       $14,000.00
101                       $18,000.00
101                       $12,500.00
Total sales for this salesperson: $44,500.00

102                       $13,500.00
102                       $14,500.00
102                       $20,000.00
Total sales for this salesperson: $48,000.00
Total of all sales: $119,500.00
```

11 Menu-Driven Programs

11.1 Introduction to Menu-Driven Programs

CONCEPT: A menu is a list of operations that are displayed by a program. The user can select one of the operations and the program will perform it.

A *menu-driven program* displays a list of operations that it can perform on the screen, and allows the user to select the operation that he or she wants the program to perform. The list of operations that is displayed on the screen is called a *menu*. For example, a program that manages a mailing list might display the menu shown in Figure 11-1.

Figure 11-1 A menu

Notice that each item in this particular menu is preceded by a number. The user selects one of the operations by entering the number that appears next to it. Entering 1, for example, allows the user to add a name to the mailing list, and entering 4 causes the program to print the mailing list. Menu-driven programs that ask the user to enter his or her selection on the keyboard typically display a character such as a number or a letter next to each menu item. The user types the character that corresponds to the menu item that he or she wants to select.

> **NOTE:** In a program that uses a graphical user interface (GUI), the user typically makes menu selections by clicking them with the mouse. You will learn about graphical user interfaces in Chapter 15.

Using a Decision Structure to Perform Menu Selections

When the user selects an item from a menu, the program must use a decision structure to perform an action based on that selection. In most languages the case structure is a good mechanism for making this happen. Let's look at a simple example. Suppose we need a program that converts the following measurements from English units to metric units:

- Convert inches to centimeters
- Convert feet to meters
- Convert miles to kilometers

Here are the formulas for making these conversions:

centimeters = inches × 2.54
meters = feet × 0.3048
kilometers = miles × 1.609

The program should display a menu, such as the following, that allows the user to select the conversion that he or she wants to perform.

```
1. Convert inches to centimeters.
2. Convert feet to meters.
3. Convert miles to kilometers.

Enter your selection.
```

Program 11-1 shows the pseudocode for the program with four sample executions of the program. The case structure in lines 21 through 48 performs the operation that the user selects from the menu. Notice that a `Default` section appears in lines 45 through 47. The `Default` section validates the user's menu selection. If the user enters any value other than 1, 2, or 3 at the menu prompt, an error message is displayed. The first three sample execution sessions show what happens when the user makes a valid selection from the menu. The last sample session shows what happens when the user makes an invalid menu selection. Figure 11-2 shows a flowchart for the program.

Program 11-1

```
 1 // Declare a variable to hold the
 2 // user's menu selection.
 3 Declare Integer menuSelection
 4
 5 // Declare variables to hold the units
 6 // of measurement.
 7 Declare Real inches, centimeters, feet, meters,
 8                miles, kilometers
 9
10 // Display the menu.
11 Display "1. Convert inches to centimeters."
12 Display "2. Convert feet to meters."
13 Display "3. Convert miles to kilometers."
14 Display
15
16 // Prompt the user for a selection
17 Display "Enter your selection."
18 Input menuSelection
19
20 // Perform the selected operation.
21 Select menuSelection
22     Case 1:
23         // Convert inches to centimeters.
24         Display "Enter the number of inches."
25         Input inches
26         Set centimeters = inches * 2.54
27         Display "That is equal to ", centimeters,
28                " centimeters."
29
30     Case 2:
31         // Convert feet to meters.
32         Display "Enter the number of feet."
33         Input feet
34         Set meters = feet * 0.3048
35         Display "That is equal to ", meters, " meters."
36
37     Case 3:
38         // Convert miles to kilometers.
39         Display "Enter the number of miles."
40         Input miles
41         Set kilometers = miles * 1.609
42         Display "That is equal to ",kilometers,
43                " kilometers."
44
45     Default:
46         // Display an error message.
47         Display "That is an invalid selection."
48 End Select
```

This displays the menu and prompts the user to enter a selection. The user's input is stored in the `menuSelection` variable.

This executes if the user enters 1.

This executes if the user enters 2.

This executes if the user enters 3.

This executes if the user enters anything other than 1, 2, or 3.

Program Output (with Input Shown in Bold)

```
1. Convert inches to centimeters.
2. Convert feet to meters.
3. Convert miles to kilometers.

Enter your selection.
1 [Enter]
Enter the number of inches.
10 [Enter]
That is equal to 25.4 centimeters.
```

Program Output (with Input Shown in Bold)

```
1. Convert inches to centimeters.
2. Convert feet to meters.
3. Convert miles to kilometers.

Enter your selection.
2 [Enter]
Enter the number of feet.
10 [Enter]
That is equal to 3.048 meters.
```

Program Output (with Input Shown in Bold)

```
1. Convert inches to centimeters.
2. Convert feet to meters.
3. Convert miles to kilometers.

Enter your selection.
3 [Enter]
Enter the number of miles.
10 [Enter]
That is equal to 16.09 kilometers.
```

Program Output (with Input Shown in Bold)

```
1. Convert inches to centimeters.
2. Convert feet to meters.
3. Convert miles to kilometers.

Enter your selection.
4 [Enter]
That is an invalid selection.
```

Although a case structure is often the easiest and most straightforward decision structure to use in a menu-driven program, other approaches can be taken as an alternative. For example, a series of nested If-Then-Else statements could be used as shown in Program 11-2. Figure 11-3 shows a flowchart for this program.

Figure 11-2 Flowchart for Program 11-1

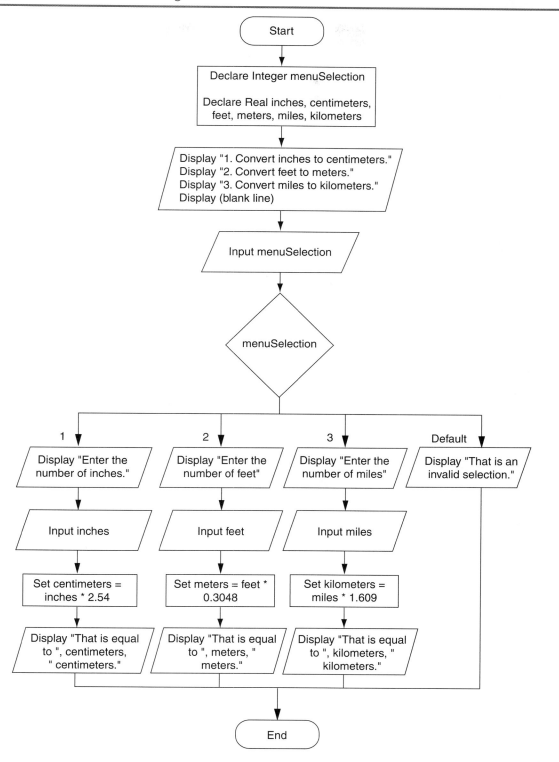

Program 11-2

```
 1 // Declare a variable to hold the
 2 // user's menu selection.
 3 Declare Integer menuSelection
 4
 5 // Declare variables to hold the units
 6 // of measurement.
 7 Declare Real inches, centimeters, feet, meters,
 8           miles, kilometers
 9
10 // Display the menu.
11 Display "1. Convert inches to centimeters."
12 Display "2. Convert feet to meters."
13 Display "3. Convert miles to kilometers."
14 Display
15
16 // Prompt the user for a selection
17 Display "Enter your selection."
18 Input menuSelection
19
20 // Perform the selected operation.
21 If menuSelection == 1 Then
22     // Convert inches to centimeters.
23     Display "Enter the number of inches."
24     Input inches
25     Set centimeters = inches * 2.54
26     Display "That is equal to ", centimeters,
27           " centimeters."
28 Else
29     If menuSelection == 2 Then
30         // Convert feet to meters.
31         Display "Enter the number of feet."
32         Input feet
33         Set meters = feet * 0.3048
34         Display "That is equal to ", meters, " meters."
35     Else
36         If menuSelection == 3 Then
37             // Convert miles to kilometers.
38             Display "Enter the number of miles."
39             Input miles
40             Set kilometers = miles * 1.609
41             Display "That is equal to ",kilometers,
42                   " kilometers."
43         Else
44             // Display an error message.
45             Display "That is an invalid selection."
46         End If
47     End If
48 End If
```

This displays the menu and prompts the user to enter a selection. The user's input is stored in the menuSelection variable.

This executes if the user enters 1.

This executes if the user enters 2.

This executes if the user enters 3.

Error message

(The output is the same as that for Program 11-1.)

Figure 11-3 Flowchart for Program 11-2

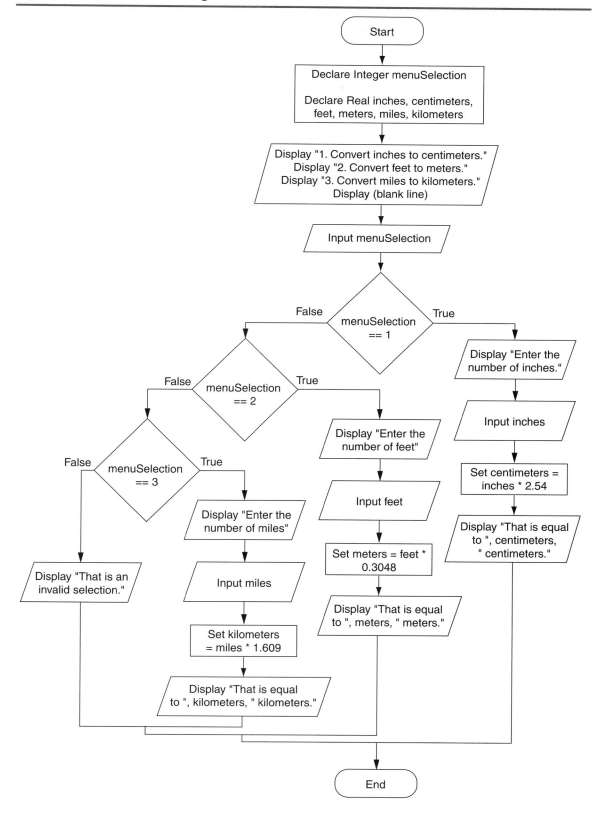

> **NOTE:** As a third alternative, the program could also be modified to use an `If-Then-Else If` statement.

Validating the Menu Selection

Any program that allows the user to select an item from a menu should validate the user's selection. Program 11-1 validated the user's menu selection with the `Default` section in the case structure (in lines 45 through 47). Program 11-2 validated the menu selection with the `Else` clause (in lines 43 through 45).

An alternative approach is to use an input validation loop immediately after the `Input` statement that reads the user's menu selection. If the menu selection is invalid, the loop displays an error message and prompts the user to enter it again. The loop repeats as long as the input is invalid.

The pseudocode in Program 11-3 shows how Program 11-1 can be modified to use an input validation loop. The input validation loop appears in lines 20 through 25. Notice that the case structure in this program does not have a `Default` section. The input validation loop makes sure the `menuSelection` variable is set to a value in the range of 1 through 3 before the program enters the case structure. Figure 11-4 shows a flowchart for the program.

Program 11-3

```
 1 // Declare a variable to hold the
 2 // user's menu selection.
 3 Declare Integer menuSelection
 4
 5 // Declare variables to hold the units
 6 // of measurement.
 7 Declare Real inches, centimeters, feet, meters,
 8           miles, kilometers
 9
10 // Display the menu.
11 Display "1. Convert inches to centimeters."
12 Display "2. Convert feet to meters."
13 Display "3. Convert miles to kilometers."
14 Display
15
16 // Prompt the user for a selection
17 Display "Enter your selection."
18 Input menuSelection
19
```

```
20 // Validate the menu selection.
21 While menuSelection < 1 OR menuSelection > 3
22     Display "That is an invalid selection. ",
23             "Enter 1, 2, or 3."
24     Input menuSelection
25 End While
26
27 // Perform the selected operation.
28 Select menuSelection
29     Case 1:
30         // Convert inches to centimeters.
31         Display "Enter the number of inches."
32         Input inches
33         Set centimeters = inches * 2.54
34         Display "That is equal to ", centimeters,
35                 " centimeters."
36
37     Case 2:
38         // Convert feet to meters.
39         Display "Enter the number of feet."
40         Input feet
41         Set meters = feet * 0.3048
42         Display "That is equal to ", meters, " meters."
43
44     Case 3:
45         // Convert miles to kilometers.
46         Display "Enter the number of miles."
47         Input miles
48         Set kilometers = miles * 1.609
49         Display "That is equal to ",kilometers,
50                 " kilometers."
51 End Select
```

Program Output (with Input Shown in Bold)

```
1. Convert inches to centimeters.
2. Convert feet to meters.
3. Convert miles to kilometers.

Enter your selection.
4 [Enter]
That is an invalid selection. Enter 1, 2, or 3.
1 [Enter]
Enter the number of inches.
10 [Enter]
That is equal to 25.4 centimeters.
```

Figure 11-4 Flowchart for Program 11-3

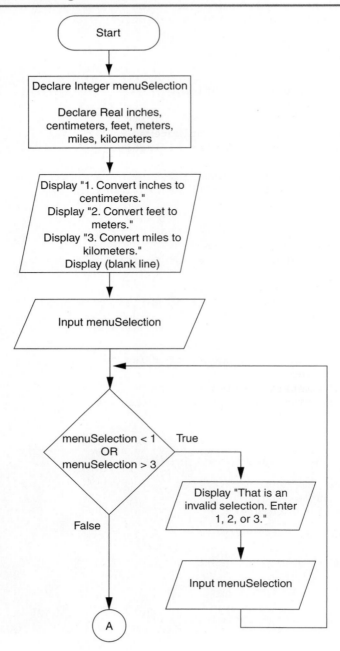

Figure 11-4 Flowchart for Program 11-3 (continued)

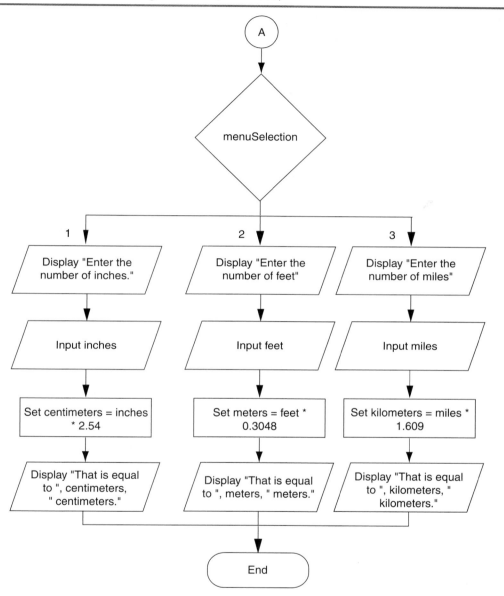

![Checkpoint]

Checkpoint

11.1 What is a menu-driven program?

11.2 The items displayed in a menu are often preceded by a number, letter, or other character. What is the purpose of this character?

11.3 What type of structure do you use in a program to perform the action that the user has selected from a menu?

11.2 Modularizing a Menu-Driven Program

> **CONCEPT:** Most menu-driven programs should be modularized, with each task written in its own module.

A menu-driven program is typically capable of performing several tasks, and allows the user to select the task that he or she wants the program to perform. In most cases, menu-driven programs should be broken down into modules that perform individual tasks. For example, look at the pseudocode in Program 11-4. This is an improved version of Program 11-3, using modules to break the program into small, manageable pieces.

Here are summaries of the modules that are used in Program 11-4:

- `main`: The `main` module is the program's starting point. It calls the other modules.
- `displayMenu`: The `displayMenu` module displays the menu on the screen, gets the user's menu selection, and validates it.
- `inchesToCentimeters`: The `inchesToCentimeters` module prompts the user to enter an amount of inches and displays that amount converted to centimeters. This module is called from the `main` module (in line 13) when the user enters 1 at the menu prompt.
- `feetToMeters`: The `feetToMeters` module prompts the user to enter an amount of feet and displays that amount converted to meters. This module is called from the `main` module (in line 16) when the user enters 2 at the menu prompt.
- `milesToKilometers`: The `milesToKilometers` module prompts the user to enter an amount of miles and displays that amount converted to meters. This module is called from the `main` module (in line 19) when the user enters 3 at the menu prompt.

Figure 11-5 shows a flowchart for the `main` module. Compare this to the flowchart for Program 11-3 (shown in Figure 11-4) and you can see how the modules have simplified the design. Figure 11-6 shows the flowcharts for the other modules.

Program 11-4

```
1 Module main()
2    // Declare a variable to hold the
3    // user's menu selection.
4    Declare Integer menuSelection
5
6    // Display the menu and get the
7    // user's selection.
8    Call displayMenu(menuSelection)
9
```

```
10      // Perform the selected operation.
11      Select menuSelection
12         Case 1:
13             Call inchesToCentimeters()
14
15         Case 2:
16             Call feetToMeters()
17
18         Case 3:
19             Call milesToKilometers()
20      End Select
21 End Module
22
23 // The displayMenu module displays the menu and
24 // prompts the user for a selection. The selected
25 // value is validated and stored in the selection
26 // parameter, which is passed by reference.
27 Module displayMenu(Integer Ref selection)
28      // Display the menu.
29      Display "1. Convert inches to centimeters."
30      Display "2. Convert feet to meters."
31      Display "3. Convert miles to kilometers."
32      Display
33
34      // Prompt the user for a selection.
35      Display "Enter your selection."
36      Input selection
37
38      // Validate the menu selection.
39      While selection < 1 OR selection > 3
40        Display "That is an invalid selection. ",
41               "Enter 1, 2, or 3."
42        Input selection
43      End While
44 End Module
45
46 // The inchesToCentimeters module converts a
47 // measurement from inches to centimeters.
48 Module inchesToCentimeters()
49      // Local variables
50      Declare Real inches, centimeters
51
52      // Get the number of inches.
53      Display "Enter the number of inches."
54      Input inches
55
56      // Convert the inches to centimeters.
57      Set centimeters = inches * 2.54
58
59      // Display the result.
60      Display "That is equal to ", centimeters,
61             " centimeters."
62 End Module
```

```
63
64 // The feetToMeters module converts a
65 // measurement from feet to meters.
66 Module feetToMeters()
67     // Local variables
68     Declare Real feet, meters
69
70     // Get the number of feet.
71     Display "Enter the number of feet."
72     Input feet
73
74     // Convert the feet to meters.
75     Set meters = feet * 0.3048
76
77     // Display the result.
78     Display "That is equal to ", meters, " meters."
79 End Module
80
81 // The milesToKilometers module converts a
82 // measurement from miles to kilometers.
83 Module milesToKilometers()
84     // Local variables
85     Declare Real miles, kilometers
86
87     // Get the number of miles.
88     Display "Enter the number of miles."
89     Input miles
90
91     // Convert the miles to kilometers.
92     Set kilometers = miles * 1.609
93
94     // Display the result.
95     Display "That is equal to ",kilometers,
96             " kilometers."
97 End Module
```

(The output is the same as that for Program 11-3.)

Figure 11-5 Flowcharts for the `main` modules in Program 11-3

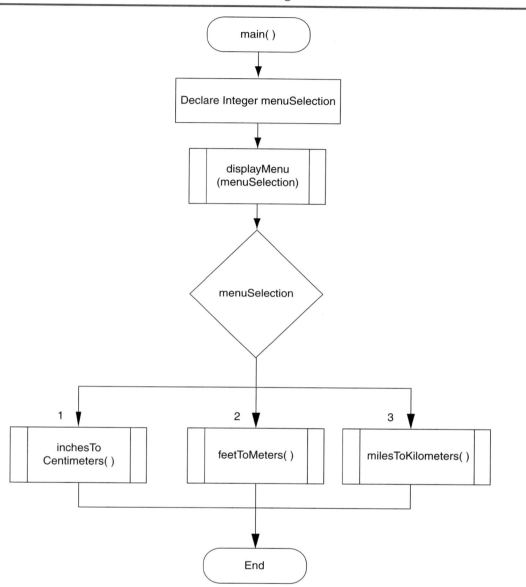

Figure 11-6 Flowcharts for the other modules in Program 11-3

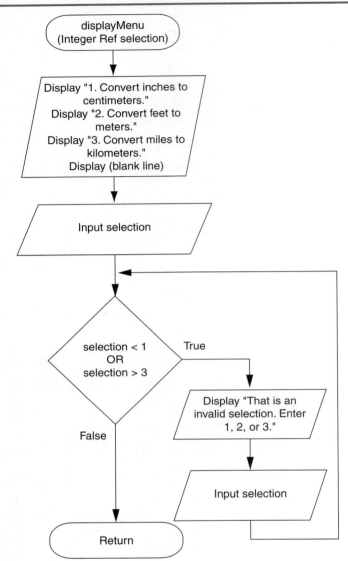

Figure 11-6 Flowcharts for the other modules in Program 11-3 (continued)

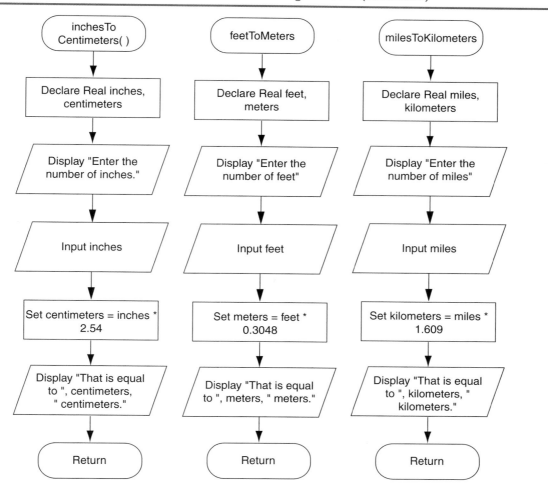

11.3 Using a Loop to Repeat the Menu

CONCEPT: Most menu-driven programs use a loop to repeatedly display the menu after a selected task is performed.

The programs you've seen so far in this chapter end immediately after performing an operation that is selected from the menu. If the user wants to select another operation from the menu, he or she has to run the program again. Having to run a program repeatedly to perform multiple operations can be inconvenient for the user, so most menu-driven programs use a loop that redisplays the menu after the user's selected action has been performed. When the user is ready to end the program, he or she selects an operation such as "End the program" from the menu.

Program 11-5 is a modification of Program 11-4. It shows how we can use a Do-While loop in the main module to display the menu repeatedly until the user is ready to end the program. Selecting item 4, End the program, causes the loop to stop and ends the program. Figure 11-7 shows a flowchart for the main module.

Program 11-5

```
 1 Module main()
 2     // Declare a variable to hold the
 3     // user's menu selection.
 4     Declare Integer menuSelection
 5
 6     Do
 7         // Display the menu and get the
 8         // user's selection.
 9         Call displayMenu(menuSelection)
10
11         // Perform the selected operation.
12         Select menuSelection
13             Case 1:
14                 Call inchesToCentimeters()
15
16             Case 2:
17                 Call feetToMeters()
18
19             Case 3:
20                 Call milesToKilometers()
21         End Select
22     While menuSelection != 4
23 End Module
24
25 // The displayMenu module displays the menu and
26 // prompts the user for a selection. The selected
27 // value is stored in the selection parameter, which
28 // is passed by reference.
29 Module displayMenu(Integer Ref selection)
30     // Display the menu.
31     Display "1. Convert inches to centimeters."
32     Display "2. Convert feet to meters."
33     Display "3. Convert miles to kilometers."
34     Display "4. End the program."
35     Display
36
37     // Prompt the user for a selection.
38     Display "Enter your selection."
39     Input selection
40
41     // Validate the menu selection.
42     While selection < 1 OR selection > 4
43         Display "That is an invalid selection. ",
44                 "Enter 1, 2, 3, or 4."
45         Input selection
46     End While
47 End Module
```

```
 48
 49  // The inchesToCentimeters module converts a
 50  // measurement from inches to centimeters.
 51  Module inchesToCentimeters()
 52      // Local variables
 53      Declare Real inches, centimeters
 54
 55      // Get the number of inches.
 56      Display "Enter the number of inches."
 57      Input inches
 58
 59      // Convert the inches to centimeters.
 60      Set centimeters = inches * 2.54
 61
 62      // Display the result.
 63      Display "That is equal to ", centimeters,
 64              " centimeters."
 65
 66      // Display a blank line.
 67      Display
 68  End Module
 69
 70  // The feetToMeters module converts a
 71  // measurement from feet to meters.
 72  Module feetToMeters()
 73      // Local variables
 74      Declare Real feet, meters
 75
 76      // Get the number of feet.
 77      Display "Enter the number of feet."
 78      Input feet
 79
 80      // Convert the feet to meters.
 81      Set meters = feet * 0.3048
 82
 83      // Display the result.
 84      Display "That is equal to ", meters, " meters."
 85
 86      // Display a blank line.
 87      Display
 88  End Module
 89
 90  // The milesToKilometers module converts a
 91  // measurement from miles to kilometers.
 92  Module milesToKilometers()
 93      // Local variables
 94      Declare Real miles, kilometers
 95
 96      // Get the number of miles.
 97      Display "Enter the number of miles."
 98      Input miles
 99
100      // Convert the miles to kilometers.
101      Set kilometers = miles * 1.609
102
```

```
103 // Display the result.
104 Display "That is equal to ",kilometers,
105         " kilometers."
106
107 // Display a blank line.
108 Display
109 End Module
```

Program Output (with Input Shown in Bold)

```
1. Convert inches to centimeters.
2. Convert feet to meters.
3. Convert miles to kilometers.
4. End the program.

Enter your selection.
1 [Enter]
Enter the number of inches.
10 [Enter]
That is equal to 25.4 inches.

1. Convert inches to centimeters.
2. Convert feet to meters.
3. Convert miles to kilometers.
4. End the program.

Enter your selection.
2 [Enter]
Enter the number of feet.
10 [Enter]
That is equal to 3.048 meters.

1. Convert inches to centimeters.
2. Convert feet to meters.
3. Convert miles to kilometers.
4. End the program.

Enter your selection.
4 [Enter]
```

TIP: A Do-While loop was chosen for Program 11-5 because it is a posttest loop, and it will always display the menu at least one time. A While loop could be used, but remember, the While loop is a pretest loop. Using it would require that the menuSelection variable be initialized with some value other than 4.

Figure 11-7 Flowchart for the `main` module in Program 11-5

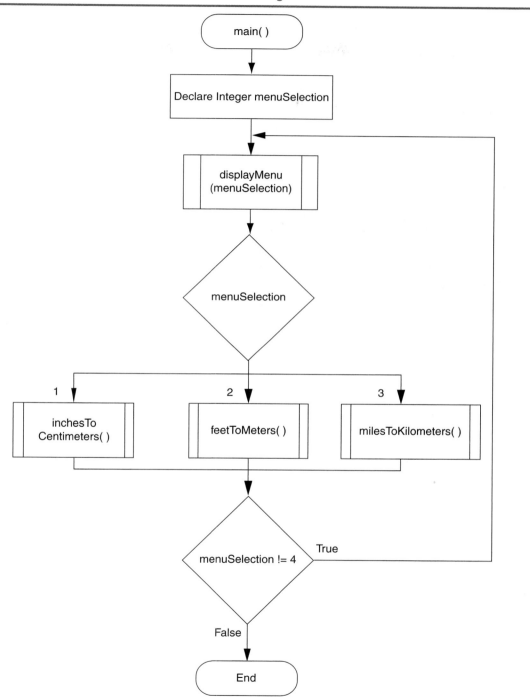

Chapter 11 Menu-Driven Programs

In the Spotlight:

Designing a Menu-Driven Program

In several of Chapter 10's *In the Spotlight* sections we stepped through the design of a series of programs for Midnight Coffee Roasters, Inc. These programs are used to manage the company's inventory of coffee. Each type of coffee that is in the inventory has a record in a file. Each record has fields indicating the name of the coffee and the quantity in stock. The programs you saw in Chapter 10 allow the user to perform the following operations:

- Add a record to the inventory file
- Search for a record
- Modify the quantity in an existing record in the inventory file
- Delete a record in the inventory file
- Display all of the records in the inventory file

Currently, all of these operations are performed by separate programs. Julie, the owner of Midnight Coffee Roasters, Inc, has asked you to consolidate all of these operations into a single program with a menu.

You decide to design a program with the following modules:

- `main`: This module executes when the program starts. It uses a loop that calls the appropriate modules to display the menu, get the user's selection, and then perform the selected operation.
- `displayMenu`: This module displays the following menu:

```
        Inventory Menu
1. Add a record.
2. Search for a record.
3. Modify a record.
4. Delete a record.
5. Display all records.
6. End the program.
```

    The `displayMenu` module also gets the user's selection, and validates the selection.
- `addRecord`: This module is called when the user selects item #1 from the menu. It allows the user to add a record to the inventory file.
- `searchRecord`: This module is called when the user selects item #2 from the menu. It allows the user to search the inventory file for a specific record.
- `modifyRecord`: This module is called when the user selects item #3 from the menu. It allows the user to modify the quantity that is stored in an existing record in the inventory file.
- `deleteRecord`: This module is called when the user selects item #4 from the menu. It allows the user to delete a record from the inventory file.
- `displayRecords`: This module is called when the user selects item #5 from the menu. It displays all of the records in the inventory file.

The pseudocode for the `main` module is shown in Program 11-6. Figure 11-8 shows a flowchart for the `main` module.

Program 11-6	Coffee inventory program: main **module**

```
 1 Module main()
 2     // Variable to hold the menu selection.
 3     Declare Integer menuSelection
 4
 5     Do
 6         // Display the menu.
 7         Call displayMenu(menuSelection)
 8
 9         // Perform the selected operation.
10         Select menuSelection
11             Case 1:
12                 Call addRecord()
13
14             Case 2:
15                 Call searchRecord()
16
17             Case 3:
18                 Call modifyRecord()
19
20             Case 4:
21                 Call deleteRecord()
22
23             Case 5:
24                 Call displayRecords()
25         End Select
26     While menuSelection != 6
27 End Module
28
```

The pseudocode for the displayMenu module follows. Figure 11-9 shows a flowchart for the displayMenu module.

Program 11-6	Coffee inventory program (continued): displayMenu **module**

```
29 // The displayMenu module displays the menu, gets
30 // the user's selection, and validates it.
31 Module displayMenu(Integer Ref selection)
32     // Display the menu.
33     Display "        Inventory Menu"
34     Display "1. Add a record."
35     Display "2. Search for a record."
36     Display "3. Modify a record."
37     Display "4. Delete a record."
38     Display "5. Display all records."
39     Display "6. End the program."
40     Display
41
```

```
42      // Get the user's selection.
43      Display "Enter your selection."
44      Input selection
45
46      // Validate the selection.
47      While selection < 1 OR selection > 6
48          Display "That is an invalid selection."
49          Display "Enter 1, 2, 3, 4, 5, or 6."
50          Input selection
51      End While
52 End Module
53
```

Figure 11-8 Flowchart for the `main` module in Program 11-6

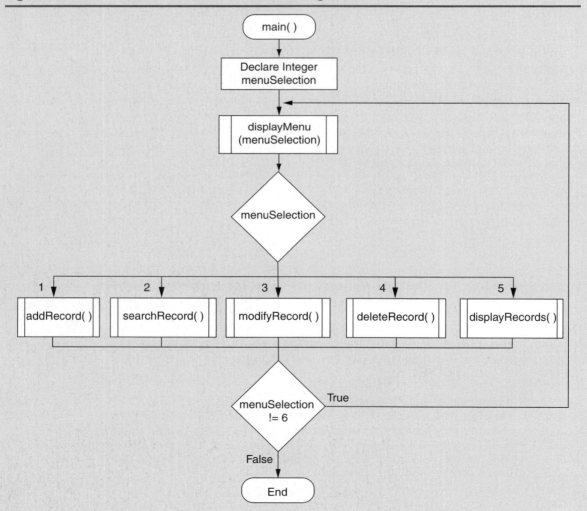

Figure 11-9 Flowchart for the displayMenu module in Program 11-6

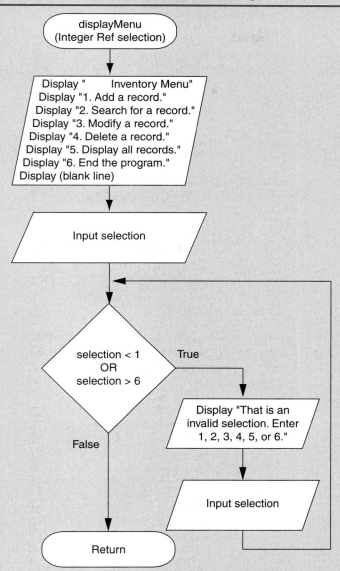

The pseudocode for the addRecord module follows. Figure 11-10 shows a flowchart for the addRecord module.

Program 11-6   **Coffee inventory program (continued): addRecord module**

```
54 // The addRecord module lets the user add a record
55 // to the inventory file.
56 Module addRecord()
57    // Variables for the fields
58    Declare String description
59    Declare Real quantity
60
61    // Variable to control the loop
62    Declare String another = "Y"
63
64    // Declare an output file in append mode.
65    Declare OutputFile AppendMode coffeeFile
66
67    // Open the file.
68    Open coffeeFile "coffee.dat"
69
70    While toUpper(another) == "Y"
71       // Get the description.
72       Display "Enter the description."
73       Input description
74
75       // Get the quantity on hand.
76       Display "Enter the quantity on hand "
77               "(in pounds)."
78       Input quantity
79
80       // Append the record to the file.
81       Write coffeeFile description, quantity
82
83       // Determine whether the user wants to enter
84       // another record.
85       Display "Do you want to enter another record? ",
86       Display "(Enter Y for yes, or anything else for no.)"
87       Input another
88
89       // Display a blank line.
90       Display
91    End While
92
93    // Close the file.
94    Close coffeeFile
95    Display "Data appended to coffee.dat."
96 End Module
97
```

Figure 11-10 Flowchart for the addRecord module in Program 11-6

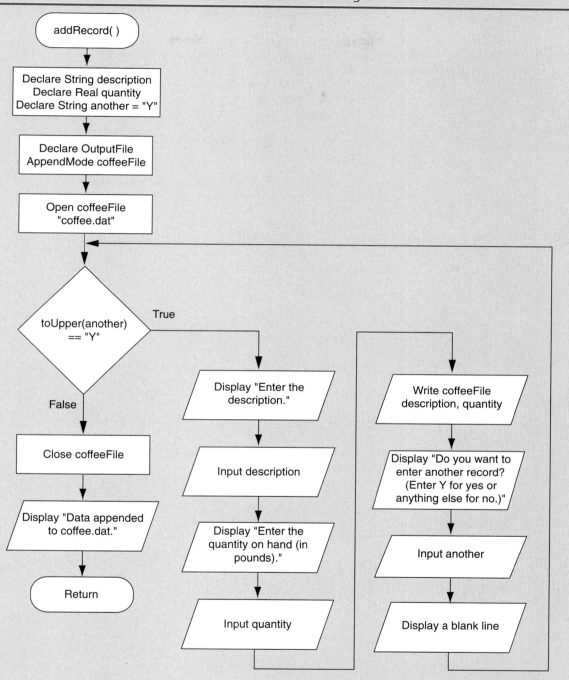

The pseudocode for the searchRecord module follows. Figure 11-11 shows a flow-chart for the searchRecord module.

| Program 11-6 | Coffee inventory program (continued): searchRecord module |

```
 98  // The searchRecord module allows the user to
 99  // search for a record in the inventory file.
100  Module searchRecord()
101      // Variables for the fields
102      Declare String description
103      Declare Real quantity
104
105      // Variable to hold the search value
106      Declare String searchValue
107
108      // Flag to indicate whether the value was found
109      Declare Boolean found = False
110
111      // Declare an input file.
112      Declare InputFile coffeeFile
113
114      // Get the value to search for.
115      Display "Enter a value to search for."
116      Input searchValue
117
118      // Open the file.
119      Open coffeeFile "coffee.dat"
120
121      While NOT eof(coffeeFile)
122          // Read a record from the file.
123          Read coffeeFile description, quantity
124
125          // If the record contains the search value,
126          // then display it.
127          If contains(description, searchValue) Then
128              // Display the record.
129              Display "Description: ", description,
130                      "Quantity: ", quantity, " pounds"
131
132              // Set the found flag to true.
133              Set found = True
134          End If
135      End While
136
137      // If the value was not found in the file,
138      // display a message indicating so.
139      If NOT found Then
140          Display searchValue, " was not found."
141      End If
142
143      // Close the file.
144      Close coffeeFile
145  End Module
146
```

Figure 11-11 Flowchart for the searchRecord module in Program 11-6

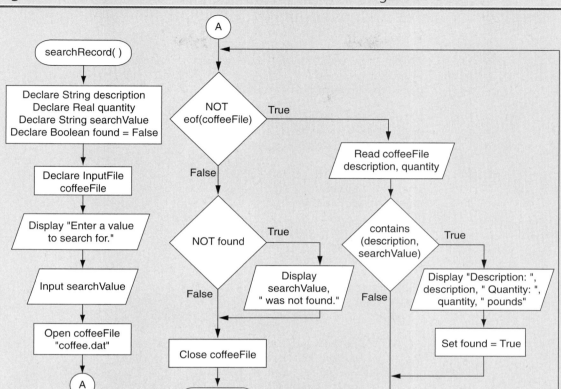

The pseudocode for the modifyRecord module follows. Figure 11-12 and Figure 11-13 show a flowchart for the modifyRecord module.

Program 11-6   **Coffee inventory program (continued): modifyRecord module**

```
147 // The modifyRecord module allows the user to modify
148 // an existing record in the inventory file.
149 Module modifyRecord()
150     // Variables for the fields
151     Declare String description
152     Declare Real quantity
153
154     // Variable to hold the search value
155     Declare String searchValue
156
157     // Variable to hold the new quantity
158     Declare Real newQuantity
159
160     // Flag to indicate whether the value was found
```

```
161      Declare Boolean found = False
162
163      // Declare an input file.
164      Declare InputFile coffeeFile
165
166      // Declare an output file to copy the original
167      // file to.
168      Declare OutputFile tempFile
169
170      // Open the files.
171      Open coffeeFile "coffee.dat"
172      Open tempFile "temp.dat"
173
174      // Get the value to search for.
175      Display "Enter the coffee you wish to update."
176      Input searchValue
177
178      // Get the new quantity.
179      Display "Enter the new quantity."
180      Input newQuantity
181
182      While NOT eof(coffeeFile)
183         // Read a record from the file.
184         Read coffeeFile description, quantity
185
186         // Write either this record to the temporary
187         // file, or the new record if this is the
188         // one that is to be changed.
189         If description == searchValue Then
190            Write tempFile description, newQuantity
191            Set found = True
192         Else
193            Write tempFile description, quantity
194         End If
195      End While
196
197      // Close the two files.
198      Close coffeeFile
199      Close tempFile
200
201      // Delete the original file.
202      Delete("coffee.dat")
203
204      // Rename the temporary file.
205      Rename("temp.dat", "coffee.dat")
206
207      // Indicate whether the operation was successful.
208      If found Then
209         Display "The record was updated."
210      Else
211         Display searchValue, " was not found in the file."
212      End If
213 End Module
214
```

Figure 11-12 First part of the flowchart for the modifyRecord module in Program 11-6

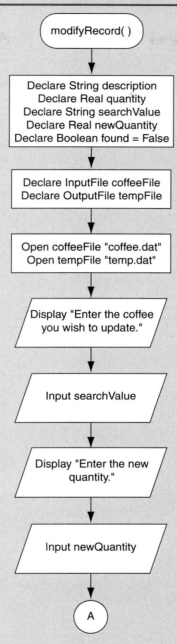

Figure 11-13 Second part of the flowchart for the `modifyRecord` module in Program 11-6

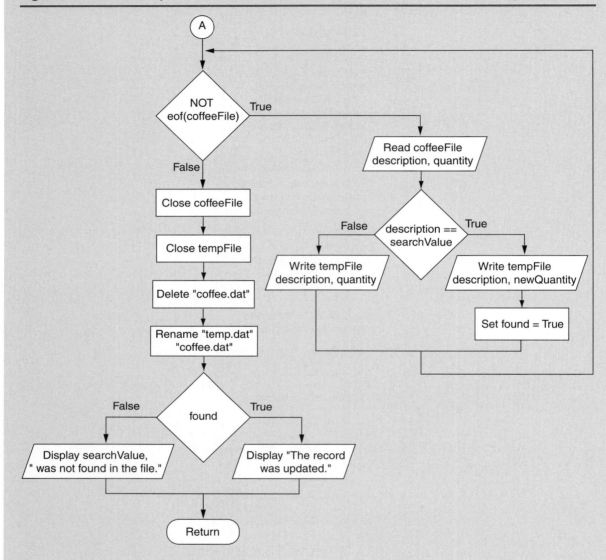

The pseudocode for the `deleteRecord` module follows. Figure 11-14 shows a flow-chart for the `deleteRecord` module.

Program 11-6	Coffee inventory program (continued): deleteRecord **module**

```
215 // The deleteRecord module allows the user to delete
216 // a record from the inventory file.
217 Module deleteRecord()
218    // Variables for the fields
219    Declare String description
220    Declare Real quantity
221
222    // Variable to hold the search value
223    Declare String searchValue
224
225    // Declare an input file.
226    Declare InputFile coffeeFile
227
228    // Declare an output file to copy the original
229    // file to.
230    Declare OutputFile tempFile
231
232    // Open the files.
233    Open coffeeFile "coffee.dat"
234    Open tempFile "temp.dat"
235
236    // Get the value to search for.
237    Display "Enter the coffee you wish to delete."
238    Input searchValue
239
240    While NOT eof(coffeeFile)
241       // Read a record from the file.
242       Read coffeeFile description, quantity
243
244       // If this is not the record to delete, then
245       // write it to the temporary file.
246       If description != searchValue Then
247          Write tempFile description, newQuantity
248       End If
249    End While
250
251    // Close the two files.
252    Close coffeeFile
253    Close tempFile
254
255    // Delete the original file.
256    Delete("coffee.dat")
257
258    // Rename the temporary file.
259    Rename("temp.dat", "coffee.dat")
260
261    Display "The file has been updated."
262 End Module
263
```

Figure 11-14 Flowchart for the `deleteRecord` module in Program 11-6

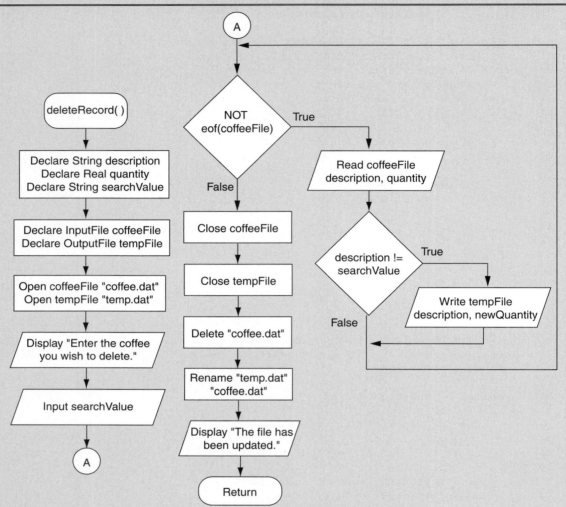

The pseudocode for the `displayRecords` module follows. Figure 11-15 shows a flow-chart for the `displayRecords` module.

Program 11-6   **Coffee inventory program (continued): `displayRecords` module**

```
264 // The displayRecords module displays all
265 // of the records in the inventory file.
266 Module displayRecords()
267    // Variables for the fields
268    Declare String description
269    Declare Real quantity
270
271    // Declare an input file.
272    Declare InputFile coffeeFile
273
```

```
274     // Open the file.
275     Open coffeeFile "coffee.dat"
276
277     While NOT eof(coffeeFile)
278        // Read a record from the file.
279        Read coffeeFile description, quantity
280
281        // Display the record.
282        Display "Description: ", description,
283               "Quantity: ", quantity, " pounds"
284     End While
285
286     // Close the file.
287     Close coffeeFile
288 End Module
```

Figure 11-15 Flowchart for the displayRecords module in Program 11-6

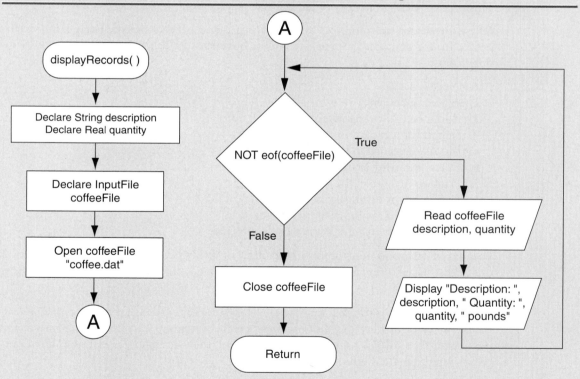

Checkpoint

11.4 Explain why most menu-driven programs use a loop to redisplay the menu after the user's selected action has been performed.

11.5 If a program uses a loop to display a menu repeatedly, how does the user end the program?

 ## 11.4 Multiple-Level Menus

CONCEPT: A multiple-level menu has a main menu and one or more submenus.

The programs that you have seen in this chapter are simple enough that all of their menu selections fit nicely in a single menu. When the user selects an operation from the menu, the program immediately performs that operation and then the program redisplays the menu (or the program ends if it does not use a loop to redisplay the menu). This type of menu system is called a *single-level menu*.

Often, programs are more complex and one menu isn't sufficient. For example, suppose you are designing a program that a business can use to perform the following operations:

1. Process a sale
2. Process a return
3. Add a record to the inventory file
4. Search for a record in the inventory file
5. Modify a record in the inventory file
6. Delete a record in the inventory file
7. Print an inventory list report
8. Print a list of inventory items by cost
9. Print a list of inventory items by age
10. Print a list of inventory items by retail value

Because there are so many items in this list, you probably shouldn't display them all in one menu. Users often have trouble sorting through the items in a menu when given too many choices.

A better approach is to use a multiple-level menu. A program that uses a *multiple-level menu* typically displays a *main menu* when the program starts, showing only a few items, and then displays smaller *submenus* when the user makes a selection. For example, the main menu might appear as follows:

```
            Main Menu
1. Process a Sale or a Return
2. Update the Inventory File
3. Print an Inventory Report
4. Exit the Program
```

When the user selects item 1 from the main menu, the following submenu would appear:

```
            Sales and Returns Menu
1. Process a Sale
2. Process a Return
3. Go Back to the Main Menu
```

When the user selects item 2 from the main menu, the following submenu would appear:

```
          Update Inventory File Menu
1. Add a Record
2. Search for a Record
3. Modify a Record
4. Delete a Record
5. Go Back to the Main Menu
```

When the user selects item 3 from the main menu, the following submenu would appear:

```
            Inventory Report Menu
1. Print an inventory list report
2. Print a list of inventory items by cost
3. Print a list of inventory items by age
4. Print a list of inventory items by retail value
5. Go Back to the Main Menu
```

Let's take a look at how the logic for this program might be designed. (We won't look at all of the modules in the program, but we will examine the ones involved in producing the menus and responding to the user's menu selections.) Figure 11-16 shows how the main module might be designed. First, a module named displayMainMenu is called. The purpose of that module is to display the main menu and get the user's selection. Next, the case structure calls the following modules:

- saleOrReturn if the user selected menu item 1
- updateInventory if the user selected menu item 2
- inventoryReport if the user selected menu item 3

If the user selects item 4, Exit the Program, the program ends.

Figure 11-17 shows the logic for the saleOrReturn module. First, a module named displaySaleOrReturnMenu is called. The purpose of that module is to display the Sales and Returns menu and get the user's selection. The case structure calls the following modules:

- processSale if the user selected menu item 1
- processReturn if the user selected menu item 2

If the user selects item 3, Go Back to the Main Menu, the program returns to the main module and the main menu is displayed again.

Figure 11-16 Logic for the main module

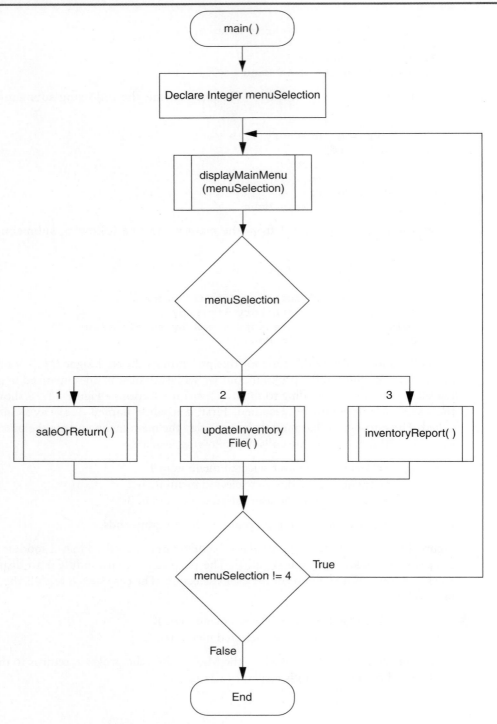

Figure 11-17 Logic for the saleOrReturn module

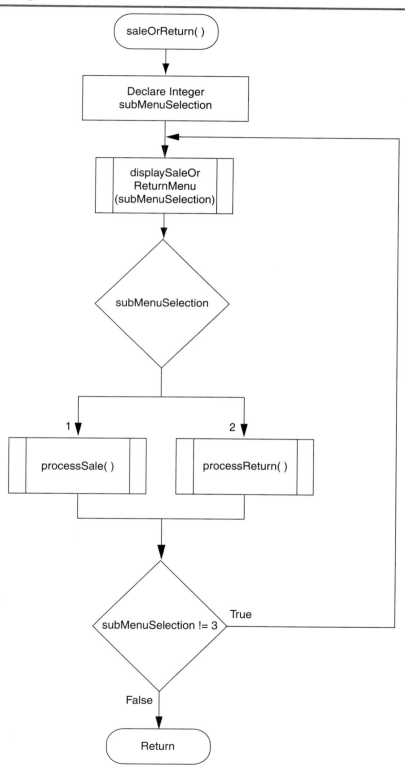

Figure 11-18 shows the logic for the updateInventory module. First, a module named displayUpdateInventoryMenu is called. The purpose of that module is to display the Update Inventory File menu and get the user's selection. The case structure calls the following modules:

- addRecord if the user selected menu item 1
- searchRecord if the user selected menu item 2
- modifyRecord if the user selected menu item 3
- deleteRecord if the user selected menu item 4

If the user selects item 5, Go Back to the Main Menu, the program returns to the main module and the main menu is displayed again.

Figure 11-18 Logic for the updateInventory module

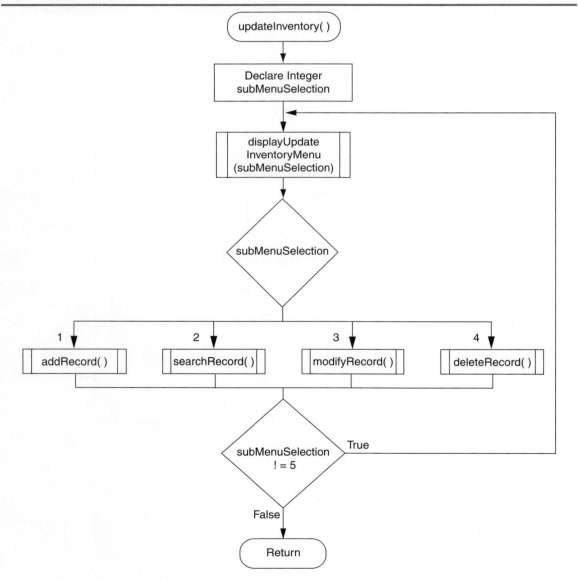

Figure 11-19 shows the logic for the inventoryReport module. First, a module named displayInventoryReportMenu is called. The purpose of that module is to display the Inventory Report menu and get the user's selection. The case structure calls the following modules:

- printInventoryList if the user selected menu item 1
- printItemsByCost if the user selected menu item 2
- printItemsByAge if the user selected menu item 3
- printItemsByRetailValue if the user selected menu item 4

If the user selects item 5, Go Back to the Main Menu, the program returns to the main module and the main menu is displayed again.

Figure 11-19 Logic for the inventoryReport module

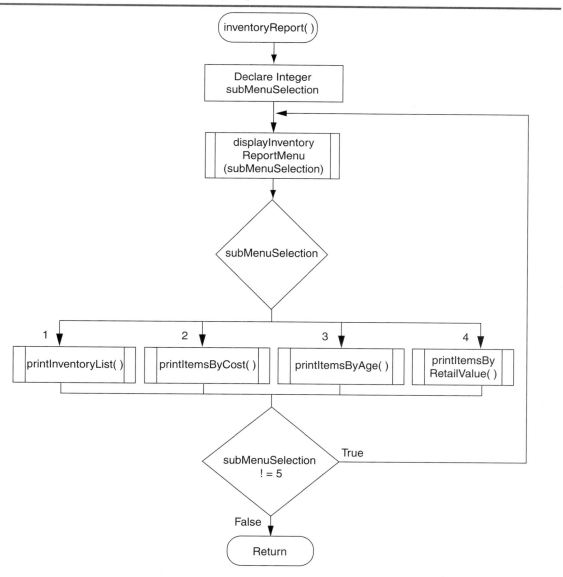

Checkpoint

11.6 What is a single-level menu?

11.7 What is a multiple-level menu?

11.8 When a program has a lot of items for the user to select from, why should you avoid displaying all of the items in one menu?

Review Questions

Multiple Choice

1. A menu is a _____.

   a. case structure that selects an operation in a program
   b. group of modules that perform individual tasks
   c. list of operations displayed on the screen that the user may choose from
   d. table of Boolean choices

2. When the user selects an item from a menu, the program must use a _____ structure to perform an action based on that selection.

   a. repetition
   b. sequence
   c. menu selection
   d. decision

3. If a menu-driven program uses a loop to redisplay the menu after a selected operation has been performed, the menu should probably have an item that the user can select to _____.

   a. end the program
   b. perform the same operation again
   c. undo the previous operation
   d. reboot the computer

4. A program that uses a multiple-level menu displays _____ when it starts.

   a. a warning to the user
   b. the main menu
   c. a submenu
   d. the grand menu

5. When the user selects an item from a multiple-level menu, _____ might be displayed next.

   a. the main menu
   b. a user information form
   c. a submenu
   d. a question asking the user if he or she wants to continue

6. When the user selects an operation from a _____, the program immediately performs that operation and then the program redisplays the menu (or the program ends if it does not use a loop to redisplay the menu).

   a. multiple-level menu
   b. single-level menu
   c. submenu
   d. master menu

7. When the user selects an operation from a _____, the program might display another menu.

   a. multiple-level menu
   b. single-level menu
   c. submenu
   d. interleaved menu

True or False

1. You cannot use nested `If-Then-Else` statements to perform the action selected by the user from a menu.

2. It is not usually necessary to validate the user's menu selection.

3. In most cases, a menu-driven program should be modularized.

4. If a menu-driven program does not use a loop to redisplay the menu after each operation, the user will have to rerun the program to select another operation from the menu.

5. In a single-level menu, the user might see a submenu appear when an item from the main menu is selected.

Short Answer

1. What type of structure do you use in a program to perform the action that the user has selected from a menu?

2. What ways for validating a user's menu selection did we discuss in this chapter?

3. How can you design a menu-driven program so that the menu is redisplayed after the selected operation has been performed?

4. What is the difference between a program that uses a single-level menu and a program that uses a multiple-level menu?

5. When a program has a lot of items for the user to select from, why should you avoid displaying all of the items on one menu?

Algorithm Workbench

1. Design an algorithm that displays the following menu, gets the user's selection, and validates the selection.

```
     Main Menu
1. Open a new document.
2. Close the current document.
3. Print the current document.
4. Exit the program.
Enter your selection.
```

2. Design a case structure that can be used with the algorithm you designed for Algorithm Workbench Question 1. The case structure should call a module named openDocument if the user selected item 1, should call a module named closeDocument if the user selected item 2, and should call a module named printDocument if the user selected item 3.

3. Put the algorithms that you designed for Algorithm Workbench Questions 1 and 2 together inside a loop that redisplays the menu after the user's selected operation is performed, or exits if the user selects item 4 from the menu.

4. Look for ways to modularize the algorithm that you designed for Algorithm Workbench Question 3 and modify it accordingly.

Programming Exercises

VideoNote
The Language
Translator
Problem

1. **Language Translator**

   Design a program that displays the following menu:

```
   Select a Language and I will say Good Morning
1. English
2. Italian
3. Spanish
4. German
5. End the Program
Enter your selection.
```

   If the user selects item 1, the program should display "Good morning." If the user selects item 2, the program should display "Buongiorno." If the user selects item 3, the program should display "Buenos dias." If the user selects item 4, the program should display "Guten morgen." If the user selects item 5, the program should end.

2. **University Meal Plan Selector**

   The university offers the following meal plans:

   > Plan 1: 7 meals per week for $560 per semester
   > Plan 2: 14 meals per week for $1,095 per semester
   > Plan 3: Unlimited meals for $1,500 per semester

   Design a menu-driven program that allows the user to select a meal plan. The program should ask the user for the number of semesters and then display the total price for the plan.

3. **Geometry Calculator**

Write a program that displays the following menu:

```
    Geometry Calculator
1. Calculate the Area of a Circle
2. Calculate the Area of a Rectangle
3. Calculate the Area of a Triangle
4. Quit
Enter your choice (1-4).
```

If the user enters 1, the program should ask for the radius of the circle and then display its area. Use the following formula to calculate the circle's area:

$$area = \pi r^2$$

Use 3.14159 for π and the radius of the circle for r.

If the user enters 2, the program should ask for the length and width of the rectangle and then display the rectangle's area. Use the following formula to calculate the rectangle's area:

$$area = length \times width$$

If the user enters 3, the program should ask for the length of the triangle's base and its height, and then display its area. Use the following formula to calculate the area of the triangle:

$$area = base \times height \times .5$$

If the user enters 4, the program should end.

4. **Astronomy Helper**

Create an application that displays the following menu:

```
    Select a Planet
1. Mercury
2. Venus
3. Earth
4. Mars
5. Exit the program
Enter your selection.
```

When the user selects a planet from the menu, the program should display data about the planet's average distance from the sun, the planet's mass, and the planet's surface temperature. Use the following data in your program:

<u>Mercury</u>

Average distance from the sun	57.9 million kilometers
Mass	3.31×10^{23} kg
Surface temperature	−173 to 430 degrees Celsius

<u>Venus</u>

Average distance from the sun	108.2 million kilometers
Mass	4.87×10^{24} kg
Surface temperature	472 degrees Celsius

<u>Earth</u>

Average distance from the sun	149.6 million kilometers
Mass	5.967×10^{24} kg
Surface temperature	−50 to 50 degrees Celsius

Mars

Average distance from the sun	227.9 million kilometers
Mass	0.6424×10^{24} kg
Surface temperature	−140 to 20 degrees Celsius

5. **Golf Score Modification**

In Programming Exercise 6 in Chapter 10 you designed the following two programs for the Springfork Amateur Golf Club:

1. A program that reads each player's name and golf score as keyboard input, and then saves these as records in a file named `golf.dat`.
2. A program that reads the records from the `golf.dat` file and displays them.

Consolidate these programs into a single program that presents a menu, allowing the user to select the operation he or she wants to perform.

8. **Phone Book Program**

Design a program that you can use to keep all of your friends' names and phone numbers in a file. The program should be menu-driven, and offer the following operations:

```
1. Add a new record
2. Search for a name.
3. Modify a phone number.
4. Delete a record.
5. Exit the program.
```

8. **The Speed of Sound**

The following table shows the approximate speed of sound in air, water, and steel.

Write a program that displays a menu allowing the user to select air, water, or steel. After the user has made a selection, he or she should be asked to enter the number of seconds the sound will travel in the selected medium. The program should then display the distance the sound will travel.

Medium	Speed
Air	1,100 feet per second
Water	4,900 feet per second
Steel	16,400 feet per second

12 Text Processing

12.1 Introduction

Sometimes the data that a program must work with comes in the form of text. Word processors, text messaging programs, email applications, Web browsers, and spell-checkers are just a few examples of programs that work extensively with text.

The earlier chapters in this book have demonstrated some text processing techniques, such as case-sensitive and case-insensitive string comparisons, sorting strings in an array, and searching for substrings within a string. In addition, Chapter 6 introduced several library functions that perform operations on strings. For your convenience, these functions are summarized in Table 12-1.

The functions shown in Table 12-1 are very useful, but sometimes you need to operate on strings at a more detailed level. Some operations require that you access or manipulate the individual characters in a string. For example, you've probably used programs or Web sites that require you to set up a password that meets certain requirements. Some systems require that passwords have a minimum length, contain at least one uppercase letter, at least one lowercase letter, and at least one numeric digit. These requirements are intended to prevent ordinary words from being used as passwords, and thus make the passwords more secure. When a new password is created, the system has to examine each of the password's characters to determine whether it meets the requirements. In the next section you will see an example of an algorithm that performs this very operation. First, however, we will discuss the process of accessing and manipulating the individual characters in a string.

Table 12-1 Common String Functions

Function	Description
length(*string*)	Returns the number of characters in *string*.
	For example, the expression length("Test") would return 4.
append(*string1*, *string2*)	Returns a string that is created by appending *string2* to the end of *string1*.
	For example, the expression append("Hello ", "World") would return the string "Hello World".
toUpper(*string*)	Returns a string that is an uppercase copy of *string*.
	For example the expression toUpper("Test") would return the string "TEST".
toLower(*string*)	Returns a string that is a lowercase copy of *string*.
	For example the expression toLower("TEST") would return the string "test".
substring(*string*, *start*, *end*)	Returns a substring of *string*. The substring is the set of characters starting at the position specified by *start* and ending at the position specified by *end*. (The first character in *string* is at position 0.)
	For example, the expression substring("Kevin", 2, 4) would return the string "vin".
contains(*string1*, *string2*)	Returns True if *string1* contains *string2*. Otherwise it returns False.
	For example the expression contains("smiley", "mile") would return True, and the expression contains("Smiley", "xyz") would return False.
stringToInteger (*string*)	Converts *string* to an Integer and returns that value.
	For example, the expression stringToInteger("77") would return the Integer value 77.
stringToReal(*string*)	Converts *string* to a Real and returns that value.
	For example, the expression stringToInteger("1.5") would return the Real value 1.5.
isInteger(*string*)	Returns True if *string* can be converted to an Integer, or False otherwise.
	For example, the expression isInteger("77") would return True, and the expression isInteger("x4yz") would return False.
isReal(*string*)	Returns True if *string* can be converted to a Real, or False otherwise.
	For example, the expression isReal("3.2") would return True, and the expression isReal("x4yz") would return False.

12.2 Character-By-Character Text Processing

CONCEPT: Some tasks require that you access and/or manipulate the individual characters that appear in a string.

Although each programming language has its own way of providing access to the individual characters in a string, many languages allow you to use subscript notation. This makes it possible to work with a string as if it were an array of characters. You use subscript 0 to access the first character, subscript 1 to access the second character, and so on. The subscript of the last character would be one less than the string's length. This is the approach that we will use in our pseudocode, as demonstrated in Program 12-1.

Program 12-1

```
 1 // Declare and initialize a string.
 2 Declare String name = "Jacob"
 3
 4 // Use subscript notation to display the
 5 // individual characters in the string.
 6 Display name[0]
 7 Display name[1]
 8 Display name[2]
 9 Display name[3]
10 Display name[4]
```

Program Output

```
J
a
c
o
b
```

In line 2 we declare `name` as a `String` variable, and initialize it with the string `"Jacob"`. The string has five characters, so we can use the subscripts 0 through 4 to access those characters, as shown in lines 6 through 10. As with arrays, an error will occur at runtime if we attempt to use an invalid subscript with a string.

Program 12-2 shows how a loop can be used to step through the characters in a string. Notice that in the `For` loop (in line 8) the `index` variable has a starting value of 0 and an ending value of `length(name) - 1`.

Program 12-2

```
 1 // Declare and initialize a string.
 2 Declare String name = "Jacob"
```

```
 3
 4 // Declare a variable to step through the string.
 5 Declare Integer index
 6
 7 // Display the characters in the string.
 8 For index = 0 To length(name) - 1
 9    Display name[index]
10 End For
```

Program Output

```
J
a
c
o
b
```

Program 12-3 shows an example of changing individual characters in a string. The program reads a string as input from the keyboard, and then changes each occurrence of the letter "t" to the letter "d."

Program 12-3

```
 1 // Declare a string to hold input.
 2 Declare String str
 3
 4 // Declare a variable to step through the string.
 5 Declare Integer index
 6
 7 // Prompt the user to enter a sentence.
 8 Display "Enter a sentence."
 9 Input str
10
11 // Change each "t" to a "d".
12 For index = 0 To length(str) - 1
13    If str[index] == "t" Then
14        Set str[index] = "d"
15    End If
16 End For
17
18 // Display the modified string.
19 Display str
```

Program Output (with Input Shown in Bold)

```
Enter a sentence:
Look at that kitty cat! [Enter]
Look ad dhad kiddy cad!
```

The programs you have seen so far in this chapter demonstrate how you can access and modify individual characters at specific locations in a string. In most programming languages, when you use a subscript or other mechanism to access an individual character position within a string, that character position must already exist or an error will occur. For example, if a string contains four characters, we cannot use subscript notation to append a fifth character to it. The following pseudocode illustrates this:

```
Declare String word = "mist"   // This string has 4 characters.
Set word[4] = "y"              // Error!
```

In the first statement the word variable is initialized with the string "mist", which has four characters. The subscript of the last character is 3. The second statement attempts to assign the character "y" to word[4], but an error will occur because that character position does not exist. If you wish to append characters to a string, you must typically use an operator or a library function that is designed for that purpose.

 WARNING! An error will also occur if you use a subscript on an uninitialized String variable. Because an uninitialized variable contains no data, you cannot access or manipulate its contents.

Character Testing Library Functions

In addition to string library functions, such as the ones shown in Table 12-1, most programming languages also provide library functions that are designed to work with single characters. Table 12-2 shows examples of commonly supported functions that test the value of a character. Note that each of the functions listed in the table returns a Boolean value of True or False.

Table 12-2 Common Character Testing Functions

Function	Description
isDigit(*character*)	Returns True if *character* is a numeric digit, or False otherwise.
isLetter(*character*)	Returns True if *character* is an alphabetic letter or False otherwise.
isLower(*character*)	Returns True if *character* is a lowercase letter or False otherwise.
isUpper(*character*)	Returns True if *character* is an uppercase letter or False otherwise.
isWhiteSpace (*character*)	Returns True if *character* is a whitespace character or False otherwise. (A whitespace character is a space, a tab, or a newline.)

Program 12-4 shows an example using one of these functions. The program reads a string as input from the keyboard, and then counts the number of uppercase characters in that string.

Program 12-4

```
 1 // Declare a string to hold input.
 2 Declare String str
 3
 4 // Declare a variable to step through the string.
 5 Declare Integer index
 6
 7 // Declare an accumulator variable to keep count
 8 // of the number of uppercase letters.
 9 Declare Integer upperCaseCount = 0
10
11 // Prompt the user to enter a sentence.
12 Display "Enter a sentence."
13 Input str
14
15 // Count the number of uppercase letters.
16 For index = 0 To length(str) - 1
17     If isUpper(str[index]) Then
18         Set upperCaseCount = upperCaseCount + 1
19     End If
20 End For
21
22 // Display the number of uppercase characters.
23 Display "That string has ", upperCaseCount, " uppercase letters."
```

Program Output (with Input Shown in Bold)

```
Enter a sentence:
Ms. Jones will arrive TODAY! [Enter]
That string has 7 uppercase characters.
```

The For loop that appears in lines 16 through 20 steps through the String variable str. The If-Then statement that begins in line 17 calls the isUpper function, passing str[index] as an argument. If that character is uppercase, the function returns True and the value of upperCaseCount is incremented in line 18. After the loop finishes, upperCaseCount will contain the number of uppercase characters in str.

In The Spotlight:

Validating a Password

Many password-protected systems allow users to setup their own passwords. For increased security, systems usually require that passwords meet minimum specifications. When a user creates a password, the system must examine the password to determine whether it meets the minimum specifications. If it does not, the system rejects the password and requires the user to create another, more secure, password.

The pseudocode shown in Program 12-5 demonstrates how a password can be validated by a system that has the following requirements:

- Passwords must be at least 8 characters long.
- Passwords must contain at least one uppercase character.
- Passwords must contain at least one lowercase character.
- Passwords must contain at least one numeric digit.

The pseudocode is modularized with functions that perform much of the validation. The main module gets a password from the user and then calls the following functions to validate that password:

- The length library function is called to determine the password's length.
- The numberUpperCase function is called with the password variable passed as an argument. This function returns the number of uppercase letters in the string argument.
- The numberLowerCase function is called with the password variable passed as an argument. This function returns the number of lowercase letters in the string argument.
- The numberDigits function is called with the password variable passed as an argument. This function returns the number of numeric digits in the string argument.

Rather than presenting the entire program at once, let's first look at the main module and then each function separately. Here is the main module:

Program 12-5   **Password validation program: main module**

```
 1 Module main()
 2     // Constant for the minimum password length
 3     Constant Integer MIN_LENGTH = 8
 4
 5     // Local variable to hold the user's password
 6     Declare String password
 7
 8     // Display some information about the program.
 9     Display "This program determines whether a password"
10     Display "meets the following requirements:"
11     Display "(1) It must be at least 8 characters long."
12     Display "(2) It must contain at least one uppercase letter."
13     Display "(3) It must contain at least one lowercase letter."
14     Display "(4) It must contain at least one numeric digit."
15     Display
16
17     // Get a password from the user.
18     Display "Enter a password."
19     Input password
20
21     // Validate the password.
22     If length(password) >= MIN_LENGTH AND
23        numberUpperCase(password) >= 1 AND
24        numberLowerCase(password) >= 1 AND
25        numberDigits(password) >= 1 Then
```

```
26            Display "The password is valid"
27     Else
28            Display "The password does not meet the requirements."
29     End If
30 End Module
31
```

Line 3 declares a constant for the minimum password length and line 6 declares a `String` variable named `password` to hold the user's password. Lines 9 through 15 display information on the screen informing the user of the password requirements. Lines 18 and 19 prompt the user to enter a password, which is read from the keyboard and assigned to the `password` variable.

The `If-Then-Else` statement that begins in line 22 evaluates a compound Boolean expression. In plain English the statement should be interpreted like this:

> If the password's length is at least 8 and
>   the number of uppercase letters in the password is at least 1 and
>   the number of lowercase letters in the password is at least 1 and
>   the number of numeric digits in the password is at least 1, Then the password is valid.
> Else
>   The password does not meet the requirements.

The `numberUpperCase` function is shown next:

Program 12-5   **Password validation program (continued): `numberUpperCase` function**

```
32 // The numberUpperCase function accepts a string
33 // argument and returns the number of uppercase
34 // letters it contains.
35 Function Integer numberUpperCase(String str)
36    // Variable to hold the number of uppercase letters
37    Declare Integer count = 0
38
39    // Variable to use stepping through str
40    Declare Integer index
41
42    // Step through str counting the number
43    // of uppercase letters.
44    For index = 0 To length(str) - 1
45       If isUpper(str[index]) Then
46          Set count = count + 1
47       End If
48    End For
49
50    // Return the number of uppercase letters.
51    Return count
52 End Function
53
```

The function accepts a string as an argument, which is passed into the parameter variable `str`. Line 37 declares an `Integer` variable named `count`, initialized with the value 0.

This variable will be used as an accumulator to hold the number of uppercase letters found in the parameter variable str. Line 40 declares another Integer variable, index. The index variable is used in the loop that begins in line 44 to step through the characters in the str parameter variable. The If-Then statement that begins in line 45 calls the isUpper library function to determine whether the character at str[index] is uppercase. If so, the count variable is incremented in line 46. After the loop has finished, the count variable will contain the number of uppercase letters found in the str parameter variable. The count variable's value is returned from the function in line 51.

The numberLowerCase function is shown next:

Program 12-5   **Password validation program (continued): numberLowerCase function**

```
54 // The numberLowerCase function accepts a string
55 // argument and returns the number of lowercase
56 // letters it contains.
57 Function Integer numberLowerCase(String str)
58     // Variable to hold the number of lowercase letters
59     Declare Integer count = 0
60
61     // Variable to use stepping through str
62     Declare Integer index
63
64     // Step through str counting the number
65     // of lowercase letters.
66     For index = 0 To length(str) - 1
67         If isLower(str[index]) Then
68             Set count = count + 1
69         End If
70     End For
71
72     // Return the number of lowercase letters.
73     Return count
74 End Function
75
```

This function is nearly identical to the numberUpperCase function, except that line 67 calls the isLower library function to determine whether the character at str[index] is lowercase. When the function ends, the statement in line 73 returns the value of the count variable, which contains the number of lowercase letters found in the str parameter variable.

The numberDigits function is shown next:

Program 12-5   **Password validation program (continued): numberDigits function**

```
76 // The numberDigits function accepts a string
77 // argument and returns the number of numeric
78 // digits it contains.
79 Function Integer numberDigits(String str)
```

```
80      // Variable to hold the number of digits
81      Declare Integer count = 0
82
83      // Variable to use stepping through str
84      Declare Integer index
85
86      // Step through str counting the number
87      // of digits.
88      For index = 0 To length(str) - 1
89          If isDigit(str[index]) Then
90              Set count = count + 1
91          End If
92      End For
93
94      // Return the number of digits.
95      Return count
96 End Function
```

This function is nearly identical to the numberUpperCase and numberLowerCase functions, except that line 89 calls the isDigit library function to determine whether the character at str[index] is a numeric digit. When the function ends, the statement in line 95 returns the value of the count variable, which contains the number of numeric digits found in the str parameter variable.

Program Output (with Input Shown in Bold)

```
This program determines whether a password
meets the following requirements:
(1) It must be at least 8 characters long.
(2) It must contain at least one uppercase letter.
(3) It must contain at least one lowercase letter.
(4) It must contain at least one numeric digit.

Enter a password.
love [Enter]
The password does not meet the requirements.
```

Program Output (with Input Shown in Bold)

```
This program determines whether a password
meets the following requirements:
(1) It must be at least 8 characters long.
(2) It must contain at least one uppercase letter.
(3) It must contain at least one lowercase letter.
(4) It must contain at least one numeric digit.

Enter a password.
loVe679g [Enter]
The password is valid.
```

Inserting and Deleting Characters in a String

Most programming languages provide library functions or modules for inserting and deleting characters in a string. In our pseudocode we will use the library modules described in Table 12-3 for these purposes.

Table 12-3 String Insertion and Deletion Modules

Function	Description
insert(*string1, position, string2*)	*string1* is a String, *position* is an Integer, and *string2* is a String. The function inserts *string2* into *string1*, beginning at *position*.
delete(*string, start, end*)	*string* is a String, *start* is an Integer, and *end* is an Integer. The function deletes from *string* all of the characters beginning at the position specified by *start*, and ending at the position specified by *end*. The character at the ending position is included in the deletion.

Here is an example of how we might use the insert module:

```
Declare String str = "New City"
insert(str, 4, "York ")
Display str
```

The second statement inserts the string "York " into the str variable, beginning at position 4. The characters that are currently in the str variable beginning at position 4 are moved to the right. In memory, the str variable is automatically expanded in size to accommodate the inserted characters. If these statements were a complete program and we ran it, we would see "New York City" displayed on the screen.

Here is an example of how we might use the delete module:

```
Declare String str = "I ate 1000 blueberries!"
delete(str, 8, 9)
Display str
```

The second statement deletes the characters at positions 8 through 9 in the str variable. The characters that previously appeared beginning at position 10 are shifted left to occupy the space left by the deleted characters. If these statements were a complete program and we ran it, we would see "I ate 10 blueberries!" displayed on the screen.

In The Spotlight:

Formatting and
Unformatting Telephone Numbers

Telephone numbers in the United States are commonly formatted to appear in the following manner:

    (XXX)XXX-XXXX

In the format, X represents a digit. The three digits that appear inside the parentheses are the area code. The three digits following the area code are the prefix, and the four digits after the hyphen are the line number. Here is an example:

    (919)555-1212

Although the parentheses and the hyphen make the number easier for people to read, those characters are unnecessary for processing by a computer. In a computer system, a telephone number is commonly stored as an unformatted series of digits, as shown here:

    9195551212

A program that works with telephone numbers usually needs to unformat numbers that have been entered by the user. This means that the parentheses and the hyphen must be removed prior to storing the number in a file or processing it in some other way. In addition, such programs need the ability to format a number so it contains the parentheses and the hyphen before displaying it on the screen or printing it on paper.

The pseudocode shown in Program 12-6 demonstrates an algorithm for unformatting telephone numbers. The main module prompts the user to enter a formatted telephone number. It then calls the isValidFormat function to determine whether the telephone number is properly formatted. If it is, it then calls the unformat module to remove the parentheses and the hyphen. The unformatted telephone number is then displayed. Rather than presenting the entire program at once, let's first look at the main module:

Program 12-6   **Phone number unformatting program:**
main module

```
 1 Module main()
 2    // Declare a variable to hold a telephone number.
 3    Declare String phoneNumber
 4
 5    // Prompt the user to enter a telephone number.
 6    Display "Enter a telephone number. The number you"
 7    Display "enter should be formatted as (XXX)XXX-XXXX."
 8    Input phoneNumber
 9
10    // If the input is properly formatted, unformat it.
11    If isValidFormat(phoneNumber) Then
12       unformat(phoneNumber)
13       Display "The unformatted number is ", phoneNumber
14    Else
```

```
15        Display "That number is not properly formatted."
16    End If
17 End Module
18
```

Line 3 declares a String variable, phoneNumber, to hold the telephone number that the user will enter. Lines 6 through 8 prompt the user to enter a properly formatted telephone number, read it from the keyboard, and store it in the phoneNumber variable.

The If-Then-Else statement that begins in line 11 passes phoneNumber as an argument to the isValidFormat function. This function returns True if the argument is properly formatted, or False otherwise. If the function returns True, line 12 passes phoneNumber as an argument to the unformat function. The unformat function receives its argument by reference, and removes the parentheses and hyphen. Line 13 then displays the unformatted telephone number.

If the telephone number that was entered by the user was not properly formatted, the isValidFormat function returns False in line 11 and the Display statement in line 15 executes.

The isValidFormat function is shown next:

Program 12-6	**Phone number unformatting program (continued):** **isValidFormat function**

```
19 // The isValidFormat function accepts a string argument
20 // and determines whether it is properly formatted as
21 // a US telephone number in the following manner:
22 // (XXX)XXX-XXXX
23 // If the argument is properly formatted, the function
24 // returns True, otherwise False.
25 Function Boolean isValidFormat(str)
26    // Local variable to indicate valid format
27    Declare Boolean valid
28
29    // Determine whether str is properly formatted.
30    If length(str) == 13 AND str[0] == "(" AND
31       str[4] == ")" AND str[8] == "-" Then
32       Set valid = True
33    Else
34        Set valid = False
35    End If
36
37    // Return the value of valid.
38    Return valid
39  End Function
40
```

The function accepts a string as an argument, which is passed into the parameter variable str. Line 27 declares a local Boolean variable named valid, which will serve as a flag to indicate whether the string in str is properly formatted as a US telephone number.

The `If-Then-Else` statement that begins in line 30 evaluates a compound Boolean expression. In plain English the statement should be interpreted like this:

> If the string's length is 13 and the character at position 0 is "(" and
>   the character at position 4 is ")" and the character at position 8 is "-" Then
>   Set `valid` to `True`.
> Else
>   Set `valid` to `False`.

After the `If-Then-Else` statement executes, the `valid` variable will be set to either `True` or `False` indicating whether `str` is properly formatted. The statement in line 38 returns the value of the `valid` variable.

The unformat module is shown next:

Program 12-6	**Phone number unformatting program (continued): `unformat` module**

```
41 // The unformat module accepts a string, by reference,
42 // assumed to contain a telephone number formatted in
43 // this manner: (XXX)XXX-XXXX.
44 // The module unformats the string by removing the
45 // parentheses and the hyphen.
46 Module unformat(String Ref str)
47    // First, delete the left paren at position 0.
48    delete(str, 0, 0)
49
50    // Next, delete the right paren. Because of the
51    // previous deletion it is now located at
52    // position 3.
53    delete(str, 3, 3)
54
55    // Next, delete the hyphen. Because of the
56    // previous deletions it is now located at
57    // position 6.
58    delete(str, 6, 6)
59 End Module
```

The module accepts a string argument by reference, passed into the parameter variable `str`. The module assumes that the string is properly formatted as `(XXX)XXX-XXXX`. Line 48 deletes the character at position 0, which is the "(" character. All of the remaining characters are automatically shifted left by one position to occupy the space left by the deleted character. Next, line 53 deletes the character at position 3, which is the ")" character. The characters that previously appeared beginning at position 4 are automatically shifted left to occupy the space left by the deleted character. Next, line 58 deletes the character at position 6, which is the hyphen. The characters previously appearing to the right of the hyphen are automatically moved left by one position. After this statement executes, the string in `str` will be unformatted, appearing simply as a string of digits.

Program Output (with Input Shown in Bold)

```
Enter a telephone number. The number you
enter should be formatted as (XXX)XXX-XXXX.
(919)555-1212 [Enter]
The unformatted number is 9195551212
```

Now let's look at an algorithm that takes an unformatted telephone number, which is a series of 10 digits, and formats it by inserting the parentheses and hyphen at the correct locations. The main module is shown here:

Program 12-7   **Phone number formatting program: main module**

```
 1 Module main()
 2     // Declare a variable to hold a telephone number.
 3     Declare String phoneNumber
 4
 5     // Prompt the user to enter a telephone number.
 6     Display "Enter an unformatted 10 digit telephone number."
 7     Input phoneNumber
 8
 9     // If the input is 10 characters long, format it.
10     If length(phoneNumber) == 10 Then
11         format(phoneNumber)
12         Display "The formatted number is ", phoneNumber
13     Else
14         Display "That number is not 10 digits."
15     End If
16 End Module
17
```

Line 3 declares a String variable, phoneNumber, to hold the telephone number that the user will enter. Line 6 prompts the user to enter an unformatted 10 digit telephone number, and line 7 stores the user's input in the phoneNumber variable. The If-Then statement that begins in line 10 calls the length library function to determine whether the user's input is 10 characters long. If it is, the format function is called in line 11 with phoneNumber passed as an argument. The format function accepts its argument by reference, and inserts the parentheses and the hyphen at the proper locations so it appears in the form (XXX)XXX-XXXX. The formatted telephone number is then displayed in line 12. If the user's input is not 10 characters long, an error message is displayed in line 14.

The format module is shown next:

Program 12-7   **Phone number formatting program (continued): format module**

```
18 // The format module accepts a string, by reference,
19 // assumed to contain an unformatted 10 digit telephone
20 // number. The module formats the string in the following
```

```
21 // manner: (XXX)XXX-XXXX.
22 Module format(String Ref str)
23    // First, insert the left paren at position 0.
24    insert(str, 0, "(")
25
26    // Next, insert the right paren at position 4.
27    insert(str, 4, ")")
28
29    // Next, insert the hyphen at position 8.
30    insert(str, 8, "-")
31 End Module
```

The module accepts a string argument by reference, passed into the parameter variable str. Line 24 calls the insert library module to insert the "(" character at position 0. All of the characters in the string are automatically shifted right one space to accommodate the inserted character. Line 27 inserts the ")" character at position 4, shifting the characters that previously appeared beginning at position 4 to the right one space. Line 30 inserts the "-" character at position 8, shifting the characters that previously appeared beginning at position 8 to the right one space. After this statement executes, the string in str will be formatted as (XXX)XXX-XXXX.

Program Output (with Input Shown in Bold)

```
Enter an unformatted 10 digit telephone number.
9195551212 [Enter]
The formatted number is (919)555-1212
```

 **Checkpoint**

12.1 Assume the following declaration appears in a program:

```
Declare String name = "Joy"
```

What would the following statement display?

```
Display name[2]
```

12.2 Assume the following declaration appears in a program:

```
Declare String str = "Tiger"
```

Write a statement that changes the str variable's first character to "L".

12.3 Design an algorithm that determines whether the first character in the String variable str is a numeric digit, and if it is, deletes that character.

12.4 Design an algorithm that determines whether the first character in the String variable str is uppercase, and if it is, changes that character to "0".

12.5 Assume the following declaration appears in a program:

```
Declare String str = "World"
```

Write a statement that inserts the string `"Hello "` at the beginning of the str variable. After the statement executes, the str variable should contain the string `"Hello World"`.

12.6 Assume the following declaration appears in a program:

```
Declare String city = "Boston"
```

Write a statement that deletes the first three characters in the str variable.

Review Questions

Multiple Choice

1. Which pseudocode statement displays the first character in the `String` variable str?
   a. `Display str[1]`
   b. `Display str[0]`
   c. `Display str[first]`
   d. `Display str`

2. Which pseudocode statement displays the last character in the `String` variable str?
   a. `Display str[-1]`
   b. `Display str[length(str)]`
   c. `Display str[last]`
   d. `Display str[length(str) - 1]`

3. If the str variable contains the string `"berry"`, which pseudocode statement changes its contents to `"blackberry"`?
   a. `Set str[0] = "black"`
   b. `Set str = str + "black"`
   c. `insert(str, 0, "black")`
   d. `insert(str, 1, "black")`

4. If the str variable contains the string `"Redmond"`, which pseudocode statement changes its contents to `"Red"`?
   a. `delete(str, 3, length(str))`
   b. `delete(str, 3, 6)`
   c. `Set str = str - "mond"`
   d. `Set str[0] = "Red"`

5. What will the following pseudocode result in?
   ```
   Declare String name = "Sall"
   Set name[4] = "y"
   ```
   a. An error will occur.
   b. The variable name will contain the string `"Sally"`.
   c. The variable name will contain the string `"Saly"`.
   d. The variable name will contain the string `"Sall y"`.

True or False

1. When subscripts are used to specify character positions in a string, the first character's subscript is 0.

2. When subscripts are used to specify character positions in a string, the last character's subscript is the same as the string's length.

3. If the `String` variable `str` contains the string `"Might"`, then the statement `Set str[5] = "y"` will change its contents to `"Mighty"`.

4. The `insert` library module automatically expands the size of the string to accommodate the inserted characters.

5. The `delete` library module does not actually remove characters from a string, but replaces them with spaces.

6. The `isUpper` library function converts a character to uppercase, and the `isLower` library function converts a character to lowercase.

7. An error will occur if you use a subscript on an empty `String` variable.

Short Answer

1. When using subscript notation to specify a character position in a string, what are the subscripts of the first and last characters?

2. If the following pseudocode were a actual program, what would it display?
```
Declare String greeting = "Happy"
insert(greeting, 0, "Birthday")
Display greeting
```

3. If the following pseudocode were a actual program, what would it display?
```
Declare String str = "Yada yada yada"
delete(str, 4, 9)
Display str
```

4. If the following pseudocode were a actual program, what would it display?
```
Declare String str = "AaBbCcDd"
Declare Integer index
For Index = 0 To length(str) - 1
    If isLower(str[index]) Then
        Set str[index] = "-"
    End If
End For
Display str
```

5. If the following pseudocode were a actual program, what would it display?
```
Declare String str = "AaBbCcDd"
delete(str, 0, 0)
delete(str, 3, 3)
delete(str, 3, 3)
Display str
```

Algorithm Workbench

1. Design an algorithm that counts the number of digits that appear in the `String` variable `str`.

2. Design an algorithm that counts the number of lowercase characters that appear in the `String` variable `str`.

3. Design an algorithm that counts the number of uppercase characters that appear in the `String` variable `str`.

4. Design an algorithm that deletes the first and last characters in the `String` variable `str`.

5. Design an algorithm that converts each occurrence of the character "t" in the `String` variable `str` to uppercase.

6. Design an algorithm that replaces each occurrence of the character "x" in the `String` variable `str` with a space.

7. Assume the following declaration exists in a program:

   ```
   Declare String str = "Mr. Bean"
   ```

   Design an algorithm that replaces "Mr." with "Mister" in the variable.

Programming Exercises

VideoNote
The Backward
String Problem

1. **Backward String**

   Design a program that prompts the user to enter a string and then displays the string contents backward. For instance, if the user enters "gravity" the program should display "ytivarg."

2. **Sentence Capitalizer**

   Design a program that prompts the user to enter a string containing multiple sentences, and then displays the string with the first character of each sentence capitalized. For instance, if the user enters "hello. my name is Joe. what is your name?" the program should display "Hello. My name is Joe. What is your name?" (*Hint:* The `toUpper` library function can be used to convert a single character to uppercase.)

3. **Vowels and Consonants**

   Design a program that prompts the user to enter a string. The program should then display the number of vowels and the number of consonants in the string.

4. **Sum of Digits in a String**

   Design a program that asks the user to enter a string containing a series of single digit numbers with nothing separating them. The program should display the sum of all the single digit numbers in the string. For example, if the user enters 2514, the method should return 12, which is the sum of 2, 5, 1, and 4. (*Hint:* The `stringToInteger` library function can be used to convert a single character to an integer.)

5. **Alphabetic Telephone Number Translator**

Many companies use telephone numbers like 555-GET-FOOD so the number is easier for their customers to remember. On a standard telephone, the alphabetic letters are mapped to numbers in the following fashion:

A, B, and C = 2
D, E, and F = 3
G, H, and I = 4
J, K, and L = 5
M, N, and O = 6
P, Q, R, and S = 7
T, U, and V = 8
W, X, Y, and Z = 9

Design a program that asks the user to enter a 10-character telephone number in the format XXX-XXX-XXXX. The program should display the telephone number with any alphabetic characters that appeared in the original translated to their numeric equivalent. For example, if the user enters 555-GET-FOOD the program should display 555-438-3663.

6. **Word Separator**

Design a program that accepts as input a sentence in which all of the words are run together, but the first character of each word is uppercase. Convert the sentence to a string in which the words are separated by spaces and only the first word starts with an uppercase letter. For example, the string "StopAndSmellTheRoses." would be converted to "Stop and smell the roses." (*Hint:* The toLower library function can be used to convert a single character to lowercase.)

7. **Pig Latin**

Design a program that reads a sentence as input and converts each word to "Pig Latin." In one version of Pig Latin you convert a word by removing the first letter, placing that letter at the end of the word, and then appending "ay" to the word. Here is an example:

English: I SLEPT MOST OF THE NIGHT
Pig Latin: IAY LEPTSAY OSTMAY FOAY HETAY IGHTNAY

8. **Morse Code Converter**

Design a program that asks the user to enter a string, and then converts that string to Morse code. Morse code is a code where each letter of the English alphabet, each digit, and various punctuation characters are represented by a series of dots and dashes. Table 12-4 shows part of the code.

Table 12-4 Morse code

Character	Code	Character	Code	Character	Code	Character	Code
space	*space*	6	-....	G	--.	Q	--.-
comma	--..--	7	--...	H	....	R	.-.
period	.-.-.-	8	---..	I	..	S	...
?	..--..	9	----.	J	.---	T	-
0	-----	A	.-	K	-.-	U	..-
1	.----	B	-...	L	.-..	V	...-
2	..---	C	-.-.	M	--	W	.--
3	...--	D	-..	N	-.	X	-..-
4	....-	E	.	O	---	Y	-.--
5	.....	F	..-.	P	.--.	Z	--..

CHAPTER

13 Recursion

TOPICS

13.1 Introduction to Recursion

> **CONCEPT:** A recursive module is a module that calls itself.

You have seen instances of modules calling other modules. In a program, the main module might call module A, which then might call module B. It's also possible for a module to call itself. A module that calls itself is known as a *recursive module*. For example, look at the message module shown in Program 13-1.

Program 13-1

```
1 Module main()
2    Call message()
3 End Module
4
5 Module message()
6    Display "This is a recursive module."
7    Call message()
8 End Module
```

Program Output

```
This is a recursive module.
This is a recursive module.
This is a recursive module.
This is a recursive module.
```
. . . and this output repeats infinitely!

The `message` module displays the string "This is a recursive module." and then calls itself. Each time it calls itself, the cycle is repeated. Can you see a problem with the module? There's no way to stop the recursive calls. This module is like an infinite loop because there is no code to stop it from repeating.

Like a loop, a recursive module must have some way to control the number of times it repeats. The pseudocode in Program 13-2 shows a modified version of the `message` module. In this program, the `message` module receives an `Integer` argument that specifies the number of times the module should display the message.

Program 13-2

```
1 Module main()
2     // By passing the argument 5 to the message module,
3     // we are telling it to display the message
4     // five times.
5     Call message(5)
6 End Module
7
8 Module message(Integer times)
9     If times > 0 Then
10        Display "This is a recursive module."
11        Call message(times - 1)
12    End If
13 End Module
```

Program Output

```
This is a recursive module.
This is a recursive module.
This is a recursive module.
This is a recursive module.
This is a recursive module.
```

The `message` module in this program contains an `If-Then` statement (in lines 9 through 12) that controls the repetition. As long as the `times` parameter is greater than zero, the message "This is a recursive module." is displayed, and then the module calls itself again. Each time it calls itself, it passes `times - 1` as the argument.

The `main` module calls the `message` module passing the argument 5. The first time the module is called the `If-Then` statement displays the message and then calls itself with 4 as the argument. Figure 13-1 illustrates this.

Figure 13-1 First two calls of the module

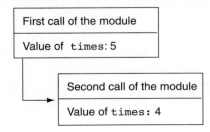

The diagram shown in Figure 13-1 illustrates two separate calls of the `message` module. Each time the module is called, a new instance of the `times` parameter is created in memory. The first time the module is called, the `times` parameter is set to 5. When the module calls itself, a new instance of the `times` parameter is created, and the value 4 is passed into it. This cycle repeats until finally, zero is passed as an argument to the module. This is illustrated in Figure 13-2.

Figure 13-2 Six calls to the `message` module

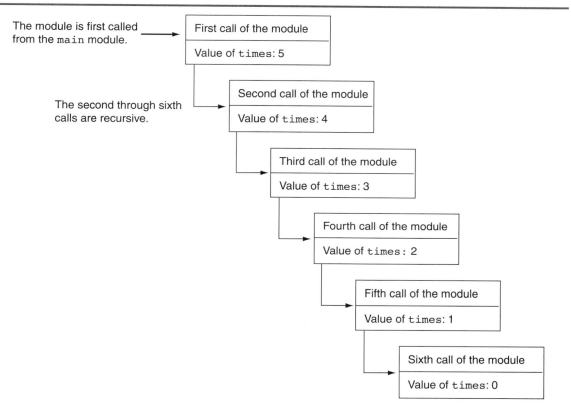

As you can see in the figure, the module is called six times. The first time it is called from the `main` module, and the other five times it calls itself. The number of times that a module calls itself is known as the *depth of recursion*. In this example, the depth of recursion is five. When the module reaches its sixth call, the `times` parameter is set to 0. At that point, the `If-Then` statement's conditional expression is false, so the module returns. Control of the program returns from the sixth instance of the module to the point in the fifth instance directly after the recursive module call. This is illustrated in Figure 13-3.

Figure 13-3 Control returns to the point after the recursive module call

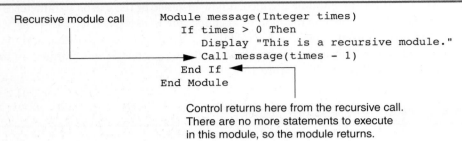

Recursive module call

```
Module message(Integer times)
    If times > 0 Then
        Display "This is a recursive module."
        Call message(times - 1)
    End If
End Module
```

Control returns here from the recursive call.
There are no more statements to execute
in this module, so the module returns.

Because there are no more statements to be executed after the module call, the fifth instance of the module returns control of the program back to the fourth instance. This repeats until all instances of the module return.

13.2 Problem Solving with Recursion

CONCEPT: A problem can be solved with recursion if it can be broken down into successive smaller problems that are identical to the overall problem.

The pseudocode shown in Program 13-2 demonstrates the mechanics of a recursive module. Recursion can be a powerful tool for solving repetitive problems and is commonly studied in upper-level computer science courses. It may not yet be clear to you how to use recursion to solve a problem.

First, note that recursion is never required to solve a problem. Any problem that can be solved recursively can also be solved with a loop. In fact, recursive algorithms are usually less efficient than loops. This is because the process of calling a module requires several actions to be performed by the computer. These actions include allocating memory for parameters and local variables, and storing the address of the program location where control returns after the module terminates. These actions, which are sometimes referred to as *overhead,* take place with each module call. Such overhead is not necessary with a loop.

Some repetitive problems, however, are more easily solved with recursion than with a loop. Where a loop might result in faster execution time, the programmer might be able to design a recursive algorithm faster. In general, a recursive module works as follows:

- If the problem can be solved now, without recursion, then the module solves it and returns
- If the problem cannot be solved now, then the module reduces it to a smaller but similar problem and calls itself to solve the smaller problem

In order to apply this approach, first, we identify at least one case in which the problem can be solved without recursion. This is known as the *base case*. Second, we determine a way to solve the problem in all other circumstances using recursion. This is called the *recursive case*. In the recursive case, we must always reduce the problem to a smaller version of the original problem. By reducing the problem with each recursive call, the base case will eventually be reached and the recursion will stop.

Using Recursion to Calculate the Factorial of a Number

The previous examples demonstrated recursive modules. Most programming languages also allow you to create recursive functions. Let's take an example from mathematics to examine an application of recursive functions. In mathematics, the notation $n!$ represents the factorial of the number n. The factorial of a nonnegative number can be defined by the following rules:

If $n = 0$ then $n! = 1$
If $n > 0$ then $n! = 1 \times 2 \times 3 \times \ldots \times n$

Let's replace the notation $n!$ with factorial(n), which looks a bit more like computer code, and rewrite these rules as follows:

If $n = 0$ then factorial(n) = 1
If $n > 0$ then factorial(n) = $1 \times 2 \times 3 \times \ldots \times n$

These rules state that when n is 0, its factorial is 1. When n is greater than 0, its factorial is the product of all the positive integers from 1 up to n. For instance, factorial(6) is calculated as $1 \times 2 \times 3 \times 4 \times 5 \times 6$.

When designing a recursive algorithm to calculate the factorial of any number, first we identify the base case, which is the part of the calculation that we can solve without recursion. That is the case where n is equal to 0 as follows:

If $n = 0$ then factorial(n) = 1

This tells how to solve the problem when n is equal to 0, but what do we do when n is greater than 0? That is the recursive case, or the part of the problem that we use recursion to solve. This is how we express it:

If $n > 0$ then factorial(n) = $n \times$ factorial($n - 1$)

This states that if n is greater than 0, the factorial of n is n times the factorial of $n - 1$. Notice how the recursive call works on a reduced version of the problem, $n - 1$. So, our recursive rule for calculating the factorial of a number might look like this:

If $n = 0$ then factorial(n) = 1
If $n > 0$ then factorial(n) = $n \times$ factorial($n - 1$)

The pseudocode in Program 13-3 shows how we might design a factorial function in a program.

Program 13-3

```
1 Module main()
2    // Local variable to hold a number
3    // entered by the user.
4    Declare Integer number
5
6    // Local variable to hold the
7    // factorial of the number
8    Declare Integer numFactorial
9
10   // Get a number from the user.
11   Display "Enter a nonnegative integer."
12   Input number
13
14   // Get the factorial of the number.
15   Set numFactorial = factorial(number)
16
17   // Display the factorial.
18   Display "The factorial of ", number,
19           " is ", numFactorial
20 End Module
21
22 // The factorial function uses recursion to
23 // calculate the factorial of its argument,
24 // which is assumed to be nonnegative.
25 Function Integer factorial(Integer n)
26    If n == 0 Then
27       Return 1
28    Else
29       Return n * factorial(n - 1)
30    End If
31 End Function
```

Program Output (with Input Shown in Bold)

```
Enter a nonnegative integer.
4 [Enter]
The factorial of 4 is 24
```

In the sample run of the program, the factorial function is called with the argument 4 passed into n. Because n is not equal to 0, the If statement's Else clause executes the following statement:

```
Return n * factorial(n - 1)
```

Although this is a Return statement, it does not immediately return. Before the return value can be determined, the value of factorial(n - 1) must be determined. The factorial function is called recursively until the fifth call, in which the n parameter will be set to zero. Figure 13-4 illustrates the value of n and the return value during each call of the function.

Figure 13-4 The value of n and the return value during each call of the function

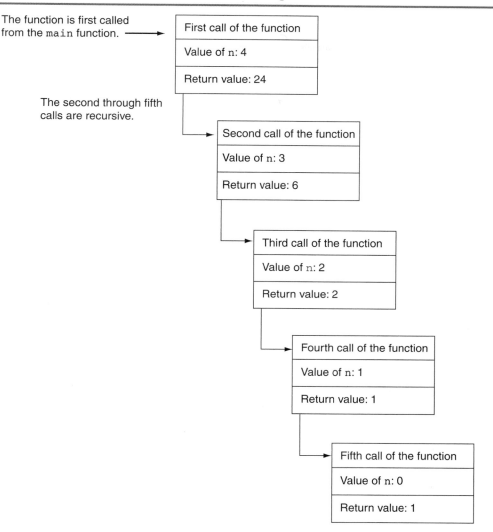

The figure illustrates why a recursive algorithm must reduce the problem with each recursive call. Eventually, the recursion has to stop in order for a solution to be reached.

If each recursive call works on a smaller version of the problem, then the recursive calls work toward the base case. The base case does not require recursion, so it stops the chain of recursive calls.

Usually, a problem is reduced by making the value of one or more parameters smaller with each recursive call. In our factorial function, the value of the parameter n gets closer to 0 with each recursive call. When the parameter reaches 0, the function returns a value without making another recursive call.

Direct and Indirect Recursion

The examples we have discussed so far show recursive modules or functions that directly call themselves. This is known as *direct recursion*. There is also the possibility of creating indirect recursion in a program. This occurs when module A calls module B, which in turn calls module A. There can even be several modules involved in the recursion. For example, module A could call module B, which could call module C, which calls module A.

 Checkpoint

13.1   It is said that a recursive algorithm has more overhead than an iterative algorithm. What does this mean?

13.2   What is a base case?

13.3   What is a recursive case?

13.4   What causes a recursive algorithm to stop calling itself?

13.5   What is direct recursion? What is indirect recursion?

 13.3   ## Examples of Recursive Algorithms

Summing a Range of Array Elements with Recursion

In this example, we look at a function named rangeSum that uses recursion to sum a range of array elements. The function takes the following arguments: an Integer array that contains the range of elements to be summed, an Integer specifying the starting element of the range, and an Integer specifying the ending element of the range. Here is an example of how the function might be used:

```
Constant Integer SIZE = 9
Declare Integer numbers[SIZE] = 1, 2, 3, 4, 5, 6, 7, 8, 9
Declare Integer sum;
Set sum = rangeSum(numbers, 3, 7)
```

The last statement in this pseudocode specifies that the rangeSum function should return the sum of elements 3 through 7 in the numbers array. The return value, which in this case would be 30, is assigned to the sum variable. Here is the pseudocode definition of the rangeSum function:

```
Function Integer rangeSum(Integer array[], Integer start,
                          Integer end)
    If start > end Then
       Return 0
    Else
       Return array[start] + rangeSum(array, start + 1, end)
    End If
End Function
```

This function's base case is when the start parameter is greater than the end parameter. If this is true, the function returns the value 0. Otherwise, the function executes the following statement:

```
Return array[start] + rangeSum(array, start + 1, end)
```

This statement returns the sum of array[start] plus the return value of a recursive call. Notice that in the recursive call, the starting element in the range is start + 1. In essence, this statement says "return the value of the first element in the range plus the sum of the rest of the elements in the range." The pseudocode in Program 13-4 demonstrates the function.

Program 13-4

```
 1 Module main()
 2     // Declare a constant for the array size.
 3     Constant Integer SIZE = 9
 4
 5     // Declare an Integer array.
 6     Declare Integer numbers[SIZE] = 1, 2, 3, 4, 5, 6, 7, 8, 9
 7
 8     // Declare a variable to hold a sum.
 9     Declare Integer sum
10
11     // Get the sum of elements 2 through 5.
12     Set sum = rangeSum(numbers, 2, 5)
13
14     // Display the sum.
15     Display "The sum of elements 2 through 5 is ", sum
16 End Module
17
18 // The rangeSum function returns the sum of a specified
19 // range of elements in array. The start parameter
20 // specifies the starting element. The end parameter
21 // specifies the ending element.
22 Function Integer rangeSum(Integer array[], Integer start,
23                           Integer end)
24     If start > end Then
25        Return 0
26     Else
27        Return array[start] + rangeSum(array, start + 1, end)
28     End If
29 End Function
```

Program Output

```
The sum of elements 2 through 5 is 18
```

The Fibonacci Series

Some mathematical problems are solved recursively. One well-known example is the calculation of Fibonacci numbers. The Fibonacci numbers, named after the Italian mathematician Leonardo Fibonacci (born circa 1170), are the following sequence:

0, 1, 1, 2, 3, 5, 8, 13, 21, 34, 55, 89, 144, 233, . . .

Notice that after the second number, each number in the series is the sum of the two previous numbers. The Fibonacci series can be defined as follows:

If $n = 0$ then Fib(n) = 0
If $n = 1$ then Fib(n) = 1
If $n >= 2$ then Fib(n) = Fib($n - 1$) + Fib($n - 2$)

A recursive function to calculate the nth number in the Fibonacci series is shown here:

```
Function Integer fib(Integer n)
    If n == 0 then
        Return 0
    Else If n == 1 Then
        Return 1
    Else
        Return fib(n - 1) + fib(n - 2)
    End If
End Function
```

Notice that this function actually has two base cases: when n is equal to 0, and when n is equal to 1. In either case, the function returns a value without making a recursive call. The pseudocode in Program 13-5 demonstrates this function by displaying the first 10 numbers in the Fibonacci series.

Program 13-5

```
 1 Module main()
 2     // Local variable to use as a counter.
 3     Declare Integer counter
 4
 5     // Display an introductory message.
 6     Display "The first 10 numbers in the ",
 7             "Fibonacci series are:"
 8
 9     // Use a loop to call the fib function, passing
10     // the values 1 through 10 as an argument.
11     For counter = 1 To 10
12         Display fib(counter)
13     End For
14 End Module
15
16 // The fib function returns the nth number
17 // in the Fibonacci series.
18 Function Integer fib(Integer n)
19     If n == 0 then
20         Return 0
21     Else If n == 1 Then
22         Return 1
23     Else
24         Return fib(n - 1) + fib(n - 2)
```

```
25      End If
26 End Function
```

Program Output

```
The first 10 numbers in the Fibonacci series are:
0 1 1 2 3 5 8 13 21 34
```

Finding the Greatest Common Divisor

Our next example of recursion is the calculation of the greatest common divisor (GCD) of two numbers. The GCD of two positive integers, x and y, is determined as follows:

> If x can be evenly divided by y, then $\gcd(x, y) = y$
> Otherwise, $\gcd(x, y) = \gcd(y, \text{remainder of } x/y)$

This definition states that the GCD of x and y is y if x/y has no remainder. This is the base case. Otherwise, the answer is the GCD of y and the remainder of x/y. The pseudocode in Program 13-6 shows a recursive method for calculating the GCD.

Program 13-6

```
 1 Module main()
 2      // Local variables to hold user input.
 3      Declare Integer num1, num2
 4
 5      // Get a number from the user.
 6      Display "Enter an integer."
 7      Input num1
 8
 9      // Get another number from the user.
10      Display "Enter another integer."
11      Input num2
12
13      // Display the GCD.
14      Display "The greatest common divisor of these"
15      Display "two numbers is ", gcd(num1, num2)
16 End Module
17
18 // The gcd function returns the greatest common
19 // divisor of the arguments passed into x and y.
20 Function Integer gcd(Integer x, Integer y)
21      // Determine whether x can be divided evenly by y.
22      // If so, we've reached the base case.
23      If x MOD y == 0 Then
24         Return y
25      Else
26         // This is the recursive case.
27         Return gcd(x, x MOD y)
28      End If
29 End Function
```

Program Output

```
Enter an integer.
49 [Enter]
Enter another integer.
28 [Enter]
The greatest common divisor of these two numbers is 7
```

A Recursive Binary Search Function

In Chapter 9, you learned about the binary search algorithm and saw an example that uses a loop. The binary search algorithm can also be implemented recursively. For example, the procedure can be expressed as follows:

> *If* `array[middle]` *equals the search value, then*
>   *the value is found.*
> *Else if* `array[middle]` *is less than the search value, then*
>   *perform a binary search on the upper half of the array.*
> *Else if* `array[middle]` *is greater than the search value, then*
>   *perform a binary search on the lower half of the array.*

When you compare the recursive algorithm to its counterpart that uses a loop, it becomes evident that the recursive version is much more elegant and easier to understand. The recursive binary search algorithm is also a good example of repeatedly breaking a problem down into smaller pieces until it is solved. Here is the pseudocode for a recursive `binarySearch` function:

```
Function Integer binarySearch(Integer array[],
        Integer first, Integer last, Integer value)
    // Local variable to hold the subscript of the element
    // in the middle of the search area.
    Declare Integer middle

    // First, see if there are any elements to search.
    If first > last Then
        Return -1
    End If

    // Calculate the mid point of the search area.
    Set middle = (first + last) / 2

    // See if the value is found at the mid point . . .
    If array[middle] == value Then
        Return middle
    End If

    // Search either the upper or lower half.
    If array[middle] < value Then
        Return binarySearch(array, middle + 1, last, value)
    Else
        Return binarySearch(array, first, middle - 1, value)
    End If
End Function
```

The first parameter, `array`, is the array to be searched. The next parameter, `first`, holds the subscript of the first element in the search area (the portion of the array to be searched). The next parameter, `last`, holds the subscript of the last element in the search area. The last parameter, `value`, holds the value to be searched for. Like the `binarySearch` function shown in Chapter 9, this function returns the subscript of the value if it is found, or −1 if the value is not found. Program 13-7 demonstrates the function.

Program 13-7

```
1 Module main()
2     // Declare a constant for the array size.
3     Constant Integer SIZE = 20
4
5     // Declare an array of employee ID numbers.
6     Declare Integer numbers[SIZE] = 101, 142, 147, 189, 199,
7                                     207, 222, 234, 289, 296,
8                                     310, 319, 388, 394, 417,
9                                     429, 447, 521, 536, 600
10
11    // Declare a variable to hold an ID number.
12    Declare Integer empID
13
14    // Declare a variable to hold the search results.
15    Declare Integer results
16
17    // Get an employee ID number to search for.
18    Display "Enter an employee ID number."
19    Input empID
20
21    // Search for the ID number in the array.
22    result = binarySearch(numbers, 0, SIZE - 1, empID)
23
24    // Display the results of the search.
25    If result == -1 Then
26       Display "That employee ID number was not found."
27    Else
28       Display "That employee ID number was found ",
29               "at subscript ", result
30    End If
31
32 End Module
33
34 // The binarySearch function performs a recursive binary search
35 // on a range of elements in an Integer array. The parameter
36 // array holds the array to be searched. The parameter first
37 // holds the subscript of the range's starting element, and the
38 // parameter last holds the subscript of the range's last element.
39 // The parameter value holds the search value. If the search value
40 // is found, its array subscript is returned. Otherwise, -1 is
41 // returned indicating the value is not in the array.
42 Function Integer binarySearch(Integer array[],
43               Integer first, Integer last, Integer value)
44    // Local variable to hold the subscript of the element
```

```
45        // in the middle of the search area.
46        Declare Integer middle
47
48        // First, see if there are any elements to search.
49        If first > last Then
50           Return -1
51        End If
52
53        // Calculate the mid point of the search area.
54        Set middle = (first + last) / 2
55
56        // See if the value is found at the mid point . . .
57        If array[middle] == value Then
58           Return middle
59        End If
60
61        // Search either the upper or lower half.
62        If array[middle] < value Then
63           Return binarySearch(array, middle + 1, last, value)
64        Else
65           Return binarySearch(array, first, middle - 1, value)
66        End If
67 End Function
```

Program Output (with Input Shown in Bold)

```
Enter an Employee ID number.
521 [Enter]
That ID is found at subscript 17
```

The Towers of Hanoi

The Towers of Hanoi is a mathematical game that is often used in computer science textbooks to illustrate the power of recursion. The game uses three pegs and a set of discs with holes through their centers. The discs are stacked on one of the pegs as shown in Figure 13-5.

Figure 13-5 The pegs and discs in the Towers of Hanoi game

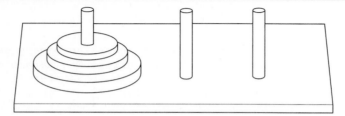

Notice that the discs are stacked on the leftmost peg, in order of size with the largest disc at the bottom. The game is based on a legend where a group of monks in a temple in Hanoi have a similar set of pegs with 64 discs. The job of the monks is to move the discs from the first peg to the third peg. The middle peg can be used as a temporary holder. Furthermore, the monks must follow these rules while moving the discs:

- Only one disk may be moved at a time
- A disk cannot be placed on top of a smaller disc
- All discs must be stored on a peg except while being moved

According to the legend, when the monks have moved all of the discs from the first peg to the last peg, the world will come to an end.

To play the game, you must move all of the discs from the first peg to the third peg, following the same rules as the monks. Let's look at some example solutions to this game, for different numbers of discs. If you only have one disc, the solution to the game is simple: move the disc from peg 1 to peg 3. If you have two discs, the solution requires three moves:

- Move disc 1 to peg 2
- Move disc 2 to peg 3
- Move disc 1 to peg 3

Notice that this approach uses peg 2 as a temporary location. The complexity of the moves continues to increase as the number of discs increases. To move three discs requires the seven moves shown in Figure 13-6.

Figure 13-6 Steps for moving three pegs

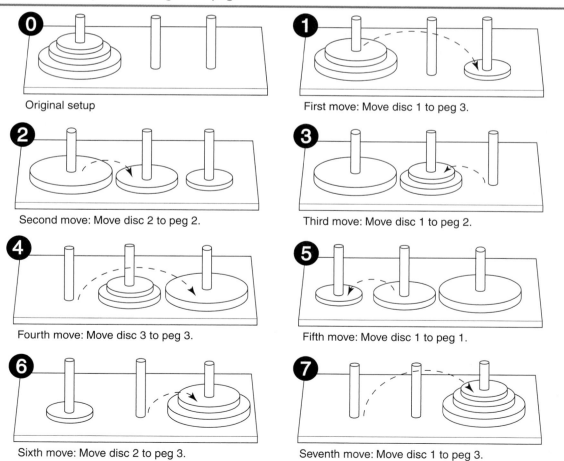

Original setup

First move: Move disc 1 to peg 3.

Second move: Move disc 2 to peg 2.

Third move: Move disc 1 to peg 2.

Fourth move: Move disc 3 to peg 3.

Fifth move: Move disc 1 to peg 1.

Sixth move: Move disc 2 to peg 3.

Seventh move: Move disc 1 to peg 3.

The following statement describes the overall solution to the problem:

Move n discs from peg 1 to peg 3 using peg 2 as a temporary peg.

The following summary describes a recursive algorithm that simulates the solution to the game. Notice that in this algorithm we use the variables A, B, and C to hold peg numbers.

To move n discs from peg A to peg C, using peg B as a temporary peg, do the following:
If n > 0 then
    Move n – 1 discs from peg A to peg B, using peg C as a temporary peg.
    Move the remaining disc from peg A to peg C.
    Move n – 1 discs from peg B to peg C, using peg A as a temporary peg.
End if

The base case for the algorithm is reached when there are no more discs to move. The following pseudocode is for a module that implements this algorithm. Note that the module does not actually move anything, but displays instructions indicating all of the disc moves to make.

```
Module moveDiscs(Integer num, Integer fromPeg,
                 Integer toPeg, Integer tempPeg)
   If num > 0 Then
      moveDiscs(num - 1, fromPeg, tempPeg, toPeg)
      Display "Move a disc from peg ", fromPeg,
              " to peg ", toPeg
      moveDiscs(num - 1, tempPeg, toPeg, fromPeg)
   End If
End Module
```

This module accepts arguments into the following parameters:

num	The number of discs to move.
fromPeg	The peg to move the discs from.
toPeg	The peg to move the discs to.
tempPeg	The peg to use as a temporary peg.

If num is greater than 0, then there are discs to move. The first recursive call is as follows:

```
moveDiscs(num - 1, fromPeg, tempPeg, toPeg)
```

This statement is an instruction to move all but one disc from `fromPeg` to `tempPeg`, using `toPeg` as a temporary peg. The next statement is as follows:

```
Display "Move a disc from peg ", fromPeg,
        " to peg ", toPeg
```

This simply displays a message indicating that a disc should be moved from `fromPeg` to `toPeg`. Next, another recursive call is executed as follows:

```
moveDiscs(num - 1, tempPeg, toPeg, fromPeg)
```

This statement is an instruction to move all but one disc from `tempPeg` to `toPeg`, using `fromPeg` as a temporary peg. The pseudocode in Program 13-8 demonstrates the module by displaying a solution for the Tower of Hanoi game.

Program 13-8

```
 1 Module main()
 2     // A constant for the number of discs to move.
 3     Constant Integer NUM_DISCS = 3
 4
 5     // A constant for the initial "from" peg.
 6     Constant Integer FROM_PEG = 1
 7
 8     // A constant for the initial "to" peg.
 9     Constant Integer TO_PEG = 3
10
11     // A constant for the initial "temp" peg.
12     Constant Integer TEMP_PEG = 2
13
14     // Play the game.
15     Call moveDiscs(NUM_DISCS, FROM_PEG, TO_PEG, TEMP_PEG)
16     Display "All the pegs are moved!"
17 End Module
18
19
20 // The moveDiscs function displays a disc move in
21 // the Towers of Hanoi game.
22 // The parameters are:
23 //     num:    The number of discs to move.
24 //     fromPeg: The peg to move from.
25 //     toPeg:   The peg to move to.
26 //     empPeg:  The temporary peg.
27 Module moveDiscs(Integer num, Integer fromPeg,
28                    Integer toPeg, Integer tempPeg)
29     If num > 0 Then
30        moveDiscs(num - 1, fromPeg, tempPeg, toPeg)
31        Display "Move a disc from peg ", fromPeg,
32               " to peg ", toPeg
33        moveDiscs(num - 1, tempPeg, toPeg, fromPeg)
34     End If
35 End Module
```

Program Output

```
Move a disc from peg 1 to peg 3
Move a disc from peg 1 to peg 2
Move a disc from peg 3 to peg 2
Move a disc from peg 1 to peg 3
Move a disc from peg 2 to peg 1
Move a disc from peg 2 to peg 3
Move a disc from peg 1 to peg 3
All the pegs are moved!
```

Recursion versus Looping

Any algorithm that can be coded with recursion can also be coded with a loop. Both approaches achieve repetition, but which is best to use?

There are several reasons not to use recursion. Recursive algorithms are certainly less efficient than iterative algorithms. Each time a module or function is called, the system incurs overhead that is not necessary with a loop. Also, in many cases a solution using a loop may be more evident than a recursive solution. In fact, the majority of repetitive programming tasks are best done with loops.

Some problems, however, are more easily solved with recursion than with a loop. For example, the mathematical definition of the GCD formula is well suited for a recursive approach. The speed and amount of memory available to modern computers diminishes the performance impact of recursion so much that inefficiency is no longer a strong argument against it. Today, the choice of recursion or a loop is primarily a design decision. If a problem is more easily solved with a loop, you should take that approach. If recursion results in a better design, you should make that choice.

Review Questions

Multiple Choice

1. A recursive module _____.
   a. calls a different module
   b. abnormally halts the program
   c. calls itself
   d. can only be called once

2. A module is called once from a program's `main` module, and then it calls itself four times. The depth of recursion is _____.
   a. one
   b. four
   c. five
   d. nine

3. The part of a problem that can be solved without recursion is the _____ case.
   a. base
   b. solvable
   c. known
   d. iterative

4. The part of a problem that is solved with recursion is the _____ case.
   a. base
   b. iterative
   c. unknown
   d. recursive

5. When a module explicitly calls itself it is called _____ recursion.
   a. explicit
   b. modal
   c. direct
   d. indirect

6. When module A calls module B, which calls module A, it is called _____ recursion.

   a. implicit
   b. modal
   c. direct
   d. indirect

7. Any problem that can be solved recursively can also be solved with a _____.

   a. decision structure
   b. loop
   c. sequence structure
   d. case structure

8. Actions taken by the computer when a module is called, such as allocating memory for parameters and local variables, are referred to as _____.

   a. overhead
   b. setup
   c. cleanup
   d. synchronization

9. A recursive algorithm must _____ in the recursive case.

   a. solve the problem without recursion
   b. reduce the problem to a smaller version of the original problem
   c. acknowledge that an error has occurred and abort the program
   d. enlarge the problem to a larger version of the original problem

10. A recursive algorithm must _____ in the base case.

   a. solve the problem without recursion
   b. reduce the problem to a smaller version of the original problem
   c. acknowledge that an error has occurred and abort the program
   d. enlarge the problem to a larger version of the original problem

True or False

1. An algorithm that uses a loop will usually run faster than an equivalent recursive algorithm.

2. Some problems can be solved through recursion only.

3. It is not necessary to have a base case in all recursive algorithms.

4. In the base case, a recursive method calls itself with a smaller version of the original problem.

Short Answer

1. In Program 13-2, presented earlier in this chapter, what is the base case of the `message` module?

2. In this chapter, the rules given for calculating the factorial of a number are as follows:

   If $n = 0$ then factorial$(n) = 1$
   If $n > 0$ then factorial$(n) = n \times$ factorial$(n - 1)$

   If you were designing a module from these rules, what would the base case be? What would the recursive case be?

3. Is recursion ever required to solve a problem? What other approach can you use to solve a problem that is repetitive in nature?

4. When recursion is used to solve a problem, why must the recursive module call itself to solve a smaller version of the original problem?

5. How is a problem usually reduced with a recursive module?

Algorithm Workbench

1. What will the following program display?
```
Module main()
    Declare Integer num = 0
    Call showMe(num)
End Module

Module showMe(Integer arg)
    If arg < 10 Then
        Call showMe(arg + 1)
    Else
        Display arg
    End If
End Module
```

2. What will the following program display?
```
Module main()
    Declare Integer num = 0
    Call showMe(num)
End Module

Module showMe(Integer arg)
    Display arg
    If arg < 10 Then
        Call showMe(arg + 1)
    End If
End Module
```

3. The following module uses a loop. Rewrite it as a recursive module that performs the same operation.
```
Module trafficSign(int n)
    While n > 0
        Display "No Parking"
        Set n = n - 1
    End While
End Module
```

Programming Exercises

VideoNote
The Recursive
Multiplication
Problem

1. **Recursive Multiplication**

   Design a recursive function that accepts two arguments into the parameters x and y. The function should return the value of x times y. Remember, multiplication can be performed as repeated addition as follows:

   $$7 \times 4 = 4 + 4 + 4 + 4 + 4 + 4 + 4$$

   (To keep the function simple, assume that x and y will always hold positive nonzero integers.)

2. **Largest Element**

   Design a function that accepts an array and the array's size as arguments, and returns the largest value in the array. The method should use recursion to find the largest element.

3. **Recursive Array Sum**

   Design a function that accepts an Integer array and the size of the array as arguments. The function should recursively calculate the sum of all the numbers in the array and return that value.

4. **Sum of Numbers**

   Design a function that accepts an integer argument and returns the sum of all the integers from 1 up to the number passed as an argument. For example, if 50 is passed as an argument, the function will return the sum of 1, 2, 3, 4, . . . 50. Use recursion to calculate the sum.

5. **Recursive Power Method**

   Design a function that uses recursion to raise a number to a power. The function should accept two arguments: the number to be raised and the exponent. Assume that the exponent is a nonnegative integer.

6. **Ackermann's Function**

   Ackermann's Function is a recursive mathematical algorithm that can be used to test how well a computer performs recursion. Design a function ackermann(m, n), which solves Ackermann's Function. Use the following logic in your function:

   If m = 0 then return n + 1
   If n = 0 then return ackermann(m − 1, 1)
   Otherwise, return ackermann(m − 1, ackermann(m, n − 1))

14 Object-Oriented Programming

14.1 Procedural and Object-Oriented Programming

CONCEPT: Procedural programming is a method of writing software. It is a programming practice centered on the procedures or actions that take place in a program. Object-oriented programming is centered on the object. Objects are created from abstract data types that encapsulate data and functions together.

There are primarily two methods of programming in use today: procedural and object-oriented. The earliest programming languages were procedural, meaning a program was made of one or more procedures. A *procedure* is simply a module or function that performs a specific task such as gathering input from the user, performing calculations, reading or writing files, displaying output, and so on. The programs that you have written so far have been procedural in nature.

Typically, procedures operate on data items that are separate from the procedures. In a procedural program, the data items are commonly passed from one procedure to another. As you might imagine, the focus of procedural programming is on the creation of procedures that operate on the program's data. The separation of data and the code that operates on the data can lead to problems, however, as the program becomes larger and more complex.

503

For example, suppose you are part of a programming team that has written an extensive customer database program. The program was initially designed so that a customer's name, address, and phone number were stored in three `String` variables. Your job was to design several modules that accept those three variables as arguments and perform operations on them. The software has been operating successfully for some time, but your team has been asked to update it by adding several new features. During the revision process, the senior programmer informs you that the customer's name, address, and phone number will no longer be stored in variables. Instead, they will be stored in a `String` array. This means that you will have to modify all of the modules that you have designed so that they accept and work with a `String` array instead of the three variables. Making these extensive modifications not only is a great deal of work, but also opens the opportunity for errors to appear in your code.

Whereas procedural programming is centered on creating procedures (which are modules and functions), *object-oriented programming* (OOP) is centered on creating objects. An *object* is a software entity that contains both data and procedures. The data contained in an object is known as the object's *fields*. An object's fields are simply variables, arrays, or other data structures that are stored in the object. The procedures that an object performs are known as *methods*. An object's methods are nothing more than modules or functions. The object is, conceptually, a self-contained unit that consists of data (fields) and procedures (methods). This is illustrated in Figure 14-1.

Figure 14-1 An object contains data and procedures

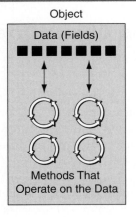

OOP addresses the problem of code/data separation through encapsulation and data hiding. *Encapsulation* refers to the combining of data and code into a single object. *Data hiding* refers to an object's ability to hide its data from code that is outside the object. Only the object's methods may then directly access and make changes to the object's data. An object typically hides its data, but allows outside code to access its methods. As shown in Figure 14-2, the object's methods provide programming statements outside the object with indirect access to the object's data.

Figure 14-2 Code outside the object interacts with the object's methods

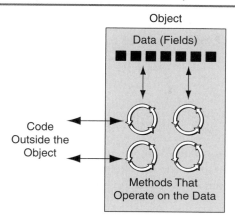

When an object's internal data is hidden from outside code and access to that data is restricted to the object's methods, the data is protected from accidental corruption. In addition, the programming code outside the object does not need to know about the format or internal structure of the object's data. The code only needs to interact with the object's methods. When a programmer changes the structure of an object's internal data, he or she also modifies the object's methods so that they may properly operate on the data. The way in which outside code interacts with the methods, however, does not change.

Object Reusability

In addition to solving the problems of code/data separation, the use of OOP has also been encouraged by the trend of *object reusability*. An object is not a standalone program, but is used by programs that need its service. For example, Sharon is a programmer who has developed an object for rendering 3D images. She is a math whiz and knows a lot about computer graphics, so her object is coded to perform all of the necessary 3D mathematical operations and handle the computer's video hardware. Tom, who is writing a program for an architectural firm, needs his application to display 3D images of buildings. Because he is working under a tight deadline and does not possess a great deal of knowledge about computer graphics, he can use Sharon's object to perform the 3D rendering (for a small fee, of course!).

An Everyday Example of an Object

Think of your alarm clock as an object. It has the following fields:

- The current second (a value in the range of 0–59)
- The current minute (a value in the range of 0–59)
- The current hour (a value in the range of 1–12)
- The time the alarm is set for (a valid hour and minute)
- Whether the alarm is on or off ("on" or "off")

As you can see, the fields are merely data values that define the *state* that the alarm clock is currently in. You, the user of the alarm clock object, cannot directly manipulate these fields because they are *private*. To change a field's value, you must use one of the object's methods. The following are some of the alarm clock object's methods:

- `Set time`
- `Set alarm time`
- `Turn alarm on`
- `Turn alarm off`

Each method manipulates one or more of the fields. For example, the `Set time` method allows you to set the alarm clock's time. You activate the method by pressing a button on top of the clock. By using another button, you can activate the `Set alarm time` method.

In addition, another button allows you to execute the `Turn alarm on` and `Turn alarm off` methods. Notice that all of these methods can be activated by you, who are outside of the alarm clock. Methods that can be accessed by entities outside the object are known as *public methods*.

The alarm clock also has *private methods,* which are part of the object's private, internal workings. External entities (such as you, the user of the alarm clock) do not have direct access to the alarm clock's private methods. The object is designed to execute these methods automatically and hide the details from you. The following are the alarm clock object's private methods:

- `Increment the current second`
- `Increment the current minute`
- `Increment the current hour`
- `Sound alarm`

Every second, the `Increment the current second` method executes. This changes the value of the current second field. If the current second field is set to 59 when this method executes, the method is programmed to reset the current second to 0, and then cause the `Increment current minute` method to execute. This method adds 1 to the current minute, unless it is set to 59. In that case, it resets the current minute to 0 and causes the `Increment current hour` method to execute. (Note that the `Increment current minute` method compares the new time to the alarm time. If the two times match and the alarm is turned on, the `Sound alarm` method is executed.)

Checkpoint

14.1 What is an object?

14.2 What is encapsulation?

14.3 Why is an object's internal data usually hidden from outside code?

14.4 What are public methods? What are private methods?

14.2 Classes

> **CONCEPT:** A class is code that specifies the fields and methods for a particular type of object.

VideoNote
Classes and
Objects

Now, let's discuss how objects are created in software. Before an object can be created, it must be designed by a programmer. The programmer determines the fields and methods that are necessary, and then creates a *class*. A class is code that specifies the fields and methods of a particular type of object. Think of a class as a "blueprint" that objects may be created from. It serves a similar purpose as the blueprint for a house. The blueprint itself is not a house, but is a detailed description of a house. When we use the blueprint to build an actual house, we could say we are building an instance of the house described by the blueprint. If we so desire, we can build several identical houses from the same blueprint. Each house is a separate instance of the house described by the blueprint. This idea is illustrated in Figure 14-3.

Figure 14-3 A blueprint and houses built from the blueprint

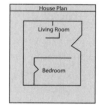

Another way of thinking about the difference between a class and an object is to think of the difference between a cookie cutter and a cookie. While a cookie cutter itself is not a cookie, it describes a cookie. The cookie cutter can be used to make several cookies, as shown in Figure 14-4. Think of a class as a cookie cutter and the objects created from the class as cookies.

Figure 14-4 The cookie cutter metaphor

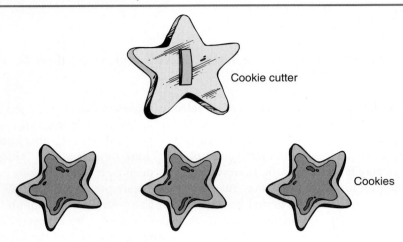

So, a class is not an object, but it can be a description of an object. When the program is running, it can use the class to create, in memory, as many objects of a specific type as needed. Each object that is created from a class is called an *instance* of the class.

For example, Jessica is an entomologist (someone who studies insects) and she also enjoys writing computer programs. She designs a program to catalog different types of insects. As part of the program, she creates a class named Insect, which specifies fields and methods for holding and manipulating data common to all types of insects. The Insect class is not an object, but a specification that objects may be created from. Next, she writes programming statements that create a housefly object, which is an instance of the Insect class. The housefly object is an entity that occupies computer memory and stores data about a housefly. It has the fields and methods specified by the Insect class. Then she writes programming statements that create a mosquito object. The mosquito object is also an instance of the Insect class. It has its own area in memory, and stores data about a mosquito. Although the housefly and mosquito objects are separate entities in the computer's memory, they were both created from the Insect class. This means that each of the objects has the fields and methods described by the Insect class. This is illustrated in Figure 14-5.

Figure 14-5 The housefly and mosquito objects are instances of the Insect class

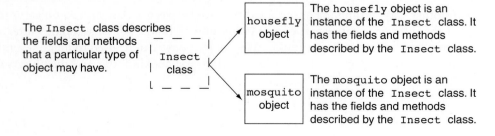

Creating a Class, Step by Step

The general format that we will use to write a class definition in pseudocode is as follows:

```
Class ClassName
    Field declarations and method definitions go here...
End Class
```

The first line starts with the word Class, followed by the name of the class. In most languages, you follow the same rules for naming variables as when naming classes. Next, you write the declarations for the class's fields and the definitions of the class's methods. (In general terms, the fields and methods that belong to a class are referred to as the class's *members*.) The words End Class appear at the end of the class definition.

Now we will demonstrate how a class is typically created in an object-oriented language. Because classes have several parts, we will not show the entire class all at once. Instead, we will put it together in a step-by-step fashion.

Suppose we are designing a program for Wireless Solutions, a business that sells cell phones and wireless service. The program will be used to keep track of the cell phones that the company has in inventory. The data that we need to keep for a cell phone is as follows:

- The name of the phone's manufacturer
- The phone's model number
- The phone's retail price

If we were designing a procedural program, we would simply use variables to hold this data. In this example, we are designing an object-oriented program, so we will create a class that represents a cell phone. The class will have fields to hold these items of data. The pseudocode in Class Listing 14-1 shows how we will start writing the class definition:

Class Listing 14-1

```
1 Class CellPhone
2     // Field declarations
3     Private String manufacturer
4     Private String modelNumber
5     Private Real retailPrice
6
7     // This class is not finished!
8 End Class
```

First, notice that in line 1 we have named the class CellPhone. In this book, we will always begin class names with an uppercase letter. This is not required, but many programmers follow this practice because it helps distinguish class names from variable names.

Lines 3, 4, and 5 declare three fields. Line 3 declares a String field named manufacturer, line 4 declares a String field named modelNumber, and line 5 declares a `Real` field named `retailPrice`. Notice that each declaration begins with the word `Private`. When the word `Private` appears before a field declaration, it specifies that the field cannot be directly accessed by any statement outside the class. In most object-oriented programming languages, the word `Private` is known as an *access specifier*. It specifies how a class field or method can be accessed.

By using the `Private` access specifier, a class can hide its data from code outside the class. When a class's fields are hidden from outside code, the data is protected from accidental corruption. It is a common practice in object-oriented programming to make all of a class's fields private and to provide access to those fields only through methods. Next, we will add the following methods to the class, which will allow code outside the class to store values in the fields:

- `setManufacturer`: The `setManufacturer` method will be a module that stores a value in the `manufacturer` field.
- `setModelNumber`: The `setModelNumber` method will be a module that stores a value in the `modelNumber` field.
- `setRetailPrice`: The `setRetailPrice` method will be a module that stores a value in the `retailPrice` field.

The pseudocode in Class Listing14-2 shows how the `CellPhone` class will appear with these methods added to it.

Class Listing 14-2

```
 1 Class CellPhone
 2     // Field declarations
 3     Private String manufacturer
 4     Private String modelNumber
 5     Private Real retailPrice
 6
 7     // Method definitions
 8     Public Module setManufacturer (String manufact)
 9        Set manufacturer = manufact
10     End Module
11
12     Public Module setModelNumber (String modNum)
13        Set modelNumber = modNum
14     End Module
15
16     Public Module setRetailPrice (Real retail)
17        Set retailPrice = retail
18     End Module
19
20     // This class is not finished!
21 End Class
```

The `setManufacturer` method appears in lines 8 through 10. This looks like a regular module definition, except that the word `Public` appears in the header. In most object-oriented languages, the word `Public` is an access specifier. When it is applied to a method, it specifies that the method can be called from statements outside the class.

The setManufacturer method has a String parameter named manufact. When the method is called, a string must be passed to it as an argument. In line 9, the value passed to the manufact parameter is assigned to the manufacturer field.

The setModelNumber method appears in lines 12 through 14. The method has a String parameter named modNum. When the method is called, a string must be passed to it as an argument. In line 13, the value passed to the modNum parameter is assigned to the modelNumber field.

The setRetailPrice method has a Real parameter named retail. When the method is called, a Real value must be passed to it as an argument. In line 17, the value passed to the retail parameter is assigned to the retailPrice field.

Because the manufacturer, modelNumber, and retailPrice fields are private, we wrote the setManufacturer, setModelNumber, and setRetailPrice methods to allow code outside the CellPhone class to store values in those fields. We must also write methods that allow code outside the class to get the values that are stored in these fields. For this purpose we will write the getManufacturer, getModelNumber, and getRetailPrice methods. The getManufacturer method will return the value stored in the manufacturer field, the getModelNumber method will return the value stored in the modelNumber field, and the getRetailPrice method will return the value stored in the retailPrice field.

The pseudocode in Class Listing 14-3 shows how the CellPhone class will appear with these methods added to it. The new methods are shown in lines 20 through 30.

Class Listing 14-3

```
 1 Class CellPhone
 2     // Field declarations
 3     Private String manufacturer
 4     Private String modelNumber
 5     Private Real retailPrice
 6
 7     // Method definitions
 8     Public Module setManufacturer(String manufact)
 9         Set manufacturer = manufact
10     End Module
11
12     Public Module setModelNumber(String modNum)
13         Set modelNumber = modNum
14     End Module
15
16     Public Module setRetailPrice(Real retail)
17         Set retailPrice = retail
18     End Module
19
20     Public Function String getManufacturer()
21         Return manufacturer
22     End Function
23
24     Public Function String getModelNumber()
25         Return modelNumber
```

```
26      End Function
27
28      Public Function Real getRetailPrice()
29         Return retailPrice
30      End Function
31 End Class
```

The `getManufacturer` method appears in lines 20 through 22. Notice that this method is written as a function instead of a module. When the method is called, the statement in line 21 returns the value stored in the `manufacturer` field.

The `getModelNumber` method in lines 24 through 26 and the `getRetailPrice` method in lines 28 through 30 are also functions. The `getModelNumber` method returns the value stored in the `modelNumber` field, and the `getRetailPrice` method returns the value stored in the `retailPrice` field.

The pseudocode in Class Listing 14-3 is a complete class, but it is not a program. It is a blueprint that objects may be created from. To demonstrate the class we must design a program that uses it to create an object, as shown in Program 14-1.

Program 14-1

```
1 Module main()
2     // Declare a variable that can reference
3     // a CellPhone object.
4     Declare CellPhone myPhone
5
6     // The following statement creates an object
7     // using the CellPhone class as its blueprint.
8     // The myPhone variable will reference the object.
9     Set myPhone = New CellPhone()
10
11    // Store values in the object's fields.
12    Call myPhone.setManufacturer("Motorola")
13    Call myPhone.setModelNumber("M1000")
14    Call myPhone.setRetailPrice(199.99)
15
16    // Display the values stored in the fields.
17    Display "The manufacturer is ", myPhone.getManufacturer()
18    Display "The model number is ", myPhone.getModelNumber()
19    Display "The retail price is ", myPhone.getRetailPrice()
20 End Module
```

Program Output

```
The manufacturer is Motorola
The model number is M1000
The retail price is 199.99
```

The statement in line 4 is a variable declaration. It declares a variable named `myPhone`. This statement looks like any other variable declaration that you have seen, except that the data type is the name of the `CellPhone` class. This is shown in Figure 14-6. When you declare a variable and specify the name of a class as the variable's data type, you are creating a class variable. A *class variable* is a special type of variable that can reference an object in the computer's memory, and work with that object. The `myPhone` variable that is declared in line 4 can be used to reference an object that is created from the `CellPhone` class.

Figure 14-6 Class variable declaration

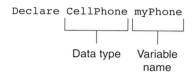

In many object-oriented languages, the act of declaring a class variable does not actually create an object in memory. It only creates a variable that can be used to work with an object. The next step is to create an object. This is done with the following assignment statement, which appears in line 9:

```
Set myPhone = New CellPhone()
```

Notice that on the right side of the = operator, the key word `New` appears. In many programming languages, the key word `New` creates an object in memory. The name of a class appears next (in this case it is `CellPhone`), followed by a set of parentheses. This specifies the class that should be used as a blueprint to create the object. Once the object is created, the = operator assigns the memory address of the object to the `myPhone` variable. The actions performed by this statement are shown in Figure 14-7.

When a class variable is assigned the address of an object, it is said that the variable *references* the object. As shown in Figure 14-8, the `myPhone` variable will reference a `CellPhone` object after this statement executes.

Figure 14-7 Creating an object and assigning its address to a class variable

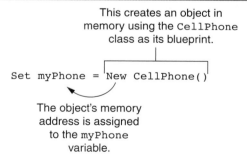

Figure 14-8 The `myPhone` variable references a `CellPhone` object

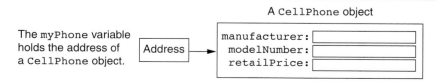

> **NOTE:** In some languages, such as C++, the act of declaring a class variable also creates an object in memory. In these languages, it is not necessary to use the New key word to create the object as we did in line 9 of Program 14-1.

The following statement, which appears in line 12, is next:

```
Call myPhone.setManufacturer("Motorola")
```

This statement calls the `myPhone.setManufacturer` method. The expression `myPhone.setManufacturer` is written in *dot notation*. It's called dot notation because programmers refer to the period as a "dot." On the left side of the dot is the name of a class variable that references an object. On the right side of the dot is the name of the method we are calling. When this statement executes, it uses the object referenced by `myPhone` to call the `setManufacturer` method, passing the string `"Motorola"` as an argument. As a result, the string `"Motorola"` will be assigned to the object's `manufacturer` field.

Line 13 calls the `myPhone.setModelNumber` method, passing the string `"M1000"` as an argument. After this statement executes, the string `"M1000"` will be stored in the object's `modelNumber` field. Line 14 calls the `myPhone.setRetailPrice` method, passing 199.99 as an argument. This causes 199.99 to be assigned to the `retailPrice` field. Figure 14-9 shows the state of the object after the statements in lines 12 through 14 execute.

Figure 14-9 The state of the object referenced by `myPhone`

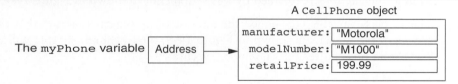

The statements in lines 17 through 19 display the values in the object's fields. Here is the statement in line 17:

```
Display "The manufacturer is ", myPhone.getManufacturer()
```

This statement calls the `myPhone.getManufacturer` method, which returns the string `"Motorola"`. The following message is displayed on the screen:

```
The manufacturer is Motorola
```

The following statement, in line 18, executes next:

```
Display "The model number is ", myPhone.getModelNumber()
```

This statement calls the `myPhone.getModelNumber` method, which returns the string `"M1000"`. The following message is displayed on the screen:

```
The model number is M1000
```

The following statement, in line 19, executes next:

```
Display "The retail price is ", myPhone.getRetailPrice()
```

This statement calls the `myPhone.getRetailPrice` method, which returns the value 199.99. The following message is displayed on the screen:

```
The retail price is 199.99
```

Accessor and Mutator Methods

As mentioned earlier, it is a common practice to make all of a class's fields private and to provide public methods for accessing and changing those fields. This ensures that the object owning those fields is in control of all changes being made to them. A method that gets a value from a class's field but does not change it is known as an *accessor method*. A method that stores a value in a field or changes the value of a field in some other way is known as a *mutator method*. In the `CellPhone` class, the methods `getManufacturer`, `getModelNumber`, and `getRetailPrice` are accessors, and the methods `setManufacturer` `setModelNumber`, and `getRetailPrice` are mutators.

NOTE: Mutator methods are sometimes called "setters" and accessor methods are sometimes called "getters."

Constructors

A constructor is a method that is automatically called when an object is created. In most cases, a constructor is used to initialize an object's fields with starting values. These methods are called "constructors" because they help construct an object.

In many programming languages, a constructor has the same name as the class that the constructor is in. That is the convention followed in this book. For example, if we write a constructor in the `CellPhone` class, we will write a module named `CellPhone`. The pseudocode in Class Listing 14-4 shows a new version of the class with a constructor added to it. The constructor appears in lines 8 through 13.

NOTE: In Visual Basic, constructors are named `New`.

Class Listing 14-4

```
 1 Class CellPhone
 2    // Field declarations
 3    Private String manufacturer
 4    Private String modelNumber
 5    Private Real retailPrice
 6
 7    // Constructor
 8    Public Module CellPhone(String manufact,
 9                            String modNum, Real retail)
10       Set manufacturer = manufact
11       Set modelNumber = modNum
12       Set retailPrice = retail
13    End Module
14
```

```
15      // Mutator methods
16      Public Module setManufacturer(String manufact)
17          Set manufacturer = manufact
18      End Module
19
20      Public Module setModelNumber(String modNum)
21          Set modelNumber = modNum
22      End Module
23
24      Public Module setRetailPrice(String retail)
25          Set retailPrice = retail
26      End Module
27
28      // Accessor methods
29      Public Function String getManufacturer()
30          Return manufacturer
31      End Function
32
33      Public Function String getModelNumber()
34          Return modelNumber
35      End Function
36
37      Public Function Real getRetailPrice()
38          Return retailPrice
39      End Function
40 End Class
```

The constructor accepts three arguments, which are passed into the manufact, modNum, and retail parameters. In lines 10 through 12, these parameters are assigned to the manufacturer, modelNumber, and retailPrice fields.

The pseudocode in Program 14-2 creates a CellPhone object and uses the constructor to initialize the object's fields. In line 9, notice that after the class name, the values "Motorola", "M1000", and 199.99 appear inside the parentheses. These arguments are passed to the manufact, modelNum, and retail parameters in the constructor. The code in the constructor then assigns those values to the manufacturer, modelNumber, and retailPrice fields.

Program 14-2

```
1 Module main()
2      // Declare a variable that can reference
3      // a CellPhone object.
4      Declare CellPhone myPhone
5
6      // The following statement creates a CellPhone
7      // object and initializes its fields with the
8      // values passed to the constructor.
9      Set myPhone = New CellPhone("Motorola", "M1000", 199.99)
10
11     // Display the values stored in the fields.
12     Display "The manufacturer is ", myPhone.getManufacturer()
13     Display "The model number is ", myPhone.getModelNumber()
14     Display "The retail price is ", myPhone.getRetailPrice()
15 End Module
```

Program Output

```
The manufacturer is Motorola
The model number is M1000
The retail price is 199.99
```

The pseudocode in Program 14-3 shows another example that uses the `CellPhone` class. This program prompts the user to enter the data for a cell phone and then creates an object containing that data.

Program 14-3

```
 1 Module main()
 2     // Variables to hold data entered by the user.
 3     Declare String manufacturer, model
 4     Declare Real retail
 5
 6     // Declare a variable that can reference
 7     // a CellPhone object.
 8     Declare CellPhone phone
 9
10     // Get the data for a cell phone from the user.
11     Display "Enter the phone's manufacturer."
12     Input manufacturer
13     Display "Enter the phone's model number."
14     Input model
15     Display "Enter the phone's retail price."
16     Input retail
17
18     // Create a CellPhone object initialized with the
19     // data entered by the user.
20     Set phone = New CellPhone(manufacturer, model, retail)
21
22     // Display the values stored in the fields.
23     Display "Here is the data you entered."
24     Display "The manufacturer is ", myPhone.getManufacturer()
25     Display "The model number is ", myPhone.getModelNumber()
26     Display "The retail price is ", myPhone.getRetailPrice()
27 End Module
```

Program Output (with Input Shown in Bold)

```
Enter the phone's manufacturer.
```
Samsung [Enter]
```
Enter the phone's model number.
```
S900 [Enter]
```
Enter the phone's retail price.
```
179.99 [Enter]
```
Here is the data you entered.
The manufacturer is Samsung
The model number is S900
The retail price is 179.99
```

Default Constructors

In most object-oriented languages, when an object is created its constructor is *always* called. But what if we do not write a constructor in the class that the object is created from? If you do not write a constructor in a class, most languages automatically provide one when the class is compiled. The constructor that is automatically provided is usually known as the *default constructor*. The actions performed by the default constructor vary from one language to another. Typically, the default constructor assigns default starting values to the object's fields.

 Checkpoint

14.5   You hear someone make the following comment: "A blueprint is a design for a house. A carpenter can use the blueprint to build the house. If the carpenter wishes, he or she can build several identical houses from the same blueprint." Think of this as a metaphor for classes and objects. Does the blueprint represent a class, or does it represent an object?

14.6   In this chapter, we use the metaphor of a cookie cutter and cookies that are made from the cookie cutter to describe classes and objects. In this metaphor, are objects the cookie cutter, or the cookies?

14.7   What is an access specifier?

14.8   What access specifier is commonly used with a class's fields?

14.9   When a class variable is said to reference an object, what is actually stored in the class variable?

14.10 What does the New key word do?

14.11 What is an accessor? What is a mutator?

14.12 What is a constructor? When does a constructor execute?

14.13 What is a default constructor?

 ## 14.3 Using the Unified Modeling Language to Design Classes

CONCEPT: The Unified Modeling Language (UML) is a standard way of drawing diagrams that describe object-oriented systems.

When designing a class, it is often helpful to draw a UML diagram. UML stands for Unified Modeling Language. It provides a set of standard diagrams for graphically depicting object-oriented systems. Figure 14-10 shows the general layout of a UML diagram for a class. Notice that the diagram is a box that is divided into three sections. The top section is where you write the name of the class. The middle section holds a list of the class's fields. The bottom section holds a list of the class's methods.

Figure 14-10 General layout of a UML diagram for a class

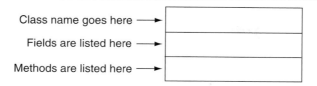

Following this layout, Figure 14-11 shows a simplified UML diagram for our `CellPhone` class.

Figure 14-11 Simplified UML diagram for the `CellPhone` class

CellPhone
manufacturer modelNumber retailPrice
CellPhone( ) setManufacturer( ) setModelNumber( ) setRetailPrice( ) getManufacturer( ) getModelNumber( ) getRetailPrice( )

Data Type and Method Parameter Notation

The UML diagram in Figure 14-11 shows only basic information about the `CellPhone` class. It does not show details such as data types and the method's parameters. To indicate the data type of a field, place a colon followed by the name of the data type after the name of the field. For example, the `manufacturer` field in the `CellPhone` class is a `String`. It could be listed in the UML diagram as follows:

```
manufacturer : String
```

The return type of a method can be listed in the same manner. After the method's name, place a colon followed by the return type. The `CellPhone` class's `getRetailPrice` method returns a `Real`, so it could be listed in the UML diagram as follows:

```
getRetailPrice() : Real
```

Parameter variables and their data types may be listed inside a method's parentheses. For example, the `CellPhone` class's `setManufacturer` method has a `String` parameter named `manufact`, so it could be listed in the UML diagram as follows:

```
setManufacturer(manufact : String)
```

Figure 14-12 shows the UML diagram for the `CellPhone` class with data type and parameter notation added to it.

Figure 14-12 UML diagram for the `CellPhone` class with data type and parameter notation

CellPhone
manufacturer : String modelNumber : String retailPrice : Real
CellPhone(manufact : String,   modelNum : String, retail : Real) setManufacturer(manufact : String) setModelNumber(modNum : String) setRetailPrice(retail : Real) getManufacturer( ) : String getModelNumber( ) : String getRetailPrice( ) : Real

Access Specification Notation

The UML diagrams in Figures 14-11 and 14-12 list all of the fields and methods in the `CellPhone` class but do not indicate which are private and which are public. In a UML diagram, you have the option to place a – character before a field or method name to indicate that it is private, or a + character to indicate that it is public. Figure 14-13 shows the UML diagram modified to include this notation.

Figure 14-13 UML diagram for the `CellPhone` class with access specification notation

CellPhone
– manufacturer : String – modelNumber : String – retailPrice : Real
+ CellPhone(manufact : String,   modelNum : String, retail : Real) + setManufacturer(manufact : String) + setModelNumber(modNum : String) + setRetailPrice(retail : Real) + getManufacturer( ) : String + getModelNumber( ) : String + getRetailPrice( ) : Real

 **Checkpoint**

14.14 The typical UML diagram for a class has three sections. What appears in these three sections?

14.15 Suppose a class has a field named `description`. The field's data type is `String`. How would you indicate the field's data type in a UML diagram?

14.16 What symbols do you use in a UML diagram to indicate private and public access specification?

14.4 Finding the Classes and Their Responsibilities in a Problem

CONCEPT: One of the first steps when designing an object-oriented program is finding the classes that should be created and determining those classes' responsibilities in the program.

So far, you have learned the basics of writing a class, creating an object from the class, and using the object to perform operations. Although this knowledge is necessary to create an object-oriented application, it is not the first step. The first step is to analyze the problem that you are trying to solve and determine the classes that you will need. The following two *In the Spotlight* sections lead you through a simple process for finding the classes in a problem and determining their responsibilities.

In the Spotlight:
Finding the Classes in a Problem

The owner of Joe's Automotive Shop has asked you to design a program that will print service quotes for customers. You decide to use an object-oriented approach to design the program. One of your first tasks is to identify the classes that you will need to create. In many cases, this means identifying the different types of real-world objects that are present in the problem, and then creating classes for those types of objects within your program.

Over the years, software professionals have developed numerous techniques for finding the classes in a given problem. One simple and popular technique involves the following steps:

1. Get a written description of the problem domain.
2. Identify all the nouns (including pronouns and noun phrases) in the description. Each of these is a potential class.
3. Refine the list to include only the classes that are relevant to the problem.

Let's take a closer look at each of these steps.

Writing a Description of the Problem Domain

The *problem domain* is the set of real-world objects, parties, and major events related to the problem. If you adequately understand the nature of the problem you are trying to solve, you can write a description of the problem domain yourself. If you do not thoroughly understand the nature of the problem, you should have an expert write the description for you.

A problem domain description should include any or all of the following:

- Physical objects, such as vehicles, machines, or products
- Roles played by people, such as manager, employee, customer, teacher, student, and so on

- The results of a business event, such as a customer order, or in this case a service quote
- Recordkeeping items, such as customer histories and payroll records

Here is a description that was written by Joe, the owner of Joe's Automotive Shop:

> Joe's Automotive Shop services foreign cars, and specializes in servicing cars made by Mercedes, Porsche, and BMW. When a customer brings a car to the shop, the manager gets the customer's name, address, and telephone number. The manager then determines the make, model, and year of the car, and gives the customer a service quote. The service quote shows the estimated parts charges, estimated labor charges, sales tax, and total estimated charges.

Identify All of the Nouns

The next step is to identify all of the nouns and noun phrases in the problem description. (If the description contains pronouns, include them too.) Here's another look at the previous problem domain description that was written by Joe. This time the nouns and noun phrases appear in bold.

> **Joe's Automotive Shop** services **foreign cars**, and specializes in servicing **cars** made by **Mercedes, Porsche,** and **BMW**. When a **customer** brings a **car** to the **shop**, the **manager** gets the **customer's name, address,** and **telephone number**. The **manager** then determines the **make, model,** and **year** of the **car**, and gives the **customer** a **service quote**. The **service quote** shows the **estimated parts charges, estimated labor charges, sales tax,** and **total estimated charges**.

Notice that some of the nouns are repeated. The following list shows all of the nouns without duplicates:

address	Mercedes
BMW	model
car	name
cars	Porsche
customer	sales tax
estimated labor charges	service quote
estimated parts charges	shop
foreign cars	telephone number
Joe's Automotive Shop	total estimated charges
make	year
manager	

Refining the List of Nouns

The nouns that appear in the problem description are merely candidates to become classes. It might not be necessary to make classes for all of them. The next step is to refine the list to include only the classes that are necessary to solve the particular problem at hand. We will look at the common reasons that a noun can be eliminated from the list of potential classes.

1. **Some of the nouns really mean the same thing.**

   In this example, the following sets of nouns refer to the same thing:

- **cars** and **foreign cars**
  Both of these refer to the general concept of a car.
- **Joe's Automotive Shop** and **shop**
  Both of these refer to the company "Joe's Automotive Shop."

We can settle on a single class for each of these. In this example, we will arbitrarily eliminate **foreign cars** from the list, and use the word **cars**. Likewise, we will eliminate **Joe's Automotive Shop** from the list and use the word **shop**. The updated list of potential classes is as follows:

address	Mercedes
BMW	model
car	name
cars	Porsche
customer	sales tax
estimated labor charges	service quote
estimated parts charges	shop
~~foreign cars~~	telephone number
~~Joe's Automotive Shop~~	total estimated charges
make	year
manager	

Because **cars** and **foreign cars** mean the same thing in this problem, we have eliminated **foreign cars**. Also, because **Joe's Automotive Shop** and **shop** mean the same thing, we have eliminated **Joe's Automotive Shop**.

2. **Some nouns might represent items that we do not need to be concerned with in order to solve the problem.**

A quick review of the problem description reminds us of what our application should do: print a service quote. In this example, we can eliminate two unnecessary classes from the list:

- We can cross **shop** off the list because our application only needs to be concerned with individual service quotes. It doesn't need to work with or determine any company-wide information. If the problem description asked us to keep a total of all the service quotes, then it would make sense to have a class for the shop.
- We will not need a class for the **manager** because the problem statement does not direct us to process any information about the manager. If there were multiple shop managers, and the problem description had asked us to record which manager generated each service quote, then it would make sense to have a class for the manager.

The updated list of potential classes at this point is as follows:

address	estimated parts charges
BMW	~~foreign cars~~
car	~~Joe's Automotive Shop~~
cars	make
customer	~~manager~~
estimated labor charges	Mercedes

model	~~shop~~
name	telephone number
Porsche	total estimated charges
sales tax	year
service quote	

Our problem description does not direct us to process any information about the **shop,** or any information about the **manager,** so we have eliminated those from the list.

3. **Some of the nouns might represent objects, not classes.**

   We can eliminate **Mercedes, Porsche,** and **BMW** as classes because, in this example, they all represent specific cars, and can be considered instances of the cars class. Also, we can eliminate the word **car** from the list. In the description, it refers to a specific car brought to the shop by a customer. Therefore, it would also represent an instance of the **cars** class. At this point the updated list of potential classes is as follows:

address	~~Mercedes~~
~~BMW~~	model
~~car~~	name
cars	~~Porsche~~
customer	sales tax
estimated labor charges	service quote
estimated parts charges	~~shop~~
~~foreign cars~~	telephone number
~~Joe's Automotive Shop~~	total estimated charges
~~manager~~	year
make	

We have eliminated **Mercedes, Porsche, BMW,** and **car** because they are all instances of the cars class. That means that these nouns identify objects, not classes.

> **TIP:** Some object-oriented designers note whether a noun is plural or singular. Sometimes a plural noun will indicate a class and a singular noun will indicate an object.

4. **Some of the nouns might represent simple values that can be stored in a regular variable and do not require a class.**

   Remember, a class contains fields and methods. Fields are related items that are stored within an object of the class, and define the object's state. Methods are actions or behaviors that may be performed by an object of the class. If a noun represents a type of item that would not have any identifiable fields or methods, then it can probably be eliminated from the list. To help determine whether a noun represents an item that would have fields and methods, ask the following questions:

- Would you use a group of related values to represent the item's state?
- Are there any obvious actions to be performed by the item?

If the answers to both of these questions are no, then the noun probably represents a value that can be stored in a regular variable. If we apply this test to each of the nouns that remain in our list, we can conclude that the following are probably not classes: **address, estimated labor charges, estimated parts charges, make, model, name, sales tax, telephone number, total estimated charges,** and **year.** These are all simple string or numeric values that can be stored in variables. The following is the updated list of potential classes:

~~address~~	~~Mercedes~~
~~BMW~~	~~model~~
~~car~~	~~name~~
cars	~~Porsche~~
customer	~~sales tax~~
~~estimated labor charges~~	service quote
~~estimated parts charges~~	~~shop~~
~~foreign cars~~	~~telephone number~~
~~Joe's Automotive Shop~~	~~total estimated charges~~
~~make~~	~~year~~
~~manager~~	

We have eliminated **address, estimated labor charges, estimated parts charges, make, model, name, sales tax, telephone number, total estimated charges,** and **year** as classes because they represent simple values that can be stored in primitive variables.

As you can see from the list, we have eliminated everything except **cars, customer,** and **service quote.** This means that in our application, we will need classes to represent cars, customers, and service quotes. In the next *In the Spotlight* section, we will write a `Car` class, a `Customer` class, and a `ServiceQuote` class.

In the Spotlight:
Determining Class Responsibilities

In the previous *In the Spotlight* section, we examined the problem domain description for the Joe's Automotive Shop program. We also identified the classes that we will need, which are `Car`, `Customer`, and `ServiceQuote`. The next step is to determine those classes' responsibilities. A class's *responsibilities* are as follows:

- The things that the class is responsible for knowing
- The actions that the class is responsible for doing

When you have identified the things that a class is responsible for knowing, then you have identified the values that will be stored in fields. Likewise, when you have identified the actions that a class is responsible for doing, you have identified its methods.

It is often helpful to ask the questions "In this program, what must the class know? What must the class do?" The first place to look for the answers is in the description of the problem domain. Many of the things that a class must know and do will be mentioned. Some class responsibilities, however, might not be directly mentioned in the problem domain, so brainstorming is often required. Let's apply this methodology to the classes we previously identified from our problem domain.

The Customer Class

In this program, what must the Customer class know? The problem domain description directly mentions the following items:

- The customer's name
- The customer's address
- The customer's telephone number

These are all values that can be represented as strings and stored in the class's fields. The Customer class can potentially know many other things. One mistake that can be made at this point is to identify too many things that an object is responsible for knowing. In some programs, a Customer class might know the customer's email address. This particular problem domain does not mention that the customer's email address is used for any purpose, so we should not include it as a responsibility.

Now, let's identify the class's methods. In this program, what must the Customer class do? The following are the only obvious actions:

- Create an object of the Customer class
- Set and get the customer's name
- Set and get the customer's address
- Set and get the customer's telephone number

From this list, we can see that the Customer class will have a constructor, as well as accessor and mutator methods for each of its fields. Figure 14-14 shows a UML diagram for the Customer class. Class Listing 14-5 shows the pseudocode for a class definition.

Figure 14-14 UML diagram for the Customer class

Customer
− name : String − address : String − phone : String
+ Customer(n : String, a : String,   p : String) + setName(n : String) + setAddress(a : String) + setPhone(p : String) + getName( ) : String + getAddress( ) : String + getPhone( ) : String

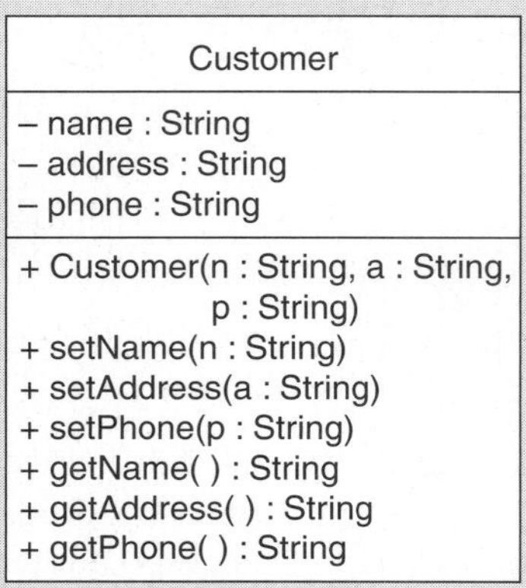

Class Listing 14-5

```
 1 Class Customer
 2    // Fields
 3    Private String name
 4    Private String address
 5    Private String phone
 6
 7    // Constructor
 8    Public Module Customer(String n, String a,
 9                               String p)
10       Set name = n
11       Set address = a
12       Set phone = p
13    End Module
14
15    // Mutators
16    Public Module setName(String n)
17       Set name = n
18    End Module
19
20    Public Module setAddress(String a)
21       Set address = a
22    End Module
23
24    Public Module setPhone(String p)
25       Set phone = p
26    End Module
27
28    // Accessors
29    Public Function String getName()
30       Return name
31    End Function
32
33    Public Function String getAddress()
34       Return address
35    End Function
36
37    Public Function String getPhone()
38       Return phone
39    End Function
40 End Class
```

The Car Class

In this program, what must an object of the Car class know? The following items are all attributes of a car, and are mentioned in the problem domain:

- the car's make
- the car's model
- the car's year

Now let's identify the class's methods. In this program, what must the Car class do? Once again, the only obvious actions are the standard set of methods that we will find in most classes (constructors, accessors, and mutators). Specifically, the actions are as follows:

- create an object of the Car class
- set and get the car's make
- set and get the car's model
- set and get the car's year

Figure 14-15 shows a UML diagram for the Car class, and Class Listing 14-6 shows the pseudocode for a class definition.

Figure 14-15 UML diagram for the Car class

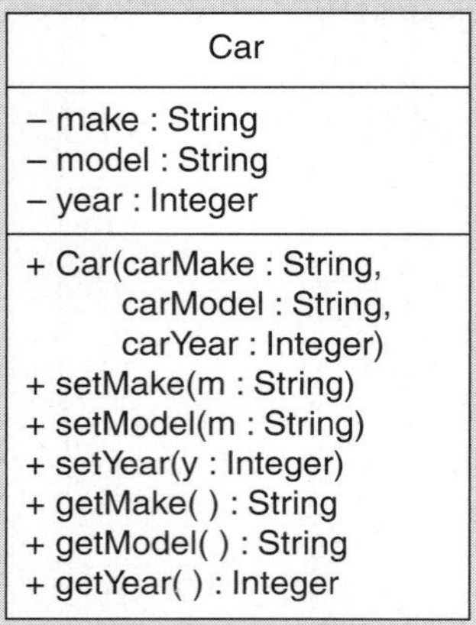

```
                    Car

        – make : String
        – model : String
        – year : Integer

        + Car(carMake : String,
              carModel : String,
              carYear : Integer)
        + setMake(m : String)
        + setModel(m : String)
        + setYear(y : Integer)
        + getMake( ) : String
        + getModel( ) : String
        + getYear( ) : Integer
```

Class Listing 14-6

```
 1 Class Car
 2    // Fields
 3    Private String make
 4    Private String model
 5    Private Integer year
 6
 7    // Constructor
 8    Public Module Car(String carMake,
 9        String carModel, Integer carYear)
10      Set make = carMake
11      Set model = carModel
12      Set year = carYear
13    End Module
14
15    // Mutators
16    Public Module setMake(String m)
17      Set make = m
18    End Module
19
20    Public Module setModel(String m)
21      Set model = m
22    End Module
```

```
23
24    Public Module setYear(Integer y)
25       Set year = y
26    End Module
27
28    // Accessors
29    Public Function String getMake()
30       Return make
31    End Function
32
33    Public Function String getModel()
34       Return model
35    End Function
36
37    Public Function Integer getYear()
38       Return year
39    End Function
40 End Class
```

The `ServiceQuote` Class

In this program, what must an object of the `ServiceQuote` class know? The problem domain mentions the following items:

- the estimated parts charges
- the estimated labor charges
- the sales tax
- the total estimated charges

Careful thought and a little brainstorming will reveal that two of these items are the results of calculations: sales tax and total estimated charges. These items are dependent on the values of the estimated parts and labor charges. Instead of storing these values in fields, we will provide methods that calculate these values and return them. (In a moment we will explain why we take this approach.)

The other methods that we will need for this class are a constructor and the accessors and mutators for the estimated parts charges and estimated labor charges fields. Figure 14-16 shows a UML diagram for the `ServiceQuote` class and Class Listing 14-7 shows the pseudocode for a class definition.

Figure 14-16 UML diagram for the `ServiceQuote` class

```
                    ServiceQuote
-------------------------------------------------
 – partsCharges : Real
 – laborCharges : Real
-------------------------------------------------
 + ServiceQuote(pc : Real, lc : Real)
 + setPartsCharges(pc : Real)
 + setLaborCharges(lc : Real)
 + getPartsCharges( ) : Real
 + getLaborCharges( ) : Real
 + getSalesTax(taxRate : Real) : Real
 + getTotalCharges( ) : Real
```

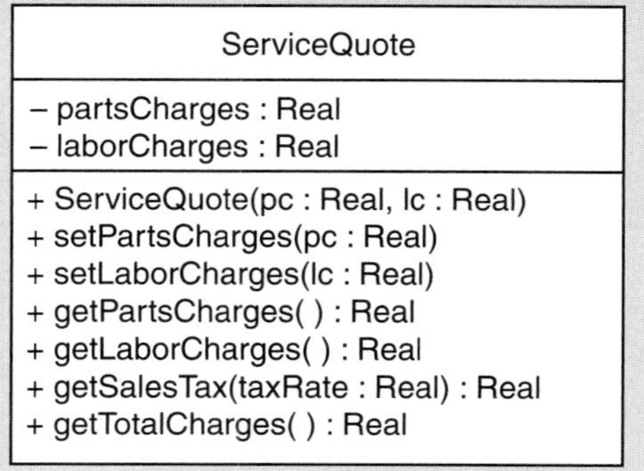

Class Listing 14-7

```
 1 Class ServiceQuote
 2    // Fields
 3    Private Real partsCharges
 4    Private Real laborCharges
 5
 6    // Constructor
 7    Public Module ServiceQuote(Real pc, Real lc)
 8       Set partsCharges = pc
 9       Set laborCharges = lc
10    End Module
11
12    // Mutators
13    Public Module setPartsCharges(Real pc)
14       Set partsCharges = pc
15    End Module
16
17    Public Module setLaborCharges(Real lc)
18       Set laborCharges = lc
19    End Module
20
21    // Accessors
22    Public Function Real getPartsCharges()
23       Return partsCharges
24    End Function
25
26    Public Function Real getLaborCharges()
27       Return laborCharges
28    End Function
29
30    Public Function Real getSalesTax(Real taxRate)
31       // Sales tax is charged only on parts.
32       Return partsCharges * taxRate
33    End Function
34
35    Public Function Real getTotalCharges(Real taxRate)
36       Return partsCharges + laborCharges + getSalesTax(taxRate)
37    End Function
38 End Class
```

First, notice that the getSalesTax method, in lines 30 through 33, accepts a Real argument for the tax rate. The method returns the amount of sales tax in line 32, which is the result of a calculation.

The getTotalCharges method, in lines 35 through 37, returns the total charges estimate. The value that is returned by this method is the result of a calculation. The value that is returned in line 36 is the result of the expression partsCharges + laborCharges + getSalesTax(taxRate). Notice that this expression calls one of the object's own methods: getSalesTax.

Avoiding Stale Data

In the ServiceQuote class, the getPartsCharges and getLaborCharges methods return the values stored in fields, but the getSalesTax and getTotalCharges methods return the results of calculations. You might be wondering why the sales tax and the total charges are not stored in fields, like the parts charges and labor charges. These values are not stored in fields because they could potentially become *stale*. When the value of an item is dependent on other data and that item is not updated when the other data is changed, it is said that the item has become stale. If the sales tax and total charges were stored in fields, the values of those fields would become incorrect as soon as the partsCharges or laborCharges fields changed.

When designing a class, you should take care not to store in a field any calculated data that can potentially become stale. Instead, provide a method that returns the result of the calculation.

 Checkpoint

14.17 What is a problem domain description?

14.18 What technique was described in this section for finding the classes in a particular problem?

14.19 What are classes' responsibilities?

14.20 What causes an item of data to become stale?

14.5 Inheritance

CONCEPT: Inheritance allows a new class to extend an existing class. The new class inherits the members of the class it extends.

Generalization and Specialization

In the real world, you can find many objects that are specialized versions of other more general objects. For example, the term "insect" describes a very general type of creature with numerous characteristics. Because grasshoppers and bumblebees are insects, they have all the general characteristics of an insect. In addition, they have special characteristics of their own. For example, the grasshopper has its jumping ability, and the bumblebee has its stinger. Grasshoppers and bumblebees are specialized versions of an insect. This is illustrated in Figure 14-17.

Figure 14-17 Bumblebees and grasshoppers are specialized versions of an insect

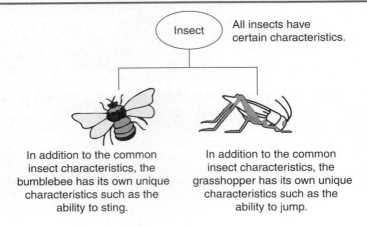

In addition to the common insect characteristics, the bumblebee has its own unique characteristics such as the ability to sting.

In addition to the common insect characteristics, the grasshopper has its own unique characteristics such as the ability to jump.

Inheritance and the "Is a" Relationship

When one object is a specialized version of another object, there is an "is a" relationship between them. For example, a grasshopper is an insect. Here are a few other examples of the "is a" relationship:

- A poodle is a dog.
- A car is a vehicle.
- A flower is a plant.
- A rectangle is a shape.
- A football player is an athlete.

When an "is a" relationship exists between objects, it means that the specialized object has all of the characteristics of the general object, plus additional characteristics that make it special. In object-oriented programming, inheritance is used to create an "is a" relationship among classes. This allows you to extend the capabilities of a class by creating another class that is a specialized version of it.

Inheritance involves a superclass and a subclass. The *superclass* is the general class and the *subclass* is the specialized class. You can think of the subclass as an extended version of the superclass. The subclass inherits fields and methods from the superclass without any of them having to be rewritten. Furthermore, new fields and methods may be added to the subclass, and that is what makes it a specialized version of the superclass.

NOTE: Superclasses are also called *base classes,* and subclasses are also called *derived classes*. Either set of terms is correct. For consistency, this text will use the terms superclass and subclass.

Let's look at an example of how inheritance can be used. Most teachers assign various graded activities for their students to complete. A graded activity can be given a numeric score such as 70, 85, 90, and so on, and a letter grade such as A, B, C, D, or F.

Figure 14-18 shows a UML diagram for the GradedActivity class, which is designed to hold the numeric score of a graded activity. The setScore method sets a numeric score, and the getScore method returns the numeric score. The getGrade method returns the letter grade that corresponds to the numeric score. Class Listing 14-8 shows the pseudocode for the class. The pseudocode in Program 14-4 demonstrates how the class works.

Figure 14-18 UML diagram for the GradedActivity class

GradedActivity
− score : Real
+ setScore(s : Real) + getScore( ) : Real + getGrade( ) : String

Class Listing 14-8

```
1 Class GradedActivity
2    // The score field holds a numeric score.
3    Private Real score
4
5    // Mutator
6    Public Module setScore(Real s)
7       Set score = s
8    End Module
9
10   // Accessor
11   Public Function Real getScore()
12      Return score
13   End Function
14
15   // getGrade method
16   Public Function String getGrade()
17      // Local variable to hold a grade.
18      Declare String grade
19
20      // Determine the grade.
21      If score >= 90 Then
22         Set grade = "A"
23      Else If score >= 80 Then
24         Set grade = "B"
25      Else If score >= 70 Then
26         Set grade = "C"
27      Else If score >= 60 Then
28         Set grade = "D"
29      Else
30         Set grade = "F"
31      End If
32
```

```
33          // Return the grade.
34          Return grade
35     End Function
36 End Class
```

Program 14-4

```
1 Module main()
2     // A variable to hold a test score.
3     Declare Real testScore
4
5     // A class variable to reference a
6     // GradedActivity object.
7     Declare GradedActivity test
8
9     // Create a GradedActivity object.
10    Set test = New GradedActivity()
11
12    // Get a test score from the user.
13    Display "Enter a numeric test score."
14    Input testScore
15
16    // Store the test score in the object.
17    test.setScore(testScore)
18
19    // Display the grade for the object.
20    Display "The grade for that test is ",
21            test.getGrade()
22 End Module
```

Program Output (with Input Shown in Bold)

```
Enter a numeric test score.
89 [Enter]
The grade for that test is B
```

Program Output (with Input Shown in Bold)

```
Enter a numeric test score.
75 [Enter]
The grade for that test is C
```

The GradedActivity class represents the general characteristics of a student's graded activity. Many different types of graded activities exist, however, such as quizzes, midterm exams, final exams, lab reports, essays, and so on. Because the numeric scores might be determined differently for each of these graded activities, we can create subclasses to handle each one. For example, we could create a FinalExam class that would be a subclass of the GradedActivity class. Figure 14-19 shows the UML diagram for such a class, and Class Listing 14-9 shows its definition in pseudocode. The class has fields for the number of questions on the exam (numQuestions), the number of points each question is worth (pointsEach), and the number of questions missed by the student (numMissed).

Figure 14-19 UML diagram for the `FinalExam` class

FinalExam
− numQuestions : Integer − pointsEach : Real − numMissed : Integer
+ FinalExam(questions : Integer,   missed : Integer) + getPointsEach( ) : Real + getNumMissed( ) : Integer

Class Listing 14-9

```
 1 Class FinalExam Extends GradedActivity
 2     // Fields
 3     Private Integer numQuestions
 4     Private Real pointsEach
 5     Private Integer numMissed
 6
 7     // The constructor sets the number of
 8     // questions on the exam and the number
 9     // of questions missed.
10     Public Module FinalExam(Integer questions,
11                             Integer missed)
12        // Local variable to hold the numeric score.
13        Declare Real numericScore
14
15        // Set the numQuestions and numMissed fields.
16        Set numQuestions = questions
17        Set numMissed = missed
18
19        // Calculate the points for each question
20        // and the numeric score for this exam.
21        Set pointsEach = 100.0 / questions
22        Set numericScore = 100.0 - (missed * pointsEach)
23
24        // Call the inherited setScore method to
25        // set the numeric score.
26        Call setScore(numericScore)
27     End Module
28
29     // Accessors
30     Public Function Real getPointsEach()
31         Return pointsEach
32      End Function
33
34      Public Function Integer getNumMissed()
35         Return numMissed
36      End Function
37 End Class
```

Notice that the first line of the FinalExam class declaration uses the Extends key word, which indicates that this class extends another class (a superclass). The name of the superclass is listed after the word extends. So, this line indicates that FinalExam is the name of the class being declared and GradedActivity is the name of the superclass it extends.

If we want to express the relationship between the two classes, we can say that a FinalExam is a GradedActivity. Because the FinalExam class extends the GradedActivity class, it inherits all of the public members of the GradedActivity class. Here is a list of the members of the FinalExam class:

Fields:

numQuestions	Declared in the FinalExam class
pointsEach	Declared in the FinalExam class
numMissed	Declared in the FinalExam class

Methods:

Constructor	Declared in the FinalExam class
getPointsEach	Declared in the FinalExam class
getNumMissed	Declared in the FinalExam class
setScore	Inherited from the GradedActivity class
getScore	Inherited from the GradedActivity class
getGrade	Inherited from the GradedActivity class

Notice that the GradedActivity class's score field is not listed among the members of the FinalExam class. That is because the score field is private. In most languages, private members of the superclass cannot be accessed by the subclass, so technically speaking, they are not inherited. When an object of the subclass is created, the private members of the superclass exist in memory, but only methods in the superclass can access them. They are truly private to the superclass.

To see how inheritance works in this example, let's take a closer look at the FinalExam constructor in lines 10 through 27. The constructor accepts two arguments: the number of test questions on the exam, and the number of questions missed by the student. In lines 16 and 17 these values are assigned to the numQuestions and numMissed fields. Then, in lines 21 and 22, the number of points for each question and the numeric test score are calculated. In line 26, the last statement in the constructor reads as follows:

```
Call setScore(numericScore)
```

This is a call to the setScore method, which is inherited from the GradedActivity class. Although the FinalExam constructor cannot directly access the score field (because it is declared private in the GradedActivity class), it can call the setScore method to store a value in the score field.

The pseudocode in Program 14-5 demonstrates the FinalExam class.

Program 14-5

```
1 Module main()
2    // Variables to hold user input.
3    Declare Integer questions, missed
```

```
 4
 5     // Class variable to reference a FinalExam object.
 6     Declare FinalExam exam
 7
 8     // Prompt the user for the number of questions
 9     // on the exam.
10     Display "Enter the number of questions on the exam."
11     Input questions
12
13     // Prompt the user for the number of questions
14     // missed by the student.
15     Display "Enter the number of questions that the ",
16             "student missed."
17     Input missed
18
19     // Create a FinalExam object.
20     Set exam = New FinalExam(questions, missed)
21
22     // Display the test results.
23     Display "Each question on the exam counts ",
24             exam.getPointsEach(), " points."
25     Display "The exam score is ", exam.getScore()
26     Display "The exam grade is ", exam.getGrade()
27 End Module
```

Program Output (with Input Shown in Bold)

```
Enter the number of questions on the exam.
20 [Enter]
Enter the number of questions that the student missed.
3 [Enter]
Each question on the exam counts 5 points.
The exam score is 85
The exam grade is B
```

In line 20, the following statement creates an instance of the `FinalExam` class and assigns its address to the exam variable:

```
Set exam = New FinalExam(questions, missed)
```

When a `FinalExam` object is created in memory, not only does it have the members declared in the `FinalExam` class, but also it has the non-private members declared in the `GradedActivity` class. Notice in lines 25 and 26, shown here, that two public methods of the `GradedActivity` class, `getScore` and `getGrade`, are directly called with the exam object:

```
Display "The exam score is ", exam.getScore()
Display "The exam grade is ", exam.getGrade()
```

When a subclass extends a superclass, the public members of the superclass become public members of the subclass. In this program, the `getScore` and `getGrade` methods can be called with the exam object because they are public members of the object's superclass.

Inheritance in UML Diagrams

You show inheritance in a UML diagram by connecting two classes with a line that has an open arrowhead at one end. The arrowhead points to the superclass. Figure 14-20 is a UML diagram showing the relationship between the `GradedActivity` and `FinalExam` classes.

Figure 14-20 UML diagram showing inheritance

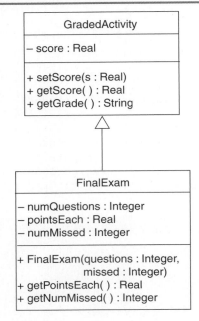

Inheritance Does Not Work in Reverse

In an inheritance relationship, the subclass inherits members from the superclass, not the other way around. This means it is not possible for a superclass to call a subclass's methods. For example, if we create a `GradedActivity` object, it cannot call the `getPointsEach` or the `getNumMissed` methods because they are members of the `FinalExam` class.

 Checkpoint

14.21 In this section, we discussed superclasses and subclasses. Which is the general class and which is the specialized class?

14.22 What does it mean to say there is an "is a" relationship between two objects?

14.23 What does a subclass inherit from its superclass?

14.24 Look at the following pseudocode, which is the first line of a class definition. What is the name of the superclass? What is the name of the subclass?

```
Class Canary Extends Bird
```

14.6 Polymorphism

CONCEPT: Polymorphism allows you to create methods with the same name in different classes (that are related through inheritance) and gives you the ability to call the correct method depending on the type of object that is used to call it.

The term *polymorphism* refers to an object's ability to take different forms. It is a powerful feature of object-oriented programming. In this section, we will look at two essential ingredients of polymorphic behavior:

1. The ability to define a method in a superclass, and then define a method with the same name in a subclass. When a subclass method has the same name as a superclass method, it is often said that the subclass method *overrides* the superclass method.
2. The ability to declare a class variable of the superclass type, and then use that variable to reference objects of either the superclass or the subclass types.

The best way to describe polymorphism is to demonstrate it, so let's look at a simple example. Class Listing 14-10 shows pseudocode for a class named Animal.

Class Listing 14-10

```
 1 Class Animal
 2    // showSpecies method
 3    Public Module showSpecies()
 4       Display "I'm just a regular animal."
 5    End Module
 6
 7    // makeSound method
 8    Public Module makeSound()
 9       Display "Grrrrr"
10    End Module
11 End Class
```

The class has two methods: showSpecies and makeSound. Here is an example of pseudocode that creates an instance of the class and calls the methods:

```
Declare Animal myAnimal
Set myAnimal = New Animal()
Call myAnimal.showSpecies()
Call myAnimal.makeSound()
```

If this were actual code, it would display the following:

```
I'm just a regular animal.
Grrrrr
```

Next, look at Class Listing 14-11, which shows the pseudocode for the Dog class. The Dog class is a subclass of the Animal class.

Class Listing 14-11

```
 1 Class Dog Extends Animal
 2    // showSpecies method
 3    Public Module showSpecies()
 4       Display "I'm a dog."
 5    End Module
 6
 7    // makeSound method
 8    Public Module makeSound()
 9       Display "Woof! Woof!"
10    End Module
11 End Class
```

Even though the Dog class inherits the showSpecies and makeSound methods that are in the Animal class, those methods are not adequate for the Dog class. So, the Dog class has its own showSpecies and makeSound methods, which display messages that are more appropriate for a dog. We say that the showSpecies and makeSound methods in the Dog class *override* the showSpecies and makeSound methods in the Animal class. Here is an example of pseudocode that creates an instance of the Dog class and calls the methods:

```
Declare Dog myDog
Set myDog = New Dog()
Call myDog.showSpecies()
Call myDog.makeSound()
```

If this were actual code, it would display the following:

```
I'm a dog.
Woof! Woof!
```

Class Listing 14-12 shows pseudocode for the Cat class, which is also a subclass of the Animal class.

Class Listing 14-12

```
 1 Class Cat Extends Animal
 2    // showSpecies method
 3    Public Module showSpecies()
 4       Display "I'm a cat."
 5    End Module
 6
 7    // makeSound method
 8    Public Module makeSound()
 9       Display "Meow"
10    End Module
11 End Class
```

The Cat class also has methods named showSpecies and makeSound. Here is an example of pseudocode that creates an instance of the Cat class and calls the methods:

```
Declare Cat myCat
Set myCat = New Cat()
Call myCat.showSpecies()
Call myCat.makeSound()
```

If this were actual code, it would display the following:

```
I'm a cat.
Meow
```

Because of the "is a" relationship between a superclass and a subclass, an object of the Dog class is not just a Dog object. It is also an Animal object. (A dog is an animal.) Because of this relationship, we can use an Animal class variable to reference a Dog object. For example, look at the following pseudocode:

```
Declare Animal myAnimal
Set myAnimal = New Dog()
Call myAnimal.showSpecies()
Call myAnimal.makeSound()
```

The first statement declares myAnimal as an Animal variable. The second statement creates a Dog object and stores the object's address in the myAnimal variable. In most object-oriented languages this type of assignment is perfectly legal because a Dog object is also an Animal object. The third and fourth statements use the myAnimal object to call the showSpecies and makeSound methods. If this pseudocode were actual code, it would display the following in most programming languages:

```
I'm a dog.
Woof! Woof!
```

Similarly, we can use an Animal variable to reference a Cat object, as shown here:

```
Declare Animal myAnimal
Set myAnimal = New Cat()
Call myAnimal.showSpecies()
Call myAnimal.makeSound()
```

If this pseudocode were actual code, it would display the following in most programming languages:

```
I'm a cat.
Meow
```

This aspect of polymorphism gives us a great deal of flexibility when designing programs. For example, look at the following module:

```
Module showAnimalInfo(Animal creature)
    Call creature.showSpecies()
    Call creature.makeSound()
End Module
```

This module displays information about an animal. Because it has an Animal variable as its parameter, you can pass an Animal object to the module when you call it. The module then calls the object's showSpecies method and makeSound method.

The showAnimalInfo module works with an Animal object, but what if you also need modules that display information about Dog objects and Cat objects? Do you need to write additional modules for each of these types? Because of polymorphism, the answer is *no*. In addition to Animal objects, you can also pass Dog objects or Cat objects as arguments to the `showAnimalInfo` module previously shown. The pseudocode in Program 14-6 demonstrates this.

Program 14-6

```
1 Module main()
2     // Declare three class variables.
3     Declare Animal myAnimal
4     Declare Dog myDog
5     Declare Cat myCat
6
7     // Create an Animal object, a Dog object,
8     // and a Cat object.
9     Set myAnimal = New Animal()
10    Set myDog = New Dog()
11    Set myCat = New Cat()
12
13    // Show info about an animal.
14    Display "Here is info about an animal."
15    showAnimalInfo(myAnimal)
16    Display
17
18    // Show info about a dog.
19    Display "Here is info about a dog."
20    showAnimalInfo(myDog)
21    Display
22
23    // Show info about a cat.
24    Display "Here is info about a cat."
25    showAnimalInfo(myCat)
26 End Module
27
28 // The showAnimalInfo module accepts an Animal
29 // object as an argument and displays information
30 // about it.
31 Module showAnimalInfo(Animal creature)
32    Call creature.showSpecies()
33    Call creature.makeSound()
34 End Module
```

Program Output

```
Here is info about an animal.
I'm just a regular animal.
Grrrrr

Here is info about a dog.
I'm a dog.
Woof! Woof!

Here is info about a cat.
I'm a cat.
Meow
```

Although these examples are very simple, polymorphism has many practical uses. For example, a university's software processes a lot of data about students, so it might use a `Student` class. One of the methods in the `Student` class might be called `getFees`. This method would return the amount of a typical student's fees for a semester.

In addition, the software might have a `BiologyStudent` class as a subclass of the `Student` class (because a biology student *is a* student). Because of additional lab charges, a biology student's fees are usually more than those of the typical student. So, the `BiologyStudent` class would have its own `getFees` method that returns the fees for a biology student.

 **Checkpoint**

14.25 Look at the following pseudocode class definitions:

```
Class Vegetable
    Public Module message()
        Display "I'm a vegetable."
    End Module
End Class
Class Potato Extends Vegetable
    Public Module message()
        Display "I'm a potato."
    End Module
End Class
```

Given these class definitions, what will the following pseudocode display?

```
Declare Vegetable v
Declare Potato p
Set v = New Potato()
Set p = New Potato()
Call v.message()
Call p.message()
```

Review Questions

Multiple Choice

1. A(n) _____ programming practice is centered on creating modules and functions that are separate from the data that they work on.

    a. modular
    b. procedural
    c. functional
    d. object-oriented

2. A(n) _____ programming practice is centered on creating objects.

    a. object-centric
    b. objective
    c. procedural
    d. object-oriented

Object-Oriented Programming

3. A(n) _____ is a member of a class that holds data.

   a. method
   b. instance
   c. field
   d. constructor

4. The _____ specifies how a class's field or method may be accessed by code outside the class.

   a. field declaration
   b. `New` key word
   c. access specifier
   d. constructor

5. A class's fields are commonly declared with the _____ access specifier.

   a. `Private`
   b. `Public`
   c. `ReadOnly`
   d. `Hidden`

6. A _____ variable is a special type of variable that can reference an object in the computer's memory.

   a. memory
   b. procedural
   c. class
   d. dynamic

7. In many programming languages, the _____ key word creates an object in memory.

   a. `Create`
   b. `New`
   c. `Instantiate`
   d. `Declare`

8. A(n) _____ method gets a value from a class's field but does not change it.

   a. retriever
   b. constructor
   c. mutator
   d. accessor

9. A(n) _____ method stores a value in a field or changes the value of a field in some other way.

   a. modifier
   b. constructor
   c. mutator
   d. accessor

10. A(n) _____ method is automatically called when an object is created.

    a. accessor
    b. constructor
    c. setter
    d. mutator

11. A set of standard diagrams for graphically depicting object-oriented systems is provided by _____.

   a. the Unified Modeling Language
   b. flowcharts
   c. pseudocode
   d. the Object Hierarchy System

12. When the value of an item is dependent on other data, and that item is not updated when the other data is changed, we say that the value has become _____.

   a. bitter
   b. stale
   c. asynchronous
   d. moldy

13. A class's responsibilities are _____.

   a. objects created from the class
   b. things the class knows
   c. actions the class performs
   d. both b and c

14. In an inheritance relationship, the _____ is the general class.

   a. subclass
   b. superclass
   c. slave class
   d. child class

15. In an inheritance relationship, the _____ is the specialized class.

   a. superclass
   b. master class
   c. subclass
   d. parent class

16. The _____ characteristic of object-oriented programming allows a superclass variable to reference a subclass object.

   a. polymorphism
   b. inheritance
   c. generalization
   d. specialization

True or False

1. The practice of procedural programming is centered on the creation of objects.

2. Object reusability has been a factor in the increased use of object-oriented programming.

3. It is a common practice in object-oriented programming to make all of a class's fields public.

4. One way to find the classes needed for an object-oriented program is to identify all of the verbs in a description of the problem domain.

5. The superclass inherits fields and methods from the subclass.

6. Polymorphism allows a class variable of the superclass type to reference objects of either the superclass or the subclass types.

Short Answer

1. What is encapsulation?
2. Why is an object's internal data usually hidden from outside code?
3. What is the difference between a class and an instance of a class?
4. In many programming languages, what does the New key word do?
5. The following pseudocode statement calls an object's method. What is the name of the method? What is the name of the variable that references the object?

```
Call wallet.getDollar()
```

6. What is stale data?
7. What does a subclass inherit from its superclass?
8. Look at the following pseudocode, which is the first line of a class definition. What is the name of the superclass? What is the name of the subclass?

```
Class Tiger Extends Felis
```

Algorithm Workbench

1. Suppose myCar is the name of a class variable that references an object, and go is the name of a method. (The go method does not take any arguments.) Write a pseudocode statement that uses the myCar variable to call the method.

2. Look at this partial class definition, and then follow the subsequent instructions:

```
Class Book
    Private String title
    Private String author
    Private String publisher
    Private Integer copiesSold
End Class
```

a. Write a constructor for this class. The constructor should accept an argument for each of the fields.
b. Write accessor and mutator methods for each field.
c. Draw a UML diagram for the class, including the methods you have written.

3. Look at the following description of a problem domain:

The bank offers the following types of accounts to its customers: savings accounts, checking accounts, and money market accounts. Customers are allowed to deposit money into an account (thereby increasing its balance), withdraw money from an account (thereby decreasing its balance), and earn interest on the account. Each account has an interest rate.

Assume that you are writing a program that will calculate the amount of interest earned for a bank account.

a. Identify the potential classes in this problem domain.
b. Refine the list to include only the necessary class or classes for this problem.
c. Identify the responsibilities of the class or classes.

4. In pseudocode, write the first line of the definition for a Poodle class. The class should extend the Dog class.

5. Look at the following pseudocode class definitions:

```
Class Plant
    Public Module message()
        Display "I'm a plant."
    End Module
End Class
Class Tree Extends Plant
    Public Module message()
        Display "I'm a tree."
    End Module
End Class
```

Given these class definitions, what will the following pseudocode display?

```
Declare Plant p
Set p = New Tree()
Call p.message()
```

Programming Exercises

VideoNote

The Pet Class Problem

1. **Pet Class**

   Design a class named `Pet`, which should have the following fields:

   - name: The name field holds the name of a pet.
   - type: The type field holds the type of animal that a pet is. Example values are "Dog", "Cat", and "Bird".
   - age: The age field holds the pet's age.

   The Pet class should also have the following methods:

   - setName: The setName method stores a value in the name field.
   - setType: The setType method stores a value in the type field.
   - setAge: The setAge method stores a value in the age field.
   - getName: The getName method returns the value of the name field.
   - getType: The getType method returns the value of the type field.
   - getAge: The getAge method returns the value of the age field.

   Once you have designed the class, design a program that creates an object of the class and prompts the user to enter the name, type, and age of his or her pet. This data should be stored in the object. Use the object's accessor methods to retrieve the pet's name, type, and age and display this data on the screen.

2. **Car Class**

   Design a class named `Car` that has the following fields:

   - **yearModel**: The yearModel field is an Integer that holds the car's year model.
   - **make**: The make field references a String that holds the make of the car.
   - **speed**: The speed field is an Integer that holds the car's current speed.

   In addition, the class should have the following constructor and other methods:

   - **Constructor**: The constructor should accept the car's year model and make as arguments. These values should be assigned to the object's yearModel and make fields. The constructor should also assign 0 to the speed field.
   - **Accessors**: Design appropriate accessor methods to get the values stored in an object's yearModel, make, and speed fields.
   - **accelerate**: The accelerate method should add 5 to the speed field each time it is called.

- **brake:** The brake method should subtract 5 from the speed field each time it is called.

Next, design a program that creates a Car object, and then calls the accelerate method five times. After each call to the accelerate method, get the current speed of the car and display it. Then call the brake method five times. After each call to the brake method, get the current speed of the car and display it.

3. **Personal Information** Class

Design a class that holds the following personal data: name, address, age, and phone number. Write appropriate accessor and mutator methods. Also, design a program that creates three instances of the class. One instance should hold your information, and the other two should hold your friends' or family members' information.

4. **Employee and ProductionWorker** Classes

Design an Employee class that has fields for the following pieces of information:

- Employee name
- Employee number

Next, design a class named ProductionWorker that extends the Employee class. The ProductionWorker class should have fields to hold the following information:

- Shift number (an integer, such as 1, 2, or 3)
- Hourly pay rate

The workday is divided into two shifts: day and night. The shift field will hold an integer value representing the shift that the employee works. The day shift is shift 1 and the night shift is shift 2. Design the appropriate accessor and mutator methods for each class.

Once you have designed the classes, design a program that creates an object of the ProductionWorker class and prompts the user to enter data for each of the object's fields. Store the data in the object and then use the object's accessor methods to retrieve it and display it on the screen.

5. **Essay** Class

Design an Essay class that extends the GradedActivity class presented in this chapter. The Essay class should determine the grade a student receives for an essay. The student's essay score can be up to 100 and is determined in the following manner:

- Grammar: up to 30 points
- Spelling: up to 20 points
- Correct length: up to 20 points
- Content: up to 30 points

Once you have designed the class, design a program that prompts the user to enter the number of points that a student has earned for grammar, spelling, length, and content. Create an Essay object and store this data in the object. Use the object's methods to get the student's overall score and grade and display this data on the screen.

15

GUI Applications and Event-Driven Programming

15.1 Graphical User Interfaces

CONCEPT: A graphical user interface allows the user to interact with the operating system and other programs using graphical elements such as icons, buttons, and dialog boxes.

VideoNote

Graphical User Interfaces

A computer's *user interface* is the part of the computer that the user interacts with. One part of the user interface consists of hardware devices, such as the keyboard and the video display. Another part of the user interface lies in the way that the computer's operating system accepts commands from the user. For many years, the only way that the user could interact with an operating system was through a *command line interface*, such as the one shown in Figure 15-1. A command line interface typically displays a prompt, and the user types a command, which is then executed.

Many computer users, especially beginners, find command line interfaces difficult to use. This is because there are many commands to be learned, and each command has its own syntax, much like a programming statement. If a command isn't entered correctly, it will not work.

Figure 15-1 A command line interface

```
C:\>cd \MyPrograms

C:\MyPrograms>dir
 Volume in drive C has no label.
 Volume Serial Number is 2414-0F08

 Directory of C:\MyPrograms

12/05/2006  09:51 AM    <DIR>          .
12/05/2006  09:51 AM    <DIR>          ..
04/17/2007  04:23 PM               250 Payroll.java
               1 File(s)            250 bytes
               2 Dir(s)  29,789,757,440 bytes free

C:\MyPrograms>_
```

In the 1980s, a new type of interface known as a graphical user interface came into use in commercial operating systems. A *graphical user interface (GUI)* (pronounced "gooey"), allows the user to interact with the operating system through graphical elements on the screen. GUIs also popularized the use of the mouse as an input device. Instead of requiring the user to type commands on the keyboard, GUIs allow the user to point at graphical elements and click the mouse button to activate them.

Much of the interaction with a GUI is done through *dialog boxes*, which are small windows that display information and allow the user to perform actions. Figure 15-2 shows an example of a dialog box that allows the user to change his or her Internet settings in the Windows operating system. Instead of typing cryptic commands, the user interacts with graphical elements such as icons, buttons, and slider bars.

Figure 15-2 A dialog box

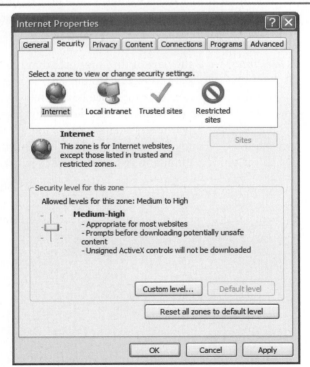

If you are developing software in an operating system that uses a GUI, such as Windows, Mac OS X, or Linux, you can also use the GUI in the programs that you write. This allows you to incorporate standard GUI elements such as dialog boxes with icons, buttons, and so on into your programs.

GUI Programs Are Event-Driven

In a text-based environment, such as a command line interface, programs determine the order in which things happen. For example, consider a program that calculates the area of a rectangle. First, the program prompts the user to enter the rectangle's width. The user enters the width and then the program prompts the user to enter the rectangle's length. The user enters the length and then the program calculates the area. The user has no choice but to enter the data in the order that it is requested.

In a GUI environment, however, the user determines the order in which things happen. For example, Figure 15-3 shows a GUI program that calculates the area of a rectangle. The user can enter the length and the width in any order he or she wishes. If a mistake is made, the user can erase the data that was entered and retype it. When the user is ready to calculate the area, he or she clicks the *Calculate Area* button and the program performs the calculation. Because GUI programs must respond to the actions of the user, it is said that they are *event-driven*. The user causes events to take place, such as the clicking of a button, and the program must respond to the events.

Figure 15-3 A GUI program

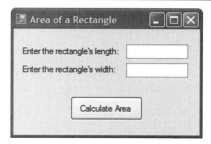

Creating a GUI Program

Many of the steps involved in creating a GUI program are the same as those that you have used to create text-based programs throughout this book. For example, you must understand the task that the program is to perform and determine the steps that must be taken to perform the task.

In addition, you must design the on-screen GUI elements that make up each window in the program's user interface. You must also determine how the program will flow from one window to the next as the user interacts with it. Some programmers find it helpful to draw a *user interface flow diagram*. Figure 15-4 shows an example of such a diagram. Each box represents a window that is displayed by the program. If actions performed in one window can cause another window to open, then an arrow appears between the two windows in the diagram. In the diagram, notice that an arrow points away from Window 1 to Window 2. This means that actions in Window 1 can cause

Window 2 to open. When a double-headed arrow appears between two windows, then either window can open the other.

Figure 15-4 A user interface flow diagram

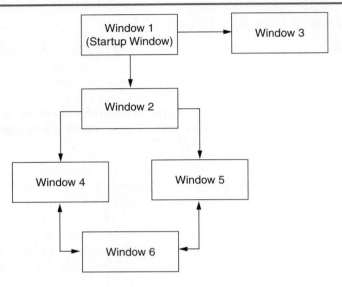

 Checkpoint

15.1 What is a user interface?

15.2 How does a command line interface work?

15.3 When the user runs a program in a text-based environment, such as the command line, what determines the order in which things happen?

15.4 What is an event-driven program?

15.5 What is a user interface flow diagram?

15.2 Designing the User Interface for a GUI Program

CONCEPT: When creating a GUI program you must design the program's windows and all of the graphical components that appear in them.

A GUI program's user interface consists of one or more windows that appear on the screen when the program is running. While creating a GUI program, one of your tasks is to design the windows and all of the graphical elements that appear in them.

In the early days of GUI programming, creating a set of graphical windows for a program was a complex and time consuming endeavor. Programmers had to write code that constructed the windows, create graphical elements such as icons and buttons, and set each element's color, position, size, and other properties. Even a simple GUI program that displayed a message such as "Hello world" required the programmer to write a hundred or more lines of code. Furthermore, the programmer could not actually see the program's user interface until the program was compiled and executed.

Today, there are several integrated development environments (IDEs) that allow you to construct a program's windows and its graphical elements visually without writing a single line of code. For example, Microsoft Visual Studio allows you to create GUI programs using the Visual Basic, C++, and C# programming languages. Sun Microsystem's NetBeans and Embarcadero® JBuilder® are popular IDEs for creating GUI programs in Java. There are several other IDEs as well.

Most IDEs display a window editor that allows you to create windows, and a "toolbox" that displays all of the items that you can place in a window. You construct a window by dragging the desired items from the toolbox to the window editor. This is shown in Figures 15-5 and 15-6. The screen in Figure 15-5 is from Visual Basic, and the screen in Figure 15-6 is from NetBeans. As you visually construct the user interface in the window editor, the IDE automatically generates the code needed to display it.

Figure 15-5 Visually constructing a window in Visual Basic

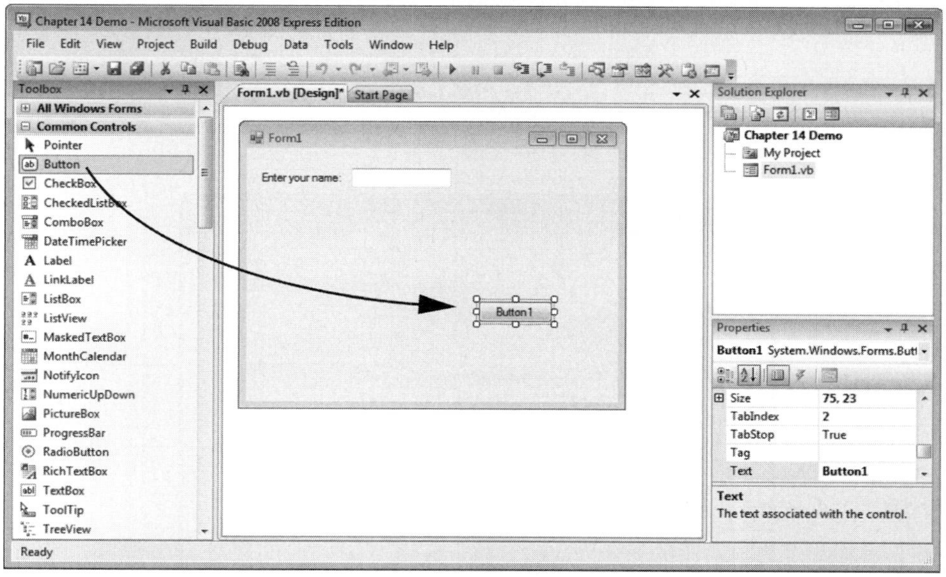

Figure 15-6 Visually constructing a window in NetBeans

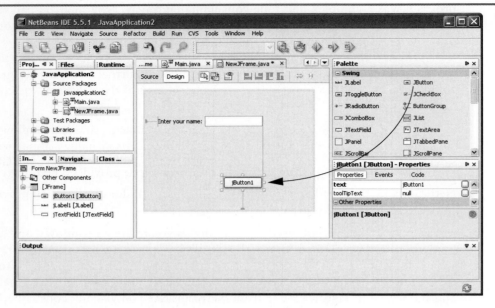

Components

The items that appear in a program's graphical user interface are known as *components*. Some of the common GUI components are buttons, labels, text boxes, check boxes, and radio buttons. Figure 15-7 shows an example of a window with a variety of components. Table 15-1 describes the components that appear in the window.

Figure 15-7 Various components in a GUI window

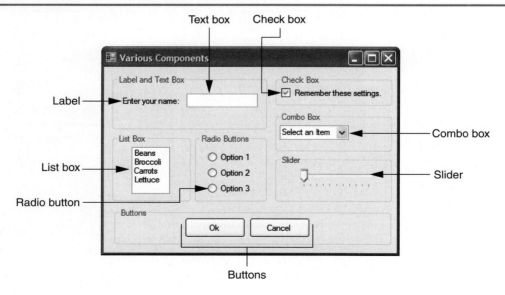

Table 15-1 Common GUI components

Component	Description
Button	A component that causes an action to occur when it is clicked
Label	An area that can display text
Text box	An area in which the user may type a single line of input from the keyboard
Check box	A component that has a box that may be checked or unchecked
Radio button	A component that can be either selected or deselected; usually appears in groups and allows the user to select one of several options
Combo box	A component (combination of a list and a text box) that displays a drop-down list of items from which the user may select; provides a text box in which the user may type input
List box	A list from which the user may select an item
Slider	A component that allows the user to select a value by moving a slider along a track

NOTE: GUI components are also known as *controls* and *widgets*.

Component Names

In most IDEs, you must assign unique names to the components that you place in a window. A component's name identifies the component in the program, in the same way that a variable's name identifies the variable. For example, Figure 15-8 shows a window from a program that calculates gross pay. The figure also shows the names that the programmer assigned to each component in the window. Notice that each component's name describes the component's purpose in the program. For example, the text box that the user enters the number of hours worked into is named `hoursTextBox`, and the button that calculates the gross pay is named `calcButton`. Additionally, in most programming languages, the rules for naming components are the same as the rules for naming variables.

Figure 15-8 Components and their names

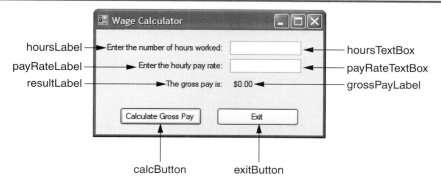

> **NOTE:** In most IDEs, if you look at the code that is generated to display a window, you will see that each component in the window is an object, and the name that you have assigned to the component is used as the name of the object.

Properties

Most GUI components have a set of *properties* that determines how the component appears on the screen. Typically, components have properties that specify the component's color, size, and position. Like variables, properties can be set to values. When you set a property to a value, it changes some aspect of the component that it belongs to.

Let's look at an example from Visual Basic. Suppose you have placed a button in a window and you want to display the text "Show Result" on the button. In Visual Basic, the `Text` property controls the text that is displayed on a component, so you change the value of the button's `Text` property to "Show Result." This causes the text "Show Result" to be displayed on the button, as shown in Figure 15-9.

Figure 15-9 A button with its Text property set to "Show Result"

```
Show Result
```

Most components in Visual Basic also have a property named `BackColor` that specifies the component's color, and another property named `ForeColor` that specifies the color of any text that is displayed on the component. For example, if you want to change the color of the text that is displayed on a button to blue, you set its `ForeColor` property to the value `Blue`.

Most IDEs allow you to set a component's properties while you are constructing the window. Typically, IDEs provide a *property window* that displays all of a component's properties, and allows you to change the properties to the desired values.

Constructing a Window—A Summary

Now that you have an idea of how GUI windows are created in an IDE, let's look at a simple set of steps that you can follow to construct a window.

1. **Sketch the window.**

   You should draw a sketch of the window before you start constructing it in the IDE. By doing this you will determine the components that are needed. At this point, it is often helpful to make a list of the necessary components.

2. **Create the necessary components and name them.**

   After sketching the window and determining the components you will need, you can start constructing it in the IDE. As you place each component in the window, you should assign it a unique and meaningful name.

3. Set the components' properties to the desired values.

A component's properties control its visual characteristics, such as color, size, position, and any text that is displayed on the component. To get the visual appearance that you want, set each component's properties to the desired values. In most IDEs, you will use a property window to set the starting values for the properties of each component.

In the Spotlight:
Designing a Window

Kathryn teaches a science class. In Chapter 4, we stepped through the development of a program that her students can use to calculate the average of three test scores. The program prompts the student to enter each score, and then it displays the average. She has asked you to design a GUI program that performs a similar operation. She would like the program to have three text boxes that the test scores can be entered into, and a button that causes the average to be displayed when clicked.

First, we need to draw a sketch of the program's window, as shown in Figure 15-10. The sketch also shows the type of each component. (The numbers that appear in the sketch will help us when we make a list of all the components.)

Figure 15-10 A sketch of the window

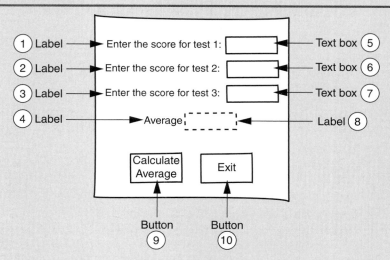

By examining the sketch we can make a list of all the components that we need. As we make the list, we will include a brief description of each component and a name that we will assign to each component when we construct it.

Component Number in the Sketch	Component Type	Description	Name
1	Label	Instructs the user to enter the score for test 1.	`test1Label`
2	Label	Instructs the user to enter the score for test 2.	`test2Label`
3	Label	Instructs the user to enter the score for test 3.	`test3Label`
4	Label	Identifies the average, which will be displayed next to this label.	`resultLabel`
5	Text box	This is where the user will enter the score for test 1.	`test1TextBox`
6	Text box	This is where the user will enter the score for test 2.	`test2TextBox`
7	Text box	This is where the user will enter the score for test 3.	`test3TextBox`
8	Label	The program will display the average test score in this label.	`averageLabel`
9	Button	When this button is clicked, the program will calculate the average test score and display it in the `averageLabel` component.	`calcButton`
10	Button	When this button is clicked the program will end.	`exitButton`

Now that we have a sketch of the window and a list of the components we will need, we can use our IDE to construct it. As we place the components, we will set the appropriate properties to make the components look the way we want them to. Assuming we are constructing the window in Visual Basic, we will set the following properties:

- The `test1Label` component's `Text` property will be set to "Enter the score for test 1:"
- The `test2Label` component's `Text` property will be set to "Enter the score for test 2:"
- The `test3Label` component's `Text` property will be set to "Enter the score for test 3:"
- The `resultLabel` component's `Text` property will be set to "Average"
- The `calcButton` component's `Text` property will be set to "Calculate Average"
- The `exitButton` component's `Text` property will be set to "Exit"
- The `averageLabel` component's `BorderStyle` property will be set to `FixedSingle`. This will cause a thin border to appear around the label, as shown in the sketch.

TIP: Although the properties listed here are specific to Visual Basic, other languages have similar properties. The names, however, may be different.

Figure 15-11 shows an example of how the window will appear. The figure shows the name of each component.

Figure 15-11 The completed window

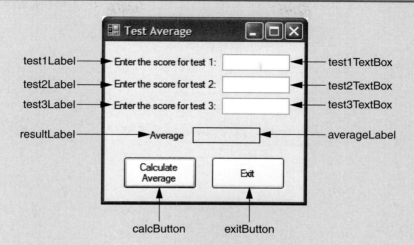

In the next *In the Spotlight* section we will continue developing this program by writing pseudocode that responds to the user's actions.

 **Checkpoint**

15.6 Why was GUI programming complex and time consuming in the early days of GUI technology?

15.7 In an IDE that allows you to visually construct a window, how do you place an item such as a button in the window?

15.8 What is a component?

15.9 Why must components be assigned names?

15.10 What do a component's properties do?

 15.3 Writing Event Handlers

CONCEPT: If you want a GUI program to perform an action when an event occurs, you must write code, known as an event handler, which responds to that event.

After you create a GUI program's user interface, you can write the code that responds to events. As previously mentioned, an *event* is an action that takes place within a program, such as the clicking of a button. Part of writing a GUI application is creating event handlers. An *event handler* is a module that automatically executes when a specific event occurs. If you want a program to perform an operation when a particular event occurs, you must create an event handler that responds when that event takes place. In pseudocode, our event handlers will be written in the following general format:

```
Module ComponentName_EventName()
    The statements that appear here
    are executed when the event occurs.
End Module
```

In the general format, *ComponentName* is the name of the component that generated the event, and *EventName* is the name of the event that occurred. For example, suppose a window contains a button component named `showResultButton`, and we want to write an event handler that executes when the user clicks it. The event handler would be written in the following format:

```
Module showResultButton_Click()
    statement
    statement
    etc.
End Module
```

Predefined names are given to all of the events that can be generated in a GUI system. In this example, you saw that a `Click` event occurs when the user clicks a component. There are many other events that can be generated as well. For example, an event with a name such as `MouseEnter` will be generated when the mouse cursor is moved over a component, and an event with a name such as `MouseLeave` will be generated when the mouse cursor is moved off of a component.

NOTE: If an event occurs and there is no event handler to respond to that event, the event is ignored.

Let's look at an example of how we can write an event handler in pseudocode. Previously in this chapter, you saw a GUI window for a program that calculates an employee's gross pay. For your convenience the window is shown again, in Figure 15-12. The figure also shows the names of the components.

Figure 15-12 A GUI window

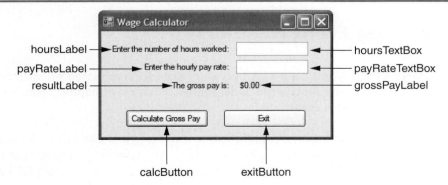

When this program runs, there are two possible events that we want it to respond to: the user clicking the `calcButton` component and the user clicking the `exitButton` component. If the user clicks the `calcButton` component, we want the program to calculate the gross pay and display it in the `grossPayLabel` component. If the user clicks the `exitButton` component, we want the program to end.

To handle the event that occurs when the user clicks the `calcButton`, we would write the following event handler in pseudocode:

```
 1 Module calcButton_Click()
 2    // Local variables to hold the hours worked, the
 3    // pay rate, and the gross pay.
 4    Declare Real hours, payRate, grossPay
 5
 6    // Get the number of hours worked from the
 7    // hoursTextBox component.
 8    Set hours = stringToReal(hoursTextBox.Text)
 9
10    // Get the pay rate from the payRateTextBox
11    // component.
12    Set payRate = stringToReal(payRateTextBox.Text)
13
14    // Calculate the gross pay.
15    Set grossPay = hours * payRate
16
17    // Display the gross pay in the grossPayLabel
18    // component.
19    Set grossPayLabel.Text = realToString(grossPay)
20 End Module
```

Let's take a closer look at each statement in this event handler.

- Line 4 declares three local variables: `hours`, `payRate`, and `grossPay`.
- Line 8 gets the value that has been typed into the `hoursTextBox` component and assigns it to the `hours` variable. A lot of things are happening in this line, so it deserves a thorough explanation.

  When the user types a value into a text box component, the value is stored in the component's `Text` property. In pseudocode, we use dot notation to refer to a component's `Text` property. For example, to refer to the `hoursTextBox` component's `Text` property, we write `hoursTextBox.Text`.

  In many languages, you cannot assign the value of a component's `Text` property directly to a numeric variable. For example, if line 8 were written as follows, an error would occur:

  ```
  Set hours = hoursTextBox.Text
  ```

  This logic will cause an error because the `Text` property holds strings, and strings cannot be assigned to numeric variables. So, we need to convert the value in the `Text` property to a real number. This can be done with the `stringToReal` function, as follows:

  ```
  Set hours = stringToReal(hoursTextBox.Text)
  ```

  (We discussed the `stringToReal` function in Chapter 6.)
- Line 12 gets the value that has been typed into the `payRateTextBox` component, converts it to a real number, and assigns it to the `payRate` variable.

- Line 15 multiplies `hours` by `payRate` and assigns the result to the `grossPay` variable.
- Line 19 displays the gross pay. It does this by assigning the value of the `grossPay` variable to the `grossPayLabel` component's `Text` property. Notice that a function, `realToString`, is used to convert the `grossPay` variable to a string. This is necessary because in many languages an error will occur if we try to assign a `Real` number directly to a `Text` property. When we assign a value to a label component's `Text` property, that value will be displayed in the label.

To handle the event that occurs when the user clicks the `exitButton`, we would write the following event handler:

```
1   Module exitButton_Click()
2       Close
3   End Module
```

This event hander executes the `Close` statement. In pseudocode, the `Close` statement causes the window that is currently open to close. If the current window is the only one open, closing it causes the program to end.

In the Spotlight:
Designing an Event Handler

In the previous *In the Spotlight* section, we designed the window shown in Figure 15-13 for Kathryn's test score averaging program.

Figure 15-13 The window for the test score averaging program

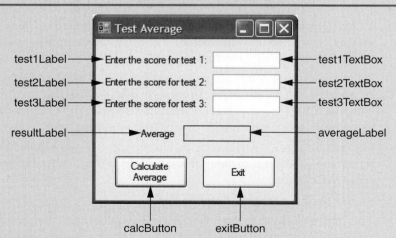

Now, we will design the program's event handlers. When the user clicks the `calcButton` component, the program should calculate the average of the three test scores and display it in the `averageLabel` component. When the user clicks the `exitButton` component, the program should end. The pseudocode in Program 15-1 shows both event handlers.

Program 15-1

```
 1 Module calcButton_Click()
 2     // Declare local variables to hold the test
 3     // scores and the average.
 4     Declare Real test1, test2, test3, average
 5
 6     // Get the first test score.
 7     Set test1 = stringToReal(test1TextBox.Text)
 8
 9     // Get the second test score.
10     Set test2 = stringToReal(test2TextBox.Text)
11
12     // Get the third test score.
13     Set test3 = stringToReal(test3TextBox.Text)
14
15     // Calculate the average test score.
16     Set average = (test1 + test2 + test3) / 3
17
18     // Display the average test score in the
19     // averageLabel component.
20     Set averageLabel.Text = realToString(average)
21 End Module
22
23 Module exitButton_Click()
24     Close
25 End Module
```

Here is a description of each statement in the `calcButton_Click` module:

- Line 4 declares local variables to hold the three test scores and the average of the test scores.
- Line 7 gets the value that has been entered into the `test1TextBox` component, converts it to a real number, and stores it in the `test1` variable.
- Line 10 gets the value that has been entered into the `test2TextBox` component, converts it to a real number, and stores it in the `test2` variable.
- Line 13 gets the value that has been entered into the `test3TextBox` component, converts it to a real number, and stores it in the `test3` variable.
- Line 16 calculates the average of the three test scores and stores the result in the `average` variable.
- Line 20 converts the value in the `average` variable to a string and stores it in the `averageLabel` component's `Text` property. Doing this displays the value in the label component.

The `exitButton_Click` module executes the `Close` statement to close the window and subsequently end the program.

Figure 15-14 shows an example of how the program's window will appear after the user has entered values into the text boxes and clicked the `calcButton` component.

Figure 15-14 The window with an average displayed

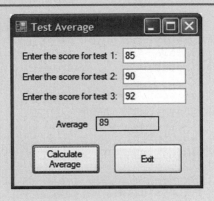

Checkpoint

15.11 What is an event?

15.12 What is an event handler?

15.13 Look at the following pseudocode and then answer the questions that follow it:

```
Module showValuesButton_Click()
    statement
    statement
    etc.
End Module
```

a. What event does this module respond to?

b. What is the name of the component that generates the event?

Review Questions

Multiple Choice

1. The _____ is the part of a computer with which the user interacts.
   a. central processing unit
   b. user interface
   c. control system
   d. interactivity system

2. Before GUIs became popular, the _____ interface was the most commonly used.
   a. command line
   b. remote terminal
   c. sensory
   d. event-driven

3. A _____ is a small window that displays information and allows the user to perform actions.

   a. menu
   b. confirmation window
   c. startup screen
   d. dialog box

4. A type of program that is typically event-driven is the _____ program.

   a. command line
   b. text-based
   c. GUI
   d. procedural

5. An item that appears in a program's graphical user interface is known as a _____.

   a. gadget
   b. component
   c. tool
   d. graphic object

6. By specifying characteristics such as color, size, and location, _____ determine how a GUI element appears on the screen.

   a. properties
   b. attributes
   c. methods
   d. event handlers

7. An _____ is an action that takes place within a program, such as the clicking of a button.

   a. event handler
   b. anomaly
   c. event
   d. exception

8. A(n) _____ is a module that automatically executes when a specific event occurs.

   a. event handler
   b. auto module
   c. startup module
   d. exception

True or False

1. Many computer users, especially beginners, find command line interfaces difficult to use.

2. Writing a GUI program today is complex and time consuming because you have to write all of the code that constructs the program's windows without seeing it on the screen.

3. A component's `Text` property typically holds string values.

4. Predefined names are given to all of the events that can be generated in a GUI system.

5. A user interface flow diagram shows how a GUI program flows from one window to the next as the user interacts with it.

Short Answer

1. When a program runs in a text-based environment, such as a command line interface, what determines the order in which things happen?

2. What determines how a component appears on the screen?

3. Describe how you typically change the color of a component.

4. Why must components be assigned names?

5. What happens if an event occurs and there is no event handler to respond to the event?

Algorithm Workbench

1. Design an event handler that will execute when the `showNameButton` component is clicked. The event handler should perform the following:

   - Store your first name in a label component named `firstNameLabel`.
   - Store your middle name in a label component named `middleNameLabel`.
   - Store your last name in a label component named `lastNameLabel`.

   (Remember, to store a value in a label component, you must store the value in the component's `Text` property.)

2. Design an event handler that will execute when the `calcAvailableCreditButton` component is clicked. The event handler should perform the following:

   - Declare the following `Real` variables: `maxCredit`, `usedCredit`, and `availableCredit`.
   - Get a value from a text box named `maxCreditTextBox` and assign it to the `maxCredit` variable.
   - Get a value from a text box named `usedCreditTextBox` and assign it to the `usedCredit` variable.
   - Subtract the value in `usedCredit` from `maxCredit` and assign the result to `availableCredit`.
   - Store the value in the `availableCredit` variable in a label component named `availableCreditLabel`.

Programming Exercises

VideoNote

The Name and Address Problem

1. **Name and Address**

Design a GUI program that displays your name and address when a button is clicked. The program's window should appear as the sketch on the left side of Figure 15-15 when it runs. When the user clicks the *Show Info* button, the program should display your name and address, as shown in the sketch on the right of the figure.

Figure 15-15 Name and address program

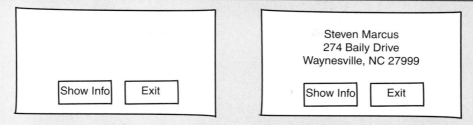

2. **Latin Translator**

   Look at the following list of Latin words and their meanings:

Latin	English
sinister	left
dexter	right
medium	center

   Design a GUI program that translates the Latin words to English. The window should have three buttons, one for each Latin word. When the user clicks a button, the program displays the English translation in a label component.

3. **Miles-per-Gallon Calculator**

   Design a GUI program that calculates a car's gas mileage. The program's window should have text boxes that let the user enter the number of gallons of gas the car holds, and the number of miles it can be driven on a full tank. When a *Calculate MPG* button is clicked, the program should display the number of miles that the car may be driven per gallon of gas. Use the following formula to calculate miles-per-gallon:

   $$MPG = \frac{miles}{gallons}$$

4. **Celsius to Fahrenheit**

   Design a GUI program that converts Celsius temperatures to Fahrenheit temperatures. The user should be able to enter a Celsius temperature, click a button, and then see the equivalent Fahrenheit temperature. Use the following formula to make the conversion:

   $$F = \frac{9}{5}C + 32$$

   F is the Fahrenheit temperature and *C* is the Celsius temperature.

5. **Property Tax**

   A county collects property taxes on the assessment value of property, which is 60 percent of the property's actual value. If an acre of land is valued at $10,000, its assessment value is $6,000. The property tax is then $0.64 for each $100 of the assessment value. The tax for the acre assessed at $6,000 will be $38.40. Design a GUI program that displays the assessment value and property tax when a user enters the actual value of a property.

A ASCII/Unicode Characters

The following table lists the ASCII (American Standard Code for Information Interchange) character set, which is the same as the first 127 Unicode character codes. This group of character codes is known as the *Latin Subset of Unicode*. The code columns show character codes and the character columns show the corresponding characters. For example, the code 65 represents the letter A. Note that the first 31 codes and code 127 represent control characters that are not printable.

Code	Character	Code	Character	Code	Character	Code	Character	Code	Character
0	NUL	26	SUB	52	4	78	N	104	h
1	SOH	27	Escape	53	5	79	O	105	i
2	STX	28	FS	54	6	80	P	106	j
3	ETX	29	GS	55	7	81	Q	107	k
4	EOT	30	RS	56	8	82	R	108	l
5	ENQ	31	US	57	9	83	S	109	m
6	ACK	32	(Space)	58	:	84	T	110	n
7	BEL	33	!	59	;	85	U	111	o
8	Backspace	34	"	60	<	86	V	112	p
9	HTab	35	#	61	=	87	W	113	q
10	Line Feed	36	$	62	>	88	X	114	r
11	VTab	37	%	63	?	89	Y	115	s
12	Form Feed	38	&	64	@	90	Z	116	t
13	CR	39	'	65	A	91	[	117	u
14	SO	40	(	66	B	92	\	118	v
15	SI	41	)	67	C	93	]	119	w
16	DLE	42	*	68	D	94	^	120	x
17	DC1	43	+	69	E	95	_	121	y
18	DC2	44	,	70	F	96	`	122	z
19	DC3	45	–	71	G	97	a	123	{
20	DC4	46	.	72	H	98	b	124	|
21	NAK	47	/	73	I	99	c	125	}
22	SYN	48	0	74	J	100	d	126	~
23	ETB	49	1	75	K	101	e	127	DEL
24	CAN	50	2	76	L	102	f		
25	EM	51	3	77	M	103	g		

B Flowchart Symbols

This page shows the flowchart symbols that are used in this book.

Terminal Symbols

Start

End

Input/Output Symbol

Processing Symbol

Connector

A

Module Call Symbol

Decision Symbol

Case Structure

C

Answers to Checkpoint Questions

This appendix can be found on the CD that accompanies this book. If a CD did not come with your book or you can't locate your CD, you can also visit `http://www.aw.com/cssupport/` to access this appendix.

Index